BROOKINGS PAPERS ON

Economic Activity

*Martin Neil Baily, Peter C. Reiss, and Clifford Winston,
Editors*

MICROECONOMICS

1998

*James R. Schneider, Editorial Consultant
Martha V. Gottron, Editorial Consultant
Takako Tsuji, Research Verifier
Kathleen M. Bucholz, Production Manager*

BROOKINGS INSTITUTION

WASHINGTON, D.C.

Contents

Purpose This issue of the *Brookings Papers on Economic Activity: Microeconomics* contains the articles, reports, and highlights of the discussions from a conference held June 19–20, 1998, at the Brookings Institution in Washington, D.C. The conference was held to promote professional research and analysis of key issues affecting the productivity and efficiency of the U.S. economy.

The expertise of the panel is concentrated on the live issues of economic performance that confront the maker of public policy and the executive in the private sector. Particular attention is devoted to recent and current economic developments that are directly relevant to the contemporary scene or especially challenging because they stretch our understanding of economic theory or previous empirical findings. Such issues are typically quantitative, and the research findings are often statistical. Nevertheless, in all the articles and reports, the reasoning and the conclusion are developed in a form intelligible to the interested, informed nonspecialist as well as useful to the expert in microeconomics. In short the papers aim at several objectives—meticulous and incisive professional analysis, timeliness and relevance to current issues, and lucid presentation.

Articles appear in this publication after presentation and discussion at a conference at Brookings. From the spirited discussion at the conference, the authors obtain new insights and helpful comments; they also receive searching criticism about various aspects of the papers. Some of these comments are reflected in the published commentaries; some are finally the product of the authors' thinking and do not imply any agreement by those attending the conference. Nor do the papers or any of the other materials in this issue necessarily represent the views of the staff members, officers, or trustees of the Brookings Institution.

1999 Subscription Rates Note: The following rates are for the two macroeconomic issues of *Brookings Papers on Economic Activity*; the Microeconomics issue is being discontinued following this 1998 issue.

	United States		Foreign	
	4th class	*1st class*	*surface*	*airmail*
Institutions	$45.00	$57.00	$61.00	$77.00
Individuals	$28.00	$40.00	$44.00	$60.00
Students	$19.00	—	—	—

Single copies: $17.00 (4th class mail)

Send subscription orders to The Brookings Institution, Department 037, Washington, D.C. 20042-0037. Or call toll free 1-800-275-1447 or (202) 797-6258. For information on the availability of this journal in microform, write to University Microfilms International, 300 North Zeeb Rd., Ann Arbor, MI 48106.

Authors for BPEA

John Adams *RAND*
Martin Neil Baily *McKinsey & Company*
Margaret Blair *Brookings Institution*
Patricia H. Born *University of Connecticut*
Axel Börsch-Supan *University of Mannheim*
Barry P. Bosworth *Brookings Institution*
Jeremy Bulow *Stanford University*
Thomas J. Campbell *U.S. House of Representatives*
Dennis Carlton *University of Chicago*
Steven Garber *RAND*
Paul Gompers *Harvard University*
Thomas Hellmann *Stanford University*
Daniel P. Kessler *Stanford University*
Paul Klemperer *Nuffield College*
Alvin Klevorick *Yale University*
Joshua Lerner *Harvard University*
Sam Peltzman *University of Chicago*
Peter C. Reiss *Stanford University*
Paul Romer *Stanford University*
Daniel Rubinfeld *U.S. Department of Justice*
George Shepherd *Emory University*
W. Kip Viscusi *Harvard University*
Larry E. Westphal *Swarthmore College*
Eric Zitzewitz *Massachusetts Institute of Technology*

Other participants in the conference

Kenneth Abraham *University of Virginia*
Ian Ayres *Yale University*
Jonathan Baker *Federal Trade Commission*
Jack Calfee *American Enterprise Institute*
Linda Cohen *University of California, Irvine*
Robert E. Litan *Brookings Institution*
Roger Noll *Stanford University*
Peter Pashigian *University of Chicago*
George Priest *Yale University*
Gregory Rosston *Stanford University*
Gary Schwartz *University of California, Los Angeles*
Lawrence White *New York University*
Matthew White *Stanford University*
Clifford Winston *Brookings Institution*
Frank Wolak *Stanford University*

Summary of the Papers

THIS ISSUE CONTAINS papers presented at the twelfth meeting of the Brookings Microeconomics Panel held at the Brookings Institution in Washington, D.C., June 19 and 20, 1998. Three of the papers study the economic and legal impacts of liability laws. The other four papers consider a broad range of economic and policy issues. Turning first to the liability papers, Steve Garber and John Adams examine the impact of product liability laws on automobile manufacturers' profitability by measuring stock market and customer reaction to verdicts in automotive personal injury cases. They find small and sometimes anomalous effects of verdicts on car sales and firms' stock prices. Patricia Born and Kip Viscusi consider the effect of liability reforms on medical malpractice and general liability insurance. They find that damage caps and several other types of state liability reforms decreased insurance premiums and yet improved the profitability of insurance companies. Thomas Campbell, Daniel Kessler, and George Shepherd provide empirical evidence on the impact of changes in liability laws on state-level productivity from 1970 to 1990. They find that states that reduced liability experienced greater increases in productivity. There also is some evidence to suggest the converse, that states that strengthened their liability laws tended to have less of an increase in productivity.

The other papers in this volume examine a range of timely economic and policy issues. Paul Gompers and Josh Lerner study the determinants of venture capital fundraising in the United States over the last twenty-five years. They find that taxes, pension fund investment laws, R&D intensity, fund performance, and fund reputations all played significant roles in determining venture fund raising. Axel Börsch-Supan's paper focuses on the role capital management plays in economic efficiency. Specifically, he compares data on capital utilization and capital productivity from Germany, Japan, and the United States. He finds that in addition to relative input prices, capital purchasing and management differences account for significant differences in capital productivity. Martin Baily and Eric Zitzewitz ask whether Korea must institute new reforms to sustain its rapid economic growth. They provide industry-level evidence suggesting that market distortions in Korea have resulted in critical misallocations of capital that have reduced productivity and lowered the rate of return to capital. Jeremy Bulow and Paul Klemperer analyze major economic and policy issues raised by the tobacco litigation in the mid- and late 1990s. They analyze how each stakeholder group (consumers, tobacco companies, federal and state governments, and lawyers) would have fared under the different proposals. They also propose improvements.

Garber and Adams on Economic Effects of Product Liability Verdicts

This paper seeks to expand our knowledge about the economic effects of product liability laws. Specifically, it tries to detect whether product liability verdicts against automobile manufacturers have economic effects beyond the direct cost of the verdict. The authors look for two types of indirect costs. The first is whether losing a liability case directly affects the automobile manufacturer's vehicle sales. The second is whether the stock market revalues manufacturers that lose product liability cases. In both instances, the loss of a case is expected to have a negative impact. The authors, however, also assert that the magnitude could depend on a variety of factors. The magnitude of a sales decline, for example, could depend on the extent and specificity of negative publicity surrounding the verdict. The magnitude of a stock market decline might depend on whether the verdict signals that the manufacturer potentially has a much bigger liability problem.

To gauge the impact of verdicts on sales and stock market values, the authors assembled a database of verdicts between 1985 and mid-1996, which included 93 judgements in favor of the plaintiffs and 116 verdicts for the manufacturers. The authors find that negative verdicts had little impact on sales of the vehicles involved in the suit. At most, sales declined by 1 to 2 percent on average. Regression evidence suggests that this result is not entirely robust or statistically significant. Additional controls for whether the verdict was punitive, there was a prior recall, the case involved dreadful injuries, or the verdict was widely publicized, while sometimes suggestive, also do not correlate with sales reductions.

The stock market analysis examines the impact of verdicts for and against automobile manufacturers. In both cases, the authors find no impact. They then use information on each verdict to try to predict the stock market reaction to that verdict. Here they find mixed evidence of systematic variations across verdicts. They conclude that some of their results are sensitive to several large verdicts. This leads them to argue that product liability verdicts have at most minor effects on company valuations.

Born and Viscusi on Effects of Tort Liability Reforms on Insurers

Did the tort liability reforms by states in the 1980s affect the performance of insurers and premium costs? This is the question that Born and Viscusi address using detailed ratemaking data from the National Association of Insurance Commissioners. In particular, the authors hope to gain insight into the economic factors that drove the rapid escalation of premiums in the mid-1980s and the ways that liability reforms may have differentially affected insurer profits.

Born and Viscusi begin by identifying the nature and extent of tort liability reforms during their sample period. The authors document a wide variety of reforms. They eschew developing a detailed set of variables summarizing these reforms in favor of using categorical variables that summarize whether the reform involved damage caps or something else. The authors use these variables to explain the decline in the ratio of insurers' general and medical malpractice liability losses to premiums from 1985 to 1991. From initial tabulations of the data, they determine that loss ratios during this period behave very differently depending on whether the firm initially has a low or high loss ratio. Born and Viscusi then go on to develop an econometric model of loss ratios that includes factors known to affect claims and premiums. These factors include macroeconomic, industry structure, and firm organization variables. A quantile regression model then allows them to examine the differential impact of these variables across firms' loss ratio distribution.

The authors find that the two liability reform variables do explain part of the decline in loss ratios from 1985 to 1991. The strength of their effect, however, differs across the distribution of loss ratios. For general liability insurers, only the damage cap variable has the predicted negative effect, which becomes more negative as one moves from initially profitable to unprofitable insurers. For medical malpractice insurance, the effect of damage cap reforms is consistently negative, and the effect of other reforms on initially unprofitable insurers is also large and negative. This implies that the financial benefits of liability reforms were concentrated mainly among inefficient or less profitable insurers. This finding shows that liability reforms, such as damage caps, may potentially reduce the costs of poor underwriting practices.

Campbell, Kessler, and Shepherd on Effects of Liability Reforms on Productivity

Campbell, Kessler, and Shepherd ask whether recent reforms in state liability laws have had measurable effects on business productivity. To date, most studies of the effects of liability laws have focused on measuring direct impacts, such as whether tougher medical malpractice law affects medical malpractice claims, awards levels, and administrative costs. This paper argues that liability laws might well have indirect effects through their influence on firms' productive scale and allocative efficiency. Campbell, Kessler, and Shepherd argue that economic models of the productive consequences of liability laws often do not make clear predictions about the consequences of liability reforms, making empirical research critical.

The authors choose to model how state liability reforms affected labor productivity, as measured by output per worker, between 1970 and 1990. Specifically, the authors develop an econometric model of state-level labor productivity data for a range of industries. Crucial to this model are variables that capture temporal, economic, demographic, and political factors affecting labor productivity. These factors include state and time fixed effects, state unemployment, political affiliations of elected officials, exports, interest group employment, asset values, and education. The authors then add qualitative variables that measure whether a state adopted more or less stringent liability reforms during the sample period. The authors painstakingly coded these variables by looking at eight different types of reforms that states adopted during this period. The paper explains in detail how the authors interpreted these reforms and mapped them into the qualitative variables used in the regressions.

Table 4 reports the authors' main finding that the private nonfarm industries of states that reduced their levels of legal liability experienced approximately a 1.7 percent increase in labor productivity. This finding is relatively robust to the choice of specification. In contrast, the private nonfarm industries of states that increased legal liability experienced only a slight negative and statistically insignificant effect on productivity. The authors also report results for the aggregate data. The results for states that reduced their levels of legal liability generally mirror the private nonfarm results. The results for states that increased the strength of their legal liability laws differ greatly across industries and are not robust to the specification employed. In subsequent tables, the authors examine the sensitivity of their results by examining productivity growth rates. From these regressions they conclude that although liability reforms do have a permanent one-time impact on productivity, they do not lead to perpetual increases or decreases in the effected states.

Gompers and Lerner on Venture Capital Fundraising

Gompers and Lerner study the rapid growth of venture capital funding in the United States between 1972 and 1994. They also examine venture capitalist success as well as industry and macroeconomic forces that spurred venture capital fundraising. Their ultimate goal is to examine the relative importance of various factors that could affect either the demand or the supply of venture capital.

The body of the paper outlines a list of industry-specific and macroeconomic factors that have influenced both the demand and supply of venture funds. These factors include economic growth, interest rates, capital gains taxes, technological innovations, and the deregulation of financial markets. The authors then attempt to identify the importance of these factors using unique data on venture capital commitments in the United States. A series of reduced form regressions suggests that tax rates, rule changes in federal pension law, and real growth in gross domestic product seem particularly important predictors of commitments. The authors explore the robustness of these findings using comparable state-level data on actual venture capital investments. Although the state-level results are generally consistent with those for the aggregate data, there are some important differences related to timing of initial public offerings.

In the latter sections of the paper, the authors examine the success of individual venture capital firms at raising funds. In particular, the authors are interested in whether ''success begets success'' and whether macroeconomic factors are very important. The main findings come from a series of discrete and continuous variable models that look at whether a firm raised funds, and if so, how much it raised. The results are mixed. The authors find some evidence that reputation matters, but this finding is sensitive to the inclusion of other variables, including firm fixed effects. The paper concludes with a discussion of policy implications.

Börsch-Supan on Capital Productivity

This paper examines why capital productivity differs among Germany, Japan, and the United States. It synthesizes evidence contained in a much larger survey of service and manufacturing productivity conducted by the McKinsey Global Institute. Börsch-Supan's main thesis is that relative price differences explain only part of why Germany and Japan are more capital intensive than the United States. He suggests that poor capital management techniques and inefficient investments account for much of the remaining difference.

Börsch-Supan begins by comparing productivity in five sectors across three countries. He finds substantial variation that is not easily explained by differences in input prices. Subsequent sections explore the gap between German and Japanese capital productivity and that of the United States. He finds some evidence that capacity utilization is much lower in most industries in Germany and Japan. He also attributes some of the capital productivity differences to differences in the composition of industry output. The remaining factors that are deemed important are classified as "capital management practices." These practices include such things as operational effectiveness and capital purchasing decisions. Through the extensive use of examples, Börsch-Supan tries to build a case that these management practices, together with regulations in Germany and Japan, have significantly lowered the productivity of capital.

Baily and Zitzewitz on Factor Productivity in Korea

This paper uses industry-level data to identify several structural economic problems that have placed a drag on Korea's factor productivity and made Korea's economy vulnerable to internal and external financial crises. The authors base much of their analysis on proprietary data developed by the McKinsey Global Institute and McKinsey and Company on eight major Korean industries. These data include information on the production practices of firms, their regulatory environment, and their capital requirements.

The paper begins with an analysis of what aggregate macroeconomic indicators suggest about Korea's productivity and its development path. These data show both that Korea has grown rapidly relative to most developed economies and that growth in input accounts for much of this overall growth. The data also reveal that capital productivity has fallen in Korea, and that in some sectors it is below that of other developed countries. This decline also is reflected in low returns to invested capital.

Baily and Zitzewitz follow up these aggregate statistics with detail from eight major Korean industries, four in manufacturing and four in services and construction. The authors find that many Korean industries have capital intensities in excess of their U.S. counterparts, despite having total factor productivities that are roughly half those in the United States. The authors then discuss institutions and regulations in Korea that might tend to encourage this overinvestment. They conclude that although moral hazard in financing arrangements may have contributed to some overinvestment, much of the explanation seems to lie in a confluence of events: the deregulation of Korean capital markets, slowing internal growth, and the East Asian financial crisis. These events, together with the failure of Korean firms to develop flexible capital management skills, exposed the overinvestment. The paper concludes with some suggestions for economic reforms.

Bulow and Klemperer on Tobacco Settlements

Bulow and Klemperer set out to analyze the economic ramifications of recent proposals for ending tobacco litigation. Their primary goal is to analyze major economic issues posed by the June 1997 tobacco resolution and congressional legislation that sought to alter the resolution. In analyzing these issues, they attempt to avoid normative conclusions and instead focus on isolating inefficient and costly provisions. They then seek to propose more efficient settlement terms.

The paper begins by describing the cigarette industry and business conditions in 1997. The authors then discuss the original settlement proposals. They first focus on the unusual taxes the resolution and legislation effectively imposed on cigarette manufacturers. They argue that the proposed fixed-revenue taxes are less efficient than ordinary specific taxes. They also argue that the proposed taxes are an extremely inefficient way of deterring teen smokers, one of the stated targets of legislative proposals. The authors next analyze company damage payment and liability protection proposals. They argue that these parts of the settlement might have unintended incentive issues.

The latter parts of the paper consider alternative proposals that would reduce teen smoking, reduce legal fees, and enforce competition in the face of a mandated rise in prices. The paper concludes by discussing the sequentially negotiated state settlements. It also makes specific suggestions for settlements.

STEVEN GARBER
RAND

JOHN ADAMS
RAND

Product and Stock Market Responses to Automotive Product Liability Verdicts

CLAIMS ABOUT DETRIMENTAL economic effects of product liability are a cornerstone of efforts by tort reformers to rally support. It seems fair to say, however, that existing evidence about economic effects of product liability is sketchy.[1] In this paper, we attempt to develop information about a narrow but important piece of a very complex puzzle. In particular, we develop quantitative evidence about a component of automobile manufacturers' incentives stemming from product liability by examining effects of trial verdicts on company stock prices and on new vehicle sales. We know of no similar study.[2]

We gratefully acknowledge financial support from the Alfred P. Sloan Foundation and the RAND Institute for Civil Justice. Our conclusions and opinions do not necessarily reflect the views of the Institute for Civil Justice, RAND, or research sponsors. We thank Dan Relles for helpful discussions and Sam Peltzman, Daniel Rubinfeld, Clifford Winston, and other conference participants for insightful comments on a previous draft. Eva Feldman, Sung-Ho Ahn, John Anderson, Darcy Byrne, Susan Mc-Glamery, Joan Schlimgen, and Roberta Shanman have provided extensive research assistance.

1. Efforts to provide empirical information about economic effects of product liability include Viscusi (1991); Huber and Litan (1991); Garber (1993); Hunziker and Jones (1994); and Manning (1994, 1997).

2. Viscusi and Hersch (1990) examine stock price effects of product liability (and regulatory enforcement) events—mostly lawsuit filings and no verdicts—for various industries. Jarrell and Peltzman (1985); Hoffer, Pruitt, and Reilly (1988); Marcus and Bromiley (1988); Bromiley and Marcus (1989); and Barber and Darrough (1996) study stock market effects of automobile recalls. Wynne and Hoffer (1976); Crafton, Hoffer, and Reilly (1981); Reilly and Hoffer (1983); and McCarthy (1989) analyze effects of

1

Efficiency effects of product liability depend on the resource costs of bringing and resolving claims and lawsuits and on how incentives emanating from product liability exposure affect manufacturer decisions and economic outcomes outside the legal system. Such outcomes include product safety and usefulness, costs of designing and manufacturing products, and rates and directions of innovation.

We focus on a component of incentives rather than directly examining economic outcomes because few of the key economic outcomes can be observed or measured by researchers. This means that researchers will be able at best to draw inferences about effects of product liability relying on assumptions about objectives of firms and information about how product liability affects the environment in which these objectives are pursued.

We focus on a single industry because liability effects on business decisions should depend on industry-specific factors such as market conditions, safety regulation, opportunities for improving product safety, and capabilities for developing evidence that products have caused injury. We chose motor vehicles because economic effects of product liability in the automobile industry have received substantial attention, and because it is possible to develop relatively extensive data for motor vehicles.[3]

We further focus the inquiry on trial verdicts. Manufacturer incentives emanating from the product liability system are a composite of many types of potential or actual "liability events" such as informal claims made (with the implicit or explicit threat of a lawsuit), lawsuit filings, negotiations about claims or suits, settlements, trial verdicts, and appeals and their resolution. We focus on trial verdicts for a combination of substantive and practical reasons, namely because verdicts are very prominent, can be documented, are sufficiently numerous to allow econometric analysis, and contain elements of surprise (that is, new information), the timing of which can be established.[4]

---

recalls on motor vehicle sales. Effects of automobile recalls on prices are studied by Hartman (1987) and Uri (1989).

3. For economic effects, see, for example, Graham (1991); Mackay (1991); Babcock (1994); and Castaing (1994).

4. Trial verdicts—unlike many other liability events such as informal claims, negotiations, and settlements (the terms of which are often confidential), and even lawsuit filings—can be documented. Concerning suit filings, there is a comprehensive database on suits in federal court, but the information it contains is not sufficiently detailed to

---

Product Liability Incentives: A Priori Considerations

Incentives for motor vehicle manufacturers to invest in safety emanating from product liability operate in conjunction with incentives resulting from the behavior of motor vehicle buyers and the National Highway Traffic Safety Administration (NHTSA), the industry's product safety regulator. Automobile companies have market-based incentives to improve the safety of their products in the ways and to the extent that these improvements translate into consumers' willingness to pay. Consumers can observe or verify the presence of seat belts, padded dashboards, and air bags.[5] Information about such other safety-related vehicle attributes as braking distances and handling in (simulated) emergency situations is available from automotive and consumer publications. In addition, the NHTSA conducts crash tests of vehicles and releases the results publicly.[6] Regulation by the NHTSA—promulgation and enforcement of motor vehicle design standards and the threat of safety-related recalls—provides additional incentives for product safety.

Product Liability Costs

Product liability may alter manufacturer behavior bearing on product safety because liability for product-related injuries can impose costs on manufacturers. It is helpful to distinguish between direct and indirect liability costs. *Direct* liability costs are incurred by companies within the product liability process. These include costs of responding to and settling informal claims that could become lawsuits; responding to, defending, negotiating over, and settling lawsuits before verdicts; trying cases; appealing, negotiating and settling lawsuits after trial verdicts; and paying trial judgments. *Indirect* liability costs are attributable to events within the liability process—they would not be incurred if it were not for these events—but are incurred outside that process. Indi-

---

support the kind of analysis reported in this paper (for example, the product involved in a suit cannot be identified), and most product liability suits are brought in the state courts.

5. Mannering and Winston (1995) estimate willingness to pay for airbags. Other recent studies providing evidence that consumer demand depends on vehicle safety include McCarthy (1990) and Dreyfus and Viscusi (1995).

6. See, for example, Hoffer, Pruitt, and Reilly (1992).

4   *Brookings Papers: Microeconomics 1998*

rect costs might result from demand decreases or regulatory actions triggered by liability events.

Product Liability Risks

When automobile companies make decisions to design, manufacture, and label a product in a particular way, the liability consequences are uncertain and will not be determined for decades. Uncertainty about eventual liability costs stems from many sources including unforeseen product hazards; doctrinal complexity and lack of precision; potential for doctrinal change; unpredictable behavior of company personnel, product users, attorneys, judges, and juries; changes in attitudes toward litigation and compensation; and unknown future capabilities for determining accident or injury causation.

The term *liability risk* is used here to refer to the potential for product liability costs, direct and indirect, encompassing both the (subjective) probabilities and magnitudes of such costs. Risk may be an essential consideration in company responses to product liability because, unlike many other business risks, product liability risks are unlimited for all practical purposes.[7]

Liability Costs, Vehicle Sales, and Stock Prices: Theory

In this section we describe what sales and stock price effects would and would not reflect and the circumstances under which such effects would be expected to be larger or smaller. First we describe case studies that provide background and motivation. Then we consider how verdicts might affect product demand and vehicle sales.

Case Studies of Liability in Motor Vehicles

Case studies and journalistic accounts of particular motor vehicle models or types of vehicles with unusually extensive and eventful product liability histories suggest that product liability costs can be very substantial. Moreover, they suggest that indirect liability costs to motor

7. This is because product liability costs usually cannot be controlled after they begin to mount, and they are not limited to any amount a company explicitly chooses to place at risk.

vehicle manufacturers may be major elements of their product liability exposure.

More specifically, the histories of product liability litigation, NHTSA action, and market developments related to various car or truck models suggest that indirect costs of litigation, if and when they exist, are part of a complicated, dynamic process. Consider the following composite scenario. Safety concerns about a vehicle model, well founded or not, arise. A complex, interdependent chain of events follows involving personal injury litigation; controversy over engineering evidence and injury causation; mass media attention, often triggered by large trial awards, many of which include punitive components; pressure on the NHTSA by groups representing consumers, victims, plaintiffs, or plaintiffs' attorneys; defect investigations by the NHTSA; safety recalls of the vehicles; and declining sales of the model. Vehicles with case histories containing many of these elements, including the possibility of demand effects and a prominent role for mass media coverage, are the Ford Pinto (concerns about fuel tank position), the Jeep CJ-5 and CJ-7 (concerns about rollovers), the Audi 5000 (concerns about sudden acceleration), and, more recently, the GM C/K (side-saddle) pickup trucks (concerns about fuel tank position).[8]

In many of these cases it is difficult to judge whether, and if so to what extent, product liability contributed to decreases in demand for vehicles involved in litigation. More important, histories and journalistic accounts are written about cases that seem atypical in various ways, including volume of litigation, sizes of awards, and the extent, char-

8. On the Pinto see Schwartz (1991). Graham (1991, p. 135) is skeptical that product liability was a fundamental factor in the declining sales of the Pinto, but he refers to speculation that "sales of all Ford models may have been adversely affected by the Pinto fuel tank controversy." In the case of the Jeep CJ-5, Graham (1991, p. 149) points to adverse publicity, resulting at least in part from efforts of plaintiff attorneys, as one cause of sharply declining sales.

On the Audi 5000, Sullivan (1990) focuses on events during 1986—most notably a report on CBS television's *60 Minutes*—and concludes that concerns about the car's alleged problem with sudden acceleration and related publicity depressed prices of used Audi 5000S and other Audi models. Brown (1986) emphasizes effects on new Audi sales. Mackay (1991, pp. 210–11) briefly recounts the Audi 5000's history, emphasizing sales declines and the roles of the plaintiffs' bar and the media, and refers to the car as "a financial disaster for the manufacturer." Huber (1991, chap. 4) provides an extensive account of and commentary on the litigation.

On the GM pickups see LaManna (1993); Thomas (1993); and Pearl and Lavin (1994).

acter, and prominence of news media coverage. Our analysis provides some perspective from a much broader class of litigation episodes.

Vehicle Sales

A verdict against a motor vehicle manufacturer would be expected to decrease demand for a vehicle model found defective only if, and to the extent that, the verdict conveys new information relevant to purchase decisions and potential buyers become aware of this information. Regarding the potential information content of a verdict, the most obvious possibility is that verdicts against manufacturers lead consumers to become more concerned about the safety characteristics of the model involved in the trial. The degree to which consumers become aware of different verdicts is likely to vary considerably. A major potential factor is the extent of news coverage.[9]

Demand decreases are quantifiable from unit sales decreases only if price does not respond. We do not observe (transactions) prices for vehicles, however. Assuming that decreases in demand are generally not entirely and quickly absorbed by decreases in price, we examine empirically the possibility of declines in unit sales shortly after verdicts are announced. If verdicts do decrease demand but demand decreases are quickly and completely accommodated by price adjustments (of which consumers are quickly well informed), demand effects would not be apparent from effects on unit sales. Demand decreases that are newly anticipated by investors at the time of the verdict would, however, be reflected in stock price responses to verdicts.

Stock Prices

A verdict for or against a motor vehicle manufacturer would be expected to affect its stock price to the extent that the verdict carries with it new information about factors relevant to future company profits, and this information becomes known to investors.[10] Future profitability

9. Garber and Bower (1998) find virtually no newspaper coverage of motor vehicle product liability trials prior to verdicts and virtually no coverage of verdicts finding manufacturers not liable. Thus, in analyzing demand effects we consider only plaintiff verdicts.

10. We think it plausible, and we investigate the possibility, that stock prices react to verdicts in favor of manufacturers as well as those holding manufacturers liable.

depends on an array of factors that are in principle sensitive to trial verdicts. These include indirect liability costs of types we have described. They also include direct liability costs, which are potentially affected through various mechanisms.

DIRECT LIABILITY COSTS IN THE CURRENT CASE. The announcement of a trial verdict should affect investor beliefs about direct costs associated with the lawsuit resulting in that verdict. Such effects of verdict announcements are complicated because a verdict does not resolve a lawsuit. For example, verdicts against manufacturers are often followed by settlement negotiations and appeals to higher courts.[11] Postverdict activities by a manufacturer's legal team generate additional direct costs, and their effectiveness determines how much will eventually be paid to the plaintiff in damages (if any).

A verdict announcement should be viewed, then, as updating investor beliefs about future direct liability costs in the lawsuit leading to the verdict, but with considerable uncertainty remaining. A verdict for a manufacturer seems safely presumed to be good news for investors about these direct liability costs. Although a verdict against a manufacturer should usually be bad news in this regard, it can in principle be less costly than what investors had expected.[12]

DIRECT LIABILITY COSTS IN OTHER CASES. Perhaps more important, verdicts may also affect direct liability costs in *other* cases, both through cases that would have been brought in any event and by affecting the number of cases. For cases that would have been brought anyway, suppose—which is not uncommon—that a company has several dozen or more other cases pending involving the same vehicle model and alleged defect. Often, a handful of cases (perhaps five or ten) will be tried, and the results of these trials could greatly affect the

11. Moreover, a jury award of damages against a manufacturer does not become a legal obligation to pay until a judgment is entered by the trial judge. Often a trial judge enters a judgment based precisely on the verdict, but sometimes the judge overrules the jury entirely or accepts the finding of liability but reduces the award. In any event, judgments for damages are often followed by appeals.

12. For example, suppose that as the jury went off to deliberate, investors believed that there was a 75 percent chance that they would find the manufacturer liable and expected the award to be $5 million. If the jury finds liability and announces damages of $1 million, investor assessments of the direct costs of this lawsuit may go down rather than up.

terms on which other cases are settled. The effect of a single verdict can be magnified in this way.

Moreover, a verdict against a manufacturer can trigger additional claims or lawsuits. For example, a large verdict against a manufacturer in a case alleging that vehicle model X is defective because of fuel tank leaks and a fire hazard may, particularly if it is widely publicized, lead people who were burned in accidents involving model X to contact an attorney. Finally, learning about the hypothetical verdict should make an attorney more willing to accept a similar case and pursue it energetically.

Samples of Verdicts

We focus on personal injury, product liability verdicts involving allegedly defective cars or light trucks. Different samples are used to study effects on vehicle sales and stock prices. We analyze sales effects for both domestic and foreign manufacturers. Lacking suitable data on stock prices for foreign manufacturers, we analyze stock price effects only for domestic manufacturers.

Sources of Verdict Information

The analyses require information about various characteristics of cases leading to verdicts, such as the model and model year of the vehicle alleged to be defective, the nature of the defect alleged, and the nature of the injuries involved in the accident. There is no comprehensive source of such information.[13] Moreover, there is no practical way of developing such information for a sample that can be reasonably viewed as random.[14]

The primary source used to identify verdicts is the *Automotive Liti-*

13. There is no database of civil cases in state courts, where most product liability lawsuits are brought, that could be used for our purposes. There is a comprehensive database of federal court cases, but it does not include the kind of information we require: for example, vehicle models or, indeed, even if cases involved a car or light truck.

14. For example, sampling cases and developing the required data would require visits to several courthouses around the country, which would be prohibitively costly.

gation Reporter (*ALR*), which was initially searched from January 1985 through July 1996.[15] This search yielded 116 verdicts for which a domestic automobile manufacturer was found not to be liable ("defendant verdicts") and other required information was reported. We judged this number to be adequate for analysis of stock price responses to defendant verdicts. This search, however, yielded only 56 verdicts in which a domestic or foreign manufacturer was held liable for money damages ("plaintiff verdicts").[16]

This original set of plaintiff verdicts was augmented by writing and following up with phone calls to plaintiff attorneys listed in the *ALR* to request unreported verdict dates. We also extended the *ALR* search through December 2, 1996; searched the index of *Jury Verdicts Weekly* (*JVW*), a publication reporting verdicts throughout California; and searched newspaper databases.[17] These efforts yielded 37 additional plaintiff verdicts for a total of 93 personal injury, product liability verdicts against automobile manufacturers from 1985 to 1996.

15. The *ALR* is sold by subscription, primarily to plaintiff and defense attorneys and law libraries. In 1994 its circulation was about 150. The cases covered in the *ALR* are an unsystematic sample of unknown completeness: almost all of the articles are based on unsolicited reports from attorneys who send information to the publisher. (Telephone interview with Nick Sullivan, editor of the *ALR*, October 1994.)

16. It is very likely that defendant verdicts are overrepresented in the *ALR* relative to plaintiff verdicts. Victorious defense attorneys have more incentive to report to the *ALR* in the hope of attracting new clients than do victorious plaintiff attorneys because potential clients of defense attorneys (for example, staff attorneys at automobile companies) are much more likely to see the *ALR* than are potential clients of plaintiff attorneys (people injured in automobile accidents). The econometric work that follows does not seek to explain trial outcomes nor does it pool defendant and plaintiff verdicts, thus this nonrandom sampling does not imply bias in our estimates.

17. The search of newspaper databases yielded only four additional plaintiff verdicts, all during 1994–96. We used selected keywords related to litigation, liability, the NHTSA, and automobile safety and company names to generate lists of titles of articles written from 1990 to 1996. We did this by searching full-text articles in the *Wall Street Journal*, the *New York Times* and the ten highest-circulation newspapers in the DIALOG PAPERS database and reviewed these titles visually. Because this process was very laborious, we automated it somewhat and searched the titles of the articles in the other DIALOG newspapers using keywords selected from the titles of articles studied in Garber and Bower (1998). The process was very costly and yielded only four verdicts over a seven-year period that had not been previously identified, so we did not attempt to identify verdicts before 1990 by searching newspapers. Attempts to locate additional verdicts by electronic searches of databases of legal publications and investment house research reports were entirely unproductive.

Sample for Vehicle Sales Analyses

The sample of plaintiff verdicts used to study sales effects is 61 of the 93 plaintiff verdicts.[18] The analysis of sales effects involves forecasting sales into the months following verdicts. Some verdicts were eliminated because the model had been discontinued by the time of the verdict. In addition, we examined the monthly sales time series and eliminated six series for which it was apparent that credible forecasts could not be produced.[19]

Samples for Stock Price Analyses

We examined stock price effects for both defendant and plaintiff verdicts. The sample sizes are 116 for defendant verdicts and 64 for plaintiff verdicts, the latter being the subset of the 93 total plaintiff verdicts for which the defendant was a domestic manufacturer.

Appendix tables A-1 and A-2 summarize the distributions of verdict years and defendant companies for the three samples.

Empirical Strategy and Variable Definitions

This section explains our approach to measuring outcomes and studying their determinants.

Outcome Variables: Sales Effects

Monthly U.S. new vehicle sales data by model were compiled from various issues of the *Automotive News Market Data Book*. We construct alternative dependent variables based on the difference between actual sales in the month after the verdict and two forecasts of what the sales would have been without the verdict. We interpret the dependent variables as alternative (noisy) estimates of sales shortfalls attributable to the verdicts.

18. We do not analyze effects of defendant verdicts on new vehicle sales because such effects seem very implausible.
19. In particular, we eliminated two verdicts for which the models were already in steep sales declines before the verdicts, three for which the models had sales of fewer than one hundred units a month, and one for which fewer than five months of preverdict sales data were available.

To construct forecasts with as little noise as possible, we considered various forecasting methods, evaluated their performance for model-level sales data during the months before their corresponding verdicts, and selected the two best performers to construct our outcome measures. We considered several forecasting approaches, including nonstatistical ones, various regression specifications, and some simple autoregressive models.[20]

To evaluate the performance of each forecasting approach, a model was repeatedly fit to subsets of each sales time series (prior to the verdict month), and a series of one-month-ahead forecasts was constructed. The forecast errors were expressed as absolute percentage errors (APEs) to make them comparable across vehicle models. Forecasting approaches were evaluated according to their mean APEs (MAPEs), which for each forecasting approach involves averaging over one-month-ahead forecasts for each vehicle model and then averaging across vehicle models.

The best forecasts, with a MAPE of 12.5 percent, resulted from a simple nonstatistical approach. In particular, using the most successful method, the forecast for a model's sales in month t (S_t) is given by

$$\hat{S}_t = \frac{C_t}{C_{t-1}} S_{t-1},$$

where C_t and C_{t-1} are company-level sales of the type of vehicle (car or truck) involved in the verdict.[21]

The forecasting method used to construct our other sales effects measure is an ordinary exponential smoother.[22] Although these forecasts had a substantially higher MAPE, 17.2 percent, we consider the

20. In the regression models we related monthly sales of an individual car (truck) model to various combinations of company sales of all cars (trucks), seasonally adjusted monthly unemployment rates, and interest rates on three- and five-year Treasury bonds adjusted to real terms by subtracting the CPI growth rate over the previous twelve months.

21. The relatively good performance of this approach may be attributable to the use of company-level sales (of the vehicle type involved in the trial) for the same month being forecast, which incorporates both seasonal and companywide effects that are not captured by the pre-forecast-month variables relied on in the other forecasting approaches.

22. This uses a geometric weighted average of past sales of a model to forecast its future sales.

method to gauge the sensitivity of our conclusions to the use of two quite different forecasting approaches.

To define the sales-effects outcome measures analyzed, let $OBSLS_j$ = the observed level of sales of the model involved in verdict j during the month after verdict j was announced; $CTPRED_j$ = the level of those sales forecasted using the nonstatistical approach; and $EXPRED_j$ = the level of those sales forecasted using the exponential-smoothing method.

The outcome measures RASLCT and RASLEX are the forecast errors expressed relative to observed sales:

$$RASLCT_j = \frac{OBSLS_j - CTPRED_j}{OBSLS_j} \text{ , and}$$

$$RASLEX_j = \frac{OBSLS_j - EXPRED_j}{OBSLS_j} \text{ .}$$

If verdicts against manufacturers typically reduce sales, we would expect actual sales to fall short of forecasts and, therefore, *RASLCT* and *RASLEX* averaged over verdicts to be negative. We also analyze cross-verdict variation in *RASLCT* and *RASLEX*.

Outcome Variables: Stock Market Effects

We develop measures of abnormal stock market responses to verdicts using standard event-study methods.[23] Daily stock price data, adjusted for splits and dividends, were obtained from the Dow Jones *Tradeline* for the four U.S. motor vehicle manufacturers.[24] For each verdict, we estimate the so-called "market model":

$$r_{it} = \alpha_i + \beta_i R_{mt} + \epsilon_{it},$$

where r_{it} = return on security i from trading day $t-1$ to day t and R_{mt} = return on the Standard & Poor's 500 index from trading day $t-1$ to day t, using data for the 120 trading days prior to the date the verdict was announced.[25] We use the estimates of α_i and β_i and to construct

23. See, for example, Campbell, Lo, and MacKinlay (1997, chap. 4); or MacKinlay (1997).

24. The early part of the sample period predates the merger of American Motors and Chrysler.

25. Returns are computed from closing prices on the indicated trading days.

CAR, the cumulative abnormal return for the next two trading days.[26] Finally, to construct *CAVAL*, a measure of abnormal *dollar* returns expressed in millions of 1996 dollars, we multiply *CAR* by the market equity of the company at the end of the month before the verdict.[27]

If verdicts against (for) manufacturers typically decrease (increase) stock prices, we would expect the cross-verdict means of *CAR* and *CAVAL* to be negative (positive) for the sample of plaintiff (defendant) verdicts. We also use regressions to analyze whether *CAVAL* varies systematically across plaintiff verdicts.

Independent Variables

It appears that no defensible model would yield identified structural equations for either sales or stock price effects.[28] Instead, we estimate various regressions intended to provide an informative description of the data. We view such equations as predictive of the outcomes of interest, but we cannot ascribe causal interpretations to them. We report but pay little attention to *t*-ratios because several specifications were estimated and because the set of verdicts analyzed is not viewed as a sample from a much larger population.

Table 1 defines the independent variables used in the regressions and reports data sources.[29] They are grouped into three categories: indirect cost, direct cost, and publicity.

PREDICTORS OF INDIRECT COSTS. Variables in this set are intended to

26. Thus if the verdict was announced on a trading day, the abnormal return incorporates the stock return on the day of the verdict and the subsequent trading day. If (as happens in a few cases) the verdict was announced on a nontrading day (a Saturday or holiday), the abnormal return variable incorporates the stock return over the following two trading days.

27. Nominal values of market capitalization and other variables were adjusted using the CPI for all items for urban consumers (CPI-U), taken from the *Economic Report of the President*, February 1997, table B-58. Market equity (capitalization) data were obtained from Standard & Poor's, Compustat.

28. For example, sales effects are expected to depend on the nature of the injuries, recall histories, the extent of publicity, and interactions. But the extent of publicity depends (see Garber and Bower, 1998) on the nature of the injuries, recall histories, and characteristics of the verdict, which in turn depend on the nature of the injuries. A defensible structural model for stock price effects would seemingly be even more complicated because stock prices are expected to depend directly on the characteristics of the verdict in addition to any factors expected to affect sales.

29. Selected interactions are also used in some regressions.

Table 1. Independent Variables for Analyses of Cross-Verdict Variation in Sales and Stock Price Effects

Variable[a]	Description	Source
Indirect cost		
DREAD	= 1 if anyone was killed, paralyzed, or seriously burned in accident leading to trial; 0 otherwise	*Automotive Litigation Reporter (ALR)*, *Jury Verdicts Weekly (JVW)*, miscellaneous newspaper articles
RLTRCL	= 1 if vehicle involved in trial was recalled prior to verdict for a related defect; 0 otherwise	Computer files from National Highway Traffic Safety Administration (NHTSA)
OTHRCL	Number of other safety recalls prior to verdict of the vehicle involved in trial	NHTSA
MDLSLS	Sales of model involved in the trial in the year prior to verdict (number of units)	*Automotive News Market Data Book*, various issues
Direct cost		
TOTDOL	Size of total award (millions of 1996 dollars)	*ALR*, *JVW*, miscellaneous news articles
COMPDOL	Size of compensatory award (millions of 1996 dollars)	*ALR*, *JVW*, miscellaneous news articles
PUNDOL	Size of punitive award (millions of 1996 dollars)	*ALR*, *JVW*, miscellaneous news articles
PUNIND	= 1 if verdict award included punitive damages; 0 otherwise	*ALR*, *JVW*, miscellaneous news articles
PIOK	= 1 if prior to verdict company disclosed related litigation on SEC form 10K; 0 otherwise	Company 10K filings
Publicity[b]		
WSJAR	= 1 if the *Wall Street Journal* covered verdict; 0 otherwise	*Wall Street Journal* on-line database
CRCOTH	Total 1992 circulation of other papers covering verdict divided by total 1992 circulation of other papers searched	*New York Times*, DIALOG (Knight Ridder) on-line databases; *Circulation 92* (Standard Rate and Data Service)
CRALL	Weighted average of *WSJAR* and *CRCOTH* based on 1992 circulation figures	*Wall Street Journal*, *New York Times*, DIALOG on-line databases; *Circulation 92*

a. Various functions and interactions also considered.
b. For the sales effects analysis, articles are counted if they appear within seven days of the verdict. For the stock price analysis, articles are counted if they appear by the second trading day that could be affected by the verdict.

control for factors that consumers might think are informative about the safety of the vehicle involved in the trial.

Injuries: Consumers might, upon learning of a verdict against a manufacturer, become more concerned about the safety of the model found defective if anyone involved in the accident leading to the trial sustained particularly severe or dreaded injuries. *DREAD* is a dichotomous variable that takes the value 1 if the accident caused any fatalities, serious burns, or paralysis.

Recall history: Upon learning of a verdict against a manufacturer, consumers may be more inclined to reduce their estimate of the safety of the model judged defective if they had some atypical preverdict reason to be concerned. To examine this possibility we use two variables summarizing the safety recall histories of the vehicles (defined by model and model year) involved in the trials. *RLTRCL* equals 1 if before the date of the verdict the vehicle had ever been recalled for a safety problem similar or related to any safety defect alleged in the trial.[30] *OTHRCL* is the number of other safety recalls—for any reason—of the vehicle involved in the trial that occurred before the verdict date.

PREDICTORS OF DIRECT COSTS. The first predictor is the size of the award. *TOTDOL* is the real dollar amount of the total damage award in millions of 1996 dollars. Its compensatory and punitive (if any) components are denoted by *COMPDOL* and *PUNDOL*.[31] The existence of a punitive component of an award is indicated by the dichotomous variable PUNIND. Including this variable in combination with total damage amounts allows for an independent effect of a finding that the manufacturer deserves to be punished.

A second predictor is whether there is an unusual amount of similar pending litigation. As discussed earlier, a verdict is expected to have a larger effect on stock prices if there are several similar cases in the litigation pipeline. A measure of the amount of pending litigation cannot

30. The vehicle components alleged to be defective and the cause of the accident or injury in the trial were coded from the litigation reporters or newspaper articles. Recall data cover all safety-related recalls, whether or not they involved a previous NHTSA investigation. We focused on the vehicle components involved in the recalls and the descriptions of how the components were believed to fail (and thereby pose a hazard). *RLTRCL* was coded as 1 if there was any indication that there had been a prior recall for reasons related to allegations made during the trial.

31. Damage amounts are those initially determined by the jury before, for example, they are reduced or overturned by the trial judge or an appeals court.

be constructed because such information is proprietary. A dichotomous variable was constructed by examining litigation sections of the 10K reports filed by the manufacturers with the Securities and Exchange Commission. The variable *P10K* equals 1 if before the verdict date the manufacturer had disclosed pending product liability litigation involving the same vehicle model and type of alleged defect.[32]

NEWSPAPER PUBLICITY VARIABLES. We focus on newspapers because very little data for television can be developed earlier than 1992 and because television coverage of verdicts appears to be very rare.[33] To measure newspaper coverage, we used procedures described fully elsewhere.[34] Briefly, we searched electronically through full-text newspaper databases for articles "triggered" by these verdicts—those for which the verdict was the reason or justification for the article. The databases are the *Wall Street Journal*, the *New York Times* and the DIALOG PAPERS database group. The DIALOG databases include fifty-eight newspapers, but the time periods covered vary from paper to paper. Generally, more papers can be searched for later years.[35] For each verdict, we searched all newspapers that could be searched given the date of the verdict. The searches were done using a keyword string of the form [(company name) or (division name) or (make name)] and [plaintiff(s) surname(s)] for the eight-day period beginning with the verdict date.[36]

32. According to general legal guidelines, firms are required to disclose information related to product liability only if such exposure is "material" according to the law. "Material" information is "information that a reasonable investor would consider significant in making an investment decision" (Hazen, 1993, p. 84).

33. See Garber (1998, pp. 280–81) for a discussion of three sources of information on television news coverage and their scopes and limitations. The data that can be developed, which include reports on the three network evening news shows over the entire sample period, suggest that it is very rare for verdicts to trigger television coverage (lead to reports at the time of or shortly after the verdict). The few exceptions are three sample verdicts involving exceptionally large damage awards, each of which included a punitive component.

34. Garber and Bower (1998).

35. For example, only eleven of the DIALOG newspapers can be searched back to 1986, twenty-four for 1988, thirty-nine for 1989, fifty-five for 1990, and a high of fifty-seven for 1994 and 1995. A few newspapers ceased publication during the analysis period.

36. Hypothetical search strings are (Chrysler or Plymouth) and Jones; (General Motors or GM or Chevrolet) and Smith; and (Ford or Mercury) and Thompson. This procedure was adopted after experimentation aimed at capturing virtually all relevant

Table 2. Descriptive Statistics for Sales Outcome Variables

Variable	Mean	Standard deviation	Minimum	Maximum
RASLCT	− 0.0225	0.233	− 1.25	0.501
RASLEX	− 0.00899	0.339	− 2.01	0.732

Source: Authors' calculations. The sample includes 61 plaintiff verdicts in cases involving makes and models for which new-vehicle unit sales could be forecast for the month following the verdict. *RASLCT* and *RASLEX* are forecast errors—which are interpreted as estimates of effects of verdicts—relative to actual sales based on two alternative methods of forecasting.

The publicity variables for the sales effect analysis are measures of coverage within this eight-day period. Because the stock price analysis examines effects within two trading days of the verdicts, the publicity measures used in that analysis incorporate only those articles published within this time period.[37]

Estimates and Interpretation

We begin by reporting and interpreting average values of the sales and stock price outcome measures. We then turn to analyses of their cross-verdict variation.

Average Values of Outcome Variables

Average sales effects. Table 2 reports descriptive statistics for *RASLCT* and *RASLEX*. These data provide at most a hint that verdicts against manufacturers typically depress sales of the vehicle model involved in the trial during the month immediately following the verdict. In particular, the means of *RASLCT* and *RASLEX* suggest that, on average, unit sales or new vehicles may be depressed by 1 to 2 percent, but these means are dwarfed by the sample standard deviations of the measures.

Average stock market responses. Table 3 reports descriptive statistics for various measures of abnormal stock returns for both the plaintiff- and defendant-verdict samples. These data provide absolutely no support for either the hypothesis that plaintiff verdicts typically depress

articles without also capturing excessive numbers of irrelevant ones (which are costly to collect and examine).

37. The discrepancies are minor because almost all relevant articles appear within two days of each verdict.

Table 3. Descriptive Statistics for Abnormal Returns, Three-Event Windows

Variable	Mean	Standard deviation	Minium	Maximum
Plaintiff verdicts (N = 64)				
Proportionate returns				
CAR	0.00104	0.0203	−0.0656	0.0521
CAR3	0.00195	0.0215	−0.0481	0.0381
CAR4	0.00617	0.0243	−0.0509	0.0487
Dollar returns (millions of 1996 dollars)				
CAVAL	25.4	558	−1,643	1,711
CAVAL3	28.6	630	−1,814	1,369
CAVAL4	147.4	710	−1,816	1,777
Defendant verdicts (N = 116)				
Proportionate returns				
CAR	−0.00225	0.0228	−0.0934	0.0719
CAR3	−0.00112	0.0259	−0.0774	0.0900
CAR4	−0.000115	0.0299	−0.0663	0.0931
Dollar returns (millions of 1996 dollars)				
CAVAL	−47.5	541	−1,936	1,834
CAVAL3	−50.0	647	−2,575	1,671
CAVAL4	−50.9	756	−2,207	2,360

Source: Authors' calculations. The samples include 64 verdicts holding U.S. manufacturers liable ("plaintiff verdicts") and 116 verdicts in which U.S. manufacturers were not found liable ("defendant verdicts"). *CAR*, *CAR3*, and *CAR4* are estimated abnormal returns during two-, three-, and four-trading-day periods beginning with the first day that could be affected by the verdict announcement. *CAVAL*, *CAVAL3*, and *CAVAL4* are the market capitalization of the defendant company at the end of the month preceding the verdict multiplied by *CAR*, *CAR3*, and *CAR4*, respectively, and are estimates of the real abnormal dollar returns associated with the verdicts over the three time intervals.

stock prices or the hypothesis that defendant verdicts typically increase them. The average values of *CAR* and *CAVAL*, which measure abnormal returns during the first two trading days that could be affected by the verdict, are in fact opposite in sign from what would be expected under these hypotheses. These means are, however, very small and are dwarfed by the sample standard deviations. To consider the possibility that investors react a bit slowly, table 3 also reports descriptive statistics for analogs to *CAR* and *CAVAL* computed over longer event windows. In particular, *CAR3* and *CAR4* are cumulative abnormal returns computed through the third and fourth trading days, respectively. *CAVAL3* and *CAVAL4* are defined analogously in terms of abnormal dollar returns. Extending the event windows by an extra day or two does nothing to change the basic conclusion.

Summary. On average, then, we find at most very weak evidence that verdicts against manufacturers typically depress sales and no evidence that verdicts for or against manufacturers typically affect stock prices. We proceed to investigate the cross-verdict variation in the outcome measures for plaintiff verdicts. Appendix table A-3 reports descriptive statistics for independent variables used in the regression analyses.

Vehicle Sales Regressions

The mean values of the proportionate sales forecast errors provide almost no evidence that product markets generally react negatively to product liability verdicts against motor vehicle manufacturers. This may be because consumers do not use verdicts to update their beliefs about the relative safety of vehicles or because verdict-driven changes in beliefs are rarely sufficient to alter purchase decisions.[38] Alternatively, verdicts may have major effects on sales in some unusual cases. For example, as might be inferred from case studies, consumers may react to verdicts that are extreme in their safety implications, are highly publicized, or both. We use regression analysis to examine such possibilities.

Table 4 reports estimates using *RASLCT,* which is based on our most accurate sales forecasting method, as the dependent variable. A weighted least-squares procedure was used to account for heteroskedasticity attributable to the greatly varying precision with which model sales are forecast.[39] The estimates in the first column of table 4 relate the relative forecast errors to *DREAD, RLTRCL,* and *OTHRCL,* three variables intended to control for potential effects of verdicts on consumers' beliefs about the safety of the vehicles involved in the trials.

38. One factor would be the importance of brand loyalty in automobile purchase decisions (Mannering and Winston, 1991).

39. The variances of $CTPRED_j$ for different verdicts were estimated from the forecast errors of one-month ahead forecasts for the ten months before the verdict month. The squared OLS residuals for the specifications in table 4 were regressed on the estimated variances of *RASLCT;* the coefficients in these regressions were statistically significant (with t-ratios on the order of 3 to 4), indicating heteroskedasticity of the maintained form. The predicted values from these regressions were then used to form the weights used to compute the estimates reported in table 4. See Judge and others (1985, pp. 434–36) for a discussion of this estimator and some asymptotically equivalent alternatives. The previous version of this paper, Garber and Adams (1998), presents OLS estimates corresponding to the GLS estimates reported in table 4 and the analogous specifications with *RASLEX* as the dependent variable. The substantive implications of these estimates are similar to those discussed here.

Table 4. Estimated Sales Effects (*RASLCT*) Regressed on Indirect Cost and Publicity Factors (*GLS*)

Independent variable	Coefficients (t-ratios)		
	1	2	3
Constant	0.00116	0.000568	−0.0126
	(0.06)	(0.02)	(−0.42)
DREAD	0.0173	0.00753	−0.000939
	(0.88)	(0.24)	(−0.03)
RLTRCL	−0.0124	0.0253	0.0554
	(−0.70)	(0.81)	(1.35)
OTHRCL	−0.0124	−0.00957	−0.00217
	(−1.66)	(−0.91)	(−0.17)
PUNIND	. . .	−0.0235	−0.0175
		(−0.58)	(−0.39)
CRALL	. . .	0.00480	0.184
		(0.07)	(0.29)
Interactions			
CRALL*DREAD	. . .	. . .	−0.0634
			(−0.10)
CRALL*RLRCL	. . .	. . .	−0.0838
			(−0.54)
CRALL*OTHRCL	. . .	. . .	−0.0911
			(−0.69)
R^2	0.04	0.03	0.06
N	61	61	61

Source: Authors' calculations. The sample include 61 plaintiff verdicts in cases involving makes and models for which new-vehicle sales could be forecast. The dependent variable is *RASLCT*, a sales forecast error relative to actual sales in the month after the verdict. Estimates are generalized (weighted) least-squares estimates allowing for heteroskedastic errors due to varying degrees of precision in forecasting sales for different observations. *DREAD* = 1 indicates that the accident involved in the verdict caused at least one fatality, case of paralysis, or serious burns. *RLTRCL* = 1 indicates that vehicles of the same make, model, and model year as the vehicle alleged defective in the trial had been previously recalled for a similar defect. *OTHRCL* counts the number of other safety recalls of vehicles of the same make, model, and model year prior to the verdict date. *PUNIND* = 1 indicates that the verdict included punitive damages. *CRALL* measures the extent of newspaper coverage of the verdict (with papers weighted by circulation). See text for explanation of coefficients.

The next column adds to the specification the variable indicating a punitive component to the award *(PUNIND)* and a variable measuring the extent of newspaper coverage of the verdict *(CRALL)*. The last column of table 4 introduces interactions of *CRALL* with *DREAD, RLTRCL,* and *OTHRCL.*

Estimates of the coefficients of *DREAD* and *RLTRCL* are, contrary to expectation, each positive in two of three cases. Taken together the estimates suggest that neither factor is relevant to predicting the sales response (if any) to verdicts against manufacturers. The estimated coefficients of *OTHRCL* are all negative, as hypothesized, and suggest perhaps a 1 percent decrease in sales for every additional recall. The hypothesis concerning punitive damages is that when a jury believes a manufacturer deserves to be punished, this leads to a product-market backlash. The estimated coefficients for *PUNIND*, although not statistically significant, suggest a decrease of perhaps 2 percent of sales.[40] The estimated coefficients of *CRALL* are opposite the sign expected. The negative coefficients of the interaction variables are of the expected sign, but in view of the estimated coefficient of *CRALL* of 0.18, are large enough to imply a negative marginal effect of publicity for only some combinations of values for *DREAD*, *RLTRCL*, and *OTHRCL*.

In sum, the estimates in table 4 provide very little indication of widespread, systematic product market reactions to verdicts against automobile manufacturers.[41] There is some indication that punitive verdicts and previous safety recalls may contribute to sales declines after verdicts. There is little if any evidence, however, that particularly dreadful injuries or the extent of newspaper coverage plays a role.

Stock Market Regressions

In principle, stock markets should react to verdicts because verdicts cannot be entirely anticipated, direct liability costs undoubtedly exist, the stakes can be substantial, and investors are generally believed to learn quickly about relevant developments. The analysis of abnormal returns averaged over verdicts, however, suggests that the stock market does not usually respond negatively to verdicts against manufacturers. We analyze the cross-verdict variation in *CAVAL* to investigate.[42]

First, consider the relationship between *CAVAL* and two features of

40. OLS estimates for *RASLCT* and *RASLEX* reported in Garber and Adams (1998), however, contradict the inference that assessment of punitive damages depresses sales.

41. Because we have focused on unit sales, however, our estimates are uninformative about the possibility that substantial demand effects exist but are accommodated largely by decreases in prices.

42. In principle, the error terms in the *CAVAL* equations are heteroskedastic because of varying degrees of precision in predicting normal stock returns for the different verdicts. OLS estimation is used to analyze stock returns, however, because regressions of squared OLS residuals on measures of the forecast variances from the estimated stock return equations did not indicate a statistically significant relationship. In addition, weighted least-squares estimates were computed for the specifications in table 5, and these estimates were very similar to the OLS estimates.

the verdict most relevant to direct costs: the size of the award *(TOT-DOL)* and the variable indicating whether the company had previously disclosed several pending cases similar to the one leading to the verdict *(P10K)*. A priori considerations suggest that *CAVAL* might be reasonably modeled as a cubic function of *TOTDOL*.[43]

The first column of table 5 reports the results of regressing *CAVAL* on a constant, *P10K, TOTDOL,* and its square and cube *(TOTSQR and TOTCUB)*. Qualitatively, the results for the polynomial in *TOTDOL* conform to expectations. In addition, the coefficient of *P10K* suggests that holding the size of an award constant, abnormal dollar *losses* (that is, minus *CAVAL*) are almost a quarter of a billion dollars larger if a verdict involves a type of case that investors had been previously warned about.

Figure 1 summarizes these results by plotting predicted values of stock market losses against the award size, assuming alternatively that *P10K* = 0 and *P10K* = 1. Note that in an intermediate range of award sizes—from roughly $25 million to $75 million—the functions are steep, with slopes of about 20. Interpreted at face value this would suggest that within this range investors anticipate an extra $20 million of (discounted) future costs for every extra $1 million in awards. Finally, the curves do flatten out as award size increases further and turn sharply downward at award sizes of about $100 million. (There are two sample verdicts in excess of $100 million.)

The second column of table 5 reports results adding *PUNIND* to the equation. The estimates of the other coefficients are largely insensitive to this change in specification. The estimated coefficient of *PUNIND* (383) suggests, however, that stock market losses are *lower* by more than a third of a billion dollars if part of the award is punitive. Although it is possible to rationalize a positive coefficient for *PUNIND* when the total award size is held constant, it seems implausible that the stock market reacts to the tune of several hundred million dollars.[44]

To probe this anomaly, the third column of table 5 decomposes the

43. This is because investors may not react to verdicts involving relatively small awards, stock market losses might increase somewhat rapidly with increasing awards within an intermediate range, and the function might tend to flatten out for exceptionally large awards because such awards (which are often primarily punitive) are often overturned or reduced by trial judges or by appeals courts.

44. For example, it appears that punitive trial awards are more often reduced or overturned.

Table 5. Abnormal Dollar Returns *(CAVAL)* Regressed on Direct Cost Variables

Independent variable	Coefficients (t-ratios)		
	1	*2*	*3*
Constant	66.6	97.0	123
	(0.66)	(0.97)	(0.97)
TOTDOL	13.8	1.99	. . .
	(1.05)	(0.14)	
TOTSQR	− 0.694	− 0.578	. . .
	(− 2.30)	(− 1.90)	
TOTCUB	0.00424	0.00387	. . .
	(2.71)	(2.49)	
COMPDOL	. . .	. . .	− 0.702
			(− 0.02)
COMPSQR	. . .	. . .	− 1.20
			(− 0.46)
COMPCUB	. . .	. . .	0.0423
			(1.06)
PUNDOL	. . .	. . .	29.4
			(1.26)
PUNSQR	. . .	. . .	− 1.72
			(− 2.29)
PUNCUB	. . .	. . .	0.0126
			(2.43)
P10K	− 242	− 313	− 223
	(− 1.30)	(− 1.67)	(− 1.10)
PUNIND	. . .	383	
		(1.72)	
R^2	0.24	0.28	0.28
N	64	64	64

Source: Authors' calculations. The sample includes 64 verdicts holding U.S. manufacturers liable. The dependent variable is *CAVAL*, the abnormal dollar return (in millions of 1996 dollars) within two trading days of the verdict announcement. Estimates are computed by ordinary least squares. *TOTDOL* is the size of the total award; *TOTSQR* and *TOTCUB* are the square and cube of *TOTDOL*. *COMPDOL* is the size of the compensatory award; *COMPSQR* and *COMPCUB* are the square and cube of *COMPDOL*. *PUNDOL* is the size of the punitive award, if any; *PUNSQR* and *PUNCUB* are the square and cube of *PUNDOL*. *P10K* = 1 if prior to the verdict the company had disclosed to investors pending litigation of the type involved in the trial. *PUNIND* = 1 indicates that the verdict included punitive damages.

total award into its compensatory *(COMPDOL)* and punitive *(PUN-DOL)* components and estimates cubic functions of each separately. The estimated coefficient of *P10K* is virtually identical to those for the other two specifications. The results for the dollar amounts are, however, baffling. In particular, when the estimates are plotted they suggest entirely implausible patterns.

To consider the potential role of indirect costs and newspaper pub-

Figure 1. Predicted Stock Market Losses versus Total Award (64 verdicts)

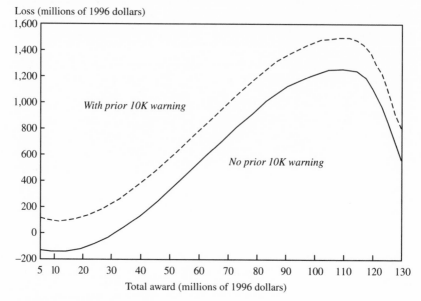

Loss (millions of 1996 dollars)

Total award (millions of 1996 dollars)

Source: Authors' calculations.

licity, in table 6 we control for size of the total award using a cubic function and add variables to the specification in the second column of table 5. First, a look across the columns of table 6 reveals that the estimated coefficients of the total award variables are similar to those in table 5 and are somewhat insensitive to the additions of the indirect cost and publicity variables. The estimated coefficients of *P10K* and *PUNIND* are even larger absolutely than in the previous table.

In the first column of table 6, results are reported from adding four variables intended to capture potential effects on vehicle sales: *DREAD*, *RLTRCL*, *OTHRCL*, and *MDLSLS*.[45] The coefficient of *DREAD* suggests that stock market losses after a verdict are $125 million larger if the case involves death, paralysis, or serious burns. The coefficients of the recall variables are positive (contrary to expectation) and are rela-

---

45. The variable MDLSLS is introduced to control for the quantity of sales potentially at stake, which was implicitly controlled in the sales effects analyses by the scaling of the dependent variables. In addition, MDLSLS may capture potential costs of liability-driven changes in vehicle design or production methods.

Table 6. Abnormal Dollar Returns (*CAVAL*) Regressed on Direct Cost, Indirect Cost, and Publicity Variables

Independent variable	Coefficients (t-ratios)		
	1	2	3
Constant	103 (0.77)	108 (0.79)	209 (1.45)
TOTDOL	3.32 (0.21)	4.32 (0.26)	12.9 (0.66)
TOTSQR	−0.592 (−1.84)	−0.570 (−1.64)	−0.866 (−1.63)
TOTCUB	0.00394 (2.42)	0.00382 (2.20)	0.00536 (1.86)
P10K	−392 (−1.69)	−387 (−1.64)	−349 (−1.45)
PUNIND	430 (1.78)	441 (1.80)	463 (1.87)
DREAD	−124 (−0.89)	−125 (−0.88)	−174 (−1.13)
RLTRCL	38.3 (0.22)	30.0 (0.17)	−68.3 (−0.37)
OTHRCL	40.5 (1.09)	36.7 (0.96)	26.3 (0.69)
MDLSLS	−0.000127 (−0.29)	−0.000146 (−0.33)	−0.000632 (−1.21)
WSJAR	. . .	−389 (−0.92)	−304 (−0.72)
CRCOTH	. . .	208 (0.23)	−2475 (−1.53)
Interactions			
CRALL*MDLSLS	. . .	. . .	0.00924 (1.40)
CRALL*DREAD	. . .	. . .	634 (0.38)
CRALL*RLTRCL	. . .	. . .	1679 (1.09)
R²	0.30	0.32	0.38
N	64	64	64

Source: Authors' calculations. The sample includes 64 verdicts holding U.S. manufacturers liable. The dependent variable is *CAVAL*, the abnormal dollar return (in millions of 1996 dollars) within two trading days of the verdict announcement. Estimates are computed by ordinary least squares. *TOTDOL* is the size of the total award; *TOTSQR* and *TOTCUB* are the square and cube of *TOTDOL*. *P10K* = 1 if prior to the verdict the company had disclosed to investors pending litigation of the type involved in the trial. *PUNIND* = 1 indicates that the verdict included punitive damages. *DREAD* = 1 indicates that the accident involved in the verdict caused at least one fatality, case of paralysis, or serious burns. *RLTRCL* = 1 indicates that vehicles of the same make, model, and model year as the vehicle alleged defective in the trial had been previously recalled for a similar defect. *OTHRCL* counts the number of other safety recalls of vehicles of the same make, model, and model year prior to the verdict dare. *MDLSLS* is the number of units sold in the year prior to the verdict of the vehicle model involved in the trial. *WSJAR* = 1 indicates that the verdict was reported in the *Wall Street Journal*. *CRCOTH* measures the extent of newspaper coverage (with papers weighted by circulation) in other newspapers. *CRALL* measures the extent of newspaper coverage of the verdict in all newspapers searched, including the *Wall Street Journal*.

tively small. If interpreted at face value, despite the small t-ratio, the coefficient of *MDLSLS* suggests extra stock market losses of about $125 for each vehicle sold during the previous calendar year of the model involved in the trial. In sum, the estimates provide only a few hints that investors anticipate negative effects of verdicts on vehicle demand.

The second column of the table adds two variables measuring newspaper coverage of the verdict during the two-trading-day event window. Here the *Wall Street Journal* and the other newspapers are considered separately because the editors of the *Journal* may be better able than other editors to judge what verdicts are of importance to investors or because *Wall Street Journal* reports may actually affect the market. In fact, the coefficient of *WSJAR* suggests that losses are almost $400 million larger when a verdict is reported in the *Journal*. (There are only five such verdicts in the sample.) The coefficient of *CRCOTH* suggests, however, that losses would be $200 million *lower* if a verdict were reported in *all* other newspapers that were included in our newspaper searches.

One would expect that negative product demand effects—if they exist—would be larger if a verdict receives more publicity. Stock market responses should reflect this if, in addition, investors observe or are able to anticipate the amount of such publicity. The third column of table 6 examines this possibility by adding interactions of a publicity measure with the three indirect cost variables that seemed most important a priori.[46] If verdicts do affect vehicle demand, and investors expect the factors captured by *DREAD, RLTRCL,* and *MDLSLS* to play a role in proportion to the amount of newspaper publicity, we would expect negative coefficients on each interaction variable. The coefficients of *DREAD, RLTRCL, MDLSLS,* and *CRCOTH* decrease substantially when the interactions are added, but clearly the three *positive* coefficients on the interactions themselves provide no support for the notion that demand effects, if any, are larger when verdicts are publicized more extensively.

The anomalous estimates reported in tables 5 and 6 for *PUNIND* and in table 5 for the compensatory and punitive components of total awards

46. A single publicity measure is used for the sake of parsimony, and we use *CRALL* (the weighted average of *WSJAR* and *CRCOTH*) because we see little reason to expect any role of *WSJ* reports on vehicle demand to be disproportionate to its share of total circulation.

Figure 2. Observed Abnormal Dollar Losses versus Total Award

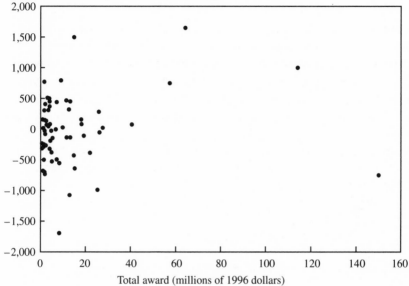

Abnormal dollars loss (millions of 1996 dollars)

Total award (millions of 1996 dollars)

Source: Authors' calculations.

suggest a closer look. A scatter plot of the data for minus *CAVAL* and *TOTDOL* is very revealing (figure 2). In particular, it suggests that the cubic shape illustrated in figure 1 is due almost entirely to the four sample observations with total awards greater than $50 million. The largest award is associated with a moderately large stock market *gain* and the next three largest awards are associated with large stock market losses. This raises the question: Which estimates in tables 5 and 6 are robust to deleting the observations corresponding to unusually large awards?[47]

The scatter diagram in figure 2 suggests that stock market reactions may be essentially random for the predominant number of verdicts less

47. Readers will likely disagree about the information content of these "outliers," but we think it useful to reexamine the data for only those verdicts of more typical sizes. Besides providing more information about patterns in the data, this exercise speaks directly to a key motivation for the present study, namely probing whether case studies or journalistic accounts focusing on atypical litigation histories are revealing about effects of more typical liability episodes.

than $30 million. But perhaps their variation is explicable by a combination of award amounts and other variables.

Table 7 presents regression results for the fifty-nine verdicts with awards less than $30 million.[48] The specifications in the table correspond to those of table 6. Looking across the columns of table 7 reveals that for all specifications the estimated effects of dollar amounts within the sample with awards less than $30 million are largely robust but very implausible.[49] A sensible interpretation is that there is no systematic stock market reaction to increasing award amounts in the range of most awards.

Although the fits reported in table 7 are much worse than their counterparts in table 6, the estimated coefficients for some key variables are similar across the tables. In particular, the existence of 10K warnings and dreadful injuries continue to predict large stock market losses, while (again, very curiously) the existence of a punitive component to an award predicts the opposite.[50]

Summary Interpretation of Estimates

We have analyzed effects of a sample of automotive product liability verdicts on two outcomes of major interest to automobile manufacturers: sales of new vehicles and stock prices. Although a priori considerations led us to view such effects as plausible—especially for stock prices—we find very little evidence of them.[51] How surprising are these results? How broad are their implications?

48. Garber and Adams (1998) report estimates for other specifications for the sample of fifty-nine verdicts, including specifications involving linear functions of the sizes of the compensatory and punitive awards separately.

49. In particular, when plotted, the cubic functions suggest negative market reactions to increasing awards up to about $15 million but sharply positive reactions to increasing awards from $15 million up to $30 million. Moreover, in specifications reported in Garber and Adams (1998) the coefficients of *COMPDOL* and *PUNDOL* are all positive, suggesting that the stock market reacts more favorably to larger awards.

50. The results for the publicity variables and their interactions are quite different across the two tables. For neither set of verdicts, however, are the estimates generally supportive of the hypothesis that more publicized verdicts involve larger losses or that more publicity tends to magnify effects of variables expected to control for effects of verdicts on consumers' views about the safety of individual vehicle models.

51. Such effects may exist, of course, despite our inability to detect them. Among factors contributing to the difficulty of detecting such effects—even if they exist—are that product liability events are unlikely to be primary determinants of automotive product demand or stock prices and that we lacked large numbers of verdicts to analyze.

Table 7. Abnormal Dollar Returns Regressed on Direct Cost, Indirect Cost, and Publicity Variables Deleting Five Largest Awards

Independent variable	Coefficients (t-ratios)		
	1	2	3
Constant	73.8	138	223
	(0.46)	(0.76)	(1.13)
TOTDOL	21.6	22.7	5.63
	(0.29)	(0.28)	(0.07)
TOTSQR	−2.90	−3.84	−2.30
	(−0.39)	(−0.49)	(−0.28)
TOTCUB	0.0928	0.121	0.0842
	(0.48)	(0.60)	(0.39)
P10K	−288	−483	−433
	(−1.38)	(−1.89)	(−1.59)
PUNIND	. . .	420	473
		(1.72)	(1.82)
DREAD	. . .	−157	−118
		(−1.07)	(−0.70)
RLTRCL	. . .	39.8	31.1
		(0.21)	(0.14)
OTHRCL	. . .	37.6	23.8
		(0.99)	(0.59)
MDLSLS	. . .	−.000345	−.000681
		(−0.73)	(−1.20)
WSJAR	. . .	. . .	132
			(0.19)
CRCOTH	. . .	. . .	−322
			(−0.11)
Interactions			
CRALL*MDLSLS	. . .	. . .	0.0110
			(1.49)
CRALL*DREAD	. . .	. . .	−2466
			(−0.65)
CRALL*RLTRCL	. . .	. . .	−1345
			(−0.36)
R²	0.04	0.13	0.18
N	59	59	59

Source: Authors' calculations. The sample includes 59 verdicts holding U.S. manufacturers liable with total awards less than $30 million (in 1996 dollars). The dependent variable is *CAVAL*, the abnormal dollar return within two trading days of the verdict announcement. Estimates are computed by ordinary least squares. *TOTDOL* is the size of the total award; *TOTSQR* and *TOTCUB* are the square and cube of *TOTDOL*. *P10K* = 1 if prior to the verdict the company had disclosed to investors pending litigation of the type involved in the trial. *PUNIND* = 1 indicates that the verdict included punitive damages. *DREAD* = 1 indicates that the accident involved in the verdict caused at least one fatality, case of paralysis, or serious burns. *RLTRCL* = 1 indicates that vehicles of the same make, model, and model year as the vehicle alleged defective in the trial had been previously recalled for a similar defect. *OTHRCL* counts the number of other safety recalls of vehicles of the same make, model, and model year prior to the verdict dare. *MDLSLS* is the number of units sold in the year prior to the verdict of the vehicle model involved in the trial. *WSJAR* = 1 indicates that the verdict was reported in the *Wall Street Journal*. *CRCOTH* measures the extent of newspaper coverage (with papers weighted by circulation) in other newspapers. *CRALL* measures the extent of newspaper coverage of the verdict in all newspapers searched, including the *Wall Street Journal*.

The lack of detectable sales effects of verdicts against manufacturers is not hard to rationalize. Our findings are consistent with various plausible conjectures, including the following three.[52] Consumers do not typically become informed about verdicts, and when they do learn of a verdict, they typically do not think it conveys much new information about the safety of the allegedly defective vehicle. In addition, cases for which trials could raise particularly serious safety concerns among consumers are rarely tried because of the settlement strategies of manufacturers. Finally, detectable sales effects would require substantial changes in consumer views about safety because of relatively strong consumer loyalty to particular vehicle brands.

The lack of detectable effects of our samples of verdicts, either for or against manufacturers, on stock prices suggests that verdicts have at most minor effects on company values relative to other events affecting stock prices on a typical trading day. For example, verdicts in cases when there are not several similar cases pending may carry little news because the stakes in a single case are relatively low, investors are relatively good at predicting trial outcomes before verdicts are announced, or both.[53] The stakes in single cases may tend to be low because verdicts do not typically have important effects on vehicle sales, manufacturers try harder to settle cases when trial losses are likely and could have costly implications for future litigation, or both. Finally, even for the purpose of predicting direct liability costs for the lawsuit at hand, investors may ascribe relatively little import to verdict announcements because of the uncertainty that remains due to the possibility of post-trial events such as successful appeals.

Before concluding, we discuss some issues that our results do *not* inform. First, our samples are dominated by individual awards of sizes that are not large relative to the values of the defendants; results averaged over our samples may mask large effects in a subset of instances. Second, our samples are dominated by cases that are not likely to affect exceptionally large numbers of related cases. In industries such as pharmaceuticals and chemicals, verdicts in individual cases that are part of

52. It is also possible that demand effects exist but take longer than a month or two to occur. This possibility was not explored because attempts to forecast sales more than one month ahead were judged too noisy to be adequate for this purpose.

53. In view of our finding that verdicts in favor of manufacturers do not tend to increase stock prices, the story cannot be as simple as "investors expect to lose."

a mass tort involving thousands or even hundreds of thousands of similar cases may have profound effects on company sales and stock values. Third, our results do not speak to effects of product liability events other than verdicts—lawsuit filings, settlements, or publicity about a set of related cases–even in the automobile industry. The accumulation of costs of numerous events within and across automotive cases, while very difficult to estimate, may be substantial, even relative to the size of automobile manufacturers.[54] Finally, our results are not informative about the effects of automobile safety regulation, litigation of types other than product liability, or other safety-related events.[55]

Economic Effects of Product Liability in the Automobile Industry

The motivation for our work is to contribute to an understanding of how product liability affects business decisions and economic efficiency. The empirical basis for drawing conclusions is still very thin. We conclude by offering some conjectures.

Let us suppose that our estimates are informative. In particular, suppose that—apart from exceptional instances such as unusually large

54. Sullivan (1990) examines effects of concerns about "sudden acceleration" in Audi 5000S, but not individual verdicts or other liability events, on prices of used vehicles and concludes that such effects are substantial. Viscusi and Hersch (1990) examine stock price reactions to events other than trial verdicts associated with diverse types of safety-related litigation. Twenty-one of the events are related to private product liability cases, and several are lawsuit filings or court rulings related to a mass tort, such as litigation involving Agent Orange, DES, and the Dalkon Shield. The only two events involving automobile manufacturers are filings of class action suits alleging property damage (not personal injury).

55. There is a substantial literature—see citations in note 2—on effects of automobile safety recalls on stock prices, new vehicle sales, and used vehicle prices; many of these studies conclude that effects are significant.

Litigation not involving product liability would include, for example, Federal Trade Commission actions alleging false advertising (Peltzman, 1981), suits related to product safety brought by government agencies (Viscusi and Hersch, 1990), private suits and civil and criminal government actions alleging corporate fraud (Karpoff and Lott, 1993), and private antitrust litigation (Bizjak and Coles, 1995).

As to other safety-related events, there are, for example, studies of effects of airplane crashes on stock prices, demand, or both. See Chalk (1987); Borenstein and Zimmerman (1988); Mitchell and Maloney (1989); Barnett, Menighetti, and Prete (1992); and Nethercutt and Pruitt (1997).

verdicts or verdicts in cases of a type that investors have been warned are pending in large numbers—demand effects of automotive product liability verdicts are not substantial and stock prices do not typically react to such verdicts.[56] The implications for economic effects of product liability depend on what automobile company decisionmakers believe about these issues. Their beliefs may or may not accurately reflect industry experience.

Do Company Decisions Reflect Well-Calibrated Expected Liability Costs?

Formal economic models of responses to product liability typically assume that firms are risk neutral.[57] Thus potential product liability costs affect decisions according to their mathematical expectations. Literature in psychology and management suggests, however, that company decisions may be influenced to a surprising extent by rare, extreme cases. Two considerations underlie this claim.

First, the "availability heuristic" of the behavioral psychology literature suggests that decisionmakers may significantly overestimate the past frequency of liability events or episodes that are highly publicized, often recounted, and unusually vexing to company decisionmakers.[58] Examples include unusually large awards, punitive damage awards, and liability when injury causation is doubtful.[59] If so, the decisionmakers are likely to greatly overestimate the likelihood of similar occurrences in the future.

Second, interviews with executives reported in management studies suggest that risk is often perceived by company decisionmakers in terms

56. Of course, stock prices may accurately reflect product liability costs even if particular liability events such as verdicts do not result in detectable, immediate responses.

57. For overviews, see Shavell (1987); Cooter and Ulen (1988); or Cooter (1991).

58. "People using this heuristic judge an event to be likely or frequent if instances of it are easy to imagine or recall" (Slovic, Fischhoff, and Lichtenstein, 1987, p. 19).

59. American Law Institute (1991, p. 235) refers to "the somewhat distorted perception one gets from reading about only the largest and most questionable punitive awards." Daniels and Martin (1990) and Rustad (1991) also argue that misconceptions about punitive damages are widespread. Cecil, Hans, and Wiggins (1991, p. 743) comment: "Often repeated 'horror stories' about jury verdicts, many of which are unconfirmed or erroneous, encourage a misleading impression of the performance of the civil jury." Finally, Viscusi (1991, p. 1) says, "Seemingly outrageous cases have come to epitomize the malfunctioning of the tort liability system."

of worst-case scenarios and that executives are willing to go to great lengths to avoid even a very small probability of an extremely bad outcome.[60] Interpreted formally, and in liability terms, executives may act as if they weigh the potential for extreme liability costs much more heavily than they would in calculating expected liability costs.

Thus company decisions may be surprisingly responsive to liability exposure because of overestimation of the probabilities of future extreme outcomes and because of overreaction, relative to behavior that maximizes expected profits, to extreme liability costs, given the subjective probabilities assigned to them.[61] In sum, although our estimates suggest that past product liability costs are less than might be inferred from case studies that focus on unusually costly episodes, the kinds of events documented in the case studies may be disproportionately influential in determining manufacturer responses to product liability exposure.

What Does Product Liability Really Deter?

Much of the theoretical literature on effects on manufacturer behavior is normative, exploring how a liability system could in principle achieve efficient levels of product safety.[62] Considering the mechanisms by which behavior is affected is also instructive for our positive purposes.

In theoretical studies, product liability is often assumed to operate as either a "negligence" or "strict liability" system. Under a negligence system a manufacturer is held liable to pay damages to an injured product user only if the injury results from failure of the manufacturer to make the product as safe as required by a legal standard. Under a strict liability system a manufacturer is held liable for all injuries resulting from use of its products.

The U.S. product liability system contains elements of both strict liability and negligence. Generally liability for injuries due to manu-

60. On management interviews see, for example, March and Shapira (1987).

61. The latter suggestion may appear to conflict with the view that firms should be viewed as risk neutral because investors can diversify risk across companies. We interpret the risk neutrality claim as normative and our claim as a positive one, referring to behavior by individual company decisionmakers who are risk averse, perceive personal risks when they make decisions, and are imperfectly controlled by stockholders.

62. See Shavell (1987); Cooter and Ulen (1988); or Cooter (1991).

facturing defects—units of a product that are not made to a manufacturer's specifications—is strict. Liability for defective product design and labeling (or warning) is based on negligence principles.

Under ideal conditions, economic efficiency can be achieved with either type of liability rule. For negligence, suppose the legal standards for avoiding liability correspond to efficient levels of care, and that manufacturers know that the standards will be faithfully applied in court. Manufacturers will then choose to comply with the standards, that is, they will behave efficiently, if the direct plus indirect costs of noncompliance are sufficiently large. As in the theory of Pigouvian pollution taxes, a strict liability system will achieve efficiency if it makes product manufacturers bear precisely, as direct and indirect costs to them, the social costs of injuries.

The theoretical literature has also explored how standard liability rules can result in inefficiency in the presence of various departures from ideal conditions.[63] And, in fact, much commentary (and some empirical evidence) by economists and others suggests that the U.S. product liability system fails to promote even approximately efficient outcomes. Among the reasons are that firms also have market and regulatory incentives to make products safer, costs of defending suits can be very large even when liability is not appropriate under the law, and negligence standards as applied are unpredictable and even on average may not correspond to efficient behavior. In addition, when liability is strict, it would be only by coincidence that the sum of expected direct and indirect liability costs were to approximate the level necessary to induce efficient responses. And finally, companies may overestimate liability exposure and overreact to worst-case scenarios.

Elsewhere, Steven Garber argues that when the potential for very large product liability costs is perceived by company decisionmakers,

63. For example, Epple and Raviv (1978) analyze imperfections in product and insurance markets and imperfect information of consumers about product characteristics. Polinsky (1980) considers long-run effects of liability on numbers of firms, market power, and product price. Polinsky and Rogerson (1983) analyze effects of market power of product sellers in the presence of underestimation of product hazards by consumers. Shavell (1984) analyzes uncertainty about whether injured parties will bring suit and the possibility that injurers will not have sufficient resources to pay judgments. Craswell and Calfee (1986) analyze uncertainty about the legal standards that will be applied in determining liability. Kolstad, Ulen, and Johnson (1990) analyze optimal use of liability in the presence of safety regulation and uncertainty about legal standards.

one should expect a mixture of efficient and inefficient company responses.[64] The basic problem, it appears, is that in many instances
company decisionmakers—with good reason—cannot be confident that
they will avoid major liability costs even if they act efficiently. One
source of the lack of confidence is instances in which companies have
been found liable for injuries in the absence of credible (to company
decisionmakers) scientific evidence of accident or injury causation.[65]
Another is the considerable risk of punitive damages being assessed for
cost-benefit balancing when risks to life and limb are involved, despite
the fact that cost-benefit balancing is necessary for achieving economic
efficiency.[66]

In sum, product liability in the real world appears to be a very
imprecise policy instrument. Rather than selectively deterring socially
undesirable behavior, the product liability system, especially as it is
perceived by manufacturers, seems to swat at a broad variety of manufacturer behavior using something more akin to a lawn rake than a
hammer, let alone a scalpel.

Would Reduced Liability Exposure Improve Automobile Industry Efficiency?

Broad reductions in liability exposure would tend to reduce anticipated liability costs resulting from both efficient and inefficient manufacturer decisions.[67] Should we expect resulting changes in behavior by

64. Garber (1993, 1998).

65. A well-known example in the automobile context is controversy about "inad-
vertent vehicle movement" (Graham, 1991, pp. 137–44), or "sudden acceleration"
(Huber, 1991, chap. 4; Center for Auto Safety, 1992), or "unintended acceleration"
(Mackay, 1991, pp. 210–11).

66. It seems widely agreed that introduction of evidence of cost-benefit balancing,
which is often portrayed in terms such as "trading off lives against dollars," makes
assessment of punitive damages particularly likely. Schwartz (1991) discusses and analyzes issues related to cost-benefit balancing in the context of Ford Pinto litigation. A
potential for punitive damages can have major effects on behavior because the sizes of
punitive damages are unlimited in any given instance, and (in the product liability
context) they can be assessed in multiple cases for the same behavior. Moreover, companies can be very averse to negative publicity, and Garber and Bower (1998) estimate
a very substantial effect of punitive damages on the extent of newspaper coverage of
verdicts.

67. Perceptions about liability exposure could change in response to various measures, including changes in legal doctrine or procedure. Some measures would tend to

automobile industry decisionmakers to be primarily efficient or inefficient? That depends on the efficiency properties of the mix of automobile company decisions deterred by product liability.

Claims about inefficient consequences of liability in the automobile
industry that invoke extensive inside knowledge of industry practices
are not hard to find. For example, one long-time industry observer
concludes that "liability has had a negative influence on innovation. It
has held back new designs, consumed resources that might otherwise
have been directed at design improvement, and added costs to the
consumer."[68] A knowledgeable industry insider, a vice president for
vehicle engineering at Chrysler, distinguishes three types of apparently
inefficient effects of product liability on decisions by automotive engineers: hesitance to pursue revolutionary or radical innovation (because radically different designs are hard to defend in court); disincen-
tives for engineers to engage in "honest and critical evaluation of
features of current and past vehicles" (for fear that internal company
communications will become damaging legal evidence if interpreted
out of context); and hesitance to improve vehicle designs quickly for
fear that changes will be alleged—and believed—to be evidence of
defects in earlier designs.[69] Such claims suggest that reductions in perceived liability exposure have the potential to ameliorate some kinds of
inefficient behavior, particularly if there are no market or regulatory
incentives encouraging such behavior.

Across-the-board reductions in perceived liability exposure would
also decrease perceived costs to manufacturers of accidents and injuries.

---

reduce perceptions of liability exposure for very broad ranges of company decisions and
behavior; others would have much more selective effects. The discussion here considers
changes that reduce perceptions of liability exposure across the spectrum of behavior.
Many of the policy reforms currently being discussed, such as damage caps, are of that
character. Garber (1993, 1998) discusses reforms aimed at improving the economic
efficiency of product liability by targeting behavior more selectively.

68. Mackay (1991, p. 220). Mackay notes: "The background for this chapter, apart
from published material, comes from personal contacts and knowledge of the industry
for over a quarter-century" (p. 192).

69. Castaing (1994, pp. 78–79). An anecdote illustrates the points that it is perceptions of legal risk, accurate or not, that determine behavior and that beliefs can differ
substantially even between decisionmakers within a company. An automobile company
attorney has reported to one of the authors on a confidential basis that a widespread
concern among engineers in his company is that design improvements will be used as
evidence of previous defects even though legal doctrine in most states does not allow
such claims to be admitted as evidence.

Would inefficient decreases in safety result? That depends largely on the extent to which market incentives and National Highway Traffic Safety Administration regulation deter behavior that is inefficiently unsafe, that is, the extent to which liability-based incentives for increases in safety are redundant or excessive. People can be expected to disagree vigorously about this. But the product liability debate could benefit greatly by recognizing the fundamental importance of this issue.

Concluding Comments

Any product liability system, like any public policy, is inevitably imperfect. The wisdom of attempting to use product liability to deter inefficiently unsafe behavior depends on

—the extent of inefficiently unsafe behavior undeterred by market forces and administrative regulation,

—the scope and importance of efficient behavior that might be deterred by product liability,

—how well the liability system will be designed and implemented, and

—the resource costs of operating the system.

For many industries or products, the potential efficiency gains from product liability may be small in comparison with the resource costs and potential inefficiencies from using product liability to try to improve matters. Often the great is the enemy of the good.

Appendix

Table A-1. Distribution of Samples by Year of Verdict

	Sales sample	Stock price sample	
Year	Plaintiff verdicts	Plaintiff verdicts	Defendant verdicts
1985	2	3	4
1986	6	8	4
1987	2	3	8
1988	3	4	8
1989	3	3	6
1990	6	4	7
1991	5	3	8
1992	8	9	9
1993	6	3	14
1994	5	4	13
1995	5	7	26
1996	10	13	9
Total	61	64	116

Source: Authors' calculations.

Table A-2. Distribution of Samples by Defendant Manufacturer

	Sales sample	Stock price sample	
Defendant	Plaintiff verdicts	Plaintiff verdicts	Defendant verdicts
GM	34	41	58
Ford	7	13	46
Chrysler	3	7	9
American Motors	2	3	3
Toyota	7	0	0
Hyundai	4	0	0
Other foreign	4[a]	0	0
Total	61	64	116

Source: Authors' calculations.
a. One each: Audi, Isuzu, Jaguar, and Suzuki.

Table A-3. Descriptive Statistics for Independent Variables, Plaintiff Verdicts

Variable	Sales sample (N = 61)		Stock price sample (N = 64)	
	Mean	Standard deviation	Mean	Standard deviation
Indirect cost				
DREAD	0.607	0.493	0.609	0.492
RLTRCL	0.196	0.401	0.281	0.453
OTHRCL	1.39	1.59	1.59	1.77
MDLSLS	a	a	120,000	155,000
Direct cost				
TOTDOL	13.4	26.7	13.4	25.1
COMPDOL	7.80	10.8	7.13	9.06
PUNDOL	5.56	20.4	6.26	20.1
PUNIND	0.180	0.388	0.203	0.406
P10K	a	a	0.156	0.366
Publicity				
WSJAR	0.0656	0.250	0.0781	0.270
CRCOTH	0.0928	0.186	0.0642	0.157
CRALL	0.0907	0.186	0.0653	0.163

Source: Authors' calculations.
a. Not used in analysis of sales effects.

References

American Law Institute. 1991. *Reporters' Study: Enterprise Responsibility for Personal Injury*, vol. 2: *Approaches to Legal and Institutional Change.* Philadelphia.

Babcock, Charles W. Jr. 1994. "Approaches to Product Liability Risk in the U.S. Automotive Industry." In *Product Liability and Innovation: Managing Risk in an Uncertain Environment*, edited by Janet R. Hunziker and Trevor O. Jones, 82–112. Washington: National Academy Press.

Barber, Brad M., and Masako N. Darrough. 1996. "Product Reliability and Firm Value: The Experience of American and Japanese Automakers, 1973–92." *Journal of Political Economy* 104 (October): 1084–99.

Barnett, Arnold, John Menighetti, and Matthew Prete. 1992. "The Market Response to the Sioux City DC-10 Crash." *Risk Analysis* 12 (March): 45–52.

Bizjak, John M., and Jeffrey L. Coles. 1995. "The Effect of Private Antitrust Litigation on the Stock-Market Valuation of the Firm." *American Economic Review* 85 (June): 436–61.

Borenstein, Severin, and Martin B. Zimmerman. 1988. "Market Incentives for Safe Commercial Airline Operation." *American Economic Review* 78 (December): 913–35.

Bromiley, Philip, and Alfred Marcus. 1989. "The Deterrent to Dubious Corporate Behavior: Profitability, Probability and Safety Recalls." *Strategic Management Journal* 10 (May): 233–50.

Brown, Warren. 1986. "Consumers Steer Clear of the Audi 5000S; Sales Plummet on Safety Allegations." *Washington Post.* December 28, 1986, p. K1.

Campbell, John Y., Andrew W. Lo, and A. Craig MacKinlay. 1997. *The Econometrics of Financial Markets.* Princeton University Press.

Castaing, François J. 1994. "The Effects of Product Liability on Automotive Engineering Practice." In *Product Liability and Innovation: Managing Risk in an Uncertain Environment*, edited by Janet R. Hunziker and Trevor O. Jones, 77–81. Washington: National Academy Press.

Cecil, Joe S., Valerie P. Hans, and Elizabeth C. Wiggins. 1991. "Citizen Comprehension of Difficult Issues: Lessons from Civil Jury Trials." *American University Law Review* 40 (Winter): 727–74.

Center for Auto Safety. 1992. "Audi 5000S Sudden Acceleration." (Collection of letters, press releases, newspaper and television accounts). Washington, D.C.

Chalk, Andrew J. 1987. "Market Forces and Commercial Airline Safety." *Journal of Industrial Economics* 36 (September): 61–81.

Cooter, Robert D. 1991. "Economic Theories of Legal Liability." *Journal of Economic Perspectives* 5 (Summer): 11–30.

Cooter, Robert, and Thomas Ulen. 1988. *Law and Economics*. Glenview, Ill.: Scott, Foresman.

Crafton, Steven M., George E. Hoffer, and Robert J. Reilly. 1981. "Testing the Impact of Recalls on the Demand for Automobiles." *Economic Inquiry* 19 (October): 694–703.

Craswell, Richard, and John E. Calfee. 1986. "Deterrence and Uncertain Legal Standards." *Journal of Law, Economics, and Organization* 2 (Fall): 279–303.

Daniels, Stephen, and Joanne Martin. 1990. "Myth and Reality in Punitive Damages." *Minnesota Law Review* 75 (October): 1–64.

Dreyfus, Mark K., and W. Kip Viscusi. 1995. "Rates of Time Preference and Consumer Valuations of Automobile Safety and Fuel Efficiency." *Journal of Law and Economics* 38 (April): 79–105.

Epple, Dennis, and Artur Raviv. 1978. "Product Safety: Liability Rules, Market Structure, and Imperfect Information." *American Economic Review* 68 (March): 80–95.

Garber, Steven. 1993. *Product Liability and the Economics of Pharmaceuticals and Medical Devices*. R-4285-ICJ. Santa Monica, Calif.: RAND.

———. 1998. "Product Liability, Punitive Damages, Business Decisions and Economic Outcomes." *Wisconsin Law Review* (1): 237–95.

Garber, Steven, and John Adams. 1998. "Product and Stock Market Responses to Automotive Product Liability Verdicts. Unpublished paper, RAND, Santa Monica, Calif. June.

Garber, Steven, and Anthony G. Bower. 1998. "An Econometric Analysis of Newspaper Coverage of Automotive Product Liability Verdicts." Unpublished paper, RAND, Santa Monica, Calif. October.

Graham, John D. 1991. "Product Liability and Motor Vehicle Safety." In *The Liability Maze: The Impact of Liability Law on Safety and Innovation*, edited by Peter W. Huber and Robert E. Litan, 120–90. Brookings.

Hartman, Raymond S. 1987. "Product Quality and Market Efficiency: The Effect of Product Recalls on Resale Prices and Firm Valuation." *Review of Economics and Statistics* 69 (May): 367–72.

Hazen, Thomas Lee. 1993. *Federal Securities Law*. Washington: Federal Judicial Center.

Hoffer, George E., Stephen W. Pruitt, and Robert J. Reilly. 1988. "The Impact of Product Recalls on the Wealth of Sellers: A Reexamination." *Journal of Political Economy* 96 (June): 663–70.

———. 1992. "Market Responses to Publicly Provided Information: The Case of Automobile Safety." *Applied Economics* 24 (July): 661–67.

Huber, Peter W. 1991. *Galileo's Revenge: Junk Science in the Courtroom*. Basic Books.

Huber, Peter W., and Robert E. Litan, eds. 1991. *The Liability Maze: The Impact of Liability Law on Safety and Innovation.* Brookings.

Hunziker, Janet R., and Trevor O. Jones, eds. 1994. *Product Liability and Innovation: Managing Risk in an Uncertain Environment.* Washington: National Academy Press.

Jarrell, Gregg, and Sam Peltzman. 1985. ''The Impact of Product Recalls on the Wealth of Sellers.'' *Journal of Political Economy* 93 (June): 512–36.

Judge, George G., and others. 1985. *The Theory and Practice of Econometrics.* Wiley.

Karpoff, Jonathan M., and John R. Lott Jr. 1993. ''The Reputational Penalty Firms Bear from Committing Criminal Fraud.'' *Journal of Law and Economics* 36 (October): 757–802.

Kolstad, Charles D., Thomas S. Ulen, and Gary V. Johnson. 1990. ''*Ex Post* Liability for Harm vs. *Ex Ante* Safety Regulation: Substitutes or Complements?'' *American Economic Review* 80 (September): 888–901.

LaManna, Sam. 1993. ''GM Verdict Could Affect Future Cases.'' *National Law Journal*, May 3: 21, 25, and 26.

Mackay, Murray. 1991. ''Liability, Safety, and Innovation in the Automotive Industry.'' In *The Liability Maze: The Impact of Liability Law on Safety and Innovation*, edited by Peter W. Huber and Robert E. Litan, 191–223. Brookings.

MacKinlay, A. Craig. 1997. ''Event Studies in Economics and Finance.'' *Journal of Economic Literature* 35 (March): 13–39.

Mannering, Fred, and Clifford Winston. 1991. ''Brand Loyalty and the Decline of American Automobile Firms.'' *Brookings Papers on Economic Activity: Microeconomics*: 67–114.

———. 1995. ''Automobile Air Bags in the 1990s: Market Failure or Market Efficiency?'' *Journal of Law and Economics* 38 (October): 265–79.

Manning, Richard L. 1994. ''Changing Rules in Tort Law and the Market for Childhood Vaccines.'' *Journal of Law and Economics* 37 (April): 247–75.

———. 1997. ''Products Liability and Prescription Drug Prices in Canada and the United States.'' *Journal of Law and Economics* 40 (April): 203–43.

March, James G., and Zur Shapira. 1987. ''Managerial Perspectives on Risk and Risk Taking.'' *Management Science* 33 (November): 1404–18.

Marcus, Alfred, and Philip Bromiley. 1988. ''The Rationale for Regulation: Shareholder Losses under Various Assumptions about Managerial Cognition.'' *Journal of Law, Economics, and Organization* 4 (Fall): 357–72.

McCarthy, Patrick S. 1989. ''Short-Term Effects of Safety-Related Recalls on New Vehicle Purchase Decisions: An Empirical Analysis'' *Transportation Research Record* (1210): 58–65.

———. 1990. "Consumer Demand for Vehicle Safety: An Empirical Study." *Economic Inquiry* 28 (July): 530–43.

Mitchell, Mark L., and Michael T. Maloney. 1989. "Crisis in the Cockpit? The Role of Market Forces in Promoting Air Travel Safety." *Journal of Law and Economics* 32 (October): 329–55.

Nethercutt, Leonard L., and Stephen W. Pruitt. 1997. "Touched by Tragedy: Capital Market Lessons from the Crash of ValuJet Flight 592." *Economics Letters* 56 (November): 351–58.

Pearl, Daniel, and Douglas Lavin. 1994. "U.S. Decision on Recall of GM Trucks Is Delayed as Agency Sees No Precedent." *Wall Street Journal.* June 6, p. A4.

Peltzman, Sam. 1981. "The Effects of FTC Advertising Regulation." *Journal of Law and Economics* 24 (December): 403–48.

Polinsky, A. Mitchell. 1980. "Strict Liability vs. Negligence in a Market Setting." *American Economic Review* 70 (May): 363–67.

Polinsky, A. Mitchell, and William P. Rogerson. 1983. "Products Liability, Consumer Misperceptions, and Market Power." *Bell Journal of Economics* 14 (Autumn): 581–89.

Reilly, Robert J., and George E. Hoffer. 1983. "Will Retarding the Information Flow on Automobile Recalls Affect Consumer Demand?" *Economic Inquiry* 21 (July): 444–47.

Rustad, Michael. 1991. *Demystifying Punitive Damages in Products Liability Cases: A Survey of a Quarter Century of Trial Verdicts.* Washington: Roscoe Pound Foundation.

Schwartz, Gary T. 1991. "The Myth of the Ford Pinto Case." *Rutgers Law Review* 43 (Summer): 1013–68.

Shavell, Steven. 1984. "A Model of the Optimal Use of Liability and Safety Regulation." *RAND Journal of Economics* 15 (Summer): 271–80.

———. 1987. *Economic Analysis of Accident Law.* Harvard University Press.

Slovic, Paul, Baruch Fischhoff, and Sarah Lichtenstein. 1987. "Behavioral Decision Theory Perspectives on Protective Behavior." In *Taking Care: Understanding and Encouraging Self-Protective Behavior*, edited by Neil D. Weinstein, 14–41. Cambridge University Press.

Sullivan, Mary. 1990. "Measuring Image Spillovers in Umbrella-branded Products." *Journal of Business* 63 (July): 309–29.

Thomas, Rich. 1993. "Just as Safe at Any Speed." *Newsweek.* May 10, 1993, p. 52.

Uri, Noel D. 1989. "Analyzing the Impact of Recalls on the Market Valuation of New Cars." *Transportation Planning and Technology* 14 (July): 37–52.

Viscusi, W. Kip. 1991. *Reforming Products Liability.* Harvard University Press.

Viscusi, W. Kip, and Joni Hersch. 1990. ''The Market Response to Product Safety Litigation.'' *Journal of Regulatory Economics* 2 (September): 215–30.

Wynne, A. James, and George E. Hoffer. 1976. ''Auto Recalls: Do They Affect Market Share?'' *Applied Economics* 8 (September): 157–63.

Comments

Comment by Sam Peltzman: Steven Garber and John Adams present a view of the tort liability system that is at odds with much recent hand-wringing. For the auto manufacturers the direct costs of jury verdicts against them are small, essentially loose change considering the size of the industry. And the indirect effects—lost sales or "goodwill" as measured by loss of stock market value—cannot reliably be distinguished from zero.

How can their results be reconciled with the seriousness with which the business community has pursued reform of the tort liability system both in Washington and in state capitals? The answer I think is that court cases, especially those reaching a decision, are only a small part of a much larger process that includes media publicity and regulatory scrutiny. Court cases are occasionally a vital part of the process, but they occur very rarely. Most are exactly what Garber and Adams show them to be—small potatoes.

I think this conclusion would stand up even if court cases were analyzed from their beginning instead of, as Garber and Adams have done, from their conclusion. The potential bias in their method is clear. By the time a case has reached a verdict, much relevant information for car buyers and stockholders has already been revealed. So lack of important effects around the date of a verdict need not preclude important effects from the whole history of the case.

The reason I think this potential bias is unimportant is that Garber and Adams's findings gibe well with others showing that, viewed in isolation, tort liability cases are not very costly. For example, Michelle White and Henry Farber tracked medical malpractice cases from their beginning and found results similar to those of Garber and Adams: the

45

expected value of a malpractice case was tiny, and the aggregate cost of all cases was a small fraction of the relevant total.[1] More recently, Jonathan Karpoff and John Lott examined the stock market response to the events engendered by the abortive effort of Republicans in Congress to limit damage awards in tort liability cases following their 1994 election victory.[2] The authors found that changes in the likely success of this effort were greeted by yawns from Wall Street. The only important exception was for a handful of companies that already had pending cases with substantial amounts at risk. But the stock market seemed to be saying that any gain from reducing expected damage costs from future cases was trivial even for firms in industries heavily exposed to liability risk.

My more important caveat concerns the focus on court cases as the unit of analysis. This gives each case equal weight and thereby, I think, obscures the role of the courts in imposing product liability costs. Consider how such costs get determined. Typically the process begins with some media publicity—a story about sticking accelerator pedals might surface in the press, for example. The ensuing evolution of the story is fraught with uncertainty. It may end with a heated denial by the manufacturer. Or it may result in regulatory scrutiny, a recall perhaps. At some point a court case could arise. This could be an individual's suit of the sort that dominates Garber and Adams's sample. Or it could be a more ominous class action case. Most of these events will end inconsequentially. Even if the action gets beyond the stage of heated denials, the likelihood of a single event mushrooming into something significant is very small. That reality is what I think Garber and Adams's results reflect. However, a handful of these cases will become truly serious. The publicity itself may be so adverse that the seller's market nearly evaporates, as happened after the television report on Audi's accelerating brake pedals. Or litigation may result in an asbestos-style class action case that bankrupts the seller.

The correct way to think about these events then is that they are drawn from a highly skewed distribution whose expected value is dominated by a small probability times a very large conditional mean. Thus for most events the actual value will ultimately be less than the expected value at

---

1. White and Farber (1991).
2. Karpoff and Lott (1997).

the beginning. This view is confirmed by analyses of events closer to their beginning than court cases. For example, a fairly common finding in analyses of regulatory initiatives on product quality is that the stock market penalty seems to *overstate* any independent assessment of the costs imposed by the particular case. This has been found for Fair Trade Commission false advertising cases, auto and drug product recalls and corporate fraud cases.[3] Large ''goodwill'' (that is, otherwise inexplicable) losses have also been found around the date of airplane accidents.[4] These things are happening early enough after the event that the stock market cannot completely ignore the small probability that they will become major occurrences. Because most will not, backward-looking analysis will most often produce an overstated reaction.

A specific example will illustrate this point. In our 1985 article Gregg Jarrell and I used the recall of the Dalkon Shield (an intrauterine birth control device with alleged health risks) to illustrate the extent to which the stock market overestimated the direct costs of product defects. We were fortunate to have a nearly decade-long record of what those costs were because the Securities and Exchange Commission forced the manufacturer, A. H. Robins, to disclose the costs separately each quarter. Even with the benefit of a decade's hindsight and a generous extrapolation of that experience, we could not come close to closing the gap between the market's devaluation of Robins and the actual costs of the recall. The ink was hardly dry on our article before a massive class action was brought against the company that ultimately forced it into bankruptcy. In the end the market had actually underestimated the cost of the recall to the company's stockholders. We needed two decades' hindsight to see this rather than one. The point of the example, however, is that the large initial reaction could reasonably have included some allowance for the possibility of the company-busting kind of loss that emerged in this rare case.

Most events like this do not take decades for the uncertainty to be resolved. And for most events the uncertainty is resolved favorably for the defendants as well as quickly. This is why samples of the events in their mature stages, such as court decisions, will usually reveal small

3. For false advertising see Peltzman (1981); for recalls see Jarrell and Peltzman (1985); and for corporate fraud see Karpoff and Lott (1993). The direct effects of most auto recalls on sales have also been found to be small and temporary. Significant negative effects are found only for severe recalls. See, for example, Reilly and Hoffer (1983).
4. See, for example, Mitchell and Maloney (1989).

effects. If something like corporate survival is no longer even remotely at stake, the effect of resolving the remaining issues, whether the liability is $30 million or $300 million, for example, will typically be drowned in the noise.

What then do Garber and Adams's results say about the costs of products liability and the proposals for reform of the liability system? If my reading is correct, they suggest the need for focusing on the main culprits, the extremely rare but outsized costs. Some—those stemming from adverse media publicity, for example—are beyond the reach of any practical change in the law. As for the rest, only something as drastic as eliminating or severely restricting the asbestos-type class action case is likely to have important effects. Garber and Adams's results imply, I think correctly, that the recent proposals for capping liability in garden variety cases are unlikely to have much meaningful effect on liability costs in most industries.[5]

Comment by Daniel L. Rubinfeld: This study by Steve Garber and John Adams focuses on the empirical determination of certain effects of product liability laws. Specifically, the authors analyze the relationship between legal verdicts and stock prices of domestic automobile manufacturers of the models involved for two, three, and four business days following the announcement of the verdict. In addition they examine postverdict sales of the models. The authors are to be commended for producing a thoughtful and balanced empirical analysis. They should also be praised for the balance they show in interpreting their results. The most interesting result is in fact a nonresult; although one might expect to see a product liability verdict affect both stock prices and product sales, the authors find little evidence of such an effect.

My comments on the Garber-Adams paper come in two parts. First, I discuss some methodological issues surrounding their empirical analysis. I argue that one should not be surprised by the nonresult, once one reflects on the sample selection process that underlies the data analyzed. Second, I comment on some of the normative implications that one might draw from their paper. I emphasize the need to be

5. There will, of course, always be counterexamples. Manning (1994) describes the particularly dramatic one of childhood vaccines where nearly all of the wholesale price is product liability costs.
Marilyn Simon provided helpful comments.

extremely wary before drawing *any* normative implications from the study.

The Empirical Analysis

In their analysis Garber and Adams consider both direct product liability costs (those costs stemming directly from product liability litigation, including the costs of defending and settling lawsuits and judgments paid), and indirect product liability costs (the costs associated with decreases in demand related to the verdict and regulatory actions related to the liability events). The effect on sales, an indirect effect, and the effect on stock prices, a combination of direct and indirect effects, are estimated separately. The authors note that these measured effects are limited to the extent to which liability verdicts carry new information to the potential consumer about the quality of the vehicle and to the market about factors that are relevant to measuring future profitability. The nonresult obtained by the authors tells us that the verdicts carried little incrementally new information to consumers; it does not tell us that product liability cases have no deterrent effect.

The data used in the study are based on verdicts announced between January 1985 and December 2, 1996. In their empirical work the authors implicitly assume there was little publicity about a case before the announcement of the verdict. Although they have made some efforts to follow publicity, a more complete analysis would pursue the presence of publicity in greater depth, much as Garber has done in some earlier work.[6] To determine whether there had been preverdict publicity, it would be necessary to search other media and to broaden the search to include articles that may not name the plaintiff explicitly but that nevertheless refer to litigation about the defect during this time.

Sample selection is an important problem here: to the extent that there might have been preverdict publicity about either the defect or the case, that publicity could affect the selection of cases to be tried rather than settled. As a consequence, one's ability to draw implications from measurements of the immediate effect of the verdict on sales or profitability is limited. The measured effect is related only to the additional information given by the verdict and any uncertainty that the verdict might resolve. For example, a verdict in favor of the plaintiff might

6. Garber and Bower (1998).

actually increase the defendant's sales or profitability if before the announcement potential consumers and investors had expected a significantly higher verdict in favor of the plaintiff. I wonder, however, whether the largely negative results are due in part to the fact that there were expectations of possible adverse decisions that had already been capitalized into sales or profitability.

As an example of the informational concern that I just raised, consider one of the authors' chosen regression variables, the one that measures whether there had been a recall on the make and model. This variable is assumed by the authors to measure whether consumers might be more inclined to reduce their estimate of the safety of the model after the announcement of the verdict than if they had not previously heard of the recall. However, there are other possible interpretations of the informational content of this variable. One is that consumers might have adjusted their estimate of the safety of the vehicle when they learned of the recall, and as a result additional significant adjustment would not have occurred at the time of the verdict. Further, it is not clear whether consumers would react positively or negatively to the recall information, because the nature of recall and the manufacturer's handling of it will determine whether it signals poor design or quality control or constructive and effective measures that respond to the reports of a defect and consequently improve future production of the model.

The verdicts included in the sample are of necessity limited; the authors' sample is based on listings in the *Automotive Litigation Reporter* (a sample of unsolicited reports submitted by attorneys), as well as proplaintiff verdicts listed in a California publication, *Jury Verdicts Weekly*, and proplaintiff verdicts found through a newspaper search. Although not necessary for the purposes of this paper, it is important to remember that the chosen data base may not be an unbiased sample of all vehicle product liability cases. It is quite possible that other events such as recall announcements are not included in the event study and may have affected the estimated forecasting model. Remember the authors' focus on the measurement of the difference between forecast and actual sales in the month following the verdict. Limiting the analysis to a forecast one period ahead increases the likelihood that the forecast itself will include data on sales for a period during which other significant informational events occurred.

Put in econometric terms, the sample selection problem that I have been discussing has the following interpretation. Suppose that all factors that affected the likelihood of plaintiff's success in a product liability case are filtered out by the settlement-discovery process (including information, risk aversion, and the differential stakes of the parties). Then any randomness associated with the outcomes of those cases that are tried will be a "white noise" process relating to factors that are trial-specific (for example, reflecting differential jury composition) and not related to the information about liability (and harm) that is available to the parties.[7] Put in signal-noise terms, as a consequence it is possible that trial verdicts' information will provide a diffuse signal of the effects of information relating to product liability on consumer behavior.

To close this section, let me add a few minor technical econometric points. First, why emphasize forecasts only one period ahead, when multiperiod forecasting would better incorporate prior information? I believe there are sufficient data to do this. This would help eliminate the problem that most of the effect of the adverse verdict will have already been felt if the expectations of the relevant parties had been continually updated over time. It would also allow one to test the extent to which information had previously been capitalized. (Ideally, one would like a measure of the "expected outcome" of the case before trial.) Second, I worry about robust estimation issues (the sensitivity of the result to individual data points), since the sample is relatively small. Finally, it seems clear that the forecasting methodology works better with company variables. I would have found it interesting if the authors had reported the results of a regression approach or an approach that mixed regression and ARIMA (time-series) modeling in the forecasting part of their work.[8]

Normative Issues

After finding little evidence of a shift in demand for the model or the stock market price in the period following the announcement of the verdict, the authors explore other ways in which product liability might affect automobile company decisionmakers. The authors point correctly to the difficulties of drawing normative implications from their study.

7. See, for example, Cooter and Rubinfeld (1989); and Perloff and Ruud (1996).
8. Pindyck (1998).

I would perhaps go a step further by suggesting that any attempt to draw normative implications from this study alone is fraught with difficulties. There are a number of reasons for this.

First, we know from the law and economics literature that the extent to which economic efficiency will be achieved depends on the particular liability rule in effect. Any conclusions that Garber and Adams reach are likely to be conditioned on the current state of product liability law, not a preferred ideal alternative. The choice of liability is complicated, depending among other things on the degree of risk aversion of customers and manufacturers, the availability of information, uncertainty about the application of the liability rule, and the extent to which risks and potential harms vary across customers.[9]

Second, the normative analysis is further complicated by evidence from the psychology literature that is inconsistent with the traditional models that explain consumer risk preferences. Findings that decision-makers overestimate the past frequency of liability events that are highly publicized lead one to conclude that these people might overreact to highly publicized liability events. Similarly, in the management literature, interviews with executives indicating that risk is evaluated by considering worst-case scenarios imply that there would be a premium placed on avoiding a small probability of an extremely bad outcome. Any normative interpretation of the empirical results based on a relatively small sample of information about low-probability events will consequently be difficult to make.

Third, because the authors have chosen to focus only on the effects on consumers of information provided at one stage of the litigation process, it is inappropriate to draw normative implications that apply to the entire process. Although useful in itself, the evidence presented in this paper does not allow one to conclude that there is either under- or overdeterrence from product defects. Garber and Adams are to be commended for avoiding such an inappropriate normative conclusion. If there is anything normative that I would draw from this study, it is the confirmation of my view that trials provide noisy information and that the effectiveness of jury verdicts in deterring bad acts is limited.

9. See, for example, Simon (1981).

Commentator's References

Cooter, Robert, and Daniel L. Rubinfeld. 1989. "Economic Analysis of Legal Disputes and their Resolution." *Journal of Economic Literature* 27 (September): 1067–97.

Garber, Steven, and Anthony G. Bower. 1998. "An Econometric Analysis of Newspaper Coverage of Automotive Product Liability Verdicts." Unpublished paper. RAND, Santa Monica, Calif. October.

Jarrell, Gregg, and Sam Peltzman. 1985. "The Impact of Product Recalls on the Wealth of Sellers." *Journal of Political Economy* 93 (June): 512–36.

Karpoff, Jonathan M., and John R. Lott Jr. 1993. "The Reputational Penalty Firms Bear from Committing Criminal Fraud." *Journal of Law and Economics* 36 (October): 757–802.

———. 1998. "Punitive Damages: Their Determinants, Effects on Firm Value, and the Impact of Supreme Court and Congressional Attempts to Limit Awards." Working Paper. University of Chicago Law School. July.

Manning, Richard. 1994. "Changing Rules in Tort Law and the Market for Childhood Vaccines." *Journal of Law and Economics* 37 (April): 247–75.

Mitchell, Mark L., and Michael T. Maloney. 1989. "Crisis in the Cockpit? The Role of Market Forces in Promoting Air Travel Safety." *Journal of Law and Economics* 32 (October): 329–55.

Peltzman, Sam. 1981. "The Effects of FTC Advertising Regulation." *Journal of Law and Economics* 24 (December): 403–48.

Perloff, Jeffrey M., Daniel L. Rubinfeld, and Paul Ruud. 1996. "Antitrust Settlements and Trial Outcomes." *Review of Economics and Statistics* 78 (August): 401–09.

Pindyck, Robert S. 1998. *Econometric Models and Economic Forecasts*, 4th ed. McGraw-Hill.

Reilly, Robert, and George Hoffer. 1983. "Will Retarding Information Flow on Automobile Recalls Affect Consumer Demand?" *Economic Inquiry* 21 (July): 444–47.

Simon, Marilyn. 1981. "Imperfect Information, Costly Information, and Product Quality." *Bell Journal of Economics* 12 (Spring): 171–84.

White, Michelle J., and Henry S. Farber. 1991. "Medical Malpractice: An Empirical Examination of the Litigation Process." *RAND Journal of Economics* 22 (Summer): 199–217.

PATRICIA H. BORN
University of Connecticut

W. KIP VISCUSI
Harvard University

The Distribution of the Insurance Market Effects of Tort Liability Reforms

THE MID-1980s marked a period of tremendous escalation in liability insurance premiums, particularly for medical malpractice, product liability, and environmental liability.[1] Whereas some insurance lines, such as automobile insurance, were comparatively stable, premiums for general liability and medical malpractice insurance doubled from 1984 to 1986.[2] Increased prices were accompanied by problems with insurance availability and insurance rationing. Many observers suggested that these substantial price increases had widespread economic effects. Motels removed diving boards from their swimming pools, pharmaceutical firms stopped innovation for products with high liability risks such as those for pregnant women, and entire industries, such as the private aircraft industry, were seriously threatened.

The irony of these effects, many critics suggested, was that increased liability was not making lives safer because potentially health-enhancing products, such as new prescription drugs and other innovations, were prevented from reaching the market. The rise in medical malprac-

Kenneth Abraham, Dennis Carlton, Cliff Winston, and Brookings conference participants provided helpful comments. Viscusi's research was supported by the Harvard Olin Center for Law, Business, and Economics and by the Sheldon Seevak Research Fund.

1. For discussion of the liability crisis, see Abraham (1987); American Law Institute (1991); Dewees, Duff, and Trebilcock (1996); Huber (1998); Huber and Litan (1991); Litan and Winston (1988); Priest (1987); Schuck (1991); Schwartz (1988); Viscusi (1991); Weiler (1991); and Weiler and others (1993).

2. These data are drawn from Insurance Information Institute (1992, pp. 28–29).

tice liability raised similar concerns. The high insurance costs seem to have led to a decrease in the proportion of doctors in obstetrics, anesthesiology, and other specialties with very high insurance costs, although such conclusions are based largely on case study evidence.

Another observation was that rising medical malpractice costs led to defensive medicine. Physicians ordered unnecessary tests or procedures that might ultimately affect liability but did not significantly help in treating patients.[3] Much of the debate in the 1990s over increased health care costs focused on medical malpractice insurance as potentially contributing to the rising cost of medical care in the U.S. economy.

This study does not concentrate on the causes of the liability crisis or its economic ramifications. Rather, its emphasis is on the effects on the insurance market of states' response to this medical insurance crisis—the tort reform measures enacted during the mid- and late 1980s. What was the character of these reforms, and how did they affect the functioning of liability insurance markets?

The occurrence of an insurance liability crisis and a reform response is not unique in the history of the insurance industry. Similar reforms were initiated in response to the medical malpractice liability crisis of the 1970s.[4] The wave of liability reforms in the 1980s is of particular interest from two standpoints. First, what was the overall effect of the reforms on insurance market performance? Did the reforms in fact reduce losses, premium costs, and profitability as expected? Second, did these effects differ according to different segments of the insurance market? What was the distribution of the effects across the market? Were the benefits primarily concentrated among the largest insurance firms, the most profitable ones, or the least efficient ones?

To assess the insurance market effects, we used a very detailed microeconomic data set, the complete ratemaking files of the National Association of Insurance Commissioners, where the unit of observation is each insurance company writing medical malpractice or general liability coverage in each state by year. This is the largest database that has ever been employed in any study of effects on general liability or

3. See Danzon, Pauly, and Kington (1990); Weiler (1991); and Weiler and others (1993).
4. Danzon (1985) addressed these reform issues. A more recent discussion of medical malpractice reform generally appears in Weiler and others (1993). For product liability, see Viscusi (1991).

medical malpractice, and our study has been carried out in greater detail than any other in the literature.[5]

Our analysis identifies the nature and extent of the consequences of the reforms. What were the reforms, and did they have a significant effect on premiums, losses, loss ratios, and litigation patterns? We do not inquire into whether these effects are desirable. Many of the consequences of the reform efforts have been to decrease medical malpractice or general liability costs. Bringing liability costs under control was clearly important, especially in a period of insurance market instability that had ramifications for many economic activities. These reforms reduced uncertainty not only for insurance companies, but also for their customers. Assessing the character of the reforms and whether they in fact improved the efficiency of the tort liability system also is a consideration in any overall assessment of efforts to restrain liability costs.[6]

The most interesting and distinctive aspect of the analysis is its inquiry into the distributional consequences of the reform efforts. Which insurers benefited the most from the liability reforms? Were they the large firms or the least profitable firms, or were the effects equally distributed across all insurers? We were particularly interested in whether the reforms conferred the greatest benefits on the least profitable companies, those that were likely doing a poor job of choosing the risks they insured. Consequently, caps on damages would have reduced the penalties for poor underwriting practices. We used quantile regression methodology to assess the potential differential effects of the reforms across insurer profitability and size distributions.

Considering the effects on both medical malpractice and general liability insurance offers several advantages. First, the character and timing of the reform efforts differed across the two types of insurance, so additional information can be gained by examining both sets of reform efforts. Second, the markets themselves differed in their scale, the companies offering the coverage, and the entities purchasing insurance. Third, the reform efforts targeted firms in markets that performed

5. The principal predecessors of this study are Barker (1992); Danzon (1985); Hughes and Snyder (1989); Viscusi (1990); Viscusi and Moore (1993); Viscusi and Born (1995); Viscusi and others (1993); and Zuckerman, Bovbjerg, and Sloan (1990).

6. Numerous studies have discussed the rationale for different kinds of reform and the strengths and limitations of different reform proposals. See American Law Institute (1991).

somewhat differently in the period just before the reform efforts. The percentage change in liability premiums for general liability insurance was somewhat higher than for medical malpractice. Moreover, as we show, the profitability of the insurance also differed, with general liability insurance tending to be less profitable.

An Overview of Tort Liability Reforms

The reform efforts enacted by the states were diverse. Table 1 summarizes the types of reform efforts by state and year (1985, 1986, or 1987) for efforts affecting amounts of damages. Some states legislated strict caps on damages. Others limited the value of noneconomic damages, principally for pain and suffering and the loss experienced by survivors after the death of a family member. Unfortunately, the wide variety of restrictions in the reform efforts and the varying circumstances in which the restrictions became applicable prevented construction of a single quantitative index of the stringency of the overall reform effort.

Laws designed to limit the circumstances in which damages may be awarded took a variety of forms. In 1987 Idaho required plaintiffs to prove "oppressive, fraudulent, wanton, malicious, or outrageous conduct" in a plea for punitive damages. Missouri bifurcated the trial process in 1987, so that actions involving punitive damages first involve determining the defendant's liability for all damages sought without regard to the amount of punitive damages. In the second part of the trial, the jury determines the amount of the punitive damages. Still other reform efforts restricted punitive damages or attempted to alter the character of the liability rules applied to physician behavior. Most of the caps on compensatory (economic and noneconomic) damages for medical malpractice and general liability cases fell between $225,000 in Michigan and $875,000 in New Hampshire. Punitive damages were generally capped at a lower level, ranging from $100,000 in Alabama to $250,000 in Georgia. In two states, West Virginia and Wisconsin, where compensatory damage caps were imposed specifically on medical malpractice cases, the cap was set at $1,000,000.

Despite the flurry of activity, there has been considerable doubt about the efficacy of the reform efforts in altering the liability landscape and

Table 1. States Enacting Damages Limitations, 1985–87

	Medical malpractice		*General liability*	
Year	*State*	*Type of limitation*	*State*	*Type of limitation*
1985	Florida	3	Illinois	1
	Illinois	4	Montana	3
	Kansas	1,3	Rhode Island	1
	South Dakota	1		
1986	Kansas	2,5	Alaska	2
	Massachusetts	2	Colorado	1
	Michigan	2	Florida	2,3
	Missouri	2	Illinois	3
	South Dakota	2	Maryland	2
	Utah	2	Minnesota	2
	West Virginia	5	New Hampshire	2
	Wisconsin	2	Oklahoma	1
			Washington	2
1987	Alabama	5	Alabama	1
			California	3
			Georgia	1,3
			Hawaii	1
			Idaho	3
			Indiana	3
			Iowa	3
			Kansas	3
			Missouri	3
			Montana	3
			North Dakota	3
			Ohio	3
			Oregon	2,3
			South Carolina	2,3
			Texas	1
			Virginia	1

Source: See text. Key: 1. monetary cap on punitive damages; 2. monetary cap on noneconomic damages; 3. limitations on circumstances in which damages may be awarded; 4. punitive damages barred in medical malpractice actions; 5. monetary cap on all medical malpractice damages.

in affecting insurance costs.[7] One potential reason for skepticism is that damage caps pertain only to the highest awards. Perhaps because these tend to be the most publicized, the public's perception of the frequency

7. For example, in 1993 the chairman of the American Bar Association's Working Group on Health Care Reform expressed his skepticism by claiming that "caps on noneconomic damages have not had the dramatic impact that supporters think." See Clifford D. Stromberg, Health Line American Political Network, August 12, 1993.

of million dollar verdicts is far greater than their actual occurrence.[8] Indeed, overpayment of small economic losses is greater than large economic losses, for which the replacement rate (the ratio of payment to the dollar value of economic loss) tends to be less. The award cap also may not bind juries if they adjust other components of the award to avoid the constraint imposed by a damage limit. Whether such compensating jury behavior is consequential has not been determined.

This study extends our work reported in Viscusi and Born (1995) in which we focused primarily on case studies of the medical malpractice reforms in Michigan and Wisconsin, coupled with exploratory analysis of national data. In this study we consider the same types of reforms that were the focus of that paper, but the statistical analysis of the insurance consequences is much more extensive here. In addition, we examine the effects of these reforms on general liability insurance markets. Although both medical malpractice and general liability reforms were generally selected from a similar menu of reform efforts, the states that chose to make these reforms differed. Moreover, the type of reforms picked by particular states varied either in timing or character. For example, in 1985 Florida adopted limitations on the circumstances in which damages may be awarded for medical malpractice cases. The state then enacted similar restrictions for general liability in 1986 but also imposed a monetary cap on noneconomic damages. As is indicated in the breakdowns in table 1, many more states adopted general liability reforms over the pivotal reform years of 1985–87 than adopted reforms pertaining only to medical malpractice.

Table 1 distinguishes reforms that affected medical malpractice specifically from general liability reforms. The empirical analysis pools these reform efforts in its analysis of medical malpractice. Overall, eleven states enacted medical malpractice reforms, with most occurring in 1986, which was the last year of the 1984–86 surge in medical malpractice insurance premiums. In the case of general liability reforms, 1986 was a prominent year, but 1987 featured a greater number—sixteen states enacted reform laws then.

A particularly striking aspect about the reform efforts is the strong correlation among them. The correlation within states is reflected in patterns such as that in Kansas. That state enacted two medical malpractice

8. See Viscusi (1991).

reforms in 1985 (a monetary cap on punitive damages and limitations on circumstances in which damages may be awarded), and followed with two more medical malpractice reforms in 1986 (a monetary cap on noneconomic damages and one on all medical damages). These efforts were once again amended by a general liability reform in 1987 (a limitation on the circumstances in which damages may be awarded).

There is an additional correlation among the kinds of damage reforms enacted in any given period. Of the nine medical malpractice reforms enacted in 1986, six involved a monetary cap on noneconomic damages. Similarly, of the eighteen general liability reforms enacted in 1987, twelve limited the circumstances in which damages may be awarded. An interesting empirical question is whether these different waves of political reform activity significantly affected the functioning of the liability system.

Because of the substantial similarities among various reform efforts, it is not feasible to estimate reliably the effect of each effort. Our focus instead is on two categorizations of reforms: a zero-one categorical variable for whether a damage cap was imposed; and a zero-one categorical variable for whether some other kind of reform was enacted. Further refinement of the categorizations did not yield stable empirical estimates. Both medical malpractice and general liability reforms are pooled for this analysis of medical malpractice insurance, whereas only the general liability reforms is used in the general liability insurance analysis.

The zero-one categorical variable approach to characterizing the reforms captures the average effect of the reform efforts on the liability system. This variable does not enable one to determine whether a liability cap of $300,000 is more effective than a liability cap of $500,000, for example. Ideally, it would be useful to be able to categorize all the various reform variables in some quantitative fashion so that one would have a continuous quantitative scale for measuring the stringency of the reform. In addition to the monetary value of the cap, however, there are also qualitative restrictions placed on the award or accompanying the reform character of the liability rules. Because of this diversity, the most feasible empirical approach is to assess whether there was a shift in behavior after the advent of the reforms.

Our focus is solely on the 1980s reform efforts. As we mentioned, many states undertook similar reform efforts in the 1970s. Potentially these could also have influenced subsequent behavior, as indicated by

Danzon.[9] Our analysis of the 1970s reforms showed no long-term influence on the performance of the liability system.[10] One reason for this failure to find an effect stems from the structure of the econometric analysis. In addition to examining the effect across states, we are also concerned with the effect over time. Each equation includes in the baseline the lagged value of the dependent variable. Separate estimates in which the lagged dependent variable is not included also appear. Thus the focus is on whether liability reforms affect change in insurance market performance over time. To the extent that the 1970s reforms have already exhibited their influence through the current history of insurance premiums, their effects are already captured through the lagged dependent variable.

We proceed with our analysis on the assumption that the reforms are likely to influence insurer performance through their influence on potential and actual court case outcomes. That is, we assume that insurers in reform states operate in an environment in which a more well-defined legal liability system reduces underwriting uncertainty. Thus the reforms influence the underwriting profitability of the insurer. This assumption is potentially an issue if the causality is reversed: instead of reform efforts leading to improved performance, performance levels may lead to further reform activity. In other words the performance of the insurers in a state may be a primary determinant of states' willingness or motivation to enact reforms. If our assumption is not valid, the potential bias of our results is minimal, given the firm-level nature of our data and the large number of firms in each state.[11]

Sample Descriptions

To undertake the analysis, we have used the complete insurance financial data files compiled by the National Association of Insurance Commissioners. These data include information on every insurance

9. Danzon (1985).
10. Viscusi and Born (1995).
11. Past individual firm profitability (the loss ratio) was not found to be a significant determinant of state reform efforts. We also investigated the relationship between state reform efforts and several other measures of past performance in the state, including the average loss ratio and the upper quantiles (seventy-fifth and ninetieth percentiles) of the state loss ratio distribution but did not find any consistent significant relationships.

company writing medical malpractice insurance, general liability insurance, or both, by state and by year for the United States. Specific data elements include premiums earned and losses incurred, by line of business, for these insurers, reported separately for each state in which the insurer operates. It is the most complete data set of insurance company financial information available. For 1984–91 the sample contains more than 8,000 observations for medical malpractice insurers and 67,000 observations for general liability insurers. In our analyses with lagged dependent variables, our panel is limited to 1985–91.

Table 2 summarizes the medical malpractice insurers' sample characteristics and the general liability insurance company data. For simplicity, we present the sample means and standard deviations for two particular years in the data. The 1985 data are for the middle of the 1984–86 liability crisis and coincide with the first year in which some states enacted liability reforms. The 1991 statistics reflect the performance of insurers several years after the reforms were implemented.

An overall shift in performance of the medical malpractice insurance industry during the period is evident. Although premiums earned rose by 46 percent during the period, losses actually declined by 5 percent. The net effect is that the ratio of losses to premiums, the loss ratio, dropped from 1.6 to 1.0. If one ignores the interest earned on premiums before losses are paid, 1.0 is the break-even loss ratio amount.

The experience in the general liability insurance industry was equally striking. Premiums earned rose 24 percent while losses declined by 14 percent. The net effect is that the loss ratio dropped from 1.8 to 1.3. The loss performance and profitability of insurers writing medical malpractice and general liability insurance clearly improved dramatically over the period.

These improvements in underwriting performance overstate the improvement in profitability, however, because of interest that is earned on premiums. Because losses are paid out after premiums are paid, in periods of high interest rates such as the early 1980s, interest rates may be sufficiently high that writing insurance can be profitable even with loss ratios below 1.0. As table 2 shows, the real (inflation-adjusted) Treasury bill rate dropped from 3.7 percent in 1985 to 1.8 percent in 1991. Insurance premiums were more profitable from an investment standpoint in 1985, thus making it more feasible to write insurance coverage with more unfavorable expected loss ratios. An improvement

Table 2. Sample Statistics, Medical Malpractice and General Liability, 1985, 1991

	1985		1991	
Variable	*Mean*	*Standard deviation*	*Mean*	*Standard deviation*
	Medical malpractice			
Premiums and losses (in millions)				
Premiums earned	2.408	10.600	3.515	14.600
Premiums written	2.763	11.800	3.554	14.400
National premiums written	38.100	82.100	31.900	53.200
Losses	2.733	13.600	2.598	11.300
Loss ratio	1.603	2.287	1.029	1.995
Reform and regulation variables				
Damages	0.124	0.329	0.653	0.476
Other	0.338	0.473	0.847	0.360
Rate regulation	0.267	0.442	0.291	0.455
Firm characteristics				
Lloyds	0.003	0.052	0.001	0.030
Mutual	0.066	0.248	0.083	0.276
Rciprocal	0.022	0.147	0.043	0.203
Return on equity	−0.056	0.525	0.173	0.745
Other controls				
Four-firm concentration ratio (state)	0.794	0.104	0.683	0.130
Real state aggregate income (in thousands)	90.026	95.391	109.984	115.503
Real Treasury bill rate	3.730	0	1.750	0
Sample size	1,091	. . .	1,119	. . .

continued

in overall performance is evident in the change in the average firm's return on equity, a measure that reflects the firm's performance in both underwriting and investment activities.[12] Average return on equity was negative in 1985 but improved to an average of 0.17 in 1991.

Table 2 provides additional information on the exposure of the malpractice insurers to liability reforms and rate regulation. The principal reform variables included in the analysis are zero-one categorical variables for whether the state imposed a damage cap or undertook some other reform (affecting joint and several liability, frivolous suits, struc-

---

12. The return on equity is defined as the sum of total investment and underwriting gains divided by the firm's total equity. This measure is calculated from a firm-level data set that contains income statement and balance sheet information for all firms in our sample.

Table 2. Sample Statistics, Medical Malpractice and General Liability, 1985, 1991
(*continued*)

	1985		1991	
Variable	*Mean*	*Standard deviation*	*Mean*	*Standard deviation*
General liability				
Premiums and losses (in millions)				
Premiums earned	1.405	5.704	1.749	7.841
Premiums written	1.608	7.120	1.976	9.426
National premiums written	56.600	123.000	68.100	217.000
Losses	1.584	6.393	1.358	6.161
Loss ratio	1.833	5.044	1.302	3.889
Reform and regulation variables				
Damages	0.202	0.401	0.595	0.491
Other	0.678	0.467	0.917	0.276
Rate regulation	0.276	0.447	0.277	0.448
Firm characteristics				
Lloyds	0.003	0.051	0.003	0.057
Mutual	0.126	0.331	0.116	0.321
Reciprocal	0.013	0.114	0.018	0.134
Return on equity	−0.103	1.000	0.132	0.202
Other controls				
Four-firm concentration ratio (state)	0.231	0.071	0.268	0.060
Real state aggregate income (in thousands)	89.475	95.684	103.964	111.245
Real Treasury bill rate	3.730	0	1.750	0
Sample size	8,363	. . .	8,628	. . .

Source: See text.

tured payments, attorneys' fees, collateral source rules, and liability limits). The prevalence of each kind of reform increased dramatically. For example, only 12 percent of all medical malpractice insurers' operations were affected by damage caps in 1985, but 65 percent of the companies wrote coverage in 1991 in states where damage caps were applicable. The presence of other reforms more than doubled in importance during that time as well. The proportion of firms operating in states with strict rate regulation was fairly stable, rising from 27 percent to 29 percent.

Measures for rate regulation structures for the states were consistently insignificant in our exploratory regressions. Both general liability insurance and medical malpractice insurance tend to be purchased by corporate and institutional entities rather than by individuals, so states do not regulate pricing in these lines, whereas regulation is binding for consumer-oriented lines such as auto insurance.

The empirical analysis also includes measures of insurance firm characteristics, that is, whether the firm was a stock company, a mutual company, a reciprocal, or Lloyd's. These organizational forms may have different incentives due to the structures of the agency relationships that vary with organizational form. The dominant organizational structure for medical malpractice insurance was stock companies, which accounted for roughly 90 percent of the sample during the period. In exploratory analyses we also examined the interactive influence of stock companies and the reform variables, but these effects were not statistically significant.

We include national premiums written in our analysis to control for the size of the overall insurance organization and capture the potential for economies of scale to be reflected in the performance of the insurer at the state level. As table 2 indicates, average national premiums written fell from $38 million to about $32 million in this period.

The final set of control variables pertains to market structure and state characteristics. In particular, we take into account the four-firm concentration ratio as a measure of industry concentration and also include the value of real state aggregate income. This final variable may have many types of influences, such as reflecting the preferences of voters in the state as well as being an index of the magnitude of the financial loss associated with the lost earnings component of a medical malpractice suit.

Table 2 also shows statistics for the general liability insurance sample. The prevalence of each kind of reform also increased dramatically for these insurers. For example, only 20 percent of the general liability insurers' operations were affected by damage caps in 1985, while in 1991 about 60 percent of these companies wrote coverage in states that had caps. The presence of other reforms increased from 68 percent to 92 percent. The proportion of firms operating in states with strict rate regulation remained stable at about 28 percent throughout the period. Table 2 also indicates that stock companies are the dominant organizational structure for general liability insurers. A consistent 87 percent of all general liability insurers were stock companies.

Contrary to the trend in medical malpractice, the average national premiums written by general liability insurance companies increased, from about $57 million to $68 million. Industry concentration, at 0.24 to 0.27, was much lower than in the medical malpractice industry, where concentration fell slightly from 0.79 to 0.68. Overall profitability measured by the return on equity improved from −0.10 in 1985 to 0.13 in 1991.

Ideally, if liability reforms have their intended effect, they should decrease losses, subsequently decrease premiums charged for coverage, and improve insurance company profitability. One might expect tort liability reforms to affect premiums less than losses to the extent that insurance company operations were previously unprofitable. Higher premiums would be necessary to restore companies to their precrisis level of profitability and to a more normal level of competitive profits. Because our analysis distinguishes between states that imposed damage caps and those that did not, we are able to assess whether the rise in premiums was particularly great in states where no reforms were enacted, which is what one would expect.

Although examining the effect of liability insurance on premiums, losses, and loss ratios is instructive, it is the loss ratio that is the main index of insurance market performance. The ratio is the inverse of ex post insurance profitability and the central measure of interest, whereas the cost and premium results show the mechanisms of interest.[13]

In a competitive insurance market, firms enter and exit the industry until the loss ratio for a new entrant is just sufficient to provide a normal level of profitability. If liability reforms improve profitability, competition will ensure that the industry returns to a normal level of profitability in the long run. Even in the absence of reforms, competition will lead to long-run normal profits. The main differences are the timing of the return to profitability and possibly the mix of firms writing coverage. A reduction in premium rates could achieve such a pass-through. If all firms are identical, have similarly risky portfolios, and are affected in the same way by liability reforms, profitability will be unaffected by the cost reductions generated by the reforms. Insurance purchasers will be the principal beneficiaries of the reform effort.

13. One potential problem with the loss ratio measure is that it is derived using losses incurred, which to some extent is an estimated value. During this period it is possible that insurers' estimates of losses were not accurate, but we have no reason to believe the inaccuracies would differ across states with and without reforms.

This idealized result may not hold because of the characteristics of insurance markets. Suppose, for example, that firms differ in their level of profitability and that reforms benefit only the less profitable firms. In such cases there would be no postreform premium competition from the more profitable firms or new entrants who likewise would not benefit from the reforms. Thus the character of the reform effort and the distribution of its consequences have a fundamental effect on who benefits from the liability reforms.

Because we are concerned with the potential differential effect of liability reforms on firms that are less profitable, it is instructive to examine the stability of firm profitability over time. That is, we ask whether firms in the highest quantiles of the loss ratio distribution (the least profitable in their underwriting performance) are consistently located in the highest quantiles or if the relative performance of the insurers is variable. We expect stability over time, but we rely on some variability to add credence to the empirical analysis. Without variation, our quantile regression results reflect only the unique characteristics of the companies in the quantile (see appendix A for our quantile regression methodology).

Table 3 shows a cross-tabulation of the number of observations on medical malpractice firms by their position in the loss ratio distribution for 1985 (row) and 1991 (column). For example, the table indicates that four firms from the highest quantile in 1985 fell to the 50–75 percent range of the distribution in 1991. The bulk of observations on the diagonal suggests general stability among the firms, but the off-diagonal cells indicate a substantial amount of variation in relative performance.

The stability of performance among general liability insurers is evident. The bulk of observations is, again, located on the diagonal or in cells adjacent to the diagonal. The off-diagonal cells, however, indicate variability in relative performance among these insurers as well. There is also little evidence to suggest that firms in the highest quantiles (worst performance) are unable to recover. Interestingly, among the firms that remain in the sample for all seven years, none of the medical malpractice firms holds a position in the lowest quantile (less than the twenty-fifth percentile) for more than six years straight, and only twelve occupy the lowest quartile for three years. Similarly, only two general liability

**Table 3. Performance Stability: Medical Malpractice and
General Liability Loss Ratios**

1985 quantile	1991 quantile					
	0–10	10–25	25–50	50–75	75–90	90–100
Medical malpractice insurers[a]						
0–10	5	3	2	0	0	1
10–25	7	7	5	9	7	4
25–50	9	19	14	17	13	7
50–75	5	12	17	26	13	12
75–90	4	3	8	11	8	3
90–100	1	0	2	4	7	1
General liability insurers[b]						
0–10	56	60	89	86	45	23
10–25	50	77	171	180	76	44
25–50	70	152	275	274	168	82
50–75	64	113	209	296	176	112
75–90	24	40	87	135	106	82
90–100	23	28	32	57	54	45

Source: See text. Each cell denotes the number of firms that fell in quantile *x* in 1985 (row) and quantile *y* in 1991 (column).

a. N = 266 (firm-state level).

b. N = 13,330 (firm-state level).

insurers occupied the lowest quintile (less than the tenth percentile) for the seven years used in the analysis.

The Effect of Liability Reforms on Insurance Company Loss Ratios

The most prominent variable of interest in the empirical insurance literature is the loss ratio. Insurance premiums reflect the combined influence of the price of insurance and the quantity of insurance sold. Similarly, loss values will be higher if more coverage is written. The loss ratio, which is the ratio of losses incurred to premiums earned for policies written in year *t* serves as a measure of the ex post price of insurance. This variable simultaneously recognizes the influence of price and quantity in driving premium levels and attempts to serve as a measure of insurance company profitability. The high loss ratios—well above 1.0—experienced among malpractice and general liability insurers in the mid-1980s served as a primary impetus for many of the tort liability reform efforts.

Appendix B presents comparable results for premiums and losses. Total premiums earned is not the ideal measure for tracking the efforts of liability reforms because the number reflects the combined influence of price and quantity. No price or quantity information, such as the number of policies written or the extent of coverage, is available to disentangle these components, however.

The character of the reforms is such that they will first exert their influence by reducing the size of damage awards and their frequency. Insurance losses should be the first to reflect the reforms' effects. Once the effect on losses becomes apparent, insurance companies will revise their premium levels, but for institutional reasons, such as the need to obtain regulatory approval of rate changes, this revision occurs with a lag. Given this lag structure, there will be an improvement in firm profitability as reflected in lower loss ratios. Any reduction in premiums as a result of this enhanced profitability will lag behind the reductions in the loss ratio.

If firms were at a competitive rate of profitability before the tort liability reforms, we would expect any diminishing of loss levels to lead to a reduction in premiums. To the extent that the loss ratio is a valid index of insurance company profitability, one would expect competition to adjust so that the loss ratios would be unaffected by the reform efforts.[14] In contrast, if loss ratios were excessive, reforms restraining tort liability could accelerate insurance companies' return to profitability, particularly in states in which regulatory authorities impose limits on raising premiums.

We use a quantile regression model to assess the effects of the liability reforms on the loss ratios of medical malpractice and general liability insurers. In particular, instead of focusing on the average effects of the covariates on the loss ratio, we explore the potential differential effects across the distribution of loss ratios. Specifically, we focus on the determinants of whether the loss ratio lies within a particular quantile of the overall loss ratio distribution. Using the quantile regression methodology, we can obtain estimates of the influence of our

14. The loss ratio excludes, for example, the administrative costs and variations in the rate of return earned on premium investments.

covariates at any point of the distribution of the dependent variable. The most common form of quantile regression model is the median regression, which is very similar to ordinary least squares (OLS) regression except that the method involves minimizing the sum of the absolute residuals rather than the sum of the squares of the residuals. Unlike OLS, quantile regressions do not impose normality distributional assumptions on the error term. Because we are interested in the effects of the reforms across the distribution, we supplement median regression analysis with generalized quantile regressions estimated at the tenth, twenty-fifth, seventy-fifth, and ninetieth percentiles. To control for possible heteroscedastic errors, we use a bootstrap resampling technique to obtain standard errors. The quantile regression methodology is discussed in more detail in appendix A.

Tables 4 through 11 report the quantile regression results in which we assess the effects of the liability reforms on loss ratios. For each of the two samples of insurers, we estimate these effects following two functional forms, beginning with a standard autoregressive formulation in which the lagged dependent variable is included in the vector x. That is: $x = f$(loss ratio$_{t-1}$, zero-one indicators for damage reform and other reform, zero-one indicators for organizational form, national premiums written, four-firm industry concentration ratio, zero-one indicator for restrictive rate filing regulation, real state aggregate income, U.S. Treasury bill rate).

We also estimate a counterpart to this equation including a variable to capture the effect of the 1986 tax reforms. That is: $x = f$(loss ratio$_{t-1}$, zero-one indicators for damage reform and other reform, zero-one indicators for organizational form, national premiums written, tax reform 1986 $\times$ return on equity, four-firm industry concentration ratio, zero-one indicator for restrictive rate filing regulation, real state aggregate income, U.S. Treasury bill rate).

Because these reforms will have the greatest benefit for the more profitable firms, the variable used is the interaction between the 1986 (and thereafter) dummy variable and the return on equity, which we measure by the underwriting and investment gains divided by total equity. Unfortunately, the timing of the tax reforms coincides with the middle of the reform period from 1985 to 1987, making it very difficult to disentangle the two types of policy influences. In the subsequent results the damage cap reform variable is consistently influential for

72   *Brookings Papers: Microeconomics 1998*

both medical malpractice and general liability, but the other reform variable is more unstable in the general liability regression results.

We then proceed with the estimation of these two equations without the lagged dependent variable, which allows us to assess the long-run effects of the reforms. Each of the tables reports five sets of quantile regression results for different fractiles of the loss ratio distribution. Thus it is possible to ascertain the differential effect of liability reforms on the less profitable firms at the upper end of the loss ratio spectrum as opposed to firms at the low end. The estimated coefficients indicate the influence of the covariate at that particular portion of the distribution. Thus, by looking across the estimated quantiles, we can infer whether the influence of a covariate gets greater, or smaller, or is unvarying across the distribution.

Medical Malpractice Loss Ratios

Tables 4 through 7 pertain to the medical malpractice sample. In table 4 the importance of examining the effects of the liability reforms on different segments of the distribution is evident when one compares the estimates obtained at each of the quantiles. The results indicate that most segments of the profitability distribution are significantly affected by the reforms. Most striking is the effect of the damage cap variable— it increases steadily in terms of its coefficient size as one moves from the lower quantiles to the higher loss ratio values, where these effects are statistically significant in all cases. The other reform variable likewise is most consequential at the upper end of the loss ratio spectrum. Beginning at the median loss ratio through a remarkably high influence at the ninetieth percentile, the other reform variable decreases the value of the loss ratio substantially. The combined effect of these reform variables based on the point estimates is −0.25 at the seventy-fifth percentile and −0.41 at the ninetieth percentile. Given the mean loss ratio values of 1.60 in 1985 and 1.0 in 1991 for the sample characteristics in table 2, it is apparent that effects of this magnitude represent a substantial influence on the profitability of insurance company operations.

It is somewhat striking that the net influence of the lagged value of the loss ratio increases to a remarkable degree as one moves to the least profitable firms. For firms at the low end of the loss ratio distribution,

Table 4. Medical Malpractice, Quantile Regression Results, Model 1, Dependent Variable = Loss Ratio

Bootstrapped standard errors in parentheses

Variable	Quantile (percent)				
	10	25	50	75	90
Intercept	0.157*** (0.045)	0.308*** (0.055)	0.494*** (0.049)	0.787*** (0.118)	1.083** (0.454)
Loss ratio $(t-1)$	0.026*** (0.006)	0.089*** (0.014)	0.275*** (0.028)	0.668*** (0.044)	1.353*** (0.059)
Damage reform	-0.027*** (0.009)	-0.029* (0.017)	-0.062*** (0.010)	-0.095*** (0.024)	-0.127* (0.074)
Other reform	0.007 (0.012)	-0.013 (0.013)	-0.051*** (0.017)	-0.158*** (0.049)	-0.290** (0.113)
Mutual	-0.025*** (0.007)	-0.072*** (0.017)	-0.072*** (0.024)	-0.116*** (0.033)	-0.114 (0.121)
Lloyds	-0.059 (0.190)	0.236 (0.272)	0.428 (0.316)	3.228 (2.585)	2.626 (7.425)
Reciprocal	-0.008 (0.016)	-0.019 (0.024)	-0.022 (0.025)	-0.076*** (0.027)	-0.244 (0.173)
National premiums written	3.2E-10*** (4.9E-11)	2.9E.10*** (5.0E-11)	6.9E-11 (6.1E-11)	-1.9E-10 (1.3E-10)	-1.6E-9*** (1.6E-10)
Four-firm concentration ratio	-0.014 (0.044)	0.037 (0.033)	-0.028 (0.054)	-0.015 (0.117)	0.306 (0.316)
Rate regulation	-0.003 (0.010)	-0.000 (0.011)	0.008 (0.015)	0.018 (0.025)	-0.057 (0.064)
Real state income	1.3E-7*** (4.0E-8)	1.2E-7*** (6.6E-8)	2.6E-8 (5.7E-8)	4.0E-8 (1.7E-7)	-3.5E-7 (3.1E-7)
Treasury bill rate	0.003 (0.003)	-0.003 (0.005)	0.006 (0.005)	-0.008 (0.010)	0.003 (0.035)

Source: Authors' calculations.

*Significant at the 90 percent confidence level, two-tailed test.
**Significant at the 95 percent confidence level, two-tailed test.
***Significant at the 99 percent confidence level, two-tailed test.

the last-period loss ratio has very little influence on current loss ratio levels. Firms at the seventy-fifth and ninetieth percentiles, however, exhibit a very strong relationship across time, which is suggestive of a consistently risky and unprofitable portfolio of insurance policies written.

Table 5 reports very similar results when we include our control for the Tax Reform Act of 1986. The effects of the two reform variables are virtually unchanged, and although the new variable is only significant at the median and seventy-fifth percentiles, it has the expected negative effect on loss ratios.

Tables 6 and 7 explore the robustness of these results with regression estimates of the model without the lagged dependent variable. Apart from a substantial decrease in explanatory power, the results are similar to those in tables 4 and 5. In both models, damage reforms have a consistent significant effect in reducing loss ratios, with effects at the ninetieth percentile being more than three times as great as those for the median firm. It is the most unprofitable firms that benefit most from the damage reforms. The magnitude of the effect is slightly larger for firms above the median when the lagged dependent variable is omitted, indicating a larger long-run influence on loss ratios for the more unprofitable firms. The other reforms variable performs in a same manner, with the point estimates following the same general pattern in the upper quantiles.

General Liability Loss Ratios

The experience among general liability insurers is reported in tables 8 through 11. Here again, the quantile regression results indicate that most segments of the profitability distribution are significantly affected by the damage reforms. In each table the effect increases in magnitude as one moves from the lower quantiles (about -0.01 at the tenth percentile) to the higher loss ratio values (-0.2 to -0.3 at the ninetieth percentile, depending on the specification). Given the mean loss ratio values of 1.8 in 1985 and 1.3 in 1991 for the sample characteristics in table 2, the results in all four tables suggest damage reforms had a substantial influence on the profitability of insurance company operations. The other reform variable is found to be generally insignificant

Table 5. Medical Malpractice, Quantile Regression Results, Model 2, Dependent Variable = Loss Ratio

Bootstrapped standard errors in parentheses

Variable	Quantile (percent)				
	10	25	50	75	90
Intercept	0.164*** (0.037)	0.337*** (0.046)	0.493*** (0.060)	0.834*** (0.133)	1.074*** (0.399)
Loss ratio ($t-1$)	0.026*** (0.006)	0.088*** (0.019)	0.274*** (0.031)	0.663*** (0.054)	1.352*** (0.071)
Damage reform	−0.027*** (0.009)	−0.033*** (0.013)	−0.060*** (0.012)	−0.095*** (0.028)	−0.116* (0.069)
Other reform	0.008 (0.012)	−0.010 (0.013)	−0.042** (0.019)	−0.146*** (0.044)	−0.289*** (0.087)
Mutual	−0.017** (0.009)	−0.052** (0.024)	−0.049*** (0.018)	−0.086*** (0.039)	−0.105*** (0.175)
Lloyds	−0.061 (0.218)	0.241 (0.217)	0.417 (0.712)	3.227 (1.998)	2.616 (8.346)
Reciprocal	0.006 (0.016)	0.001 (0.029)	−0.010 (0.038)	−0.087** (0.040)	−0.266 (0.165)
National premiums written	3.5E-10*** (5.8E-11)	3.4E-10*** (5.2E-11)	1.4E-10** (6.0E-11)	−1.1E-10 (7.4E-11)	−1.6E-9*** (1.4E-10)
Tax reform 86* ROE	−0.036 (0.036)	−0.092 (0.059)	−0.154*** (0.050)	−0.141** (0.070)	−0.049 (0.179)
Four-firm concentration ratio	−0.017 (0.036)	0.041 (0.058)	−0.029 (0.066)	0.041 (0.126)	0.352 (0.344)
Rate regulation	−0.003 (0.008)	0.004 (0.010)	−0.003 (0.012)	0.015 (0.028)	−0.059 (0.080)
Real state income	1.4E-7*** (4.4E-8)	1.4E-7*** (4.4E-8)	5.7E-8 (6.3E-8)	5.2E-8 (2.1E-7)	3.3E-7 (2.8E-7)
Treasury bill rate	0.002 (0.003)	−0.007 (0.006)	0.007 (0.005)	−0.012 (0.013)	−0.001 (0.033)

Source: Authors' calculations.

*Significant at the 90 percent confidence level, two-tailed test.
**Significant at the 95 percent confidence level, two-tailed test.
***Significant at the 99 percent confidence level, two-tailed test.

Table 6. Medical Malpractice, Quantile Regression Results, Model 1, Dependent Variable = Loss Ratio, Model without Lagged Dependent Variable

Bootstrapped standard errors in parentheses

Variable	Quantile (percent)				
	10	25	50	75	90
Intercept	0.187***	0.387***	0.590**	1.286***	2.404***
	(0.032)	(0.048)	(0.076)	(0.183)	(0.785)
Damage reform	-0.026**	-0.037***	-0.091***	-0.217***	-0.344***
	(0.011)	(0.012)	(0.021)	(0.040)	(0.122)
Other reform	0.007	-0.021	-0.079***	-0.196***	-0.244*
	(0.013)	(0.013)	(0.022)	(0.031)	(0.137)
Mutual	-0.036***	-0.092***	-0.124**	-0.166***	-0.378**
	(0.008)	(0.012)	(0.021)	(0.064)	(0.172)
Lloyds	-0.051	0.295	0.504	3.101	11.576**
	(0.171)	(0.267)	(1.924)	(5.738)	(5.736)
Reciprocal	-0.015	-0.031	-0.058*	-0.221***	-0.555***
	(0.021)	(0.019)	(0.034)	(0.044)	(0.142)
National premiums written	3.2E-10***	2.9E-10***	6.9E-11	-1.9E-10	-1.6E-9***
	(4.7E-11)	(4.4E-11)	(6.1E-11)	(1.3E-10)	(1.6E-10)
Four-firm concentration ratio	-0.026	0.046	0.115	0.227*	0.844
	(0.037)	(0.037)	(0.070)	(0.116)	(0.642)
Rate regulation	-0.005	-0.006	0.006	-0.022	0.038
	(0.009)	(0.009)	(0.012)	(0.029)	(0.081)
State income	1.3E-7***	1.2E-7*	2.6E-8	4.0E-8	-3.5E-7
	(4.9E-8)	(6.3E-8)	(5.7E-8)	(1.5E-7)	(3.1E-7)
Treasury bill rate	0.002	-0.005	0.009	-0.020	-0.068
	(0.003)	(0.005)	(0.006)	(0.018)	(0.063)

Source: Authors' calculations.
*Significant at the 90 percent confidence level, two-tailed test.
**Significant at the 95 percent confidence level, two-tailed test.
***Significant at the 99 percent confidence level, two-tailed test.

Table 7. Medical Malpractice, Quantile Regression Results, Model 2, Dependent Variable = Loss Ratio, Model without Lagged Dependent Variable

Bootstrapped standard errors in parentheses

Variable	Quantile (percent)				
	10	25	50	75	90
Intercept	0.199*** (0.051)	0.420*** (0.048)	0.594*** (0.052)	1.278*** (0.139)	2.457*** (0.611)
Damage reform	-0.027*** (0.008)	-0.041*** (0.017)	-0.094*** (0.015)	-0.198*** (0.041)	-0.324*** (0.096)
Other reform	0.010 (0.011)	-0.012 (0.020)	-0.066*** (0.018)	-0.182*** (0.036)	-0.257 (0.161)
Mutual	-0.031** (0.013)	-0.069*** (0.016)	-0.101*** (0.031)	-0.160*** (0.038)	-0.383* (0.145)
Lloyds	-0.051 (0.286)	0.292 (0.269)	0.492 (0.732)	3.099 (3.867)	11.573** (5.216)
Reciprocal	-0.004 (0.019)	-0.013 (0.021)	-0.048 (0.031)	-0.196*** (0.047)	-0.632*** (0.137)
National premiums written	3.4E-10*** (5.9E-11)	3.2E-10*** (5.2E-11)	1.3E-10** (5.4E-11)	-4.7E-11 (1.4E-10)	-2.1E-9*** (2.0E-10)
Tax reform 86* ROE	-0.032 (0.042)	-0.110* (0.062)	-0.128** (0.052)	-0.193** (0.075)	-0.074 (0.083)
Four-firm concentration ratio	-0.034 (0.047)	0.045 (0.044)	0.102** (0.045)	0.283** (0.112)	0.807 (0.660)
Rate regulation	-0.005 (0.010)	-0.001 (0.010)	-3.9E-4 (0.013)	-0.035 (0.026)	0.033 (0.126)
Real state income	1.5E-7*** (5.6E-8)	2.0E-7*** (5.6E-8)	1.5E-7* (6.8E-8)	3.2E-7 (1.4E-7)	-3.7E-7 (5.4E-7)
Treasury bill rate	0.002 (0.005)	-0.010 (0.006)	0.010** (0.008)	-0.023 (0.013)	-0.069 (0.045)

Source: Authors' calculations.
*Significant at the 90 percent confidence level, two-tailed test.
**Significant at the 95 percent confidence level, two-tailed test.
***Significant at the 99 percent confidence level, two-tailed test.

except at the upper quantiles, where it has a surprising positive effect, which may reflect the fact that not all liability reforms reduce costs.

As shown in tables 8 and 9, the lagged value of the loss ratio exhibits a much less striking pattern of influence among general liability insurers than among the medical malpractice insurers. Except at the tenth percentile, the coefficients are all statistically significant, but are considerably less significant in magnitude. Again, this result is suggestive of consistently risky and unprofitable underwriting portfolios.

Tables 10 and 11 explore the robustness of the results in tables 8 and 9 with regression estimates of the model without the lagged dependent variable. Damage reforms remain a consistently significant determinant of loss ratios, and the influence is greatest among the firms with the highest ratios. The estimated effect at the ninetieth percentile is five times as great as for the median firm. Unlike the results obtained for the medical malpractice insurers, the magnitude of the effects of the damage reform do not increase relative to those obtained for the model that includes the lagged dependent variable. This result suggests that the damage reforms have led to permanent long-run reductions in loss ratios. The other reforms variable performs less consistently and, once again, exhibits a positive influence at the upper quantiles.

The Effect of Liability Reforms
on Insurance Company Premiums and Losses

We also estimated the effects of the liability reform efforts on insurance company premiums and losses, the two components of the loss ratio. Because the most frequently cited index of the liability crisis is the surge in insurance premiums that took place in the mid-1980s, we were interested in the influence of the reform efforts on the level of insurer premiums. As before, we estimated the effects of the liability reforms following two functional forms: the autoregressive formulation that includes the lagged dependent variable in the vector x, and the same model without the lagged dependent variable. In these analyses the quantile regression results allow us to examine any differential effect of the reforms on smaller firms, at the lower end of the premium

Table 8. General Liability, Quantile Regression Results, Model 1, Dependent Variable = Loss Ratio

Bootstrapped standard errors in parentheses

Variable	Quantile (percent)				
	10	25	50	75	90
Intercept	0.126*** (0.012)	0.247*** (0.017)	0.479*** (0.024)	0.874*** (0.057)	1.906*** (0.199)
Loss ratio ($t-1$)	1.6E-7 (5.0E-9)	8.0E-9 (6.6E-9)	-2.6E-7*** (9.6E-9)	-7.9E-7*** (2.5E-8)	-2.3E-6*** (9.8E-8)
Damage reform	-0.013*** (0.003)	-0.025*** (0.004)	-0.050*** (0.005)	-0.109*** (0.014)	-0.300*** (0.050)
Other reform	0.004 (0.004)	0.007 (0.006)	-0.008 (0.008)	0.016 (0.019)	0.189*** (0.068)
Mutual	-0.058*** (0.004)	-0.096*** (0.005)	-0.108*** (0.008)	-0.197*** (0.019)	-0.655*** (0.067)
Lloyds	0.033 (0.026)	0.132*** (0.037)	0.095* (0.054)	0.141 (0.131)	0.219 (0.443)
Reciprocal	-0.044** (0.010)	-0.083*** (0.014)	-0.103*** (0.020)	-0.304* (0.049)	-0.907 (0.173)
National premiums written	1.2E-10*** (7.1E-12)	1.2E-10*** (8.7E-12)	5.8E-11*** (1.1E-11)	-1.2E-10*** (2.7E-11)	-5.7E-10*** (1.2E-10)
Four-firm concentration ratio	0.022 (0.022)	0.007 (0.030)	-0.077* (0.044)	-0.084 (0.108)	-0.062 (0.386)
Rate regulation	-0.007** (0.003)	-0.007 (0.004)	-0.003 (0.006)	-0.007 (0.015)	0.037 (0.052)
Real state income	2.3E-7*** (1.4E-8)	3.6E-7*** (1.8E-8)	5.1E-7*** (2.6E-8)	8.1E-7*** (6.4E-8)	1.5E-6*** (2.3E-7)
Treasury bill rate	-0.003** (0.001)	-8.5E-5 (1.9E-3)	0.004 (0.003)	0.019*** (0.007)	0.038 (0.023)

Source: Authors' calculations.
*Significant at the 90 percent confidence level, two-tailed test.
**Significant at the 95 percent confidence level, two-tailed test.
***Significant at the 99 percent confidence level, two-tailed test.

Table 9. General Liability, Quantile Regression Results, Model 2, Dependent Variable = Loss Ratio

Bootstrapped standard errors in parentheses

Variable	Quantile (percent)				
	10	25	50	75	90
Intercept	0.137*** (0.012)	0.270*** (0.016)	0.540*** (0.023)	0.994*** (0.050)	2.094*** (0.205)
Loss ratio ($t-1$)	1.5E-7*** (4.9E-9)	-3.1E-9*** (6.4E-9)	-2.9E-7*** (9.5E-9)	-8.4E-7*** (2.1E-8)	-2.3E-6*** (1.0E-7)
Damage reform	-0.012*** (0.003)	-0.020*** (0.004)	-0.041*** (0.006)	-0.079*** (0.012)	-0.218*** (0.052)
Other reform	0.005 (0.004)	0.008 (0.005)	0.013 (0.008)	0.034** (0.017)	0.239*** (0.070)
Mutual	-0.061*** (0.004)	-0.101*** (0.005)	-0.118*** (0.008)	-0.210*** (0.017)	-0.617*** (0.069)
Lloyds	0.027 (0.026)	0.126*** (0.036)	0.108** (0.053)	0.180 (0.114)	1.240 (0.456)
Reciprocal	-0.039*** (0.010)	-0.079*** (0.014)	-0.095*** (0.020)	-0.304*** (0.043)	-0.898*** (0.177)
National premiums written	1.3E-10*** (7.1E-12)	1.2E-10*** (8.6E-12)	6.8E-11*** (1.1E-11)	-8.7E-11*** (2.4E-11)	-4.9E-10*** (1.2E-10)
Tax reform 86* ROE	-0.056*** (0.002)	-0.109*** (0.003)	-0.285*** (0.004)	-0.706*** (0.008)	-1.641*** (0.031)
Four-firm concentration ratio	0.035 (0.021)	0.025 (0.029)	-0.023 (0.043)	-0.026 (0.094)	0.231 (0.394)
Rate regulation	-0.007** (0.003)	-0.005 (0.004)	-0.001 (0.006)	-0.003 (0.013)	0.048 (0.054)
Real state income	2.2E-7*** (1.3E-8)	3.5E-7*** (1.8E-8)	4.9E-7*** (2.6E-8)	7.3E-7*** (5.6E-8)	1.5E-6*** (2.4E-7)
Treasury bill rate	-0.004*** (0.001)	-0.002 (0.002)	-0.002 (0.003)	0.008 (0.006)	0.010 (0.024)

Source: Authors' calculations.

*Significant at the 90 percent confidence level, two-tailed test.
**Significant at the 95 percent confidence level, two-tailed test.
***Significant at the 99 percent confidence level, two-tailed test.

Table 10. General Liability, Quantile Regression Results, Model 1, Dependent Variable = Loss Ratio, Model without Lagged Dependent Variable

Bootstrapped standard errors in parentheses

Variable	Quantile (percent)				
	10	25	50	75	90
Intercept	0.114***	0.235***	0.467***	0.786***	1.769***
	(0.011)	(0.014)	(0.021)	(0.052)	(0.203)
Damage reform	−0.012***	−0.022***	−0.041***	−0.097***	−0.259***
	(0.003)	(0.003)	(0.005)	(0.013)	(0.051)
Other reform	0.002	0.007	0.012	0.032*	0.209***
	(0.004)	(0.005)	(0.007)	(0.018)	(0.071)
Mutual	−0.057***	−0.102***	−0.116	−0.182***	−0.591***
	(0.004)	(0.005)	(0.007)	(0.018)	(0.070)
Lloyds	0.010	0.029	0.073	0.111	−0.707
	(0.025)	(0.031)	(0.047)	(0.115)	(0.454)
Reciprocal	−0.038***	−0.076***	−0.090	−0.257***	−0.830***
	(0.010)	(0.012)	(0.018)	(0.045)	(0.176)
National premiums written	$1.3E-10$***	$1.3E-10$***	$7.1E-11$***	$-1.1E-10$***	$-5.8E-10$***
	($7.7E-12$)	($8.5E-12$)	($1.1E-11$)	($2.7E-11$)	($1.4E-10$)
Four-firm concentration ratio	0.023	0.011	−0.028	0.043	0.443
	(0.021)	(0.026)	(0.040)	(0.099)	(0.396)
Rate regulation	−0.005	−0.006	−0.001	−0.007	0.029
	(0.003)	(0.004)	(0.005)	(0.014)	(0.053)
Real state income	$1.9E-7$***	$3.3E-7$***	$4.6E-7$***	$8.0E-7$***	$2.0E-6$***
	($1.3E-8$)	($1.6E-8$)	($2.4E-8$)	($5.9E-8$)	($2.4E-7$)
Treasury bill rate	−0.002	0.001	0.003	0.022***	0.031
	(0.001)	(0.002)	(0.002)	(0.006)	(0.024)

Source: Authors' calculations.
*Significant at the 90 percent confidence level, two-tailed test.
**Significant at the 95 percent confidence level, two-tailed test.
***Significant at the 99 percent confidence level, two-tailed test.

Table 11. General Liability, Quantile Regression Results, Model 2, Dependent Variable = Loss Ratio, Model without Lagged Dependent Variable

Bootstrapped standard errors in parentheses

Variable	Quantile (percent)				
	10	25	50	75	90
Intercept	0.124*** (0.011)	0.255*** (0.015)	0.518*** (0.020)	0.901*** (0.046)	1.901*** (0.196)
Damage reform	-0.013*** (0.003)	-0.020*** (0.004)	-0.037*** (0.005)	-0.071*** (0.012)	-0.191*** (0.049)
Other reform	0.005** (0.004)	0.008 (0.005)	0.020** (0.007)	0.051*** (0.016)	0.270*** (0.068)
Mutual	-0.061*** (0.004)	-0.106*** (0.005)	-0.123*** (0.007)	-0.198*** (0.016)	-0.573*** (0.067)
Lloyds	0.006 (0.024)	0.040 (0.032)	0.097** (0.044)	0.169 (0.103)	0.648 (0.435)
Reciprocal	-0.036*** (0.009)	-0.070*** (0.012)	-0.082*** (0.017)	-0.261*** (0.040)	-0.863*** (0.169)
National premiums written	1.3E-10*** (7.4E-12)	1.3E-10*** (8.8E-12)	8.0E-11*** (1.0E-11)	-8.7E-11*** (2.4E-11)	-5.1E-10*** (1.3E-10)
Tax reform 86* ROE	-0.043*** (0.002)	-0.098*** (0.003)	-0.235*** (0.004)	-0.624*** (0.008)	-1.538*** (0.033)
Four-firm concentration ratio	0.019 (0.020)	0.021 (0.027)	0.004 (0.037)	0.115 (0.088)	0.845 (0.379)
Rate regulation	-0.005 (0.003)	-0.004 (0.004)	-0.001 (0.005)	-0.003 (0.012)	0.042 (0.051)
Real state income	1.8E-7*** (1.3E-8)	3.2E-7*** (1.6E-8)	4.4E-7*** (2.2E-8)	7.1E-7*** (5.3E-8)	1.8E-6*** (2.3E-7)
Treasury bill rate	-0.002* (0.001)	-0.001 (0.002)	-0.002 (0.002)	0.011** (0.005)	0.009 (0.023)

Source: Authors' calculations.
*Significant at the 90 percent confidence level, two-tailed test.
**Significant at the 95 percent confidence level, two-tailed test.
***Significant at the 99 percent confidence level, two-tailed test.

distribution, as opposed to firms writing a high volume of premiums. A summary of our results is presented in appendix B.

Among medical malpractice insurers, we find that the damage reform variable is most influential in the models we estimate, and again has a differential effect across the distribution of firm premiums. When the lagged dependent variable is included in either model, the estimated effect rises steadily in magnitude from a 4 percent reduction in total premiums for firms at the twenty-fifth percentile to 13 percent at the ninetieth percentile. At the ninetieth percentile this represents a reduction of more than $1,000,000 in premiums for these firms. The effect of the other reform tort liability variable is not statistically significant when the lagged dependent variable is included in either model. Interestingly, when we omit the lagged dependent variable, the damage reform variable is less significant in each model and no longer follows the pattern exhibited in the first equation. Also, the other reform variable exerts a positive effect across the distribution.

For general liability insurers, damage reforms reduce premiums from 5.8 to 8.4 percent depending on the model specification. The estimated effects of the other reform variable are insignificant at the lower quantiles, and positive and significant at the seventy-fifth and ninetieth percentiles. When the lagged dependent variable is omitted from either model, damage reform is no longer a consistent determinant of premiums across the distribution, but the other reform variable is associated with higher total premiums. The results suggest little correlation between the size of the general liability insurer and the effects of the liability reforms.

The analysis of insurer premiums suggests that when the pertinent aspects of other factors that drive premium amounts are controlled, the damage reforms had some success in controlling premium levels. Although the initial intent of the reforms is to affect loss amounts, the ultimate economic mechanism at work should involve a pass-through of the decreased loss levels to insurance customers in the form of lower premiums. There does appear to be such a pass-through effect; the damage reforms did substantially reduce medical malpractice and general liability insurance premiums, but the effects of the other reforms and the longer-term effects of the damage reforms are less clear.

Our analysis suggests that the liability reforms reduced loss levels for a given level of premiums. We noted earlier, however, that the damage reforms had a significant effect on premiums as well. Next, we explicitly tested the effects of the reforms on loss levels using the same basic models but including contemporaneous premiums as an independent variable. These results, when compared to those obtained for the premium equations, allow us to tell a more complete story about how the reform efforts are influencing overall performance.

Among medical malpractice insurers, the two liability reform variables each indicate that the reforms were successful in restraining the level of losses. In each model estimated, the effect of these reforms on different segments of the loss distribution is fairly consistent in percentage terms in the case of the damage cap variable. For that reform measure, the decrease in losses runs from 17 percent to 24 percent and is consistently significant throughout all loss levels. As in the case of premiums, the greatest effect of the reforms is at the upper end of the distribution. Given a value of $4.7 million at the ninetieth percentile, the effect at this point of the distribution represents a reduction in losses of nearly $900,000 for these firms.

When we omit the lagged dependent variable from either model, we find that the estimated effects of the liability reform variables are virtually unaffected, suggesting that the liability reforms have led to consistent long-term reductions in the level of losses. The uniformity of the effect across the loss distribution is consistent with our earlier findings regarding premiums: there is little correlation between the size of the firm and the effects of the liability reforms.

The effect of the liability reforms on loss levels is equally striking among general liability insurers. The two variables each indicate that the reforms were successful in restraining the level of losses. In all four equations we estimated, the magnitude of the reduction is fairly consistent throughout the loss distribution, falling from 11 percent to 6 percent as one moves to the upper quantiles.

When the lagged dependent variable is omitted from the models, the estimates on the damage reform variable continue to have a negative effect on losses that is significant across the distribution and is roughly the same magnitude at all quantiles. The damage reform is largest at the tenth percentile, -0.113, and falls to -0.06 at the median. The other reform variable exhibits a significant positive effect on losses that rises as one moves to the upper quantiles.

Additional Considerations

In the preceding analysis we raised a few concerns that limit the quality of our results. Thus, we undertook steps to evaluate the robustness of the estimates we obtained, steps that address particular concerns with the theoretical and empirical approach. First we considered the possibility of omitted firm characteristics that may have biased our results. Then, we considered the possible endogeneity of the reform efforts in our analysis of loss ratios. Finally, we noted that our quantile regression approaches, viewed in unison, tell a reasonable story about the effects of the liability reforms.

Our quantile regression estimates of the effects of the liability reforms on premiums, losses, and loss ratios reveal several instances in which the effects are not uniform across the distribution. We can be fairly certain that these effects are not being driven by any particular firms in each quantile because there was substantial variability in performance over this period, as is evident in table 3. Still, it is possible that our effects are being driven by other firm characteristics that we overlooked, including firms' persistence in operating in particular types of markets or holding particular types of underwriting portfolios.

To assess the possibility that our reform variables are not simply capturing these other characteristics, we incorporated individual firm fixed-effects variables into a variant of our model.[15] Our results are consistent with those obtained in the quantile regression analysis, so we can reasonably assume that individual firm effects are not important. The results of our analysis are presented in appendix C.

We assumed in our analysis that the liability reforms were exogenous in the loss ratio equation. This assumption is reasonable given the number of firms and level of concentration in each state; it is not likely

15. For several reasons we had to adjust the equations we estimated previously. Most important, we had to omit any variables that were specific to the firm for the entire time period, which required us to drop the organizational form variables. In addition, the estimates would be biased if we included the lagged dependent variable among the regressors, so it was omitted. Although outliers in the loss ratio distribution were not a problem in the quantile regression, we chose to estimate the effects of the reforms in a logarithmic form. Finally, with more than 1,500 firms in the general liability sample, we encountered a limitation in our statistical software package: a maximum of 800 variables is allowed in any estimation procedure. We decided to take a random sample of one-half of the companies (769 to be exact), which consequently lowered the number of observations to just over 30,000 for this sample.

that any one firm's experience is the motivation for a state's reform efforts. Still, it is possible that states with the poorest insurance experience, on average, would be more likely to enact reforms than states with good experience. To explore the possible endogeneity of the reform and firm performance, we estimated several simultaneous equation models and performed Hausman specification tests, all of which suggested that one insurer's performance does not make a significant incremental contribution to the enactment of tort reform. If there is any endogeneity, it will tend to reduce the effect of the liability reforms. Enactment of reforms will reduce loss ratios. This improved profitability will decrease the impetus for additional liability reforms if there is such a simultaneous relationship.

Having identified large and significant effects of the liability reforms on loss ratios, we are particularly interested in the mechanisms behind this result, namely, the relative magnitudes of the estimated liability reform effects on losses versus premiums. In comparing the findings from our analyses of premiums and losses (see table 5), we find that the damage reforms reduce losses by about twice as much as the percentage effect on premiums. This result is consistent with the findings reported in the loss ratio table (see table 4)—that the liability reforms improve insurer profitability. Where significant, the effects of the reforms on the losses and premiums of the general liability insurers suggest the same pattern. We found, however, that the effect of the damage reform is much less uniform across the distribution of losses for the general liability insurers than for the medical malpractice insurers. Insurers with smaller loss levels are found to have been more affected by the reforms than those with larger losses. If the correlation between losses and premiums were stronger, we would have expected a corresponding strong negative effect on the lower portion of the loss ratio distribution, since we found no strong differential effects across the premium distribution. Because we did not, we suspect that a firm's relative position in the premium distribution is not strongly related to its position in the loss distribution.

Economic Implications of the Liability Reforms

The states enacted the tort liability reform efforts in response to the liability insurance crisis in the early to mid-1980s. The purpose of this paper was to assess whether these efforts were successful in promoting their intended objective. To do this we analyzed detailed data for every company in every state writing medical malpractice or general liability insurance coverage.

The impetus for these various reform efforts was the surge in losses and increases in premiums that occurred in the 1980s, which were accompanied by a decrease in insurer profitability. These adverse effects were largely concentrated among insurance lines such as general liability and medical malpractice rather than lines such as automobile insurance. The changes led to fears that America was undergoing a "liability crisis." These assessments were based largely on the magnitudes of the changes from the status quo and the decrease in firms' profitability. Change, however, is not necessarily bad. If, for example, the previous level of liability was too low, additional liability burdens would be warranted. Nonetheless, there was a general sense, supported in large part by anecdotal evidence, that the rise in liability was in fact depressing innovation and causing the withdrawal of vital products and services from the market.

As a result of this surge in liability, the states sought to restrain the insurance costs imposed on firms and physicians. During 1984–87 eleven states adopted damage reforms pertaining to medical malpractice and twenty-six states adopted damage reforms pertaining to general liability. The focus of the empirical inquiry was on whether these reforms improved profitability and restrained losses and premiums. Thus we took as the valid objective of these reforms the intent to reduce the overall liability burden and to bolster the profitability of the insurance firms, which at the time of the crisis were highly unprofitable.

To carry out our analysis we assembled what is by far the largest data set that has yet been used to assess the effect of the liability reforms. For the 1984–91 period we have information by state and firm for every company writing medical malpractice coverage and every company writing general liability coverage, leading to more than 1,000 observations a year for medical malpractice and 8,000 observations for general liability. Analyzing the effect of the liability reforms on both lines of insurance is instructive because these two lines were at the center of the liability crisis. Moreover, state legislatures sought to restrain each of these types of liability costs. These markets, however, are not identical, and the reforms also differed in their timing and their character, so there is additional variation in these efforts and in their performance that provides a fuller empirical framework for assessing the potential effects of liability reform.

Despite the wide variety of statistical explorations undertaken, the result is a remarkably uniform picture of the effect of the reforms. Damage caps and the other reforms helped control insurance company costs, which in turn led to a decrease in premiums. The profitability of writing medical malpractice and general liability insurance also increased. Viewed in the narrow terms of attempting to restrain liability costs, the reforms certainly were a success.

The most interesting aspect of these effects is the different distributional consequences of the reforms across the market. Who benefits from the liability reforms? Is it the large firms, the least profitable firms, or are the effects equally distributed? Our empirical results indicated substantial variation.

The greatest differences in the distribution of the consequences were observed for the loss ratio effects. Firms with relatively high loss ratios experienced the greatest effect of the damage reforms. Thus, the least profitable firms reaped the greatest benefits. The reforms bolstered their profitability and were not passed through in their entirety to insurance purchasers. Because the least profitable firms achieved this dubious status by writing insurance coverage for which the losses are far in excess of the premiums, the reform efforts may have conferred the greatest benefits on the firms that were least able to choose carefully the risks they insured Consequently, damage caps reduce the penalties for poor underwriting practices. It should be noted that although the profitability of firms varies considerably over time, many firms tend to remain in the same relative profitability position from year to year, which would reflect a persistence in their underwriting practices and portfolio mix.

The distribution of the reform variable effects for premiums and losses was less pronounced. Unlike the results for the loss ratios, there is no evident increase in the consequences of the liability reforms as one moves across the distribution of losses and premiums. These results indicate that it is not simply the large firms in the market that benefited from the liability reforms. Indeed, there is no systematic size-related difference in the findings. Rather, the benefits were concentrated among those firms that would have suffered the greatest decrease in profitability as a result of the large damage awards that would have been made had it not been for the restraining effect of the reforms.

Nor did the character of the reforms follow the usual textbook case in which savings are passed through to insurance purchasers with no improvement in profitability. Although all groups of firms benefited to some extent, firms with the least profitable insurance portfolios reaped the overwhelming share of the cost savings. This result may be due to the character of damage reforms.

Appendix A: Quantile Regression Methodology

The quantile regressions estimate the effect of the vector of explanatory variables x on the conditional distribution of the loss ratio, which we designate by LR. Following Koenker and Bassett, we will characterize the τth as a quantile of LR given x is linear and can be characterized by

$$(1) \qquad \text{Quant}_\tau \, (LR|x) = \beta'_\tau x,$$

where β_τ is the pertinent vector of coefficients for the τth quantile.[16] Thus, this analysis enables one to determine the differential effect of the explanatory variable vector x on loss ratios at different quantiles. The quantile regressions were estimated using an estimator that can be characterized by

$$(2) \qquad \underset{\beta}{\text{Min}} \, \frac{1}{n} \sum_{i=1}^{n} [\tau\rho(LR_i \geq \beta'x_i) + (1 - \tau)\rho(LR_i \geq \beta'x_i)]|LR_i - \beta'x_i|,$$

where n is the sample size, i is the sample, and ρ is an indicator function that takes on a value of one if the event characterized by the specified inequality holds and a value of zero if it does not. The vector x in our analysis includes the two reform variables, rate regulation, organizational form, national premiums written, four-firm concentration ratio, real state aggregate income, and the U.S. Treasury bill rate. Following Koenker and Bassett, we also assume that the conditional density of y given x in the τth quantile is independent of x. We use a bootstrapping technique to obtain the value of the asymptotic standard errors.[17]

16. Koenker and Bassett (1978, 1982).
17. Chamberlain (1991).

Appendix B: Summary of Other Quantile Regression Results

The variables that enter our premium equation are similar to those in the loss ratio equation. The dependent variable is the log of premiums earned, where the logarithmic form diminishes the role of outliers and also converts all the coefficients of the continuous variables, which are also in log form, into elasticities. As before, we estimate the effects of the liability reforms following four functional forms: the autoregressive formulation that includes the lagged dependent variable in the vector x, the same model without the lagged dependent variable, and the same two models repeated with the tax reform 1986 control variable (*TR86*). Table B-1 summarizes the quantile regression results for premiums for the two samples of insurers.

The top section of the table pertains to our medical malpractice insurance sample. Our quantile regression analyses of the effects of the liability reforms on premiums allow us to examine any differential effect of the reforms on smaller firms, at the lower end of the premium distribution, as opposed to larger firms at the high end. The damage reform variable is most influential in the models with the lagged dependent variable. Although there is no significant effect for firms at the bottom tenth percentile of premiums, the effect of the damage cap rises steadily from a 4 percent reduction for firms at the twenty-fifth percentile to a high value of 12 percent at the ninetieth percentile. Damage caps do not appear to have a uniform effect across the distribution of premiums. Instead, they have a differential incidence in affecting premiums at the firms writing a high volume of premium amounts. The effect of the "other reform" tort liability variable is not statistically significant.

We examine the robustness of the damage reform effects on premiums by estimating the equation without the lagged dependent variable. As in the loss ratio equations, the omission of the lagged dependent variable reduces the explanatory power. Interestingly, the effect of the damage reform on premiums no longer follows the pattern exhibited in the first equation, and the estimated coefficients are significant only at the median and seventy-fifth percentile. The other reform variable takes on a surprising significant positive effect that is uniform across the distribution. Thus, in contrast to the results in the models with the

Table B-1. Summary of Other Quantile Regression Results: Medical Malpractice and General Liability Premiums

Bootstrapped standard errors in parentheses

Variable	*Quantile (percent)*				
	10	*25*	*50*	*75*	*90*
Medical malpractice					
Model 1 with lagged dependent variable					
Damage reform	−0.000	−0.043***	−0.063***	−0.101***	−0.121***
	(0.019)	(0.011)	(0.016)	(0.029)	(0.055)
Other reform	−0.008	0.001	−0.025	−0.024	0.038
	(0.026)	(0.013)	(0.019)	(0.029)	(0.054)
Model 1 without lagged dependent variable					
Damage reform	−0.113	−0.062	−0.088***	−0.157*	−0.119
	(0.108)	(0.065)	(0.035)	(0.086)	(0.091)
Other reform	0.156	0.250***	0.173***	0.334***	0.312***
	(0.129)	(0.045)	(0.057)	(0.088)	(0.053)
Model 2 with lagged dependent variable					
Damage reform	0.004	−0.041***	−0.061***	−0.095***	−0.130***
	(0.026)	(0.010)	(0.009)	(0.025)	(0.041)
Other reform	−0.009	0.001	−0.020	−0.030	0.040
	(0.024)	(0.015)	(0.018)	(0.025)	(0.051)
Model 2 without lagged dependent variable					
Damage reform	−0.088	−0.069	−0.090*	−0.156**	−0.116
	(0.082)	(0.079)	(0.048)	(0.070)	(0.074)
Other reform	0.139**	0.271***	0.166***	0.317***	0.288***
	(0.066)	(0.064)	(0.041)	(0.072)	(0.095)
General liability					
Model 1 with lagged dependent variable					
Damage reform	−0.016	−0.027***	−0.033***	−0.022***	0.019
	(0.012)	(0.006)	(0.006)	(0.008)	(0.015)
Other reform	−0.034	−0.033***	−0.043***	−0.042***	−0.015
	(0.022)	(0.007)	(0.011)	(0.014)	(0.020)
Model 1 without lagged dependent variable					
Damage reform	0.427***	0.428***	0.458***	0.560***	0.568***
	(0.042)	(0.033)	(0.023)	(0.024)	(0.028)
Other reform	0.052	0.017	−0.002	0.079**	0.165***
	(0.057)	(0.042)	(0.032)	(0.031)	(0.039)
Model 2 with lagged dependent variable					
Damage reform	−0.058***	−0.056***	−0.069***	−0.084***	−0.068***
	(0.011)	(0.006)	(0.005)	(0.007)	(0.012)
Other reform	0.005	0.002	0.009	0.029***	0.060***
	(0.015)	(0.008)	(0.007)	(0.010)	(0.017)
Model 2 without lagged dependent variable					
Damage reform	−0.055	−0.042**	−0.016	0.047***	0.087***
	(0.034)	(0.019)	(0.014)	(0.014)	(0.021)
Other reform	0.303	0.283***	0.340***	0.315***	0.354***
	(0.049)	(0.027)	(0.019)	(0.019)	(0.030)

Source: Authors' calculations.
*Significant at the 90 percent confidence level, two-tailed test.
**Significant at the 95 percent confidence level, two-tailed test.
***Significant at the 99 percent confidence level, two-tailed test.

lagged dependent variables, these results are less powerful in suggesting a relationship between firm size and the effects of the liability reforms.

The bottom section of table B-1 pertains to the premiums in our general liability insurance sample. The covariates are similar to those included in the loss ratio equations. However, three variables were omitted from the regression due to problems with the estimation in the quantile regressions: log national premiums written, the log four-firm concentration ratio, and log state aggregate income. The results in the table indicate that both reform measures were influential. In the models with the lagged dependent variable, damage reforms are negative wherever they are significant, and have a fairly uniform effect across the distribution. The size of the effect differs between the two models, with a larger effect found in the model that controls for the influence of *TR86*. The estimated effects of the other reform variable are inconsistent across the models. Also, the effect of the damage reform becomes positive when the lagged dependent variable is omitted. These positive relationships may be an indication of a long-run influence of damage reform on the general size of firms operating in reform states. These results also suggest little correlation between the size of the general liability insurer and the effects of the liability reforms.

The results in tables B-1 suggest that when the pertinent aspects of other factors that drive premium amounts are controlled, the tort liability reforms had some success in controlling premium levels. Although the initial intent of the reforms was to affect loss amounts, the ultimate economic mechanism at work involved a pass-through of the decreased loss levels in lower premiums. There appears to be such a pass-through effect because the reforms did substantially reduce medical malpractice and general liability insurance premiums, but the longer-term effects among general liability insurers are less clear.

The statistical model analyzing the effect of the liability reforms on levels of insurance losses is similar to that for premiums. The main difference is that each model also includes the current value of premiums earned as an explanatory variable. The amount of losses should vary with the extent of insurance coverage written, and this variable captures the presence of this relationship.

Table B-2 shows the quantile regression results for losses for the sample of medical malpractice and general liability insurers for each of the four models. The top section of the table pertains to the medical

Table B-2. Summary of Other Quantile Regression Results:
Medical Malpractice and General Liability Losses

Variable	Quantile (percent)				
	10	25	50	75	90

Medical malpractice

Model 1 with lagged dependent variable

Damage reform	−0.211***	−0.169***	−0.187***	−0.241***	−0.186***
	(0.040)	(0.036)	(0.022)	(0.031)	(0.047)
Other reform	−0.006	−0.028	−0.131***	−0.188***	−0.095**
	(0.051)	(0.041)	(0.027)	(0.042)	(0.044)

Model 1 without lagged dependent variable

Damage reform	−0.208***	−0.168***	−0.171***	−0.254***	−0.231***
	(0.042)	(0.035)	(0.026)	(0.028)	(0.049)
Other reform	−0.016	−0.061**	−0.170***	−0.181***	−0.093**
	(0.045)	(0.033)	(0.033)	(0.046)	(0.040)

Model 2 with lagged dependent variable

Damage reform	−0.210***	−0.166***	−0.174***	−0.232***	−0.181***
	(0.038)	(0.023)	(0.024)	(0.045)	(0.044)
Other reform	−0.018	−0.027	−0.113***	−0.176***	−0.093*
	(0.064)	(0.028)	(0.029)	(0.043)	(0.051)

Model 2 without lagged dependent variable

Damage reform	−0.210***	−0.168***	−0.180***	−0.238***	−0.226***
	(0.050)	(0.039)	(0.026)	(0.034)	(0.039)
Other reform	−0.018	−0.046	−0.150***	−0.182***	−0.079
	(0.055)	(0.045)	(0.031)	(0.035)	(0.051)

General liability

Model 1 with lagged dependent variable

Damage reform	−0.115***	−0.080***	−0.082***	−0.060***	−0.043***
	(0.024)	(0.013)	(0.009)	(0.012)	(0.018)
Other reform	−0.057*	−0.047***	−0.048***	−0.029*	−0.019
	(0.031)	(0.022)	(0.016)	(0.017)	(0.025)

Model 1 without lagged dependent variable

Damage reform	−0.150***	−0.114***	−0.085***	−0.093***	−0.055**
	(0.019)	(0.014)	(0.010)	(0.015)	(0.022)
Other reform	−0.028	−0.021	−0.042***	−0.028	−0.011
	(0.032)	(0.025)	(0.015)	(0.020)	(0.031)

Model 2 with lagged dependent variable

Damage reform	−0.111***	−0.083***	−0.085***	−0.083***	−0.059***
	(0.025)	(0.013)	(0.011)	(0.013)	(0.018)
Other reform	0.012	0.020	0.016	0.033*	0.059**
	(0.035)	(0.019)	(0.016)	(0.018)	(0.025)

Model 2 without lagged dependent variable

Damage reform	−0.113***	−0.081***	−0.059***	−0.072***	−0.085***
	(0.023)	(0.012)	(0.009)	(0.013)	(0.020)
Other reform	0.054	0.060***	0.064***	0.094***	0.186***
	(0.034)	(0.017)	(0.014)	(0.018)	(0.028)

Source: Authors' calculations.
*Significant at the 90 percent confidence level, two-tailed test.
**Significant at the 95 percent confidence level, two-tailed test.
***Significant at the 99 percent confidence level, two-tailed test.

malpractice sample. The two liability reform variables each indicate that the reforms were successful in restraining losses. In each of the four models the effect of the damage reforms on different segments of the loss distribution is fairly consistent, ranging from 17 percent to 25 percent, and is consistently significant throughout all loss levels. By contrast, the other reform variable is statistically significant in the quantile regression results for losses at the median loss level or higher. The combined effect of both tort liability reform variables is greatest at the seventy-fifth percentile, with the second largest effect being at the median. The influence at the ninetieth percentile is not significantly different from that at the median loss level. As in the case of premiums, the greatest effect of the reforms is at the upper end of the distribution. However, the extreme outliers at the upper right tail (ninetieth percentile) do not exhibit a relatively greater influence than do the high-end loss levels in the quantiles just below at that amount. Our most striking finding is that the estimated effects of the liability reform variables are virtually unaffected when the lagged value of log losses is omitted from the model, suggesting that the liability reforms have led to consistent long-term reductions in the level of losses. The uniformity of the effect across the loss distribution is consistent with our earlier findings with regard to premiums: there is little correlation between the size of the firm and the effects of the liability reforms.

The effect of the liability reforms on loss levels is equally striking when we examine their influence among general liability insurers (see the bottom section of table B-2). The results for the first model indicate that both damage and other reforms were successful in restraining losses. In the case of damage reforms, the loss effects are consistently significant across the loss distribution and are fairly consistent throughout the distribution, falling slightly from 15 percent to 4 percent as one moves to the upper quantiles. The results for the other reform variable with the lagged dependent variable are significant only in the quantile regression results below the ninetieth percentile. When the lagged dependent variable is omitted, both liability reform variables remain negative, except for the other reform variable at the ninetieth percentile; they are fairly close in magnitude to the estimates in the previous models. In the first model the other reform variable has a significant effect only at the median, where its effect is estimated at about -0.05. Interestingly, although the damage cap has a similar effect in the two models, the other reform has a positive effect in the second model. This finding is consistent with the results obtained in the premiums regresssions, and may be capturing changes in the size of firms operating in states that enact these measures.

Appendix C: Fixed-Effects Analysis

To assess the possibility that our reform variables are not simply capturing these other characteristics, we complete our analysis by incorporating individual firm fixed-effects variables into our model. For several reasons we had to adjust the equations we estimated previously. Most important, we had to omit any variables that were specific to the firm for the entire time period, which required us to drop the organizational form variables. In addition, the estimates would be biased if we included the lagged dependent variable among the regressors, so it is omitted. Although outliers in the loss ratio distribution were not a problem in the quantile regression, we chose to estimate the effects of the reforms on our three key variables in logarithmic form. Finally, with more than 1,500 firms in the general liability sample, we encountered a limitation in our statistical software package: a maximum of 800 variables is allowed in any estimation procedure. We took a random sample of one-half of the companies (769 to be exact), which consequently lowered the number of observations to just over 30,000 for this sample.

Specifically, we use ordinary least squares methodology to estimate the following equations:

$$Log\ Loss\ Ratio_{ijt} =$$

$$\alpha + \beta_1\ Damages\ Reform_{jt} + \beta_2\ Other\ Reform_{jt}$$

(3)
$$+ \beta_3\ Log\ National\ Premiums_{it} + \beta_4\ Number\ of\ States_{it}$$

$$+ \beta_5\ (TaxRef'86* ROE)_{it} + \beta_6\ Log\ Concentration\ Ratio_{jt}$$

$$+ \beta_7\ Rate\ Regulation_{jt} + \beta_8\ Log\ State\ Income_{jt}$$

$$+ \beta_9\ Log\ Treasury\ Bill\ Rate_t + \sum_{i=1}^{N-1} \varphi_j\ Firm_i + \varepsilon_{ijt}$$

Log Premium Earned$_{ijt}$ =

$$\alpha + \beta_1 \text{ } Damages \text{ } Reform_{jt} + \beta_2 \text{ } Other \text{ } Reform_{jt}$$

(4) $+ \beta_3 \text{ } Log \text{ } National \text{ } Premiums_{it} + \beta_4 \text{ } Number \text{ } of \text{ } States_{it}$

$$+ \beta_5 \text{ } (TaxRef'86* \text{ } ROE)_{it} + \beta_6 \text{ } Log \text{ } Concentration \text{ } Ratio_{jt}$$

$$+ \beta_7 \text{ } Rate \text{ } Regulation_{jt} + \beta_8 \text{ } Log \text{ } State \text{ } Income_{jt}$$

$$+ \beta_9 \text{ } Log \text{ } Treasury \text{ } Bill \text{ } Rate_t + \sum_{i=1}^{N-1} \varphi_j \text{ } Firm_i + \varepsilon_{ijt}$$

Log Losses Incurred$_{ijt}$ =

$$\alpha + \delta_1 \text{ } Log \text{ } Premiums_{ijt} + \beta_1 \text{ } Damages \text{ } Reform_{jt}$$

$$+ \beta_2 \text{ } Other \text{ } Reform_{jt}$$

(5) $+ \beta_3 \text{ } Log \text{ } National \text{ } Premiums_{it} + \beta_4 \text{ } Number \text{ } of \text{ } States_{it}$

$$+ \beta_5 \text{ } (TaxRef'86* \text{ } ROE)_{it} + \beta_6 \text{ } Log \text{ } Concentration \text{ } Ratio_{jt}$$

$$+ \beta_7 \text{ } Rate \text{ } Regulation_{jt} + \beta_8 \text{ } Log \text{ } State \text{ } Income_{jt}$$

$$+ \beta_9 \text{ } Log \text{ } Treasury \text{ } Bill \text{ } Rate_t + \sum_{i=1}^{N-1} \varphi_j \text{ } Firm_i + \varepsilon_{ijt}$$

for firm i in state j at time t.

The results for the medical malpractice sample, presented in the top section of table C-1, indicate a strong negative effect of the damage reform on the log loss ratio. The effects of this reform variable on premiums and losses are consistent with this finding in that the downward effect on losses is almost three times as great as the negative effect on premiums. The other reform variable is not significant in the loss ratio equation, while it appears to have a positive effect on average premiums and a negative (though insignificant) effect on loss levels.

The results for the general liability sample are fairly similar to those for the medical malpractice sample (see the bottom section of table C-1). Interestingly, the effect of the damage reform on the log loss ratio is very close to the effect found among the medical malpractice insurers, an effect that suggests a 9 to 10 percent reduction in loss ratios due to

Table C-1. Fixed-Effects Regression Results: Medical Malpractice and General Liability 50 Percent Sample[a]

Standard errors in parentheses

	Dependent variable (N=6,982)		
Variable	Log loss ratio	Log premiums earned	Log losses incurred
	Medical malpractice		
Intercept	2.726***	−2.610*	2.877***
	(0.886)	(1.378)	(0.899)
Log premiums (t)	. . .	. . .	0.946***
			(0.008)
Damages	−0.097***	−0.056	−0.152***
	(0.025)	(0.039)	(0.025)
Other reform	0.001	0.151***	−0.036
	(0.028)	(0.044)	(0.029)
Log national premiums written	−0.095***	0.547***	−0.066***
	(0.018)	(0.028)	(0.019)
Log number of states of operation	0.112***	−0.507***	0.112***
	(0.028)	(0.043)	(0.028)
Tax reform 1986 ROE	−0.078***	−0.003	−0.095***
	(0.023)	(0.038)	(0.023)
Log four-firm concentration ratio	−0.136*	−0.931***	−0.382***
	(0.074)	(0.116)	(0.076)
Rate regulation	−4.2E-4	−0.166***	−0.019
	(0.025)	(0.039)	(0.025)
Log state income	0.009	0.844***	0.045***
	(0.012)	(0.019)	(0.014)
Log Treasury bill rate	−0.039	−0.067	−0.195
	(0.046)	(0.072)	(0.047)
Adjusted R^2	0.226	0.745	0.902
	General Liability 50 percent Sample		
Intercept	15.636***	0.408**	−1.740***
	(0.304)	(0.178)	(0.142)
Log premiums (t)	. . .	. . .	0.896***
			(0.005)
Damages	−0.099***	0.012	−0.052***
	(0.008)	(0.019)	(0.016)
Other reform	−0.571***	0.300***	0.129***
	(0.011)	(0.028)	(0.022)
Log national premiums written	−1.400***	4.9E-22	8.7E-22
	(0.023)	(2.6E-21)	(2.1E-21)
Log number of states of operation	0.834***	0.082***	−0.030
	(0.040)	(0.025)	(0.020)
Tax reform 1986 ROE	0.380***	−0.005	−0.089***
	(0.016)	(0.028)	(0.023)
Log four-firm concentration ratio	0.977***	0.239***	0.023
	(0.021)	(0.041)	(0.033)
Rate regulation	−0.653***	−0.051**	0.055***
	(0.010)	(0.020)	(0.016)
Log state income	0.209***	0.971***	0.182***
	(0.006)	(0.009)	(0.009)
Log Treasury bill rate	−0.505***	−0.066*	−0.053*
	(0.022)	(0.036)	(0.029)
Adjusted R^2	0.417	0.620	0.809

Source: Authors' calculations.

a. Medical malpractice equations include a set of 264 firm dummy variables. General liability 50 percent sample equations include a set of 769.

*Significant at the 90 percent confidence level, two-tailed test.

**Significant at the 95 percent confidence level, two-tailed test.

***Significant at the 99 percent confidence level, two-tailed test.

the reform efforts. This result is surprising given the independent effects of the damage reform on premiums and losses. It is not inconsistent with the results we obtained in the quantile regression analysis, however, which may indicate a limited value in including the fixed effects in the model.

References

Abraham, Kenneth S. 1987. "Making Sense of the Liability Insurance Crisis." *Ohio State Law Journal* 48 (Spring): 399–411.

American Law Institute. 1991. *Reporter's Study—Enterprise Responsibility for Personal Injury*, vols. 1 and 2. Philadelphia.

Barker, Drucilla K. 1992. "The Effects of Tort Reform on Medical Malpractice Insurance Markets: An Empirical Analysis." *Journal of Health Politics, Policy, and Law* 17 (Spring): 143–61.

Chamberlain, Gary. 1991. "Quantile Regression, Censoring, and the Structure of Wages." Discussion paper. Harvard Institute of Economic Research, Cambridge, Mass. June.

Danzon, Patricia M. 1985. *Medical Malpractice: Theory, Evidence, and Public Policy*. Harvard University Press.

Danzon, Patricia M., Mark V. Pauly, and Raynard S. Kington. 1990. "The Effects of Malpractice Litigation on Physicians' Fees and Incomes." *American Economic Review* 80 (May): 122–27.

Dewees, Don, David Duff, and Michael Trebilcock. 1996. *Exploring the Domain of Accident Law: Taking the Facts Seriously*. Oxford University Press.

Huber, Peter W. 1988. *Liability: The Legal Revolution and Its Consequences*. Basic Books.

Huber, Peter W., and Robert E. Litan, eds. 1991. *The Liability Maze: The Impact of Liability Law on Safety and Innovation*. Brookings.

Hughes, James W., and Edward A. Snyder. 1989. "Evaluating Medical Malpractice Reforms." *Contemporary Policy Issues* 7 (April): 83–98.

Insurance Information Institute. 1992. *The Fact Book: 1992 Property/Casualty Insurance Facts*. New York.

Koenker, Roger, and Gilbert Bassett Jr. 1978. "Regression Quantiles." *Econometrica* 46 (January): 33–50.

———. 1982. "Robust Tests for Heteroscedasticity Based on Regression Quantiles." *Econometrica* 50 (January): 43–61.

Litan, Robert E., and Clifford Winston, eds. 1988. *Liability: Perspectives and Policy*. Brookings.

Priest, George L. 1987. "The Current Insurance Crisis and Modern Tort Law." *Yale Law Journal* 96 (June): 1521–90.

Schuck, Peter H., ed. 1991. *Tort Law and the Public Interest: Competition, Innovation, and Consumer Welfare*. Norton.

Schwartz, Alan. 1988. "Proposals for Products Liability Reform: A Theoretical Synthesis." *Yale Law Journal* 97 (February): 353–419.

Viscusi, W. Kip. 1990. "The Performance of Liability-Insurance in States with Different Products Liability Statutes." *Journal of Legal Studies* 19 (June): 809–36.

————. 1991. *Reforming Products Liability*. Harvard University Press.

Viscusi, W. Kip, and Patricia Born. 1995. "Medical Malpractice Insurance in the Wake of Liability Reform." *Journal of Legal Studies* 24 (June): 463–90.

Viscusi, W. Kip, and Michael J. Moore. 1993. "Product Liability, Research and Development, and Innovation." *Journal of Political Economy* 101 (February): 161–84.

Viscusi, W. Kip, and others. 1993. "The Effect of 1980s Tort Reform Legislation on General Liability and Medical Malpractice Insurance." *Journal of Risk and Uncertainty* 6 (April): 165–86.

Weiler, Paul C. 1991. *Medical Malpractice on Trial*. Harvard University Press.

Weiler, Paul C., and others. 1993. *A Measure of Malpractice: Medical Injury, Malpractice Litigation, and Patient Compensation*. Harvard University Press.

Zuckerman, Stephen, Randall R. Bovbjerg, and Frank A. Sloan. 1990. "Effects of Tort Reforms and Other Factors on Medical Malpractice Insurance Premiums." *Inquiry* 27 (Summer): 167–82.

Comment

Comment by Dennis W. Carlton: This paper is a thorough and thoughtful empirical analysis of the consequences of certain reform measures introduced to deal with the insurance crisis of the 1980s. The authors are clear that the paper's focus is empirical, not theoretical. The findings are noteworthy and robust and should stimulate theoretical work to explain the phenomena of crises in insurance.

The crisis in medical malpractice and general liability insurance in the 1980s manifested itself in huge premium increases (medical malpractice premiums doubled in two years), widespread concern that products were not being offered for sale because of the unavailability of affordable insurance, and the unavailability of certain previously sold lines of insurance. Despite much litigation (plaintiffs sued on antitrust grounds in some states, alleging the cause of the crisis to be conspiracy) and study (academic articles plus studies by various government agencies), the reasons for the crisis as well as our understanding of it merit more attention. It is clear that some enormous and well-publicized damage awards created uncertainty in the industry, but it is not so clear how to link that uncertainty to price and unavailability, although some academic work, especially by George Priest and Ralph Winter, takes important steps in improving our understanding.[1] Nor is it clear how that uncertainty should affect the interpretation of Patricia Born and W. Kip Viscusi's findings, but I hope further work here is forthcoming.

Born and Viscusi's empirical findings seem (subject to some minor criticisms later) robust and striking. The reforms that some states adopted appear to have solved the crisis in the sense that the profitability

1. Priest (1987); Winter (1988).

of insurance companies (as measured by the loss ratio) has improved. Moreover, the reforms seem to have helped most those insurance companies that were the least profitable. This sounds as if the reforms were successful, but that conclusion is unwarranted, and Born and Viscusi are careful not to endorse it. How the reforms affected the long-run availability of insurance remains unclear.

The authors' results raise the issue of how long it takes for long-run equilibrium to be achieved in the insurance sector. If the reforms still had such enormous effects in 1991—for example, the loss ratio for medical malpractice of the firm at the seventy-fifth percentile was about 26 percent lower in reform states than in nonreform states—what does that say about the long-run equilibrium in nonreform states? Either the long-run equilibrium has not yet been reached or insurance companies in nonreform states make a lot less money in long-run equilibrium. Moreover, if, as the paper finds, malpractice premiums are lower in reform states than in nonreform states, yet loss ratios are also lower in reform states (the ratio of premiums to loss is higher), doesn't that mean that a lot less insurance is sold in reform states? It is unclear what theory could generate the authors' results, and that is what is so good about this paper. It challenges researchers to improve their theories to explain the facts. Let me try to explain the theoretical challenge that the results in this paper pose.

Theoretical Comments

In a simple model of insurance with identical firms ex ante, each firm sets premiums so as to cover expected losses (including costs of operations). Thus the expected loss ratio (expected costs divided by premiums) should equal one.[2] The actual loss ratio for any firm will of course depend on the firm's subsequent random loss experience. Identical firms ex ante will look very different ex post. When each firm writes a *new* policy, however, its expected loss ratio will equal one again. This means that, in long-run equilibrium, loss ratios should hover

2. Loss ratios raise a host of complicated accounting and economic problems. For example, one must calculate and discount to present value future costs caused by harms manifested many years after the premiums are written, and one must account for the interest earned on premiums. I will abstract from these important matters here to highlight the key theoretical points.

around one. In other words even if jury awards skyrocket as they did in 1984, firms would be harmed relative to their expectations and would suffer high loss ratios for policies already written, but absent regulatory constraints, they would not be harmed on the next new policy written. In the short run, reforms will benefit firms by limiting losses and preventing the loss ratio from being too high; but in the long run there should be no effect on the loss ratio. Mere cost increases should not cause a crisis of availability nor should they affect the profits of firms at all, and certainly not differentially. Yet that is what seems to be the description of the insurance crisis that the literature and this paper provide.

Because the simple model fails to explain the facts, the model must be too simple. Let me suggest two extensions. First, it must be that the increased uncertainty of awards (as distinct from the amount of the award) matters, either through firms' risk aversion (hard to believe) or because the uncertainty itself increases underwriting costs and the problems caused by the moral hazard of insureds so as to make certain lines unprofitable to write. Thus the reforms affect loss ratios through their effect on the uncertainty of loss.

Second, ex ante firms must have permanent profitability differences, and these differences must become worse during uncertain times. For example, suppose that in long-run equilibrium, firms have differential efficiency (for example, they experience systematically different loss ratios), perhaps because they have different expertise and specialize in different types of niche coverages. When uncertainty increases, the comparative costs of firms change because the underwriting costs in different niches change; thus there can be differential profit effects. The authors' results suggest that in response to the crisis in the 1980s the costs of low-profit firms rose relative to those of the marginal firm in each niche so that profits of low-profit firms got squeezed.

Although this is only one possible explanation for the results—and Born and Viscusi do not attempt to provide one—it can be tested. Indeed, the advantage of developing some theory to explain the results is precisely that the implications can be tested. For example, does the evidence show that the ''availability'' problem diminished in states enacting reforms compared with other states, as would be expected if loss uncertainty were reduced? Or did the reforms simply prevent some insurance coverage from being written? Did loss ratio variability decline in reform states? For example, does the variance of the error in the loss ratio model in the appendix decline with reforms?

The differential efficiency of insurance firms is a key element of the results, as is the differential effect of reforms on these insurance firms. It would seem then that the enactment of the reforms should have large differential effects on the stock market value of different insurance companies. Can any event studies be done? Moreover, how stable can the long-run equilibrium be if it involves very different firms? Why don't the most profitable firms expand over a period of several years? Are there limits on special expertise in niche segments of insurance?

Econometric Comments

I have some quibbles and comments with the econometrics, although given the robustness of the results, I would not expect major changes in empirical results to emerge if my concerns were addressed. First, the inclusion and exclusion of the lagged variable is not a choice between a short-run or long-run model. If the lagged variable belongs in, it should be there, and standard econometric procedures for dealing with possible error structures can be followed. The long-run equilibrium can be calculated in a standard way. To the extent that there is a lagged adjustment period, I would like to know why. What is preventing rapid price adjustment, and how do the reforms affect the speed of adjustment? Regulation should affect the speed of adjustment. Does it?

Second, I am not convinced that the endogenity of reform has been completely handled. If a state's decision to enact reform is driven by the unexpected loss of a large number of carriers in the state, then reform will occur in those states where many (low-profit) firms would be hurt. This would seem to strengthen the authors' results because the nonreform states are in a sense too good a benchmark to use to judge the effect of reform: if no reform were enacted in the reform states, the adverse results would have presumably been more severe than in nonreform states (where the results were not so severe as to merit reform laws).

Third, it is somewhat puzzling that even though the damage caps vary widely across reform states and therefore have large and different truncation effects, there is no empirical detection of such an effect.

Finally, if the differential efficiency of firms is, as the paper suggests, affected by tort reform, it is not obvious that a fixed-effects model will be appropriate. The firm's specific effect depends on the reform.

In conclusion, this is a fine piece of empirical work, and the findings should guide theoretical explanations for insurance crises and lead to a better understanding of these puzzling events.

Commentator's References

Priest, George L. 1987. "The Current Insurance Crisis and Modern Tort Law." *Yale Law Journal* 96 (June): 1521–90.

Winter, Ralph A. 1988. "The Liability Crisis and the Dynamics of Competitive Insurance Markets." *Yale Journal on Regulation* 5 (Summer): 455–500.

THOMAS J. CAMPBELL
Member, U.S. House of Representatives
Stanford University

DANIEL P. KESSLER
Stanford University
Hoover Institution
National Bureau of Economic Research

GEORGE B. SHEPHERD
Emory University School of Law

The Link between Liability Reforms and Productivity: Some Empirical Evidence

TORT LAW HAS two principal goals: compensation of injured parties, and optimal deterrence of potential injurers. During the past fifty years, however, changes in legal doctrine have emphasized the compensation goal. Through such changes as the expansion of strict liability, the switch from contributory to comparative negligence,[1] and the rejection of contractual limitations of liability,[2] the tort system has become increasingly a vehicle for insuring individuals against accidental injury.

The authors thank James Alt, Ian Ayres, Gerald Carlino, Morris Fiorina, Robert Hall, Gary King, Al Klevorick, Keith Krehbiel, Ralph Landau, Roger Noll, George Priest, Al Pross, Robert Rabin, David Scharfstein, Scott Stern, Cliff Winston, and Stanford seminar participants for generously providing comments and data. Campbell and Shepherd are grateful for support from the Center for Economic Policy Research at Stanford University. Kessler is grateful for support from the Harvard/MIT Research Training Group in Positive Political Economy, the John M. Olin Foundation, and the State Farm Companies Foundation. All errors are the authors' own.
    1. Contributory negligence bars plaintiffs who are at all at fault from recovery; comparative negligence apportions damages on the basis of fault.
    2. See, for example, Huber (1988).

107

In addition, as Priest points out, common law tort doctrine has also undergone several other, more subtle changes that reflect this change in the law's ambition.[3]

Notwithstanding the debate over the social desirability of expansive compensation to tort claimants, the concomitant expansion of penalties imposed on potential injurers may have important welfare effects through its impact on productivity.[4] Previous empirical research suggests, for example, that high levels of liability may affect the rate of both new innovations and the implementation of existing innovations.[5] Furthermore, in industries with important agency problems such as health care, the expansion of liability may have either increased or reduced productive efficiency, depending on the competing effects of insurance-induced moral hazard.[6]

Despite the important role that certain well-defined changes in liability law have played in expanding tort awards, empirical investigation of the effect of these changes on productivity has been limited. Although substantial work investigates the impact of liability law reforms on liability insurance market outcomes,[7] the comprehensive literature on state and regional differences in productivity, output, and employment has paid little attention to the influence of reforms in state liability law on the determination of macroeconomic outcomes.[8] Nor has the extensive research on the impact of liability pressure on productivity focused on the role of liability law reforms in that process.[9]

This paper seeks to fill that gap. We use a newly collected data set of state liability reforms and other political and economic characteristics of states, matched with data on productivity by state by industry for the twenty years from 1970 to 1990, to provide empirical evidence on how

3. Priest (1991).
4. See Calfee and Winston (1993) on the social desirability of expansive compensation; see Priest (1987), Litan and Winston (1988), and Kessler (1995) on expanded penalties.
5. See, for example, Viscusi and Moore (1993) and Huber and Litan (1991).
6. Kessler and McClellan (1996).
7. See, for example, Viscusi (1990), Blackmon and Zeckhauser (1991), Viscusi and others (1993), Born and Viscusi (1994), and Viscusi and Born (1995).
8. See, for example, Beeson (1987), Beeson and Husted (1989), Carlino and Voith (1992), Dertouzos and Karoly (1992), Blanchard and Katz (1992), and Jayaratne and Strahan (1996).
9. See Huber and Litan (1991, chap. 1) for an extensive review of that research.

changes in liability rules have affected productivity. The key issue in identifying the effect of liability reforms on productivity is the potential endogeneity of reforms, that is, the correlation with reforms of unobserved determinants of productivity. Ideally, we would use instrumental variables (IV) methods to estimate the effect of reforms; however, IV identification requires the assumption that some political or economic determinants of reforms do not affect productivity, an assumption with no strong theoretical basis. To address the potential endogeneity of reforms, we control for a wide range of time-varying and time-invariant characteristics of states that may affect productivity and the propensity to reform, and we allow different types of states to have different underlying time trends in productivity. Our basic approach, discussed in detail later, estimates the effect of reforms as the differential growth in productivity over time in those states that changed their liability laws, relative to productivity growth in those states where liability law remained the same.

We find that states that changed their liability laws to decrease levels of liability experienced greater increases in aggregate productivity than states that did not. Conversely, in several industries, states that changed their laws to increase levels of liability experienced smaller increases in productivity than states that did not, although this result is not as robust to choice of specification. In particular, states that decreased liability pressure showed statistically significant productivity increases of approximately 1 to 2 percent between 1972 and 1990, relative to states that did not, when we controlled for state fixed effects and for time-varying political and economic characteristics of states and allowed different types of states to have different underlying time trends in productivity.

We proceed as follows. First, we discuss the theoretical ambiguity of the impact of the liability system on social welfare, and review those microeconomic mechanisms found by previous research to be important channels through which the liability system affects welfare. Second, we discuss our empirical approach to estimating the impact of liability reforms on one of these channels—productivity. Third, we describe our data in detail, including the eight legal reforms that we examine. Fourth, we present our econometric models. Finally, we present our empirical results, and our conclusions.

Links between the Liability System and
the Determinants of Social Welfare

In simple models, a wide range of rules for apportioning damages from accidental injuries can result in socially optimal precautionary care decisions. But the welfare implications of any particular formulation of liability law quickly become theoretically ambiguous in more complex models that allow for either product market failures (such as those involving public goods, externalities, or informational imperfections) or an imperfectly functioning legal system. The most studied example of the interaction between product market failure and the liability system involves innovation, research, and development, which, from the perspective of social welfare, private markets may either over- or underprovide.[10] If private markets produce too much innovation, and liability pressure tends to discourage innovation, then an expansive liability system may be welfare-enhancing. Conversely, if private markets produce socially too little innovation, then a liability system that discourages innovation may be socially harmful.

A substantial literature has outlined some possible mechanisms through which liability pressure may affect innovation. For example, Viscusi and Moore model the effect of liability pressure on a firm's trade-off between product safety and product novelty.[11] They observe that liability's effect on innovation depends on the interaction between innovation and the firm's ability to produce product safety. If innovation enables the firm to increase safety at less cost, then innovation will respond positively to liability; but if innovation makes it more difficult for the firm to produce product safety, then innovation will respond negatively to liability. Based on data on U.S. firms from 1980 to 1984, Viscusi and Moore show that low to moderate levels of expected liability costs have a positive effect on product innovation but that very high levels of liability costs have a negative effect.

Other work focuses on the link between liability costs and the *adoption* (rather than the invention) of new technologies. For example, liability considerations may discourage a manufacturer from making

10. See Tirole (1988), especially section 10.3, for a discussion of this literature.
11. Viscusi and Moore (1993).

safety (or other product) improvements if juries use such improvements as evidence that the manufacturer's previous designs were defective.[12] Along these lines, liability costs may lead to the nonoptimal extension of the service life of equipment if costly safety features are effectively mandated by the tort system only for new equipment.[13]

Moral hazard due to informational imperfections can also cause otherwise optimal liability rules to be welfare-reducing (or cause otherwise nonoptimal rules to be welfare-enhancing). Consider the case of markets for health care, in which most patients' care is financed through health insurance, and most physicians' financial liability for acts of negligence is financed through malpractice liability insurance. On one hand, increasing financial penalties for physicians above the expected costs of medical injuries may be welfare-improving if moral hazard from malpractice insurance leads physicians to take too few precautions. On the other hand, if moral hazard from health insurance is more important, then decreasing financial penalties below the expected costs of injuries may be welfare-improving.[14] Because patients (and physicians) do not bear the costs of care in any particular case, they may have the incentive to consume (and produce) precautionary medical care that has social marginal costs greater than social marginal benefits. In this situation, even compensation *equal to* the expected costs of medical injury may result in social losses due to "defensive medicine"—precautionary treatments with minimal medical benefit administered out of fear of legal liability. Based on data on elderly medicare beneficiaries treated for serious heart disease between 1984 and 1990, Kessler and McClellan show that doctors do practice defensively: malpractice liability reforms that directly reduce provider liability pressure lead to reductions of 5 to 9 percent in medical expenditures, without substantial effects on mortality or medical complications.[15]

The welfare analysis of specific liability rules is further complicated if the assumption of a perfectly functioning legal system is relaxed. For

12. Graham (1991).
13. See Martin (1991) for a discussion of this as it applies to the aircraft industry.
14. This would be true if the liability system imposed uninsurable, nonfinancial penalties on physicians, such as damage to professional reputation, that were sufficient to induce careful behavior.
15. Kessler and McClellan (1996).

example, if judges and juries impose liability with error, and if additional investment in safety reduces the probability of liability, then potential injurers may take socially excessive precautions.[16] Excessive care results from the all-or-nothing nature of the liability decision: small increases in precaution above the optimal level can lead to large decreases in expected liability.

Empirical Approach

As a review of the literature suggests, identifying the general equilibrium social welfare effects of the liability system, either theoretically or empirically, is difficult.[17] For this reason, this paper identifies the impact of reforms to states' liability law on a single important determinant of social welfare—productivity. We hypothesize that the differential costs and benefits to political interest groups of liability reforms may be correlated with states' propensity to adopt reforms.[18] Under the assumption that such measures of interest-group strength or size are uncorrelated with productivity, except through their influence on the propensity to adopt liability reforms, IV methods could use these factors to identify the impact of reforms on productivity. Unfortunately, such measurable determinants of reforms also may affect states' legal and regulatory environments in other ways that influence productivity. And in fact, measurable determinants of reforms may themselves be an important vehicle through which liability reforms affect productivity. For example, the concentration of lawyers in a state may affect the prevalence of liability reforms, but liability reforms may also affect the concentration of lawyers, which in turn may affect statewide productivity through other channels. Thus, it is not clear a priori whether controlling for political or interest group strength or size is appropriate in calculating the impact of liability reform. We present regression estimates of the impact of changes in liability rules on productivity that do and do not control for several state and time-varying measures of interest group strength and size.

16. Cooter and Ulen (1986); Craswell and Calfee (1986).
17. See Huber and Litan (1991, chap. 1).
18. See, for example, Noll (1989) and Winston and Crandall (1994).

In addition to these political and interest-group factors, all of our models control for other factors that may be correlated with the propensity to adopt reforms and with productivity. First, we control for state fixed effects to account for time-invariant differences across states. Second, because states have substantially different growth rates that may be correlated with the propensity to adopt legal reforms but that are not actually caused by such reforms, we allow different types of states to have different baseline time paths of productivity.[19] Most importantly, states that adopt reforms may have different productivity growth paths than states that do not. Thus, we include separate time fixed effects for states that adopted liability-decreasing reforms and states that adopted liability-increasing reforms during our sample period. This means that our estimated effect of reforms is identified solely by the timing of reforms in adopting states, not by the fact that adopting states may have different trends in productivity for other reasons. In addition, because states that adopted reforms before our sample period may have different trends in productivity and be differentially likely to adopt reforms in the future, we include separate time fixed effects for states that adopted liability-decreasing reforms effective before 1972 and for states that adopted liability-increasing reforms effective before 1972. Finally, to address the concern that states in different regions of the country may have different productivity trend growth and be differentially likely to change their liability system, we include a separate vector of time fixed effects for Sun Belt states (census regions Southeast, Southwest, Rocky Mountain, and Far West).

Third, we control for time-varying economic factors that may affect both state legislative activity and productivity. Because the legislative activity associated with liability reform occurs at least a year before the reforms take effect, we control for contemporaneous, once-, and twice-lagged time-varying economic factors. In particular, we control for the state unemployment rate, to capture the effect of state and regional business cycles, and for a set of resource-base characteristics of states, to capture the level of investment in physical and nonphysical infrastructure.

---

19. On state differences in growth rates, see, for example, Blanchard and Katz (1992).

Data

We use annual data by state for 1970 to 1990 from several different sources.

First, we use data on gross state product (GSP) and total employment by state by industry, from the U.S. Department of Commerce Bureau of Economic Analysis. GSP is equal to gross output (sales and receipts and other operating income, plus inventory change) minus intermediate inputs (consumption of goods and services purchased from other industries or imported). Total employment is equal to total full-time plus total part-time employment. We focus on labor productivity—GSP divided by total employment—in our analysis.[20]

Second, we assemble information on states that adopted liability reforms, and when they adopted them, by carefully reviewing each state's statutes and published judicial decisions. We distinguish reforms that apply generally from those that apply only to claims for medical malpractice. For purposes of this paper, we analyze only those reforms that apply generally.[21]

Third, we use data on states' economic and political environments and resource bases from several different sources.[22] Data on the political parties of elected officials by state are from the Council of State Governments. Data on lawyers per capita for 1970, 1980, 1985, and 1988 are from the American Bar Foundation; intervening years were calculated by linear interpolation. We confirm the validity of the interpolated data on lawyers by replacing it in the analyses with data on total employment in the legal services sector from the Bureau of Economic Analysis Table SA25, which is available by state for every year in our study period; using total employment in legal services did not alter our results. Data on physicians per capita for 1970, 1975, 1980, 1985, and 1990 are from the American Medical Association; intervening years were calculated by linear interpolation. Data on states' economic con-

20. Gross state product data are described further in Parker (1993); employment data are from Bureau of Economic Analysis (various years: table SA25). Data limitations precluded our use of a more comprehensive measure of performance such as total factor productivity.

21. See Kessler and McClellan (1996) for discussion of medical malpractice reforms specifically.

22. Special thanks to Morris Fiorina and Gary King for making these data available in machine-readable form.

ditions and resource bases, including information on unemployment rates, commercial bank assets per capita, higher education enrollment per capita, and highway mileage per square mile of land, are from the Bureau of the Census.[23]

Data on Liability Law Reforms

We investigate the effects of eight types of legal reforms: caps on damage awards, abolition of punitive damages, mandatory prejudgment interest, collateral source rule reform, caps on contingency fees, mandatory periodic payments, joint and several liability reform, and comparative negligence. Our definition of these reforms is identical to that used in Kessler and McClellan and is summarized in table 1.[24]

—*Caps on damage awards.* Several states have placed dollar limits on the amount that a plaintiff can recover, either in total or for damages due to pain and suffering. For example, a reform statute might state that the plaintiff can recover no more than $250,000, regardless of the severity of a plaintiff's injuries or of a defendant's culpability.

—*Abolition of punitive damages.* Although we have tracked modifications to punitive damages statutes, for purposes of comparability we catalog as reforms only those statutes that eliminate punitive damages. As discussed later, we group together caps on damage awards, collateral source rule reforms, and reforms restricting punitive damages. Given the distributions of punitive and compensatory damages, a restriction on punitive damages would likely need to be more strict than a restriction on compensatory damages in order to reduce total liability by the same amount.[25]

—*Mandatory prejudgment interest.* The common law entitled a plaintiff to interest on the value of a loss only from the date of judgment, not from the time of the loss. If a plaintiff did not receive judgment until two years after a loss, the plaintiff received no interest on the loss

23. Council of State Governments (1970–90); American Bar Foundation (1971, 1985, 1991); American Medical Association (1970–90); Bureau of the Census (1970–90).
24. Since Kessler and McClellan (1996) analyzed the impact of tort reforms on the costs of defensive medical treatment, that paper did not investigate comparative negligence, which is generally not important in medical malpractice litigation.
25. See Peterson, Sarma, and Shanley (1987, tables 3.1, 3.7) for data on the distributions of punitive and compensatory damages.

Table 1. Legal Reforms Used in Analysis

Reform	Description of reform	Predicted impact on liability
Caps on damage awards	Either noneconomic (pain and suffering) or total damages payable are capped at a statutorily specified dollar amount	Decrease
Abolition of punitive damages	Defendants are not liable for punitive damages under any circumstances	Decrease
Reform of collateral source rule	Total damages are statutorily reduced by all or part of the dollar value of collateral source payments to the plaintiff	Decrease
Caps on contingency fees	The proportion of an award that a plaintiff can contractually agree to pay a contingency-fee attorney is capped at a statutorily specified level	Decrease
Mandatory periodic payments	Part or all of damages must be disbursed in the form of an annuity that pays out over time	Decrease
Reform of joint and several liability	Joint and several liability is abolished for noneconomic or total damages, either for all claims or for claims in which defendants did not act in concert	Decrease
Comparative negligence	Damages are apportioned according to the plaintiff's relative fault, instead of barring plaintiffs who are at all at fault from recovery (contributory negligence)	Increase
Mandatory prejudgment interest	Interest on either noneconomic or total damages accruing from either the date of the injury or the date of filing of the lawsuit is mandatory	Increase

Source: Authors' tabulations.

for the two-year period. Several states have altered this rule to entitle plaintiff to interest either from the time of injury or from the time plaintiff filed suit, which increases defendants' liability.

　　—*Collateral source rule reform.* The collateral source rule, an old common law tort doctrine, states that the defendant must bear the full cost of the injury suffered by the plaintiff, even if the plaintiff were compensated for all or part of the cost by an independent or "collateral" source. This means that a defendant liable for personal injuries must always bear the cost of plaintiff's medical care, for example, even if the treatment were financed by the patient's own health insurance.

Either the plaintiff enjoys double recovery (the plaintiff recovers from the defendant and his own health insurance for medical expenses attributable to the injury) or the defendant reimburses the plaintiff's health insurer, depending on the plaintiff's insurance contract and state or federal law. Reforms to the collateral source rule may reduce the extent of a defendant's liability for plaintiff's injuries in either case by reducing the defendant's responsibility to finance damages arising out of an insured injury.

—*Caps on contingency fees.* Traditionally, a client and his or her attorney were free to agree to any size attorney fee. Several states have altered this rule by imposing limits on the fraction of any damage award that an attorney can receive on contingency. This change to tort law may reduce liability by restricting certain plaintiffs' ability to obtain representation and sue, in those cases in which the capped contingency fee fails to cover an attorney's fixed costs of representation.

—*Mandatory periodic payments.* At common law, a plaintiff would receive compensation for damages from future losses in a lump sum at the time of judgment, calculated by the jury without instruction or expert assistance. It has been argued that juries do not discount future losses adequately; thus, requiring that future damages be paid periodically may reduce liability.

—*Joint and several liability reform.* Traditionally, if several defendants' acts combined to injure a plaintiff, then each defendant was liable for the judgment's full amount, regardless of how minor a defendant's contribution was to the injury. For example, if a first defendant was 95 percent responsible for a plaintiff's injury and a second was only 5 percent responsible, joint and several liability required the second defendant to pay the entire judgment if the first defendant lacked sufficient resources to pay her or his share. The rule's rationale was that if a defendant became insolvent, then other culpable defendants should suffer, not the innocent plaintiff. The elimination or qualification of the rule reduces defendants' liability by not holding any defendant liable for the acts of another defendant due to that defendant's insolvency.

—*Comparative negligence.* Regardless of a defendant's culpability, the common law doctrine of contributory negligence completely denied recovery to a plaintiff who had been at all negligent. Comparative negligence modified this sometimes harsh result so that the negligent plaintiff's recovery would decline not to zero, but only by plaintiff's fraction of the total negligence: if plaintiff had been 15 percent negligent and defendant had been 85 percent negligent, then plaintiff would recover 85 percent of her damages. Although comparative negligence does not directly specify that defendants' liability is to be increased, it does empirically increase awards.[26]

Liability reforms, then, fall into two categories. We call those reforms that may increase the level of liability by increasing the expected size of trial judgments and settlement amounts "increase" reforms. They include comparative negligence and mandatory prejudgment interest. The remaining six reforms—caps on damage awards, abolition of punitive damages, collateral source rule reform, caps on contingency fees, mandatory periodic payments, and joint and several liability reform—are all "decrease" reforms predicted to decrease judgments' size.

Table 2 reports the status of states' liability systems at the beginning of the period analyzed by our models and shows which states changed their liability laws during our sample period.[27] The first two columns indicate which states adopted decrease and increase reforms effective before 1972; the second two columns report the earliest effective date of decrease and increase reforms that became effective between 1972 and 1990. The effective date, usually the year after the reform's legislative enactment, was obtained from state statutes. Twenty-eight states adopted decrease reforms and thirty states adopted increase reforms effective during our sample period. Of the twenty-eight states adopting decrease reforms during our sample period, eight did not adopt increase reforms—these states changed their liability system to decrease unambiguously the level of liability. Additionally, seven states adopted decrease reforms and twenty adopted increase reforms effective before 1972; as discussed later, we allow these states to have different 1972–

26. Kessler (1995). Some states adopted "pure" comparative negligence: a plaintiff would recover for defendant's share of the negligence regardless of plaintiff's share. Other states enacted "modified" comparative negligence, which denies recovery to a plaintiff whose negligence exceeds 50 percent.

27. Because the degrees of freedom in our data are limited, we distinguish only between the effects of decrease reforms and the effects of increase reforms in our analysis. Although this distinction is important (because the two types of reforms have theoretically opposing effects on the liability system), our categorization of laws into these two groups may neglect substantial variation in states' liability systems.

Table 2. Chronology of Legal Reforms through 1990, by State

State	Reforms adopted before sample period Decrease	Increase	Reforms adopted during sample period Decrease	Increase
Alabama			1987	
Alaska		*	1976	1975
Arizona		*	1988	1984
Arkansas				1975
California			1986	
Colorado		*	1986	
Connecticut			1986	1973
Delaware				1984
Florida			1976	1973
Georgia		*	1986	
Hawaii		*	1986	
Idaho		*	1986	
Illinois			1986	1981
Indiana			1985	1985
Iowa			1975	1981
Kansas	*		1974	1974
Kentucky		*		1984
Louisiana	*	*		1980
Maine				
Maryland		*	1986	
Massachusetts	*			
Michigan			1981	1979
Minnesota		*	1986	
Mississippi		*		
Missouri			1986	1983
Montana			1987	1975
Nebraska	*	*		
Nevada				1973
New Hampshire		*	1986	
New Jersey		*	1976	1973
New Mexico			1987	1981
New York	*		1986	1975
North Carolina				1981
North Dakota			1987	1973
Ohio			1988	1980
Oklahoma		*	1978	1973
Oregon		*	1987	
Pennsylvania				1976
Rhode Island		*		
South Carolina				1974
South Dakota		*		
Tennessee				
Texas			1986	1973
Utah				1973
Vermont	*	*		
Virginia				
Washington	*		1986	1974
West Virginia				1979
Wisconsin		*		
Wyoming			1986	1973

Source: Authors' tabulations.

Notes: Sample period is from 1972 through 1990, inclusive. Date shown is the effective date for the earliest reform adopted during the sample period.

90 time trends in productivity to allow for the possibility that reforms have a long-run impact on productivity growth.

Data on Political and Interest-Group Characteristics

We use data on four types of political and interest-group characteristics:

—*Lawyers per capita*. A simple political economy model would predict that the greater the number of lawyers per capita, the greater will be the political power that lawyers will exert against reforms that harm lawyers and for reforms that help them. The smaller judgments and settlements likely under decrease reforms may harm lawyers; increase reforms are likely to provide corresponding benefits. An attorney who receives payment from a client under a contingency agreement suffers directly from smaller judgments that decrease reforms cause. In addition, smaller expected judgments deter potential plaintiffs from filing suit; expected judgments will exceed expected litigation costs in fewer disputes. Fewer lawsuits will harm all attorneys, whether they receive payment by the hour or under contingency agreements, and whether they represent plaintiffs or defendants. According to this reasoning, lawyers would favor increase reforms and oppose decrease reforms. However if all changes in the law, whether they increase or decrease liability, require lawyers to interpret and implement them, then lawyers may favor both increase and decrease reforms. Lawyers benefit from any change in legal regime if the change increases demand for their expertise.

—*Physicians per capita*. Physicians are a powerful political interest generally thought to favor decrease reforms: smaller judgments benefit doctors by reducing both pecuniary and nonpecuniary malpractice expenses, because smaller awards lead to fewer malpractice lawsuits. The fact that several states have passed decrease reforms that apply only to medical malpractice claims is evidence that physicians may play an important role in the political process on this issue.

—*Importance of manufacturing exports*. A simple political economy model would predict that states that export a large fraction of their manufacturing output would be less likely to adopt increase reforms and more likely to adopt decrease reforms. In states with high exports, all else constant, voters and consumer organizations will demand less in the way of increase reforms and more in the way of decrease reforms. Some nonresident plaintiffs will choose to sue the state's firms within the state, and they will do so increasingly as the level of liability in the state rises. Thus, if residents are disproportionate stakeholders in local firms (for example, by virtue of employment), then increase reforms may transfer relatively more in states with high exports from residents to nonresidents. Similarly, because the costs to residents of decrease reforms will be lower in states with high exports (relative to low-export states, nonvoting nonresidents will bear a greater fraction of decrease reforms' costs), residents will be more likely to support decrease reforms than their counterparts in low-export states.

—*Republican or Democratic state politics.* State party politics may be correlated both with the propensity to adopt changes to liability law and with other state-level public policies that affect economic performance. We measure a state's party politics with the party of the state's governor, and whether Democrats are in the majority in one or both chambers of the state legislature.[28]

Models

We estimate the effects of reforms as the differential growth over time in productivity in states that changed their liability laws, relative to productivity growth in states that did not, controlling for time-invariant and time-varying characteristics of states. In particular, we control for state fixed effects α_s (forty-nine dichotomous state indicator variables); for time fixed effects θ_t, where θ_t is allowed to differ for states adopting decrease and increase reforms effective before 1972, for states adopting decrease and increase reforms effective during the sample period, and for Sun Belt states (six sets of eighteen dichotomous year indicator variables); for contemporaneous, once-, and twice-lagged political and interest-group characteristics of states X_{st}; and for contemporaneous, once-, and twice-lagged economic characteristics of states Z_{st}.

We define $L_{st}^D = 1$ if state s adopted a decrease reform during our

28. We also include an interaction term to control for whether Democrats control the governorship and one or both chambers of the state legislature.

sample period and that change in law was effective on or before year t ($L_{st}^D = 0$ otherwise), and $L_{st}^I = 1$ if state s adopted an increase reform during our sample period and that reform was effective on or before year t ($L_{st}^I = 0$ otherwise). Thus, the basic models of the impact of liability reforms on productivity are of the following form:

$$
(1) \quad \ln(P_{st}^j) = \alpha_s^j + \theta_t^j + \beta_D^j L_{st}^D + \beta_I^j L_{st}^I + \lambda_X^j X_{st} + \lambda_{X1}^j X_{st-1}
$$
$$
+ \lambda_{X2}^j X_{st-2} + \lambda_Z^j Z_{st} + \lambda_{Z1}^j Z_{st-1} + \lambda_{Z2}^j Z_{st-2} + v_{st}^j,
$$

where P_{st}^j represents productivity, as measured by GSP per worker, in state s and industry j during year t, and v_{st}^j is an error term. Because the dependent variable in equation 1 is in log form, the coefficients of interest, β_D^j and β_I^j, can be interpreted as the percentage difference in productivity growth between reform and nonreform states.

However, liability reforms might have important dynamic effects on productivity growth; changes in laws may have different short-run and long-run effects. For example, reforms may not influence macroeconomic outcomes immediately but may take several years to reach their full effect. Indeed, if the relationship between liability reform and productivity were causal, one would expect reforms to have greater long-run than short-run effects, because of the time it would take for reforms to change firms' and individuals' behavior. We investigate this possibility with a "time-since-adoption" model that estimates separately the impact of reforms on changes over time in productivity shortly after adoption and long after adoption:

$$
\ln(P_{st}^j) = \alpha_s^j + \theta_t^j + \beta_{D1}^j L_{st}^D * SA_{st}^D + \beta_{D2}^j L_{st}^D * LA_{st}^D
$$
$$
(2) \quad + \beta_{I1}^j L_{st}^I * SA_{st}^I + \beta_{I2}^j L_{st}^I * LA_{st}^I + \lambda_X^j X_{st} + \lambda_{X1}^j X_{st-1}
$$
$$
+ \lambda_{X2}^j X_{st-2} + \lambda_Z^j Z_{st} + \lambda_{Z1}^j Z_{st-1} + \lambda_{Z2}^j Z_{st-2} + v_{st}^j,
$$

where $SA_{st}^D = 1$ if a year t was less than two years after the effective date of the earliest decrease reform adopted during our sample period, $SA_{st}^D = 0$ otherwise; and $LA_{st}^D = 1$ if a year t was two or more years after the effective date of the earliest decrease reform adopted during our sample period, $LA_{st}^D = 0$ otherwise. SA_{st}^I and LA_{st}^I are defined similarly.

We estimate equations 1 and 2 for all nonfarm single-digit SIC (standard industrial classification) industries and for states' private-sector

nonfarm economies as a whole. We report results for the service industries at a more disaggregated level, because tort reforms are likely to
have different impacts on different service industries. For example,
decreases in liability in the health care sector may improve productivity
if liability reductions lead providers to employ fewer tests and procedures that have minimal medical benefit.[29] Decreases in liability may
reduce measured productivity for the same reason, however: value-
added in health care is partially a function of the number of tests and
procedures performed, whether or not they are medically necessary.
The effect of liability reductions on the legal services sector is also
ambiguous. On one hand, decrease reforms may impose costs on lawyers if they reduce contingency fee payments and the number of lawsuits; this would imply that decrease reforms would lower GSP per
worker in the legal services sector. On the other hand, if all changes in
the law require lawyers to interpret and implement them, then reforms
may increase attorneys' productivity.

As discussed earlier, political and interest-group factors may themselves be an important vehicle through which liability reforms affect
productivity. But they may also affect states' propensity to adopt reforms and influence states' legal and regulatory environment in other
ways that affect productivity. For this reason, we present estimates that
do and do not control for political and interest-group characteristics X.

Empirical Results

Table 3 presents descriptive statistics for all of the variables in our
model for the eight states (Alabama, Colorado, Hawaii, Idaho, Maryland, Minnesota, New Hampshire, and Oregon) that changed their liability systems between 1972 and 1990 to achieve unambiguous reductions in liability (that is, adopting decrease but not increase reforms,
described below as "unambiguous decrease" states) versus the then
forty-two states and previews the results of our analysis. (We separate
states into unambiguous decrease states and all other states for purposes
of table 3 because increase and decrease reforms may be correlated).

29. We excluded doctors per capita from X_{st} when estimating equations 1 and 2 for
the health care sector; we excluded lawyers per capita from X_{st} when estimating the two
equations for the legal services sector.

Table 3. Average Productivity and Political, Economic, and Other Characteristics of Reforming and Nonreforming States, 1972 and 1990

Variable	*States adopting decrease but not increase reforms, 1972–90*			*All other states, 1972–90*		
	1972	*1990*	*Percent change**	*1972*	*1990*	*Percent change**
Private nonfarm labor productivity (1987 dollars per worker)	31,042 (2,412)	34,073 (2,226)	9.8	36,148 (10,972)	37,004 (9,630)	2.4
Democratic governor only	0.125	0.250	12.5	0.143	0.048	−9.5
Democratic house or senate only	0.125	0	−12.5	0.048	0.048	0
Democratic legislature only	0	0.125	12.5	0.167	0.357	19.0
Governor + one chamber Democratic	0	0	0	0.119	0.214	9.5
Governor + both chambers Democratic	0.500	0.500	0	0.333	0.214	−11.9
Unemployment rate	0.052 (0.013)	0.051 (0.012)	−1.9	0.052 (0.017)	0.054 (0.011)	3.8
Percentage of manufacturing exported	0.282 (0.038)	0.285 (0.057)	1.0	0.294 (0.069)	0.305 (0.062)	3.7
Doctors per 1,000 population	1.505 (0.366)	2.338 (0.650)	55.3	1.351 (0.369)	2.136 (0.512)	58.1
Lawyers per 1,000 population	1.589 (0.409)	2.851 (0.612)	79.4	1.614 (0.397)	2.657 (0.751)	64.6
Commercial bank assets per population (thousands of 1987 dollars)	6.698 (1.417)	9.436 (2.867)	40.9	7.822 (2.373)	12.481 (14.400)	59.6
Higher education enrollment per population	0.045 (0.008)	0.056 (0.006)	24.4	0.043 (0.010)	0.055 (0.010)	27.9
Highway mileage per square mile of land	1.343 (0.714)	1.387 (0.768)	3.3	1.750 (1.071)	1.821 (1.192)	4.1

Sources: Authors' calculations. Standard deviations are in parentheses. See text for full explanation.
*Changes for dichotomous variables expressed in percentage points.

States unambiguously decreasing liability levels show higher growth in productivity over the 1972–90 period. Specifically, average private nonfarm real labor productivity growth in the eight unambiguous decrease states was 9.8 percent during the sample period, compared with 2.4 percent growth in all other states. Thus, the raw version of our estimator suggests that liability reforms increase productivity substantially, by 7.4 percent (9.8 − 2.4). This simple comparison, however, does not control for fixed differences across states, for differential time trends in productivity in different types of states, and for differences in time-varying state economic, political, and resource-base characteristics. In addition, the comparison does not permit analysis of the dynamic effects of reforms. Nonetheless, it anticipates the principal result that follows.

The political and economic characteristics of unambiguous decrease and all other states do not follow a clear pattern. In the eight unambiguous decrease states Democrats were less likely to have only a legislative majority in 1972 and 1990; in addition, in none of these states did Democrats hold both the governor's seat and only a single chamber of the legislature in either 1972 or 1990. On the other hand, four of the eight states had both a Democratic governor and a Democratic legislature, compared with fourteen of the forty-two other states in 1972 and nine in 1990.

Trends in manufacturing exports and the concentration of physicians and lawyers also exhibit no clear pattern. A simple political economy model would predict that states with high levels or growth rates of manufacturing exports would be more likely to adopt reforms decreasing liability: in such states decrease reforms could result in net transfers into the state. But unambiguous decrease states had both a lower initial level and a slower growth rate of the share of manufacturing exports than did other states. Similarly, a simple political economy model would predict that states with lower concentrations of lawyers and higher concentrations of physicians would adopt liability-decreasing reforms. However, although unambiguous decrease states had approximately 1.5 percent fewer lawyers per resident in 1972 [(1.589 − 1.614)/1.614], they experienced substantially greater growth in lawyers over the sample period, and by 1990 had approximately 7.3 percent more lawyers per capita [(2.851 − 2.657)/2.657] than did other states. Conversely, unambiguous decrease states have higher baseline levels but lower growth rates of the concentration of physicians.

Table 4 presents least-squares estimates of the effect of liability reforms on the natural log of productivity per private nonfarm worker by industry, based on the basic model given by equation 1. That equation estimates the effect of reforms as the differential growth over time in productivity in those states that changed their liability laws, relative to productivity growth in those states whose liability laws remained the same. The leftmost two columns present estimates from models that exclude controls for state-and time-varying political and interest-group characteristics; the rightmost columns present estimates that control for all political, economic, and resource-base variables X and Z listed in table 3. Because our econometric models use data on inputs and outputs aggregated to the state level from individual firms of different sizes, we weight each observation by the level of real GSP.

As the estimates in table 4 show, states that reduce their levels of legal liability experience greater increases in productivity than states that do not, measured in terms of constant-dollar GSP per worker. In particular, states adopting decrease reforms experience approximately 1.7 percent greater aggregate productivity growth than states that do not. The magnitude and statistical significance of this result is robust to the inclusion of controls for states' political and interest-group characteristics. Evaluated at the mean value of states' labor productivity over the sample period, this finding suggests that decrease reforms are associated with a $603 increase in GSP per worker per year, in 1987 dollars.

Conversely, in several industries, states that changed their liability laws to increase levels of liability experienced lesser increases in productivity than states that did not. However, states adopting increase reforms do not experience significantly less productivity growth in aggregate than states that do not adopt such reforms; in addition, the estimated effect of increase reforms across industries is not as robust to the inclusion of political and interest-group controls.

Reforms have the greatest impact on industries likely to be subject to the highest levels of liability and on the insurance industry. According to the Insurance Services Office, the most common sources of commercial liability insurance claims (other than medical malpractice) in 1987 were (in decreasing order of frequency) auto accidents, unsafe

Table 4. Effects of Tort Reforms on Productivity by Industry, Basic Model, 1972–90

Industry	Without controls for political and interest-group characteristics		With controls for political and interest-group characteristics		Average productivity (thousands of 1987 $ per worker)
	Liability-decreasing reforms	Liability-increasing reforms	Liability-decreasing reforms	Liability-increasing reforms	
Total private nonfarm	0.017** (0.007)	−0.001 (0.009)	0.017** (0.006)	−0.001 (0.007)	35.5 [8.9]
Mining	−0.203** (0.094)	0.390** (0.076)	−0.050 (0.058)	0.098** (0.047)	73.3 [10.0]
Construction	0.000 (0.012)	−0.015 (0.009)	0.001 (0.009)	0.003 (0.008)	33.2 [11.1]
Manufacturing	0.020** (0.010)	−0.025** (0.010)	0.027** (0.008)	−0.009 (0.007)	37.6 [7.8]
Transportation, communications, utilities	−0.006 (0.009)	−0.036** (0.008)	0.001 (0.009)	−0.029** (0.007)	62.2 [14.7]
Wholesale trade	0.017** (0.005)	−0.018** (0.006)	0.010** (0.005)	−0.020** (0.005)	40.5 [6.9]
Retail trade	−0.001 (0.006)	−0.024** (0.007)	−0.002 (0.006)	−0.016** (0.006)	19.2 [2.5]
Finance, insurance, real estate	0.031** (0.014)	0.012 (0.011)	0.031** (0.012)	0.018* (0.009)	76.1 [17.2]
Services net of hotels, amusement, health, legal	0.007 (0.007)	−0.011** (0.005)	0.003 (0.006)	−0.002 (0.005)	16.8 [3.4]
Hotels, lodging places	0.017 (0.012)	−0.010 (0.012)	0.019* (0.011)	−0.007 (0.009)	22.6 [5.6]
Amusement, recreation	0.006 (0.011)	−0.056** (0.013)	0.003 (0.011)	−0.051** (0.011)	14.0 [4.4]
Health care	−0.003 (0.006)	−0.010** (0.005)	−0.003 (0.005)	−0.007 (0.005)	28.8 [4.8]
Legal services	−0.003 (0.009)	−0.014 (0.009)	0.001 (0.007)	−0.006 (0.007)	49.8 [9.6]

Source: Authors' calculations. Heteroscedasticity-consistent standard errors are in parentheses. Standard deviations of average productivity are in brackets. Regression coefficients are percentage changes because the dependent variable in the model is ln(productivity). Standard errors of estimates calculated with White's (1980) method. N = 950 except for mining; services net of hotels, amusement, health, legal; and amusement, recreation, for which N = 948 due to missing data.
* = significant at the 0.10 level.
** = significant at the 0.05 level.

premises, defective products, and operations of contractors, construction, and design firms.[30] By industry, liability for auto accidents is likely to fall on transportation-related industries; liability for unsafe premises is likely to fall on the retail trade, hotel, and amusement industries; liability for defective products is likely to fall on manufacturers and wholesalers; and liability for operations of contractors is likely to fall on the construction industry.

Correspondingly, decrease reforms improve productivity the most in the manufacturing and the finance, insurance, and real estate sectors (FIRE). According to estimates that control for political and interest-group factors, states that adopt decrease reforms experience 2.7 percent greater manufacturing productivity growth (statistically significant at the 5 percent level) than states that do not. Evaluated at the mean value of manufacturing labor productivity for the sample period, this finding suggests that decrease reforms are associated with a $1,015 increase in GSP per worker per year, in 1987 dollars. Industries experiencing smaller positive but still statistically significant effects of decrease reforms include hotels and lodging places—and wholesale trade, with 1.9 percent (standard error 1.1) and 1.0 percent (standard error 0.5) greater productivity growth, respectively, than in those same industries in states that did not adopt decrease reforms.

Increase reforms reduce productivity the most in the amusement and recreation sector (subject to high levels of premises liability) and the transportation sector (subject to high levels of auto liability). Estimates calculated controlling for political and interest-group factors indicate that states that adopt increase reforms show 5.1 percent (standard error 1.1) lower productivity growth in the amusement and recreation sector and 2.9 percent (standard error 0.7) lower productivity growth in the transportation sector compared with states that do not. Industries experiencing smaller negative but still statistically significant effects of increase reforms include wholesale trade (subject to products liability) and retail trade (subject to premises liability), of approximately 1 to 2 percent.

The strong estimated effect of reforms on the FIRE sector parallels

30. Insurance Services Office (1988, p. 94). Ostrom and Kauder (1994, p. 30) similarly report that the most common sources of tort case filings (other than medical malpractice) in state courts are (in decreasing order of frequency) auto accidents, unsafe premises, intentional torts, and defective products.

the findings of other research on liability reform and the performance of the insurance industry. Both decrease and increase reforms lead to statistically significant increases in productivity in the FIRE sector, although the positive impact of increase reforms is only a short-run phenomenon, as the later discussion of table 5 indicates. Because labor productivity is likely to be strongly correlated with profitability in the insurance industry, the estimated effect of decrease reforms is consistent with evidence that liability reforms adopted in the 1980s reduced insurers' losses and premiums and improved insurer profitability.[31]

The large, positive impact of increase reforms on productivity in the mining industry may be due to the fact that labor productivity is a poor measure of performance in industries heavily dependent on natural resources. A more detailed examination of trends in the mining industry shows that several states exhibited dramatic declines in labor productivity. During the sample period labor productivity in mining declined more than 40 percent in twenty states; no other industry in any state experienced the same or greater declines. Exhaustion of mineral lands is the likely cause of these declines. For example, Hawaii, an unambiguous decrease reform state, exhibited the greatest decline in mining labor productivity during the sample period—approximately 85 percent—and had 1992 book values of mineral land and rights per worker that were approximately one-quarter as large as the U.S. national average ($2,500, compared with a national average of $10,900).[32] More comprehensive analysis along these lines is limited by incomplete information on land and mineral values.[33]

The theoretical ambiguity of the impact of liability reforms on measured productivity in the health care and legal sectors is reflected in table 4. The estimated impacts on productivity trends of both decrease and increase reforms in the health care and legal services sectors are small in magnitude and statistically indistinguishable from zero. Our findings are thus consistent with the hypothesis that increase and decrease reforms may have opposing effects in these two sectors.

As noted earlier, liability reforms might have important dynamic

31. See, for example, Born and Viscusi (1994) and Blackmon and Zeckhauser (1991).
32. Bureau of the Census (1992).
33. In 1992, for example, data by state on the value of mineral land and rights are withheld for confidentiality reasons for eight states.

effects on productivity growth. Changes in laws may have different short-and long-run effects; it may take several years for reforms to reach their full effect. Indeed, if the relationship between liability reform and productivity were causal, one would expect reforms to have greater long-run than short-run effects, because of the time it would take for reforms to change firms' and individuals' behavior. Table 5 reports results from the "time-since-adoption" model specified in equation 2 to investigate this possibility. That equation estimates separately the impact of reforms on changes over time in productivity shortly after adoption (no more than two years after the effective date, generally no more than three years after enactment) and long after adoption (two or more years after the effective date, generally three or more years after enactment).

As table 5 shows, the estimates from the dynamic models have the same general pattern as those from the basic models, except that the effects of liability reforms are generally larger in the long run than in the short run. In the economy as a whole, decrease reforms lead to 1.1 percent greater productivity growth shortly after adoption (significant at the 10 percent level), but to 2.7 percent greater productivity growth long after adoption (significant at the 5 percent level), holding all else constant. Similarly, decrease reforms increase manufacturing productivity growth by 2.0 percent in the short run and by 4.6 percent in the long run. In addition, the counterintuitive statistically significant positive effect of increase reforms on productivity in the FIRE sector reported in table 4 disappears in the long run. Although growth in GSP per worker in FIRE is 2.4 percent higher in states that adopt increase reforms no more than two years after the reforms' effective date, this effect shrinks to 1.0 percent and becomes statistically insignificant two or more years after the reforms take effect.

We estimated several alternative models to explore further the relationship between liability reforms and productivity. We estimated the effect of reforms on the differential growth over time in productivity *growth rates* in those states that changed their liability laws, relative to the change in growth rates in those states whose liability law remained the same. That is, in equation 1, we substituted $\ln(P_{st}^j) - \ln(P_{st-1}^j)$ for $\ln(P_{st}^j)$. Although changes in liability law are associated with significant and permanent one-time effects on productivity growth, they are not

Table 5. Effects of Tort Reforms on Productivity by Industrial, Time-Since-Adoption Model, 1972–90

	With controls for political and interest-group characteristics				Average productivity (thousands of 1987 $ per worker)
	Liability-decreasing reforms		Liability-increasing reforms		
Industry	Shortly after adoption	Long after adoption	Shortly after adoption	Long after adoption	
Total private nonfarm	0.011* (0.006)	0.027** (0.008)	0.000 (0.008)	0.002 (0.008)	35.5 [8.9]
Mining	0.036 (0.058)	−0.169** (0.071)	0.093* (0.049)	0.046 (0.052)	73.3 [10.0]
Construction	−0.002 (0.011)	0.007 (0.011)	0.008 (0.008)	−0.002 (0.010)	33.2 [11.1]
Manufacturing	0.020** (0.011)	0.046** (0.010)	0.001 (0.007)	−0.020** (0.008)	37.6 [7.8]
Transportation, communications, utilities	−0.006 (0.011)	0.010 (0.011)	−0.032** (0.008)	−0.021** (0.008)	62.2 [14.7]
Wholesale trade	0.006 (0.005)	0.020** (0.006)	−0.015** (0.005)	−0.025** (0.006)	40.5 [6.9]
Retail trade	0.000 (0.006)	−0.003 (0.007)	−0.010 (0.006)	−0.024** (0.006)	19.2 [2.5]
Finance, insurance, real estate	0.029** (0.012)	0.040** (0.015)	0.024** (0.010)	0.010 (0.011)	76.1 [17.2]
Services net of hotels, amusement, health, legal	−0.002 (0.006)	0.013* (0.007)	0.002 (0.005)	−0.004 (0.005)	16.8 [3.4]
Hotels, lodging places	0.010 (0.012)	0.032** (0.013)	−0.004 (0.010)	−0.006 (0.011)	22.6 [5.6]
Amusement, recreation	0.009 (0.011)	−0.002 (0.014)	−0.047** (0.012)	−0.060** (0.012)	14.0 [4.4]
Health care	0.001 (0.005)	−0.009 (0.005)	−0.006 (0.005)	−0.011** (0.005)	28.8 [4.8]
Legal services	0.005 (0.007)	−0.009 (0.010)	−0.011 (0.008)	−0.004 (0.007)	49.8 [9.6]

Source: Authors' calculations. Heteroscedasticity-consistent standard errors are in parentheses. Standard deviations of average productivity are in brackets. Regression coefficients are percentage changes because the dependent variable in the model is ln(productivity). Standard errors of estimates calculated with White's (1980) method. N = 950 except for mining; services net of hotels, amusement, health, legal; and amusement, recreation, for which N = 948 due to missing data.
* = significant at the 0.10 level.
** = significant at the 0.05 level.

associated with systematic significant perpetual effects on the productivity growth rate.

We also estimated models that allowed the effect of reforms adopted during our sample period to vary in states that did and did not have pre-1972 reforms, and models that allowed the estimated effect of reforms to vary with the number of reforms adopted during the 1972–90 sample period. Results from these models provide no clear support for several hypotheses about the interaction effects between reforms. First, there is no support for the hypothesis that changes in the liability system, in and of themselves, affect productivity. For example, the effect on aggregate productivity of decrease reforms adopted during the sample period does not vary between states with and without pre-1972 increase reforms; the effect of increase reforms adopted during the sample period does not vary between states with and without pre-1972 decrease reforms. Second, there is at most weak support for the hypothesis that reforms have a cumulative or complementary effect. The magnitude of the effect of decrease reforms adopted during the sample period is significantly greater in states with pre-1972 decrease reforms, as is the magnitude of the effect of increase reforms adopted 1972–1990 in states with pre-1972 increase reforms). However, the estimated effects of neither decrease nor increase reforms adopted during the sample period varied significantly with the number of adopted decrease or increase reforms, respectively (one versus two or more).

Conclusion

We provide empirical evidence on the impact of liability reforms using a newly collected data set of state tort laws and other political and economic characteristics of states, matched with data by state by industry on productivity during the period 1970–90. We find that states that changed their liability laws during this period to decrease levels of liability experienced greater increases in productivity in aggregate and in most industries than states that did not. Conversely, states that changed their liability laws to increase levels of liability experienced smaller increases in productivity in several industries than did states that did not, although this result is not as robust to choice of specification.

In particular, states that adopted reforms to decrease levels of legal liability but none to increase liability showed substantially greater raw productivity growth during 1972–90 than other states. Much, but not all, of these differences in productivity growth across states is attributable to factors other than liability reform. Controlling for state fixed effects and for time-varying political and economic characteristics of states, and allowing different types of states to have different underlying time trends in productivity reduces substantially the magnitude of the estimated impact of changes in liability rules. After accounting for these factors, however, we find that states adopting liability-decreasing reforms show statistically significant increases in trends in aggregate productivity of approximately 1 to 2 percent. Evaluated at the mean value of states' labor productivity over the 1972–90 period, this finding suggests that decrease reforms lead to a $603 increase in GSP per worker per year in 1987 dollars, holding all else constant. In some industries, states adopting liability-increasing reforms show statistically significant decreases in trends in productivity of a similar magnitude.

The key issue in identifying the effect of liability reforms on productivity is the potential endogeneity of the reforms, that is, the correlation with reforms of unobserved determinants of productivity. Ideally, we would estimate the impact of reforms by IV methods. IV identification, however, requires an observable factor that would be correlated with the propensity to reform but not with productivity (except through its impact on the likelihood of reform), and there is no strong theoretical argument that any such factor exists. Instead, we estimate the impact of liability reforms on productivity, controlling for a wide range of time-varying and time-invariant characteristics of states, and we allow different types of states to have different underlying time trends in productivity.

We take two approaches to investigate whether our least-squares estimates represent a causal link between reforms and productivity, and both approaches suggest that our estimates are valid. First, we find that productivity growth is most responsive to liability reform in industries likely to be subject to the most common sources of commercial liability insurance claims and tort cases—auto accidents, unsafe premises, and defective products. Second, we find that the long-run effects of liability reform on productivity growth (two or more years after the reforms' effective date, generally three or more years after enactment) are greater than the short-run effects (no more than two years after the effective date, generally no more than three years after enactment).

These results are consistent with the hypothesis that marginal reductions in liability from a maximal level improve efficiency. Notwithstanding the issues of endogeneity discussed earlier, however, the results are also consistent with two other hypotheses. First, the results may be due to a "Delaware effect" in liability law, whereby capital migrates from high-liability to low-liability states. If the Delaware hypothesis is true, then the observed positive association between GSP per worker and liability reforms could be due to zero-sum flows of capital among states rather than to a more efficient use of resources. In this world, liability reforms affect the distribution of wealth but not true productive efficiency. Second, the results may not account for externalities created by reductions in the level of liability. Specifically, firms from states with relatively low levels of liability may have relatively low costs because they do not bear the true costs of production; this could cause a positive association between observed productivity and liability reform even if reform results in the inefficient deployment of resources into externality-intensive uses.

Our findings on the causes and effects of liability reforms indicate that further research into the forces that generate the empirical regularities outlined in this paper remains to be done. Additional research into models of the political processes by which liability reforms are adopted may illuminate the search for a valid instrument with which to estimate the impact of reforms on economic and social outcomes. Analysis of the choice and timing of state legislatures in enacting liability reform might also provide a vehicle with which to investigate theories of legislative politics. Finally, more extensive analysis of industry-specific microdata may be the best route to evaluate the extent to which the estimated impact of liability reform on productivity represents a true efficiency gain.

References

American Bar Foundation. 1971, 1985, 1991. *The Lawyer Statistical Report.* Chicago.

American Medical Association. 1970–90. *Physician Characteristics and Distribution in the U.S.* Chicago.

Beeson, Patricia E. 1987. "Total Factor Productivity Growth and Agglomeration Economics in Manufacturing, 1959–1973." *Journal of Regional Science* 27:183–99.

Beeson, Patricia. E., and Steven Husted. 1989. "Patterns and Determinants of Productive Efficiency in State Manufacturing." *Journal of Regional Science* 29 (February):15–28.

Blackmon, Glenn, and Richard Zeckhauser. 1991. "State Tort Reform Legislation: Assessing Our Control of Risks." In *Tort Law and Public Interest: Competition, Innovation, and Consumer Welfare,* edited by Peter H. Schuck. W. W. Norton.

Blanchard, Olivier Jean, and Lawrence F. Katz. 1992. "Regional Evolutions." *Brookings Papers on Economic Activity:* 1–61.

Born, Patricia H., and W. Kip Viscusi. 1994. "Insurance Market Responses to the 1980s Liability Reforms: An Analysis of Firm Level Data." *Journal of Risk and Insurance* 61 (June): 192–218.

Bureau of the Census, U.S. Department of Commerce. 1970–90. *Statistical Abstract.*

———. 1992. *Census of Mineral Industries: General Summary.*

Bureau of Economic Analysis, U.S. Department of Commerce. Various years. "Full-Time and Part-Time Employment by Industry." www.bea.doc.gov/bea/dr/spitbl-e.htm.

Calfee, John E., Clifford Winston, and W. Kip Viscusi. 1993. "The Consumer Welfare Effects of Liability for Pain and Suffering: An Exploratory Analysis." *Brookings Papers on Economic Activity: Microeconomics:*1: 133–16.

Carlino, Gerald A., and Richard Voith. 1992. "Accounting for Differences in Aggregate State Productivity." *Regional Science and Urban Economics* 22 (November): 597–617.

Cooter, Robert D., and Thomas S. Ulen. 1986. "An Economic Case For Comparative Negligence." *New York University Law Review* 61: 1067–1110.

Council of State Governments. 1970–90. *Book of the States.* Chicago.

Craswell, Richard, and Calfee, John E. 1986. "Deterrence and Uncertain Legal Standards." *Journal of Law, Economics, and Organization* 2: 279–303.

Dertouzos, James N., and Lynn A. Karoly. 1992. *Labor-Market Responses to Employer Liability.* R-3989-ICJ. RAND, Institute for Civil Justice, Santa Monica, Calif.

Graham, John D. 1991. "Product Liability and Motor Vehicle Safety." In Huber and Litan (1991), pp. 120–90.

Huber, Peter W. 1988. *Liability: The Legal Revolution and its Consequences.* Basic Books.

Huber, Peter W, and Robert E. Litan, eds. 1991. *The Liability Maze: The Impact of Liability Law on Safety and Innovation.* Brookings.

Insurance Services Office. 1988. "Claim File Data Analysis: Technical Analysis of Study Results." ISO Data, Inc., New York. December.

Jayaratne, Jith, and Philip E. Strahan. 1996. "The Finance-Growth Nexus: Evidence from Bank Branch Deregulation." *Quarterly Journal of Economics* 111 (August): 639–70.

Kessler, Daniel P. 1995. "Fault, Settlement, and Negligence Law." *RAND Journal of Economics* 26 (Summer): 296–313.

Kessler, Daniel P., and Mark McClellan. 1996. "Do Doctors Practice Defensive Medicine?" *Quarterly Journal of Economics* 111 (May): 353–90.

Litan, Robert E., and Clifford Winston, eds. 1988. *Liability: Perspectives and Policy.* Brookings.

Martin, Robert. 1991. "General Aviation Manufacturing: An Industry Under Siege." In Huber and Litan (1991), pp. 478–99.

Noll, Roger G. 1989. "Economic Perspective on the Politics of Regulation." In *Handbook of Industrial Organization,* edited by Richard Schmalensee and Robert D. Willig. Vol. 2, pp. 1253–82. Amsterdam: North-Holland.

Ostrom, Brian J., and Neal B. Kauder. 1994. "Examining the Work of State Courts, 1994: A National Perspective from the Court Statistics Project." National Center for State Courts, State Justice Institute, Williamsburg, Va.

Parker, Robert P. 1993. "Gross Product by Industry, 1977–90." *Survey of Current Business* 73 (May): 33–54.

Peterson, Mark A., Syam Sarma, and Michael G. Shanley. 1987. "Punitive Damages: Empirical Findings." R-3311-ICJ. RAND, The Institute for Civil Justice, Santa Monica, Calif.

Priest, George L. 1987. "The Current Insurance Crisis and Modern Tort Law." *Yale Law Journal* 96 (June): 1521–89.

———. 1991. "The Modern Expansion of Tort Liability." *Journal of Economic Perspectives* 5 (Summer): 31–50.

Tirole, Jean. 1988. *The Theory of Industrial Organization.* MIT Press.

Viscusi, W. Kip. 1990. "The Performance of Liability Insurance in States with Different Products-Liability Statutes." *Journal of Legal Studies* 19 (June): 809–36.

Viscusi, W. Kip, and Patricia H. Born. 1995. "The General-Liability Reform Experiments and the Distribution of Insurance-Market Outcomes." *Journal of Business and Economic Statistics* 13 (April): 183–88.

Viscusi, W. Kip, and Michael J. Moore. 1993. "Product Liability, Research and Development, and Innovation." *Journal of Political Economy* 101 (February): 161–84.

Viscusi, W. Kip, and others. 1993. "The Effect of 1980s Tort Reform Legislation on General Liability and Medical Malpractice Insurance." *Journal of Risk and Uncertainty* 6 (April): 165–86.

White, Halbert. 1980. "A Heteroskedasticity-Consistent Covariance Matrix Estimator and a Direct Test for Heteroskedasticity." *Econometrica* 48 (May): 817–38.

Winston, Clifford, and Robert W. Crandall. 1994. "Explaining Regulatory Policy." *Brookings Papers on Economic Activity: Microeconomics*: 1–31.

Comment

Comment by Alvin K. Klevorick: Debates about liability rules and their reform often begin by focusing on the prevention of accidents, the compensation of those who are injured in such accidents, and the costs of administering the legal system that decides who should pay and how much they should pay for such maloccurrences. Such discussions rather speedily broaden in scope, however, to the interesting and important general question of the effect of liability rules on overall economic welfare. In the context of law reform, the issue is framed in terms of the effect on welfare of changes in liability rules. As Campbell, Kessler, and Shepherd correctly argue, resolving these questions requires an empirical approach because the welfare implications of any particular liability law—and hence of any tort reform—can become ambiguous in a theoretical model that is even plausibly complex. The authors undertake just such an inquiry here.

Specifically, Campbell, Kessler, and Shepherd examine how a set of state-level liability reforms that were undertaken in the period 1972–90 affected labor productivity in different industries in each state and the total private nonfarm labor productivity in each state. They include as explanatory variables the adoption of liability reforms as well as political and economic characteristics of the states. The authors control for both time-invariant and time-varying characteristics of states, and then they estimate the effects of liability reforms by the difference *between* the change in labor productivity in states that changed their liability rules *and* the change in labor productivity in states that did not undertake such reforms.

Among the political characteristics for which they control are the strength of various interest groups (lawyers per capita, physicians per

139

capita), the importance of manufacturing exports, and the party characteristics of state politics—the party of the governor and the party in
control of the legislature. The economic or resource-base controls include variables for unemployment rates, commercial bank assets per
capita, higher education enrollment per capita, and highway mileage
per square mile of land. In addition, the authors include state fixed
effects and time fixed effects, and they allow separate time fixed effects
for those states that had adopted reforms strengthening or weakening
their liability rules before the sample period began, that is, before 1972,
for states making such changes within the sample period, and for Sun
Belt states.

The authors' first comparison is between productivity changes in
those states that during the sample period adopted liability-decreasing
reforms but not liability-enhancing ones, which they dub the "unambiguous decrease" states, and productivity changes in all other states.
They find that the unambiguous decrease states experienced greater
growth in productivity during the 1972–90 sample period. But they find
no clear pattern distinguishing the political and economic characteristics
of the unambiguous decrease states from the others.

Following this first rough-cut comparison, the authors go on to estimate their regression models with more attention to the timing of
reforms that strengthened or weakened the liability pressure on economic actors. They reach several major conclusions. First, states that
reduced the levels of legal liability experienced greater increases in
productivity, on the order of 1–2 percent over the sample period, than
states that did not make such reforms. The magnitude and statistical
significance of this result is robust to the inclusion of variables controlling for the political party and interest-group characteristics of the
states. Second, states that adopted reforms that *increased* liability pressure did not experience significantly less productivity growth over the
period than did other states, although this productivity reduction effect
did appear in several industries. The estimated effect of the liability-
increasing reforms in the latter industries was not robust, however, to
the inclusion of variables to control for political and interest-group
characteristics. Finally, the long-run effects of liability reform on productivity change—with the long run being two or more years after the
effective date of the reform—are larger than the short-run effects of
such reform (no more than two years after the effective date). But even

in the long run, liability-increasing reforms still display no significant effect on productivity at the level of total private nonfarm activity in a state.

The authors have made a useful contribution to our understanding of the effects of liability rules on labor productivity and, more generally, on social welfare. There are, however, limitations on what this particular study and, more generally, others of its genre can teach us about the welfare effects of tort law. Let me suggest the sources of these limitations and their implications.

The Performance Measure—Labor Productivity

First, in analyzing and assessing liability rules it is important to recognize, as the authors do, the numerous channels through which those rules affect welfare and the multiplicity of the tort system's effects. Liability rules have an impact beyond the number of accidents, the costs of those accidents, and the directly apparent costs of preventing those accidents. The multiplicity of the tort system's effects can be decomposed in any number of ways. For example, in the Huber and Litan volume, *The Liability Maze*, the authors and editors adopt the analytical dichotomy of separating the impact of liability rules into effects on safety and effects on innovation.[1] The latter encompasses both invention and the adoption of new technologies. In an alternative approach, Viscusi and Moore examine the trade-off between product safety and product novelty.[2] As a final example, when, in a 1996 paper, Kessler and McClellan answer affirmatively that doctors do in fact practice defensive medicine, they focus on whether malpractice liability engendered productive inefficiency before reforms took place.[3]

In the current paper, Campbell, Kessler, and Shepherd examine the effect of liability reforms on productivity, defined as gross state product (GSP) divided by total employment. This measure does not seem to be as ''orthogonal'' to safety as were the measures in the earlier studies just cited. Changes in the labor productivity measure appear to be an amalgam of the effects on safety or accident-cost reduction and the effects on the capacity of a firm, an industry, or an economy to deploy

1. Huber and Litan (1991).
2. Viscusi and Moore (1993).
3. Kessler and McClellan (1996).

its resources effectively. The authors hint at this mixture of effects when they observe, in one of their concluding remarks, that their

> results may not account for externalities created by reductions in the level of liability. Specifically, firms from states with relatively low levels of liability may have relatively low costs because they do not bear the true costs of production; this could cause a positive association between observed productivity and liability reform even if reform results in the inefficient deployment of resources into externality-intensive uses.

It is not apparent how much of the true costs of production are reflected in the GSP measure—recall that it is calculated as gross output (sales and receipts and other operating income, plus inventory change) *minus* intermediate inputs (consumption of goods and services purchased from other industries or imported). One factual accounting question is whether the GSP computation counts damage judgments as firm costs. I could not ascertain this from the paper itself or from the several issues of the *Survey of Current Business* discussing the measurement of GSP that I checked. A second, more substantive question about the interpretation of the GSP measure for the assessment of how liability rules affect social welfare is whether information is disseminated well enough and insurance premiums calculated precisely enough that the accident costs a firm engenders are fully reflected in the prices of its products and the costs of its insurance policies. And, of course, whether the impact of accident costs is felt by the firm and thereby included in the GSP measure will depend on the liability rule in effect.

The overall point is that it is difficult to know with confidence what aspects of the effects of liability rules a productivity measure based on GSP data is capturing. Under one scenario, *if all* of the true costs of production are being reflected to the firm, then the authors' concern about externalized costs is unwarranted. But then the GSP data are reflecting *all* the effects of liability and not just those beyond safety. The more likely case is that the GSP data reflect some, but not all, of the ''true costs of production.'' Then the GSP figure is a hybrid measure as it incorporates both safety and nonsafety ramifications of the choice of a liability rule and of reforms of that rule.

Even within the set of productivity measures, there is the further question about why one should focus on the authors' chosen measure—labor productivity. Campbell, Kessler, and Shepherd provide the straightforward response that data constraints precluded their using a more comprehensive performance measure such as total factor productivity. This is unfortunate because despite its pitfalls, some measure of total factor productivity does seem more appropriate if one is trying to assess the effect of liability rules or their reform on society's or an industry's ability to improve its capacity to make the most of its resource base. In particular, if a liability-reform-induced change in relative prices were to change the optimal factor proportions, and specifically the labor-capital mix, the resulting substitution between capital and labor would be reflected as a change in productivity—when measured, as here, by labor productivity—when in fact there has been no shift in the relevant isoquants. We would be detecting a certain amount of movement along the isoquant in capital-labor space and be labeling it, instead, as our having managed to shift the curve.

The authors themselves raise concerns about the insight the labor productivity measure can provide in three industries. First, they express concern that labor productivity is a poor measure of performance in industries, such as mining, that depend heavily on natural resources. They suggest that particular weakness of the labor-based measure as an explanation of the large, positive impact that liability-increasing reforms have on productivity in mining. A second area in which changes in measured labor productivity may provide inaccurate signals of liability reform effects, the authors observe, is health care. If liability reductions lead providers to engage in less defensive medicine—by employing fewer tests and procedures that are of minimal benefit to health—that will increase actual productivity. It may, however, reduce measured productivity because value-added in the health care sector is partially a function of the number of tests and procedures performed, regardless of some objective measure of their medical necessity and medical value. Finally, the authors are concerned about using the labor productivity measure in the legal services sector. They observe that liability reductions have an ambiguous effect on legal services. Liability-decreasing reforms may impose costs on lawyers if the number of lawsuits and the size of contingency-fee payments decline, and this would reduce GSP per worker in the sector. But such reforms may increase lawyers' measured productivity if all legal changes require lawyers' interpretation and implementation. As a result of these counterbalancing impacts, the effect of liability-decreasing reforms on lawyers' productivity is uncertain. Despite the authors' expressed concern, the resulting ambiguity does not seem to undercut application of the productivity measure itself to legal services. The problem with using labor productivity in the legal sector is quite different from that resulting from its use as a measure in health care—unless one believes that lawyers' interpretation and implementation services are unproductive!

The Liability Law Reforms

The second set of concerns that I have about the this study relates to the measurement of reforms of liability law. Campbell, Kessler, and Shepherd use data that they have compiled on states' adoption of eight types of legal reform. These include caps on damage awards, abolition of punitive damages, mandatory prejudgment interest, collateral source rule reform, caps on contingency fees, mandatory periodic payments of damages, reform of joint and several liability, and the introduction of comparative negligence. The authors divide these reforms into two categories, which they characterize as decrease reforms and increase reforms. The latter are hypothesized to increase liability by raising the expected size of trial judgments and settlement amounts, and they include the introduction of comparative negligence and the payment of mandatory prejudgment interest. The authors classify all the other tort-system changes as decrease reforms, which reduce the pressure of the legal system on potential defendants.

The authors develop their very useful data base by reviewing each state's statutes and published judicial decisions. Of central importance to them is *when* the liability reform was adopted. Indeed, they observe that "our estimated effect of reforms is identified solely by the timing of reforms in adopting states. . . ."

This importance of the timing of reforms for their study raises interesting questions in the context of judicially adopted reforms. How did the authors assign a time for the adoption of such reforms? What level of state court must reach the decision for it to be included? Does one decision constitute the reform? To be sure, there is ambiguity about the timing of a legislative reform and the assessment of when such a reform is truly effective, in part because this depends on how courts treat and interpret the statute. But there seems to be much more ambiguity about the timing of judicially introduced reforms. I would also expect that the diffusion of behavioral effects may differ for statutory and judicial reforms. This may have implications for (a) the lags on the time-varying economic factors that the authors consider and (b) the distinction between short-run and long-run effects of the reforms on which they focus. In assessing the possible effects that differences in the routes to reform may have for the analysis, it would be useful to know more about the source—legislative or judicial—of the reforms included in the data set.

The authors recognize that their dichotomous classification of reforms—into liability-decreasing and liability-increasing changes—may mask substantial variations in states' liability systems. Another complication, not explicitly discussed, is that the effect of a given reform on an industry depends on whether firms in that industry are plaintiffs or defendants in tort cases. Some firms may be in different positions in different cases—for example, a firm may regularly be a defendant in product liability actions deriving from the output it sells to consumers but also a plaintiff in actions relating to intermediate goods it purchases. The latter could include claims for economic loss that is parasitic on property damage or suits for pure economic loss if the jurisdiction takes an expansive view of such recovery, for example, for particularly foreseeable plaintiffs.

The authors do partially come to grips with differential effects of reforms on different lines of business when they examine most closely the insurance industry and the industries that are subject to the highest levels of liability. They focus on the enterprises in these industries because they are the ones that, arguably, will feel the greatest impact of reforms. In fact, however, except for manufacturing and wholesale trade, liability-decreasing reforms have an insignificant effect on these liability-prone industries. As table 4 reveals, the bigger impact on them is the deleterious productivity effect of liability-increasing reforms.

Although the authors' dichotomous classification of tort reforms necessarily glosses over differences in different states' systems, even the raw compilation of reform data presented in table 2 reflects an interesting pattern. With few exceptions, when a state had both decrease *and* increase reforms in the sample period, the liability-reducing change followed the increase reform. This seems an accurate characterization of the spirit of tort reform during the two decades covered by the study. For a richer picture of liability reform, however, it would be useful to know whether the same state had multiple increase or multiple decrease reforms in this sample period and the timing of such changes where they occurred. But table 2 does not show this; it reports only the earliest effective date of decrease and increase reforms that became effective in each state in the 1972–90 sample period.

Another bit of information about reforms that the table 2 chronology omits concerns the presample period. In their analysis, the authors are careful to allow states that undertook reforms, whether liability-increasing or liability-decreasing, before the sample period to have different 1972–90 time trends in productivity so that reforms are allowed to have a long-run impact on productivity growth. But it would be helpful to know for each state the date of the last pre-1972 reform of each type that the state adopted. The impact of such a reform may well depend on how long it was in effect, and the conjecture that the reform's age matters is especially plausible in light of the authors' results on the long-run versus short-run impacts of within-sample reforms.

The authors' carefully constructed database may enable them to shed light on one aspect of the more general debate about law's effects, namely, the impact of legal uncertainty. The uncertain application of the law is often cited as having a negative effect on the decisionmaking and performance of individual agents—for example, firms. The analogue at the systemic level in this paper might be the impact of uncertainty resulting from a sequence of reforms of liability law on an industry's or a state economy's performance. Is it possible that a sequence of reforms—any liability reforms, regardless of direction—could retard productivity growth? If firms choose different techniques in response to different liability rules, repeated changes in the rules may engender uncertainty about whether the switch in technique is worthwhile, they may make firms more tentative about R & D and long-term investments, and they may reduce learning by doing. At the close of their section on empirical results, the authors refer to alternative models they have estimated that provide "no support for the hypothesis that changes in the liability system, in and of themselves, affect productivity." That is an interesting finding, although before drawing definite conclusions, one would want to use their rich data set to develop and test the effect of other measures of reform uncertainty on productivity.

The Descriptive Statistics

The authors begin their presentation of the empirical results by comparing the productivity growth during the sample period of "the unambiguous decrease" states with productivity change in all other states during that period. The unambiguous decrease states show substantially greater raw productivity growth, on the order of 7.5 percent, during the sample period. The authors observe that much, but not all, of this difference in raw productivity growth across states is due to factors other than liability reforms, and they go on to their regression analysis to produce an estimate that controls for these other factors.

I find it curious, however, that when the authors discuss whether there are clear patterns in the economic and political characteristics of the unambiguous decrease states and the characteristics of the other states, they give little weight to the timing of reforms, which becomes— and rightfully so—crucial in their regression analysis. Specifically, in concluding that there is no clear pattern of differences between those states that undertook decrease, but not increase, reforms during the 1972–90 period and all the other states, the authors refer to the states' political and economic characteristics in 1972, in 1990, and the change between those years. When the relative levels of the particular characteristic in the two sets of states remained the same over the entire sample period, the authors' comparison is informative. But if the relative positions of the groups of states being compared changed within the sample period, their own theory suggests that the relevant comparison is between the levels of these characteristics at the time that the reform was introduced and not the values at the period's endpoints.

Interjurisdictional Competition

The authors observe that their empirical results are consistent both with the hypothesis that reductions in liability from its level at the beginning of the 1970s have improved efficiency and with a "Delaware effect" in liability law. This alternative hypothesis would suggest that capital migrates from high-liability to low-liability states. Under this alternative, the observed positive relation between state-level labor productivity and reforms that reduce liability pressure then could reflect zero-sum capital flows among the states, not a more efficient allocation of resources at the national level.

This alternative interpretation suggests that liability reform be viewed as one of the instruments of interjurisdictional competition that states can use in their race with each other—whether to the bottom, to the top, or to the middle. In comparing the effects of liability reform on state-level variables, then, one would want to take account of other measures that states and localities are using contemporaneously to attract mobile resources. Such information might help to disentangle the effect of liability reform itself as well as to shed light on the allocative versus distributional effects of such reforms.

The Importance of the Microeconomic Approach

The message with which Campbell, Kessler, and Shepherd conclude their paper bears emphasis. They call for ''more extensive analysis of industry-specific microdata'' as that ''may be the best route to evaluate the extent to which the estimated impact of liability reform on productivity represents a true efficiency gain.'' I fully concur. The aggregate analysis in the current piece is interesting and suggestive. But I believe that we will learn most about the panoply of effects that liability rules and, as a corollary, liability reforms have by focusing sharply on the effects in individual firms and industries. To my mind, we need more truly microeconomic studies like the excellent one that Kessler and McClellan produced earlier on the impact of liability laws on the practice of medicine.

Commentator's References

Huber, Peter W., and Robert E. Litan, eds. 1991. *The Liability Maze: The Impact of Liability Law on Safety and Innovation.* Brookings.

Kessler, Daniel P., and Mark McClellan. 1996. ''Do Doctors Practice Defensive Medicine?'' *Quarterly Journal of Economics* 111 (May): 353–90.

Viscusi, W. Kip, and Michael J. Moore. 1993. ''Product Liability, Research and Development, and Innovation.'' *Journal of Political Economy* 101 (February): 161–84.

PAUL A. GOMPERS
Harvard University
National Bureau of Economic Research

JOSH LERNER
Harvard University
National Bureau of Economic Research

What Drives Venture Capital Fundraising?

DURING THE PAST twenty years, commitments to the U.S. venture capital industry have grown dramatically. This growth has not been uniform: it has occurred in concentrated areas of the country, and peaks in fundraising have been followed by major retrenchments. Despite the importance of the venture capital sector in generating innovation and new jobs, few academic studies have explored the dramatic movements in venture fundraising.

In this paper we examine the forces that affected fundraising by independent venture capital organizations from 1972 through 1994. We study both industry fundraising patterns and the success of individual venture organizations. We find that regulatory changes affecting pension funds, capital gains tax rates, overall economic growth, and research and development expenditures, as well as firm-specific performance and reputation, affect fundraising. The results are potentially important for understanding and promoting venture capital investment.

Margaret Blair, Diane Denis, Martin Feldstein, Thomas Hellmann, James Poterba, Peter Reiss, Andrei Shleifer, and participants at the Harvard-MIT Public Finance seminar, the Brookings Panel on Economic Activity, the Conference on European Venture Capital at Università Bocconi, and the American Finance Association annual meeting provided helpful comments and suggestions. We would also like to thank Gabe Biller, Kay Hashimoto, and Qian Sun for excellent research assistance. Dan Feenberg provided us with state-level tax data. Chris Allen helped in collecting data. Support for this project was provided by the Advanced Technology Program and the Division of Research, Harvard Business School.

Various factors may affect the level of commitments to venture capital organizations. James Poterba has argued that many of the changes in fundraising could arise from changes in either the supply of or the demand for venture capital.[1] When we refer to the supply of venture capital, we mean the desire of investors to place money into venture capital funds. Demand is then the desire of entrepreneurs to attract venture capital investment in their firm. For example, decreases in capital gains tax rates might increase commitments to venture capital funds through increases in the desire of taxable investors to make new commitments to funds as well as through increases in the demand for venture capital investments when workers have greater incentives to become entrepreneurs. Our research methodology attempts to distinguish between supply and demand factors that affect the quantity of venture capital.

We find that demand-side factors appear to have had an important impact on commitments to venture capital funds. Capital gains tax rates have a significant effect at the industry, state, and firm levels. Decreases in the capital gains tax rates are associated with greater venture capital commitments. The effect, however, appears to occur through the demand for venture capital: rate changes affect both taxable and tax-exempt investors. Similarly, R&D expenditures, especially expenditures by industrial firms, are positively related to venture investments in particular states.

We also find that the Department of Labor's clarification of its "prudent man" rule, which enabled pension funds to freely invest in venture capital, and the performance and reputation of individual venture firms influence fundraising. Higher recent returns (as measured by the value of equity held in firms taken public) lead to greater capital commitments to new funds. Older and larger organizations also attract more capital. Finally, we examine factors that affect venture organizations' decisions to raise funds targeted at early-stage, start-up firms. These funds are potentially the most important for generating new companies and innovation. We find that smaller, West Coast venture organizations are more likely to have raised an early-stage venture fund.

1. Poterba (1989).

The Institution of Venture Capital

Many new firms require substantial capital.[2] A company's founder
may not have sufficient funds to finance company projects and might
therefore seek outside financing. Entrepreneurial firms that are characterized by significant intangible assets, expect years of negative earnings, and have uncertain prospects are unlikely to receive bank loans
or other debt financing. For many of these young companies, the tremendous uncertainty and asymmetric information may make venture
capital the only potential source of financing. Venture capital organizations finance these high-risk, potentially high-reward projects, purchasing equity stakes while the firms are still privately held. Venture
capitalists have backed many high-technology companies including Ap-
ple Computer, Cisco Systems, Genentech, Intel, Microsoft, Netscape,
and Sun Microsystems. A substantial number of successful service firms
(including Federal Express, Staples, Starbucks, and TCBY) have also
received venture financing.

Venture capitalists are often active investors, monitoring the progress of firms, sitting on boards of directors, and meting out financing
based on the attainment of milestones. Whereas banks monitor the
financial health of firms that they lend to, venture capitalists monitor
strategy and investment decisions and take an active role in advising
firms. Venture capitalists often retain important rights that allow them
to intervene in the company's operations when necessary. In addition,
these capitalists provide entrepreneurs with access to consultants, investment bankers, and lawyers. Alon Brav and Paul Gompers have
shown that venture capital backing adds value even after the initial
public offering: the returns of venture-backed companies are substantially better than those without venture capital in the five years after
going public.[3]

The first modern venture capital firm, American Research and Development (ARD), was formed in 1946 by MIT President Karl Comp-
ton, Harvard Business School Professor Georges F. Doriot, and local
business leaders. A small group of venture capitalists made high-risk

2. Much of this discussion is based on Gompers and Lerner (1996).
3. Brav and Gompers (1997).

investments in emerging companies that were based on technology developed for World War II. The success of the investments ranged widely: almost half of ARD's profits during its twenty-six-year existence as an independent entity came from its $70,000 investment in Digital Equipment Company in 1957, which grew in value to $355 million. Because institutional investors were reluctant to invest, ARD was structured as a publicly traded, closed-end fund and marketed mostly to individuals.[4] The few other venture organizations begun in the decade after ARD's formation were also structured as closed-end funds.

The first venture capital limited partnership, Draper, Gaither, and Anderson, was formed in 1958. Imitators soon followed, but limited partnerships accounted for a minority of the venture pool during the 1960s and 1970s. Most organizations raised money either through closed-end funds or small business investment companies (SBICs), federally guaranteed risk-capital pools that proliferated during the 1960s. Although the market for SBICs in the late 1960s and early 1970s was strong, the incentives to take greater risks than government guarantees created ultimately led to the collapse of the sector. The annual flow of money into venture capital during its first three decades never exceeded a few hundred million dollars and usually was much less.

One change in the venture capital industry during the past twenty years has been the rise of the limited partnership as the dominant organizational form. Limited partnerships also have an important advantage that makes them attractive to tax-exempt institutional investors: capital gains taxes are not paid by the limited partnership. Instead taxes are paid only by the (taxable) investors. Venture partnerships have predetermined, finite lifetimes (usually ten years, although extensions are often allowed). Investors in the fund are limited partners. To maintain limited liability, investors must not become involved in the day-to-day management of the fund.

The Economics of Venture Capital

The predominance of limited partnerships in the venture capital industry—the typical venture organization raises a fund every few

4. Liles (1977).

Figure 1. Supply and Demand in Venture Capital

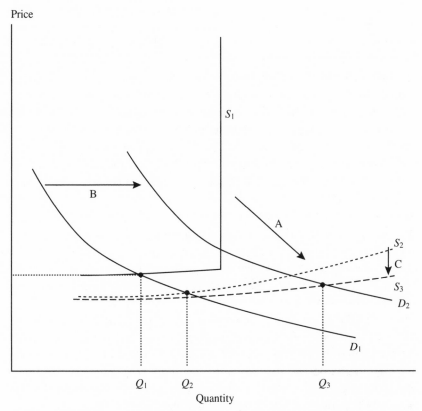

Source: Authors' construction. Equilibrium before the clarification of ERISA is represented by Q_1. After ERISA, the supply curve shifts from S_1 down to S_2 (A) and the new equilibrium quantity of venture capital is Q_2. Capital gains tax reductions move both demand to D_2 (B) and supply to S_3 (C) and the equilibrium quantity of venture capital moves to Q_3.

years—makes it easier to track venture fundraising. We can therefore examine marketwide and firm-specific influences on fundraising.

Supply and Demand in Venture Capital

In this section we develop predictions about what factors might influence the quantity of venture capital in an economy. To understand the mechanism through which these factors work, it is important to discuss supply and demand in the venture capital market. Figure 1 presents a simple illustration of equilibrium in the venture capital market. The supply of venture capital is determined by the willingness of investors to provide funds to venture firms. The willingness of investors to commit money depends on the expected rate of return on venture investments. Therefore, in the venture capital market, price is the expected rate of return on new venture capital investments. Higher expected returns lead to a greater desire of investors to supply venture capital—that is, like most supply schedules, this one slopes upward.

The demand schedule is simply the number of entrepreneurial firms seeking venture capital that can supply a particular expected rate of return. As the price increases, that is, as the expected return increases, fewer entrepreneurial firms demand capital because the number of projects meeting that threshold declines. The demand schedule therefore slopes downward.

We discuss the equilibria in the supply and demand framework by examining the quantity of venture capital. Although any supply and demand equilibrium also implies a particular price (an expected rate of return), we cannot measure the anticipated rate of return in the venture capital market. Nor does the actual rate of return provide a useful proxy. Returns from venture capital investments can only be observed many years after the original investments because private firms are valued at cost until they are sold or taken public many years later. Because of these accounting policies, the stated returns for venture funds are exceedingly variable and somewhat misleading.[5] We feel fairly comfortable that the expected rate of return, or price, does not vary much across the sample period. As we discuss later, however, supply curves for venture capital are likely to be very elastic. Thus changes in equilibrium will have a significantly larger effect on quantities than on prices.

The supply schedule for venture capital is likely to be flat. Investors choose to place money in financial assets because of their monetary returns. Because close substitutes for these cash flows exist, either through a single security or combination of securities, investors have a particular expected return on venture capital that just compensates for

5. See the discussion in Gompers and Lerner (1997). In addition, practices of reporting valuations of companies are often very different from one venture organization to another. Finally, information on fund returns is closely guarded, and even the intermediaries who specialize in compiling the data do not have very comprehensive coverage.

the systematic riskiness of the investments.[6] If perfect substitutes for venture capital existed, the supply curve should be totally flat. We draw supply curves as sloping slightly upward in figure 1. One source of an upward slope would be differential taxes. Because the return on venture capital investments is taxable, investors with higher tax rates would require progressively higher expected rates of return to induce them to invest in venture funds versus some tax-free investment.

The Employment Retirement Income Security Act and Venture Commitments

One policy decision that potentially had an effect on commitments to venture funds through supply changes was the Department of Labor's clarification of the "prudent man" rule in the Employment Retirement Income Security Act (ERISA). Through 1978 the rule stated that pension managers had to invest with the care of a prudent man. Consequently, many pension funds avoided investing in venture capital entirely: it was believed that a fund's investment in a start-up company could be viewed as imprudent. In early 1979 the Department of Labor ruled that portfolio diversification was a consideration in determining the prudence of an individual investment. Thus the ruling implied that allocating a small part of a portfolio to venture capital funds would not be seen as imprudent. The clarification opened the door for pension funds to invest in venture capital.

We conjecture that the supply curve for venture capital before the clarification of ERISA might have looked like S_1 in figure 1. The upward inelastic segment of S_1 results because pension funds, which control substantial amounts of capital, were unable to invest in venture funds. The supply of venture capital may have been limited at any expected rate of return. If the initial demand for venture capital is represented by D_1, the equilibrium quantity of venture capital would be given by Q_1.

After ERISA, the supply curve moved to S_2. The supply curve moved down and flattened out because pension funds, which are tax exempt, required a lower expected rate of return on venture investments than did taxable investors. The curve would not have an inelastic segment

6. Scholes (1972).

because the resources of pension funds could now be invested in venture capital funds. When we looked at the data, we expected that the quantity of venture capital supplied would increase to Q_2 after ERISA was clarified. This effect should be significant only for contributions by pension funds because ERISA regulations have no bearing on other types of investors.

Capital Gains Taxes and Venture Capital Fundraising

The effect of capital gains tax rates on commitments to the venture capital industry has been debated in academic studies as well as political circles. The effect of reductions in the capital gains tax rate on commitments was one of the intended benefits of the 1994 reduction of the tax from 28 percent to 14 percent on investments in small companies held for five years.

Poterba argued that it was unlikely that capital gains taxes affected venture capital by shifting the supply curve.[7] The supply effect of capital gains tax reductions is illustrated by C in figure 1. A reduction in the capital gains tax rate would lower the required expected (pretax) rate of return on venture investments for taxable investors. This would cause the right-hand side of supply curve S_2 to shift down to S_3. Most investors in venture capital after 1980 have been tax-exempt institutions, and the supply effect may therefore have been small.

Poterba then developed a model of the decision to become an entrepreneur. He argues that the capital gains tax rate could have a dramatic effect on this choice. Lower capital gains tax rates make it relatively more attractive for a manager or worker to start his or her own company. Most of a manager's compensation comes in the form of salary and cash bonuses that are taxed at the ordinary income tax rate. Most of the compensation from being an entrepreneur is in the form of capital appreciation on the equity of the company. Poterba argues that it is possible that reductions in the capital gains tax rates could have a first-order effect on the demand for venture capital as more people are induced to become entrepreneurs and better projects are brought to market. This outcome would increase the quantity of venture capital

7. Poterba (1989).

demanded to D_2 and increase the equilibrium quantity of venture capital to Q_3.[8]

If the capital gains tax rate has an important impact on commitments to venture capital funds, we would expect a significant relation at the industry level and at the level of specific funds. Lower capital gains taxes should lead to increases in commitments to the industry as a whole as well as to individual funds. We can also shed light on whether Poterba's argument about supply and demand effects is valid. If capital gains taxes affect commitments to venture capital primarily through the demand for venture capital, we would expect that reductions in the capital gains tax rate would increase the commitments of both tax-exempt and tax-sensitive investors. If the effect is primarily due to supply changes, contributions by tax-exempt investors should be unrelated to the capital gains tax rate. Because we can separate contributions to venture funds by investor type, we should be able to determine whether the demand effects (B in figure 1) or supply effects (C) of decreases in the capital gains tax rate are more important.

Other Macroeconomic Factors and Venture Fundraising

Venture capital fundraising is potentially affected by other macroeconomic factors. Both the expected return on alternative investments and the general health of the economy could affect commitments to venture capital funds. If the economy is growing quickly, there may be more attractive opportunities for entrepreneurs to start new firms and thus increases in the demand for venture capitalists. Formally, the demand curve would shift to the right. The greater investment opportunity might be associated with greater commitments to the venture capital industry. Growth in gross domestic product (GDP), increased returns in the stock market, and greater R&D expenditures would all be potential proxies for demand conditions.

---

8. Anand (1993) examines investments by venture capital firms in private communications companies and finds that the level and composition of investment appears to be affected negatively by increases in the capital gains tax rate. The author's ability to draw conclusions, however, is limited because he looks only at one industry. Investments in one industry may be affected by many other factors, including technology shifts, tastes, or other investment opportunities. Examining the impact of capital gains tax rates on the quantity of venture capital raised appears to be a much more satisfactory way to address the issue.

Interest rates could also affect the supply of venture capital. Bonds are an alternative investment to venture capital. If interest rates rise, the attractiveness of investing in venture capital funds may deteriorate. This would decrease the willingness of investors to supply venture capital at all prices (that is, at all expected return levels).

Firm Performance and Fundraising

In addition to the marketwide factors already discussed, we look for firm-specific characteristics that may influence venture capital fundraising. First, a substantial body of research examines the relation between past performance and investment. Allocations by investors across asset classes seem to be driven, in part, by the relative performance of various sectors in the recent past. If there is short-run momentum in returns, as Grinblatt, Titman, and Wermers show, this response may be rational.[9]

The flow of money into and out of various types of financial institutions in response to performance has been documented extensively for mutual funds. Although the early research on mutual funds indicated that fund managers as a group do not significantly outperform the market, recent work has shown that cash flows appear to respond to past performance.[10] Sirri and Tufano find that performance relative to peers in the same investment category is an important determinant of new capital commitments to mutual funds.[11] They examine 690 equity mutual funds and rank them by their performance relative to funds that have the same investment focus. They find that the top performing funds in any particular investment style receive substantial new commitments in the subsequent year. The relation between performance and commitments, however, is not linear. Funds that perform poorly do not appear to be penalized in the following year: money does not leave them. Sirri and Tufano note that one exception is new funds. Money does seem to leave them if they are poor performers.

Chevalier and Ellison have examined how these patterns affect investment incentive functions.[12] They found that funds that have under-

---

9. Grinblatt, Titman, and Wermers (1995).
10. For the earlier research, see Jensen (1968) and Ippolito (1989).
11. Sirri and Tufano (1998).
12. Chevalier and Ellison (1997).

performed their peers in the first part of a year have an incentive to increase the riskiness of their portfolios to enhance the chances that they will end up near the top of the performance charts. If they bet wrong and fail, they will lose few of their current investors.

If the evidence from mutual funds has implications for venture capital, we would expect that recent performance would be positively related to commitments to new funds. As in Sirri and Tufano's mutual fund results, the reputation of the venture organization may influence the flow of new commitments when it raises a new fund.[13] Several measures of reputation may be important. These include the age of the venture organization and the amount of capital under management. Older and larger venture organizations are likely to have more established reputations. They may therefore receive larger capital commitments than similar younger funds.

Venture Industrywide Results

We examine the implications of performance and capital gains tax rates for commitments to venture capital funds by performing two layers of analysis. The first examines the flow of venture capital commitments into the industry. We examine the commitments to new venture capital funds from 1969 through 1994, first aggregating all commitments in the United States. We then take up an analysis of the level of venture activity state by state.

Aggregate Fundraising Results

Data on annual commitments to U.S. venture capital funds come from the consulting firm Venture Economics, which has tracked venture fundraising since the 1960s. Its database not only records venture capital organizations, but also the names of their individual funds. We have checked the entries in the database against the historical information reported in more than 400 venture offering memorandums and partnership agreements, as well as against the fund profiles in the *Venture Capital Journal* and *Private Equity Analyst*.[14] This database is also

13. Sirri and Tufano (1998).
14. The construction and verification of the database are described in Gompers and Lerner (1998).

used in the analysis of information on individual organizations' fund-raising in the section on individual results.

This database includes more than 2,000 venture capital funds, SBICs, and related organizations. It is used to prepare directories such as the Venture Economics annual *Venture Capital Performance*, which is compiled from information provided by venture capitalists and institutional investors. In examining fundraising behavior, we look only at venture capital limited partnerships. First, these partnerships are the dominant organizational form in the industry, accounting for 80 percent of commitments in recent years. Furthermore, the actual size of SBICs and corporate venture affiliates is often very difficult to estimate. SBICs have access to matching government funds, often several times greater than the amount contributed by private investors. Corporate programs usually do not have a pool of capital specified in advance and are frequently disbanded before investing much capital. Limited partnerships with their well-defined size and life span offer the cleanest estimate of venture capital inflows.

We totaled commitments to venture funds each year. Commitments are defined as the pledges that venture capitalists receive for investment over the lifetime of the fund. They are not the amount of money actually invested in a given year. Typically, venture funds draw on and invest the committed capital over a two- or three-year period. For example, in 1995 Sierra Ventures raised their fifth fund with aggregate commitments of $100 million. This $100 million would be invested between 1995 and about 1999, but we classified the entire $100 million as having been committed in 1995.

We also needed some measure of returns. Ideally, we would have year-by-year performance data for individual funds, but these data present some problems. As discussed earlier, calculation of returns is hampered by policies of many venture organizations that potentially delay the write-up or write-down of assets. As a proxy for performance of the venture organizations, we used a measure of the market value of equity held by venture capitalists in firms that went public in a particular year. This measure is highly correlated with returns on venture funds. Most money in venture capital is earned on firms that eventually go public. Ignoring those that do not go public is reasonable because their impact on returns is usually small. A 1988 Venture Economics study found that a $1.00 investment in a firm that goes public provides an average cash return of $1.95 in excess of the initial investment with an average holding period of 4.2 years.[15] The next best alternative, an investment in an acquired firm, yields a cash return of only 40 cents over a 3.7 year mean holding period. Using the initial public offering (IPO) measure also makes sense because marketing documents for venture capital funds often highlight the successful public companies that have been backed by a venture organization. We therefore expected that the amount of venture capital raised would be a positive function of the value of firms taken public by venture capitalists in the previous year.

We identified potential venture-backed IPOs using three sources. The first is the listings of venture-backed IPOs published in *Venture Capital Journal*.[16] We also used listings of the securities distributions by venture funds. Venture capitalists typically unwind their successful investments by distributing the shares to their limited partners. They avoid selling the shares themselves and distributing the proceeds to their limited partners because their investors include both tax-exempt and taxpaying parties. To sell the shares would generate an immediate tax liability, which some of the limited partners may wish to avoid. We obtained lists of the distributions received by a pension fund that is among the largest venture investors and by three investment managers.[17] (These investment managers allocate funds from numerous pension funds into venture capital and other asset classes.) The investors had received distributions from 135 venture funds, most of which are managed by the oldest and most established venture organizations in the industry. Most of the successful investments by these funds can be identified from these lists.

The final sources used to identify IPOs for the sample were the offering documents issued by venture capitalists to raise new funds. Venture organizations often list in these offering memorandums their past investments that either went public or were acquired on favorable terms. We examined more than 400 of these memorandums in the files of Venture Economics.[18] We identified any investments listed as having

15. Venture Economics (1988).
16. This is the same source used by Barry and others (1990) and Megginson and Weiss (1991).
17. Gompers and Lerner (1999).
18. Gompers and Lerner (1998).

gone public. Most of the offering documents are from young venture organizations because Venture Economics' Fund Raiser Advisory Service counsels less experienced firms on strategies for raising capital.

We included in the IPO sample all firms for which a venture investor was listed in the "Management" and "Principal and Selling Shareholders" sections of the IPO prospectus and was also listed in the Venture Economics database. In many cases, it was not immediately obvious whether a venture investor or director was an exact match with a venture organization listed in the database.[19] To address these ambiguities, we consulted the edition of Venture Economics' *Pratt's Guide to Venture Capital Sources* published in the year of the IPO. We compared the addresses and key personnel of each of these ambiguous venture organizations with the information reported in the prospectus. If we were not virtually certain that a venture organization in the prospectus and the database were the same, we did not code it as a match. For each investor, we coded the venture organization, the particular venture fund investing in the firm, and the size of the stake before and after the offering. This process led to the identification of 885 IPOs in which a venture capitalist served as a director or a venture capital fund was a blockholder.

In each year we calculated the market value of the equity stakes in firms going public held by each venture capital organization. This value is the number of shares held by the venture organization multiplied by the IPO offering price. We then summed the market values for each IPO in a given year to obtain an annual performance number for each venture capital organization. We then summed across all venture organizations in a given year to get a measure of venture industry performance.

Figure 2 shows venture capital commitments and the market value of all firms brought public by venture capitalists in each year from 1969 through 1994. From 1969 through 1979 commitments to venture capital and venture-backed IPOs were low. Starting in 1980 commitments to the industry and the value of firms brought public increased. The rise of both reversed in 1984. After 1983 it appears that the shift in venture-

19. In many cases, individual investors (often called "angels") will describe themselves as venture capitalists. Groups of individual investors often make their investments through partnerships, which frequently are given a name not unlike those of venture capital organizations.

Figure 2. Venture Capital Commitments and Market Value of Venture Capital-Backed IPOs, 1969–94

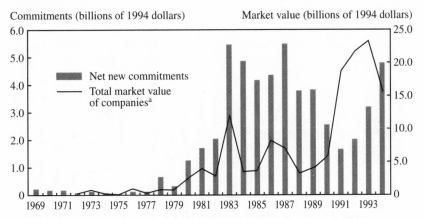

Sources: See text.

a. Annual market value of all venture capital-backed firms issuing equity in an initial public offering

backed IPO market led to changes in commitments to new venture funds. For example, increases in the market value of venture-backed IPOs in both 1986 and 1991–92 preceded resurgences in the venture capital market.

The relation between capital gains taxes and venture capital commitments is shown in figure 3. In the 1970s high capital gains tax rates were associated with low levels of venture capital fundraising. Increases in the capital gains tax rates in 1988 were followed by reductions in venture capital commitments, while the reduction of capital gains for long-held investments in 1994 was followed by a rise in venture fundraising. This negative relation is clearly only suggestive because the influence of various factors needs to be examined.

Detailed information on commitments is shown in table 1. The volatility of commitments is readily apparent. The level of fundraising (expressed in millions of 1994 dollars) can vary dramatically from one year to the next. The volatility in venture fundraising is mirrored by a similar volatility in the IPO market, both for venture-backed companies and for the entire IPO market. There is a dramatic shift from individuals to pension funds after 1978 as the primary capital source for new venture funds.

Figure 3. Net New Commitments to the Venture Capital Industry and Capital Gains Tax Rates, 1972–94

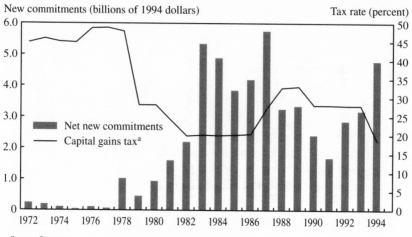

New commitments (billions of 1994 dollars)   Tax rate (percent)

Net new commitments

Capital gains tax[a]

Sources: See text.
a. Highest marginal capital gains tax rate effective in that year.

To assess the impact of each of these variables controlling for the others, we ran multivariate regressions, which are presented in table 2. Our approach here and in the individual firm regressions is to estimate reduced-form specifications and identify those factors that potentially work through demand shifts and those that work through supply shifts. The time series runs from 1972 through 1994. The dependent variable is the natural logarithm of real commitments to the venture capital industry (in millions of 1994 dollars). We present regressions for commitments to the entire venture capital industry, as well as for four subgroups: taxable investors, tax-exempt investors, individuals, and pension funds. The independent variables include the natural logarithm of the market value of firms brought public by venture organizations in the previous year (in millions of 1994 dollars), the real return on Treasury bills in the previous year, the real value-weighted stock market return in the prior year as reported by the Center for Research in Security Prices (CRSP), the previous year's real GDP growth, a dummy variable that equals one for years after 1978 when ERISA's prudent man rule was clarified, and the top marginal capital gains tax rate.

Changes in ERISA's prudent man rule are associated with greater commitments to the venture capital industry, but the effect is not sig-

Table 1. Venture Capital Industry Summary Statistics, 1978–94

Millions of 1994 dollars unless otherwise specified

	1978	1979	1980	1981	1982	1983	1984	1985	1986	1987	1988	1989	1990	1991	1992	1993	1994
Net new commitments to independent venture capital partnerships	427	483	1,245	1,712	2,089	5,453	4,839	4,191	4,427	5,378	3,718	3,458	2,507	1,529	2,011	2,545	4,766
Source of venture contributions (percent)																	
Corporations	10	17	19	17	12	12	14	12	11	10	12	20	7	5	3	8	9
Individuals	32	23	16	23	21	21	15	13	12	12	8	6	11	12	11	7	12
Pensions funds	15	31	30	23	33	31	34	33	50	39	47	36	53	42	42	59	47
Foreign	18	15	8	10	13	16	18	23	11	14	13	13	7	12	11	4	2
Endowments	9	10	14	12	7	8	6	8	6	10	11	12	13	24	18	11	21
Insurance companies	16	4	13	15	14	12	13	11	10	15	9	13	9	5	15	11	9
Venture capital-backed initial public offerings																	
Number of companies	6	4	27	68	27	121	53	46	97	81	35	39	42	122	157	165	136
Total amount raised	231	95	563	946	661	3,605	863	979	2,546	2,156	851	1,068	1,158	4,031	4,702	4,923	3,351
Total market value of companies	501	335	3,519	4,436	2,860	16,694	4,059	3,805	10,136	8,078	3,516	4,183	5,536	19,269	22,476	23,531	16,018
All IPOs																	
Number of companies	42	103	95	227	100	504	213	195	417	259	96	254	213	403	605	819	646
Total amount raised	835	1,189	1,460	3,346	1,461	11,395	2,956	3,698	10,204	6,118	2,694	14,699	10,481	26,001	41,057	58,248	33,841
Total market value of companies	2,320	4,334	7,662	13,423	6,585	48,140	12,534	13,570	37,998	27,908	13,242	46,445	28,841	72,668	104,775	. . .	. . .

Sources: Authors' analysis of Venture Economics' database; Brav and Gompers (1997); and various issues of the *Venture Capital Journal*.

Table 2. **Regressions for Industrywide Fundraising**

t-statistics in parentheses

Independent variable	Dependent variable: Natural logarithm of commitments (in millions of 1994 dollars)				
	Total	Taxable	Tax-exempt	Individuals	Pensions
Natural logarithm of value of all venture capital-backed IPOs in previous year (millions of 1994 dollars)	−0.0124 (−0.06)	−0.0300 (−0.11)	−0.2453 (−1.71)	0.0046 (0.17)	−0.3037 (−1.92)
Previous year's real GDP growth	13.28 (2.01)	16.08 (2.34)	14.48 (3.92)	14.92 (2.10)	12.38 (3.05)
Previous year's T-bill return	0.0022 (0.04)	0.0436 (0.64)	−0.1212 (−3.28)	0.0417 (0.59)	−0.1556 (−3.83)
Previous year's return of CRSP value-weighted index	0.3836 (0.48)	−0.2240 (−0.22)	0.1648 (0.30)	−0.3920 (−0.36)	−0.1092 (−0.18)
Was ERISA's prudent man rule clarified?	2.172 (3.05)	0.8598 (1.25)	2.183 (5.92)	0.6299 (0.89)	2.454 (6.05)
Capital gains tax rate	−3.835 (−1.66)	−2.068 (0.96)	−1.803 (−1.65)	−2.498 (−1.52)	−2.726 (−2.14)
Constant	6.551 (3.01)	5.3195 (1.95)	8.579 (5.85)	5.307 (1.88)	8.918 (5.53)
Summary statistics					
Adjusted R^2	0.824	0.303	0.874	0.250	0.884
p value of *F*-statistic	0.000	0.000	0.000	0.000	0.000
N	22	17	17	17	17

Sources: Authors' calculations. See text for full explanation of variables and methodology.

nificant for commitments by taxable investors and individuals. As expected, the strongest effect of ERISA's clarification is on contributions by pension funds. We conducted an *F*-test of the null hypothesis that the coefficient for pension funds does not differ from the coefficient for individuals and taxable investors and found that ERISA's effect on contributions by pension funds is different at the 5 percent confidence level. This result is consistent with a supply-side effect: the easing of pension fund restrictions increased the number of investors wishing to invest in venture capital funds.

Increases in capital gains tax rates consistently depress contributions to the venture industry, although the effect is only significant for contributions to the entire industry and contributions by pension funds.[20]

20. The coefficients on capital gains tax rates are not significantly different from one another across different investor classes. The purpose of the comparison is simply

Although we do find an effect of capital gains taxes on venture capital commitments, it does not appear to be working through the supply side. If changes in the capital gains tax rates had a first-order effect on investors' willingness to invest in venture capital, the effect would be strongest for individuals and taxable parties. The opposite is true. As Poterba suggests, the effect of changes in the capital gains tax rate is likely to come through changes in the demand for venture capital.[21] More and better-quality managers become entrepreneurs when the capital gains tax rate declines and the demand for venture capital increases. This increase in demand leads to a greater quantity of venture capital being supplied in equilibrium.

Once other factors are included, the value of firms taken public by venture organizations in the previous year does not appear to have a dramatic effect on contributions. Although we cannot rule out a role for IPOs in creating liquidity in the venture sector and potentially affecting contributions, we cannot find an effect in the multivariate regressions. This finding is contrary to the arguments of Black and Gilson, who emphasize the importance of a vibrant public market in the development of a venture capital industry.[22] It is consistent, however, with the experience of Israel and Singapore, where venture industries have experienced dramatic growth without having strong domestic public equity markets.

Of the macroeconomic variables, only real GDP growth is important. Increases in the real rate of growth lead to greater commitments to venture funds. Once again, this suggests that increasing demand for venture capital is an important determinant of the quantity. Robust economic growth creates new opportunities for entrepreneurs and increases demand for such capital.

One concern may be that because we are using time series observations on venture fundraising and the independent variables, the results may be affected by serial correlation in the error terms. The Durbin-Watson statistics for each of the regressions were between 1.88 and 2.00, indicating that serial correlation does not affect the results. As a

---

to show whether capital gains tax rates affect taxable investors only (as the supply effect would predict) or whether they affect all investors equally (as the demand effect would predict).

21. Poterba (1989).
22. Black and Gilson (1998).

diagnostic, we also ran Cochrane-Orcutt regressions using a lag term, which did not materially change the results.

State-Level Venture Activity

One difficulty with the analysis in the previous section was the relatively small number of observations. To gain additional power for our tests of marketwide venture activity, we examined venture capital activity in each of the fifty states and the District of Columbia from 1976 through 1994. We could then examine how state-level demand and supply factors affect venture investing in those states.

We employed a slightly different approach here than we used with the aggregate and firm-level data. Rather than examine the formation of venture funds in each state, we measured the actual venture capital investments. This reflects the difficulty of assigning venture organizations to particular states. Many organizations have multiple offices, which may account for differing shares of the investments. Venture organizations' headquarters may reflect the need to be proximate to their sources of capital and not their portfolio firms. For instance, many venture organizations are based in New York City, even though the city has historically been the site of few start-up firms. This pattern is particularly true for groups specializing in the later-stage investments, which typically occur after other groups (which may be geographically closer to the portfolio firm) have already joined the board.[23]

We once again used Venture Economics data to determine venture capital activity by state. In this case, we undertook a special tabulation of the number of companies financed and the dollar volume of financing in each state and year between 1976 and 1994. We included all investments by private equity groups in young entrepreneurial firms, but excluded investments in leveraged buyouts and restructurings by groups that primarily make venture capital investments.

We also collected a variety of additional data by state. Gross state product has been compiled on an annual basis by the U.S. Department of Commerce's Bureau of Economic Analysis.[24] For each state, we compiled the total amount of research performed in industry and academia, regardless of funding source. The state industrial R&D data

23. Lerner (1995).
24. Bureau of Economic Analysis (1997); and Friedenberg and Beemiller (1997).

were compiled by the National Science Foundation (NSF) as part of the Survey of Research and Development in Industry.[25] The data posed two problems. First, since 1978 this information has been collected only on a biannual basis. Thus, it was necessary to impute the missing years. Second, certain states are persistently missing. In these instances, the unassigned R&D in each region was assigned to each suppressed state on the basis of its gross state product.[26] The allocation of academic R&D expenditures by state was determined by the NSF's annual Survey of Research and Development Expenditures at Universities and Colleges.[27] We obtained the marginal state tax rate on capital gains through the use of the TAXSIM tax simulation program. We computed the impact of $1,000 of capital gains on a wealthy individual in each state and year, controlling for the possible deductibility of state taxes in federal taxes.[28]

Table 3 shows venture capital activity in each state by counting the number of companies that received venture capital and the total amount of venture capital invested from 1976 through 1994. The tremendous concentration of investment in four states is clearly evident. California has by far the most activity with nearly $20 billion invested (in 1994 dollars). Massachusetts, New York, and Texas are the next most active and account for the bulk of the remaining capital. It is also clear that many states have almost no venture capital activity. We seek to explore these patterns in a regression framework.

Table 4 shows state fixed-effects regressions for the level of venture capital investment per capita and the number of companies receiving venture capital per capita. We employ an observation for each year in each state—a balanced panel. Independent variables include market-wide measures used in the regressions in table 2 (logarithm of IPO activity, the previous year's real Treasury bill return, and the previous year's equity market return). In addition, we include several variables

25. National Science Foundation (1980, 1998b).

26. For instance, in 1977, as in earlier and later years, data for New Hampshire and Vermont are suppressed. Of the $2.4 billion of R&D spending in New England in that year, $2.3 billion is accounted for by Connecticut, Maine, Massachusetts, and Rhode Island. We divide the remaining amount between New Hampshire (65 percent) and Vermont (35 percent), proportional to their gross state product in that year.

27. National Science Foundation (1998a).

28. The program is described in Feenberg and Coutts (1993); the simulation and the resulting data are reproduced at http://www.nber.org/taxsim/state-rates.

Table 3. Venture Capital Activity, by State, 1976–94
Number of companies; amount in millions of 1994 dollars

State	Companies financed	Total venture capital invested	State	Companies financed	Total venture capital invested
Alaska	3	52.1	Montana	17	49.2
Alabama	75	199.1	Nebraska	15	8.1
Arizona	189	693.9	Nevada	22	25.8
Arkansas	12	14.7	New Hampshire	136	344.3
California	6,154	19,967.7	New Jersey	643	2,019.2
Colorado	609	1,557.0	New Mexico	38	56.5
Connecticut	486	2,094.2	New York	811	2,369.4
Delaware	26	42.6	North Carolina	239	612.2
District of Columbia	70	211.0	North Dakota	4	28.2
Florida	338	779.7	Ohio	342	1,351.2
Georgia	395	872.0	Oklahoma	60	134.8
Hawaii	4	1.2	Oregon	297	789.3
Idaho	12	58.5	Pennsylvania	575	2,292.4
Illinois	514	1,879.1	Rhode Island	85	226.6
Indiana	137	260.3	South Carolina	37	165.9
Iowa	60	143.4	South Dakota	15	7.6
Kansas	46	90.3	Tennessee	235	844.1
Kentucky	59	173.5	Texas	1,254	3,861.1
Louisiana	45	137.6	Utah	117	246.7
Maine	50	126.8	Vermont	313	969.1
Maryland	321	989.2	Virginia	17	61.6
Massachusetts	2,276	5,886.4	Washington	327	835.8
Michigan	267	808.6	West Virginia	16	33.7
Minnesota	483	837.1	Wisconsin	144	269.4
Mississippi	26	32.0	Wyoming	5	4.2
Missouri	107	611.6			

Sources: Authors' calculations. See text.

that might serve as a proxy for state-level demand conditions. These include the previous year's growth in gross state product per capita as well as measures of the previous year's academic and industrial expenditure on R&D per capita. The R&D expenditure potentially captures demand effects of high-technology firms. If R&D is higher in one state than in another, it may mean that the number of potential entrepreneurs with promising ideas is greater.

In addition, we include a dummy variable that is equal to one after 1978 to capture the effect of changes in ERISA's prudent man rule. Finally, we include several measures of the capital gains tax rate burden. We first control for state and federal capital gains taxes separately by including the maximum marginal state and federal capital gains tax rate separately. We then add the federal and state rates to create a variable that captures the total capital gains tax burden in that state.[29]

Table 4 shows that both industrial and academic R&D spending are significantly related to state-level venture capital activity. Increases in state R&D levels increase both the amount of venture capital invested as well as the number of firms receiving venture capital. This result suggests that academic and industrial R&D spending are potentially important for the creation of entrepreneurial firms that demand venture capital.

Similarly, growth in gross state product per capita is positively related to venture capital activity. This result, consistent with the aggregate results, may indicate the importance of the demand effects. That is, it is important to have a strong, growing economy to create new firms that need venture capital financing.

The dummy variable measuring the shift in ERISA policy continues to have a positive effect in the state-level regressions. After the clarification of ERISA, the amount of venture capital invested per capita as well as the number of firms receiving venture capital per capita increased. Finally, capital gains tax rates continue to matter. In the regressions including both state and federal rates, it is only the federal rate that is significantly related to venture capital activity. The state capital gains tax rate is, however, always negatively related to venture capital activity and is of the same order of magnitude as the effect of federal

29. The state tax measure includes only the marginal impact: any savings in federal taxes due to the deductibility of state taxes are factored in. All regressions include state fixed effects.

Table 4. Regressions for State-Level Venture Capital Activity, 1976–94
t-statistics in parentheses

Dependent variable	Dependent variable			
	Logarithm of real venture capital investment in the state per million residents[a]		Number of companies receiving venture financing in state per thousand residents	
Logarithm of value of all venture capital-backed IPOs in previous year (millions of 1994 dollars)	-0.2008 (-3.35)	-0.1973 (-3.37)	-0.2414 (-1.46)	-0.2372 (1.46)
Logarithm of previous year's real gross state product per capita	0.5343 (1.73)	0.5438 (1.77)	4.5621 (4.59)	4.5854 (4.68)
Previous year's real gross state product growth in the state	0.0480 (3.11)	0.0478 (3.11)	0.1609 (3.45)	0.1605 (3.45)
Logarithm of previous year's real expenditure on academic R&D per capita in the state	0.7939 (4.88)	0.8032 (5.15)	0.1898 (0.36)	0.2044 (0.39)
Logarithm of previous year's real expenditure on industrial R&D per capita in the state	0.1359 (3.23)	0.1362 (3.24)	0.3208 (2.67)	0.3211 (2.67)
Previous year's T-bill return	-0.1332 (-5.44)	-0.1337 (-5.48)	-0.1294 (-1.83)	-0.1295 (-1.83)

Previous year's return on CRSP value-weighted index	0.0386 (0.15)	0.0235 (0.09)	1.4166 (1.98)	1.3983 (1.99)
Was ERISA's problem man rule clarified?	1.1713 (6.45)	1.1830 (6.70)	1.6815 (3.32)	1.6948 (3.41)
State capital gains tax rate	-2.5838 (-0.91)	. . .	-5.0675 (-0.61)	. . .
Federal capital gains tax rate	-3.4408 (-5.14)	. . .	-6.2439 (-3.37)	. . .
Sum of the state and federal capital gains tax rate	. . .	-3.3684 (-5.45)	. . .	-6.1480 (-3.61)
Summary statistics				
Overall R^2	0.425	0.425	0.426	0.425
p-value of χ^2-statistic	0.000	0.000	0.000	0.000
N	765	765	765	765

Sources: Authors' calculations. See text for full explanation of variables. State fixed effects are not reported.
a. Investment is in millions of 1994 dollars.

rates. The combined federal and state capital gains rate is also significantly related to venture capital activity. The result confirms the earlier findings using nationwide data. Increases in capital gains tax rates do appear to dampen venture capital activity.

Individual Venture Organization Results

In this section we examine fundraising patterns by individual venture organizations. First, we present summary statistics for the database, both in its entirety and segmented by year. We then analyze factors affecting the fundraising ability of individual venture organizations. Finally, focusing on early- and seed-stage firms, we examine the decision of venture organizations to raise funds. The importance of early- and seed-stage funds in creating new firms is widely recognized. Many of the efforts to stimulate venture activity focus on stimulating seed capital funds. Understanding the unique factors affecting the decision to target these firms is important for potential policy decisions. We examine fund information collected by Venture Economics from 1961 through 1992.

Summary Statistics

Table 5 presents information on the completeness of the venture fundraising database. In all, there is information on 1,294 venture capital funds. Of those, we have information on the fund size and closing date for 846 (20 of these are missing the month of closing). The average venture organization in the sample raised 2.23 funds; the median raised only 1.00. The maximum number of venture funds raised by an organization is 25. The average venture organization raised $126 million in 1994 dollars, while the largest raised more than $2 billion.

The time series distribution of our sample is presented in table 6. There was growth in both the number of funds raised and the dollar volume of commitments in the early and mid-1980s. The sample also appears to show a slight growth in the size of funds raised (in constant 1994 dollars). The sum of all the funds in the sample shows $45.0 billion in venture funding, which represents nearly all the capital raised

Table 5. Summary Statistics for Funds in Venture Economics Venture Intelligence Database

Items in record	Observations
Completness of records in correted database	
Month and year of closing and fund size	826
Year of closing and fund size	20
Month and year of closing: no size	428
Year of closing: no month or size	20
Neither closing date nor fund size	112

Summary Information for each venture organization				
	Mean	*Median*	*Minimum*	*Maximum*
Number of funds raised	2.23	1	1	25
Total funds raised (millions of 1994 dollars)[a]	126.46	57.11	0.46	2,267.00
Closing date of first fund in sample[b]	3/82	7/83	1.63	12/92
Closing date of last fund in sample[b]	5/85	12/86	1/63	12/92

Sources: Authors' calculations. See text.

a. Does not include venture organizations for which the size of all funds cannot be determined. It does include venture organizations for which the size of some funds cannot be determined.

b. Does not include venture organizations for which the closing date of all funds cannot be determined. It does include venture organizations for which the closing date of some funds cannot be determined. Funds whose month of closing cannot be determined are regarded as closing in July.

by organized venture capital partnerships during the sample period.[30] The lack of size data for 448 of the funds does not impart bias to our results. Our data cover almost all the capital raised over the sample period, and thus the results are clearly applicable to the most important firms.

Fundraising Regression Results

We analyzed firm-level fundraising by using one yearly observation for each venture organization, starting with the year that it raised its first venture capital fund. The dependent variable is either a dummy indicating whether the venture organization raised a fund or the amount of money (in millions of 1994 dollars) raised in that year. Independent variables include the age of the organization, the amount of money it raised during the previous ten years (in millions of 1994 dollars), the value of equity held by this venture organization in firms brought public in that year and the previous year, the value of all venture-backed firms

30. The federal government does not collect numbers on venture capital inflows. The Venture Economics database, however, corresponds closely to those of another consulting firm, Asset Alternatives, as well as to estimates by practitioners.

Table 6. Venture Capital Fund Size and Closings, 1961–92

Year	Funds closed	Funds with size data	Size of funds (millions of 1994 dollars) Average	Sum
1961	2	0	. . .	. . .
1962	2	0	. . .	. . .
1963	1	0	. . .	. . .
1964	0	0	. . .	. . .
1965	1	1	41.5	41.5
1966	1	0	. . .	. . .
1967	2	0	. . .	. . .
1968	12	0	. . .	. . .
1969	16	6	73.0	437.7
1970	14	5	50.3	251.3
1971	13	5	61.3	306.6
1972	11	5	24.2	121.1
1973	13	3	36.5	109.4
1974	11	6	14.4	86.5
1975	11	0	. . .	. . .
1976	14	3	38.2	113.5
1977	9	3	28.4	85.2
1978	23	14	30.5	427.1
1979	27	11	44.0	483.5
1980	57	26	47.9	1,245.9
1981	81	47	36.4	1,712.1
1982	98	51	41.0	2,088.8
1983	147	99	55.1	5,452.5
1984	150	106	45.7	4,839.3
1985	99	74	56.6	4,190.6
1986	86	61	72.6	4,427.8
1987	112	95	56.6	5,378.3
1988	78	66	56.3	3,718.0
1989	88	70	49.4	3,457.5
1990	50	36	69.6	2,507.0
1991	34	23	66.5	1,528.7
1992	31	30	67.0	2,010.8
Total	1,294	846	53.2	45,021.7

Sources: Authors' calculations. See text.

brought public in the previous year, real GDP growth in the previous year, the previous year's Treasury bill return, the previous year's stock market return as measured by the annual return on the CRSP value-weighted market index, a dummy variable that equals one after 1978 (indicating years after the clarification of the ERISA prudent man rule), and the top marginal capital gains tax rate on individuals.[31]

We estimated a Heckman two-stage model, which estimates two equations. The first equation is the probability that a fund was raised in a given year. The second is the amount raised given that a fund was raised in a particular year. This two-stage model is appropriate if the correct decision is that venture capitalists first decide whether to raise a new fund. Once they decide to raise it, they then decide the size of fund to raise. The two equations give us insights about factors that affect the probability of raising a new fund and about factors that primarily affect the optimal fund size.

Table 7 gives the results from the Heckman models. The first regression in each model gives the probability of raising a new fund, and the second gives the size of a fund if it is raised. Neither the capital gains tax rate nor ERISA's clarification had a significant effect on the probability of a venture organization's raising a new fund. The ERISA dummy has no effect on the size of the fund either. The capital gains tax rate does, however, have a significant effect: lower capital gains tax rates are associated with larger funds. This finding would be expected if venture organizations raised new funds on a normal cycle that was typically unaffected by external factors. Changes in the capital gains tax rate may affect the quantity of good start-ups to finance as managers are induced to start firms. More good projects would lead venture capitalists to raise larger funds.

A company's performance also has a dramatic effect on fundraising. Both the value of equity held in companies taken public by the venture capital firm in the current year and in the previous year have a positive effect on the probability of raising a new fund and on the size of the fund. The effect of the previous year's IPO volume is about three times as large as the current year's. This might be due to the time it takes to raise a new fund (sometimes many months). Venture organizations go

31. We look at money raised during the previous ten years because that is the specified life span of a typical venture capital limited partnership agreement. The ten-year sum provided the best available estimate of capital under management.

Table 7. Regressions for Individual Venture Fundraising by Individual, Independent Organizations in the Venture Economics Venture Intelligence Database, 1961–92

t-statistics in parentheses

	Dependent variable			
	Model 1		Model 2	
Independent variables	*Was fund raised?*	*If so, logarithm of fund size*[a]	*Was fund raised?*	*If so, logarithm of fund size*[a]
Years since raising last fund	−0.4560 (−15.84)	−21.17 (−7.55)	−0.4692 (−21.58)	−14.15 (−7.02)
Square of the number of years since missing last fund	0.0272 (11.94)	0.8710 (3.94)	0.0291 (16.27)	0.5293 (3.28)
Age of the venture organization (years)	0.0136 (2.79)	0.9820 (2.32)	⋯	⋯
Total venture capital raised during previous ten years for venture organization (millions of 1994 dollars)	⋯	⋯	0.0004 (2.14)	0.1670 (9.56)
Value of equity held in firms brought public this year (millions of 1994 dollars)	0.0037 (3.30)	0.3326 (3.50)	0.0029 (2.46)	0.1124 (1.15)
Value of equity held in firms brought public in the previous year (millions of 1994 dollars)	0.0091 (4.39)	1.0310 (6.11)	0.0058 (2.58)	0.3742 (2.07)
Total value of firms brought public in previous year by all venture capitalists (millions of 1994 dollars)	1.3xE-6 (0.23)	−0.0006 (−1.60)	1.7xE-6 (0.34)	−0.0006 (−1.72)

Real GDP growth in the previous year	−0.0048 (−0.72)	...	0.0006 (0.08)	...
T-bill return in previous year	0.0724 (3.84)	...	0.0759 (5.45)	...
Return on the CRSP value weighted index in the previous year	0.0027 (2.37)	...	0.0036 (2.86)	...
Capital gains tax rate	0.0018 (0.31)	−1.1650 (−3.50)	0.0021 (0.41)	−1.8156 (−5.50)
Was ERISA's prudent man rule clarified?	−0.0382 (−0.37)	8.3666 (0.96)	−0.0472 (−0.44)	−5.4530 (−0.66)
Constant	−0.6230 (−2.15)	−0.5752 (−0.04)	−0.6357 (−2.27)	28.99 (1.98)
Summary statistics				
Log likelihood	−8159.3		−8197.4	
p-value of χ^2-statistic	0.000		0.000	
N	5,573		5,573	

Sources: Authors' calculations. All regressions are Heckman two-stage models. See text for full explanation of variables.
a. Fund size in millions of 1994 dollars.

on "road shows" and gauge investor interest, sign up prospective investors, and generate the necessary documents before closing. The more relevant performance is probably the previous year's returns, which are foremost in investors' minds during fundraising.

Reputation also appears to influence the size of the fund raised. Older and larger venture organizations have higher probabilities of raising funds and raise larger funds. The reputation variable potentially captures beliefs about future returns not captured in recent performance variables. The effect of venture organization size is particularly strong on the size of the fund raised. This could indicate that size is a good proxy for reputation. Size might also measure the need to raise larger funds. Large venture organizations may have more employees and general partners. To keep all of them working at capacity, the minimum fund size needed is substantially greater.

The Treasury bill return in the previous year is positively related to the probability of raising a new fund. This effect may stem from the rapid increase in funds being raised in the early 1980s at a time when real interest rates were high. Both the probability of raising a fund and the size of a new fund first decline and then increase with time from the previous fund.[32]

Table 8 shows the fixed-effects regression models. The models include dummy variables for each venture organization that are intended to pick up unmeasured firm-specific factors. If we find a result even after controlling for fixed effects, we can be confident that the effects are robust. We could not estimate the fixed-effects Heckman model. Therefore, we ran two separate regressions. The first is a fixed-effects logit that estimates the probability of raising a fund in a given year. The second is a fixed-effects least squares regression that estimates the size of funds raised if a fund is being raised. The approximation to the two-stage maximum likelihood Heckman model is consistent in the estimations without the fixed effects, so we are confident that the results in table 8 are reasonable.[33]

In both specifications, the capital gains tax rate continues to be a significant factor in venture fundraising. A decrease in the rate increases the funds raised in both specifications. In the first model, the ERISA

32. The regression results are robust to various segmentations of the data, for example, firms located on the West Coast and East Coast.
33. Maddala (1983).

dummy variable has an important impact. Controlling for firm factors, the ERISA clarification leads to a greater probability of raising a new fund.

Venture organization performance (as measured by the value of equity stakes in IPOs) continues to have a positive effect on fundraising. In the two-stage model with firm fixed effects, the probability of raising a fund increases with greater performance, but the size of the fund does not appear to be affected. The reputation variables, however, have mixed signs in the fixed-effects regression that are different from those in the regressions without the firm fixed effects. In the two-stage model, the probability of raising a fund is lower for older and larger organizations, but the fund size is larger. This lower probability may reflect the retirement of partners within older venture organizations. Unconditionally, older firms are more likely to raise a fund because of their better track record. Controlling for firm effects, however, as a firm ages, it becomes less likely to raise a fund.

Stage Focus Results

We also undertook an analysis of the ability of venture capital organizations to raise a fund that focuses on early-stage investments. The early-stage venture market is often considered critical to the success of later-stage investments. Early-stage funds provide new firms with crucial financing in their infancy.[34] Many of the policy initiatives undertaken around the world are aimed at increasing the availability of early-stage capital. Similarly, firms in their very early stages are the most prone to capital rationing and liquidity constraints because the uncertainty and asymmetric information are at their greatest. If we can understand the incentives to raise a focused fund, we might be able to understand industry dynamics better and make better recommendations about promoting new entrepreneurial firms.

We divide firms into two categories in this analysis. We indicate whether the funds analyzed earlier have a stated investment focus on early-stage firms only. (Venture Economics characterizes each fund's focus in its database.) Table 9 presents summary statistics for venture funds that have a stated early-stage focus and those that do not. Funds

34. See, for instance, Organization for Economic Cooperation and Development (1997).

Table 8. Fixed-Effects Regressions for Venture Fundraising by Individual, Independent Organizations in the Venture Economics Venture Intelligence Database, 1961–92

t-statistics in parentheses

	Dependent variable			
	Model 1		Model 2	
Independent variables	Logit—was fund raised?	OLS—if so, logarithm of fund size[a]	Logit—was fund raised?	OLS—if so, logarithm of fund size[a]
Years since raising last fund	-1.1056 (-18.80)	-2.903 (-1.02)	-1.3034 (-22.83)	2.343 (0.89)
Square of the number of years since raising last fund	0.1069 (16.91)	0.1526 (0.54)	0.1141 (18.74)	-0.2100 (-0.79)
Age of the venture organization (years)	-0.2772 (-11.23)	4.8364 (3.18)	...	...
Total venture capital raised during previous ten years for venture organization (millions of 1994 dollars)	...	...	-0.0049 (-7.10)	0.1660 (6.41)
Value of equity held in firms brought public this year (millions of 1994 dollars)	0.0049 (2.03)	0.0128 (0.10)	0.0056 (2.22)	-0.0764 (-0.59)
Value of equity held in firms brought public in the previous year (millions of 1994 dollars)	0.0138 (3.06)	0.2905 (1.38)	0.213 (4.09)	-0.1417 (-0.65)

	(1)	(2)	(3)	(4)
Total value of firms brought public in previous year (millions of 1994 dollars)	$4.1 \times$ E-6 (0.38)	-0.0001 (-0.21)	$-5.0 \times$ E-6 (-0.48)	0.0004 (0.55)
Real GDP growth in the previous year	-0.0315 (-1.42)	-1.875 (-1.42)	-0.0037 (-0.16)	-2.012 (-1.57)
T-bill return in previous year	-0.0160 (-0.43)	-1.727 (-0.77)	0.1154 (3.33)	-1.782 (-0.93)
Return on the CRSP value weighted index in the previous year	0.0009 (0.28)	-0.1847 (-0.80)	0.0061 (1.94)	-0.1959 (-0.89)
Capital gains tax rate	0.0007 (0.06)	-1.153 (-1.92)	0.0039 (0.36)	-1.506 (-2.45)
Was ERISA's prudent man rule clarified?	2.047 (5.75)	0.7768 (0.04)	0.0967 (0.35)	10.22 (0.67)
Constant	1.434 (1.62)	127.15 (2.77)	1.155 (1.26)	127.60 (2.89)
Summary statistics				
Log likelihood/adjusted R^2	-1903.6	0.212	-1939.5	0.252
p-value of χ^2/F-statistic	0.000	0.000	0.000	0.000
N	5,323	1,117	5,323	1,117

Sources: Authors' calculations. See text for a full explanation of the variables and methodology. Firm fixed effects are not reported.

a. Fund size in millions of 1994 dollars.

Table 9. Summaries of Venture Capital Commitments by Stage Focus for Funds Raised by Independent Venture Organizations in the Venture Economics Venture Intelligence Database, 1961–92

Means, in millions of 1994 dollars unless otherwise specified; median in parentheses

	Funds with stated focus on early-stage firms	Funds without stated focus on early-stage firms	Significance of the difference between early and nonearly
Size of the fund	41.98	56.95	0.000
	(24.66)	(35.88)	(0.000)
Amount of venture capital raised by organization in previous funds	92.20	87.58	0.714
	(39.54)	(26.64)	(0.000)
Organization age (years)	4.38	3.77	0.140
	(3.08)	(0.58)	(0.002)
Date of fund closing	August 1985	August 1983	0.000
	(June 1985)	(May 1984)	(0.000)
Funds raised on West Coast (percent)	38.3	30.3	0.017
Funds raised on East Coast (percent)	32.2	43.6	0.001

Sources: Authors' calculations. See text.

focusing on early-stage investments are significantly smaller, with a mean size of $42 million and a median of $25 million, than funds that do not focus on early-stage investments (mean of $57 million and a median of $36 million). This makes sense because early-stage investments are typically smaller than later-stage investments. Gompers has found that the average early-stage investment is only half as large as the mean later-stage investment.[35] Because the amount of time spent during the investment and monitoring process (in due diligence, negotiations, and so forth) and the need for oversight after the investment are similar, early-stage funds are usually smaller.

Early-stage funds also tend to be raised by venture organizations that are slightly older and larger. One possibility is that older, more experienced venture organizations have the necessary knowledge to raise a focused fund. The early-stage funds are, on average, more recent and are more likely to be raised on the West Coast. Clearly, the mix of investments on the West Coast, primarily California, is heavily concentrated on early-stage, technology-based companies. East Coast firms are more balanced and tend to have portfolios with larger proportions of later-stage companies.

Table 10 shows multivariate regressions analyzing the determinants of fund focus. We used each new venture capital fund as an observation and examined whether it had an early-stage focus. As the summary statistics suggested, smaller funds are more likely to have an early-stage focus. Similarly, firms on the West Coast are more likely to raise an early-stage fund. Finally, a venture organization has been more likely to raise a fund with an early-stage focus after the Department of Labor's clarification of ERISA's prudent man rule. This is potentially due to the clarification stating that investments would be judged prudent not by their individual risk, but by their contribution to portfolio risk. Before the amendment, early-stage funds may have been viewed as too speculative and may have had a more difficult time raising money than a later-stage or general purpose venture capital fund. After the amendment venture organizations could raise focused funds without worrying that pension funds would avoid them out of concern over their perceived riskiness.

35. Gompers (1995).

Table 10. Regressions for Stage Focus of Venture Capital Funds by Independent Organizations in the Venture Economics Venture Intelligence Database, 1961–92

t-statistics in parentheses

Independent variable	Dependent variable: Did the fund state a focus on early-stage investments?			
Size of the fund (millions of 1994 dollars)	−0.0057 (−2.82)	−0.0035 (−1.40)	...	...
Age of the venture organization (years)	0.0118 (0.75)	...	0.0018 (0.13)	...
Total venture capital raised during previous ten years for this venture organization[a]	...	0.0247 (1.62)	...	−3.24×E-7 (−0.71)
Was the fund located on the West Coast?	0.4026 (2.35)	0.4619 (2.70)	0.2280 (1.44)	0.2786 (1.79)
Was ERISA's prudent man rule clarified?	0.7659 (1.78)	0.9025 (2.11)	1.829 (4.39)	1.871 (4.52)
Capital gains tax rate	0.0208 (1.36)	0.0247 (1.62)	0.0395 (2.70)	0.0404 (2.80)
Constant	−2.244 (−3.14)	−2.502 (−3.49)	−4.333 (−6.25)	−4.401 (−6.39)
Summary statistics				
Log likelihood	−455.3	−461.9	−557.4	−571.8
p-value of χ² statistic	0.002	0.001	0.000	0.000
N	818	843	1,236	1,283

Sources: Authors' calculations. All regressions are logit estimates. See text for full explanation of variables.
a. Millions of 1994 dollars.

Alternative Explanations

Several alternative explanations may account for our findings. First, the supply and demand for venture capital may be affected by the supply of substitute financing. We have attempted to control for the cost of credit by including the real interest rate. In periods of high real interest rates, venture capital may be more attractive from the entrepreneur's perspective. Similarly, if the availability of bank financing were a major factor in the determination of venture capital commitments, we should have seen an increase in venture capital commitments in the late 1980s and early 1990s, when bank credit to young, small firms was significantly tighter. Instead, we see decreasing venture capital commitments during this period, indicating that bank credit and venture fundraising moved together.

Our results on capital gains taxes and venture commitments may reflect an inability to measure expected GDP growth accurately. If expected growth is somehow correlated with capital gains tax rates, we might be incorrectly attributing the explanatory power of growth to the tax rates. In unreported regressions, we modeled expected GDP growth using the previous four years of real growth. Instead of lagged GDP growth, we reestimated the regressions using the expected growth rate. Results were qualitatively the same as already reported. This is not surprising because the expected GDP growth rate is primarily affected by the previous year's growth.

Finally, the growth in venture capital commitments may have less to do with policy changes and more with greater technological opportunities. In fact, the state-level R&D expenditures indicate that this may be the case. If changes in technological opportunity were causing increases in venture capital investments, we would expect several measures of technological innovation to lead increases in venture fundraising. In particular, Kortum and Lerner show that a surge of patents occurred in the late 1980s and 1990s.[36] This finding suggests that some of the recent growth in venture capital fundraising in the mid-1990s may be due to increases in technological opportunities. The increase in venture fundraising in the late 1970s and 1980s (the period of our sample), however, does not seem to be caused by similar technology

36. Kortum and Lerner (1998).

shifts. Similarly, the state-level analysis shows that even controlling for R&D spending, regulatory policies still have an effect.

Conclusion

We have examined the determinants of fundraising for the venture capital industry and individual venture organizations. We examined supply and demand effects as well as the importance of individual firm performance and reputation.

We find that demand for venture capital appears critical. Higher GDP growth and increases in R&D spending lead to greater venture capital activity. Capital gains tax rates also matter: lower rates lead to more venture capital raised. The effect, however, appears to stem from a greater demand for venture capital. Commitments by tax-exempt pension funds are the most affected by changes in the capital gains tax rate. The clarification in ERISA rules governing pension fund investment has also generally increased commitments to the industry.

Fund performance is an important determinant of the ability of venture organizations to raise new capital. Firms that hold larger equity stakes in companies that have recently gone public raise funds with greater probability and raise larger funds. Reputation, in the form of firm age and size, also positively affects the ability to raise new capital.

There is also evidence that decisions to raise early-stage venture funds have been affected by pension regulations. The probability of raising a focused fund increased after ERISA's clarification. We also find greater early-stage activity in smaller funds and venture organizations on the West Coast, where technology-based start-ups are more prevalent.

Our research has a variety of implications for policymakers who wish to stimulate venture capital activity. The fundraising results indicate that regulatory reform and policy decisions may have an effect on commitments to the venture industry. Although the capital gains tax rate is an important driver of venture capital fundraising, blanket reduction in the rates may be a blunt instrument for promoting venture capital. Our analysis suggests that an important factor for the increase in venture capital is probably an increase in the number of high-quality start-ups. The greater number of good firms leads to more demand for venture capital. Policies that increase the relative attractiveness of becoming an entrepreneur and promote technology innovation probably would have more effect on venture capital investments than an across-the-board cut in the capital gains tax rate. Furthermore, the results highlight the highly localized nature of venture capital activity. Countries that wish to promote such activity may consider concentrating efforts rather than spreading resources uniformly around the country. This is in contrast to many of the efforts that various countries have instituted.

The results also raise questions for further research. In general, the importance of reputation and performance as determinants of fundraising is consistent with findings of earlier literature on other types of money managers. The decision to invest is clearly predicated on the expectation of future returns, and both past performance and reputation are components of such expectations. But in recent years many of the most established venture organizations in the United States have experienced internal corporate governance problems and have been disbanded. The issue of who carries the reputation with him or her is important. Does reputation follow general partners who start their own funds, or must they establish new reputations? In markets without experienced venture capitalists, how can the lack of reputation be overcome? Clearly, more work is necessary.

Other unanswered questions relate to the effectiveness of public efforts to transfer the venture capital model to other regions. Even if venture capital organizations spur technological innovation in the United States, it is not evident that the model can be seamlessly transferred abroad. Different employment practices, regulatory policies, or public market avenues might limit the formation of funds.[37] Even if it were feasible to transfer such efforts, public economic development programs can be subject to political manipulation such as pressures to award funds to politically connected businesses.

Overseas venture initiatives, however, may be able to benefit from the experience of venture organizations in the United States. In particular, the Israeli Yozma program seems to have successfully captured spillovers of knowledge from U.S. and British venture organizations. In contrast to many forms of government intervention to boost economic

---

37. See Black and Gilson (1998).

growth, the implementation of these programs has received little scrutiny by economists.[38] This is a ripe area for further exploration.

Venture capital is increasingly regarded as an important component of the U.S. economic landscape. Although policymakers have often tried to affect the flow of funds into the sector, little has been known about the real impact of such policy measures. Our paper begins to answer those questions and points toward areas for future research.

38. Two recent exceptions are Irwin and Klenow (1996) and Lerner (forthcoming).

References

Anand, Bharat N. 1993. "Tax Effects on Venture Capital." Unpublished working paper. Princeton University. October.

Barry, Christopher B., and others. 1990. "The Role of Venture Capital in the Creation of Public Companies: Evidence from the Going Public Process." *Journal of Financial Economics* 27 (October): 447–71.

Black, Bernard S., and Ronald J. Gilson. 1998. "Venture Capital and the Structure of Capital Markets: Banks versus Stock Markets." *Journal of Financial Economics* 47 (March): 243–77.

Brav, Alon, and Paul A. Gompers. 1997. "Myth or Reality? The Long-Run Underperformance of Initial Public Offerings: Evidence from Venture and Nonventure Capital-Backed Companies." *Journal of Finance* 52 (December): 1791–822.

Bureau of Economic Analysis. 1997. "Gross State Product by Industry: Original Experimental Estimates, 1963–1986." Unpublished data file. U.S. Department of Commerce.

Chevalier, Judith A., and Glenn D. Ellison. 1997. "Risk Taking by Mutual Funds as a Response to Incentives." *Journal of Political Economy* 105 (December): 1167–200.

Feenberg, Daniel R., and Elizabeth Coutts. 1993. "An Introduction to the TAXSIM Model." *Journal of Policy Analysis and Management* 12 (Winter): 189–94.

Friedenberg, Howard L., and Richard M. Beemiller. 1997. "Comprehensive Revision of Gross State Product by Industry, 1977–94." *Survey of Current Business* 77 (June): 15–41.

Gompers, Paul A. 1995. "Optimal Investment, Monitoring, and the Staging of Venture Capital." *Journal of Finance* 50 (December): 1461–90.

Gompers, Paul A., and Josh Lerner. 1996. "The Use of Covenants: An Empirical Analysis of Venture Partnership Agreements." *Journal of Law and Economics* 39 (October): 463–98.

———. 1997. "Risk and Reward in Private Equity Investments: The Challenge of Performance Assessment." *Journal of Private Equity* 1 (Winter): 5–12.

———. 1998. "Venture Capital Distributions: Short- and Long-Run Reactions." *Journal of Finance* 53 (December): 2161–83.

———. 1999. "An Analysis of Compensation in the U.S. Venture Capital Partnership." *Journal of Financial Economics* 51 (January): 3–44.

Grinblatt, Mark, Sheridan Titman, and Russ Wermers. 1995. "Momentum Investment Strategies, Portfolio Performance, and Herding: A Study of Mutual Fund Behavior." *American Economic Review* 85 (December): 1088–105.

Ippolito, Richard. 1989. "Efficiency with Costly Information: A Study of

Mutual Fund Performance, 1965–1984.'' *Quarterly Journal of Economics* 104 (February): 1–23.

Irwin, Douglas A., and Peter J. Klenow. 1996. "High Tech R&D Subsidies: Estimating the Effects of Sematech." *Journal of International Economics* 40 (May): 323–44.

Jensen, Michael. 1968. "The Performance of Mutual Funds in the Period 1945–1964." *Journal of Finance* 23 (May): 389–416.

Kortum, Samuel, and Josh Lerner. 1998. "Stronger Protection or Technological Revolution: What Is behind the Recent Surge of Patenting?" *Carnegie-Rochester Conference Series on Public Policy* 48 (June): 247–304.

Lerner, Josh. 1995. "Venture Capitalists and the Oversight of Private Firms." *Journal of Finance* 50 (March): 301–18.

———. Forthcoming. "The Government as Venture Capitalist: The Long-Run Effects of the SBIR Program." *Journal of Business.*

Liles, Patrick R. 1977. *Sustaining the Venture Capital Firm.* Cambridge, Mass.: Management Analysis Center, Inc.

Maddala, G. S. 1983. *Limited-Dependent and Qualitative Variables in Econometrics.* Cambridge University Press.

Megginson, William C., and Kathleen A. Weiss. 1991. "Venture Capital Certification in Initial Public Offerings." *Journal of Finance* 46 (July): 879–903.

National Science Foundation, Division of Science Resource Studies. 1980. *Research and Development in Industry—1979.* Washington.

———. 1998a. "Survey of Research and Development Expenditures at Universities and Colleges." http://caspar.nsf.gov.

———. 1998b. "Survey of Research and Development in Industry." http://www.nsf.gov/sbe/srs/indus/start.htm.

Organization for Economic Cooperation and Development. 1997. *Government Venture Capital for Technology-Based Firms.* Paris.

Poterba, James. 1989. "Venture Capital and Capital Gains Taxation." In *Tax Policy and the Economy*, edited by Lawrence H. Summers. MIT Press.

Scholes, Myron S. 1972. "The Market for Securities: Substitution versus Price Pressure and the Effects of Information on Share Prices." *Journal of Business* 45 (April): 179–211.

Sirri, Erik R., and Peter Tufano. 1998. "Costly Search and Mutual Fund Flows." *Journal of Finance* 53 (October): 1589–622.

Venture Economics. 1988. *Exiting Venture Capital Investments.* Needham, Mass.

———. 1996. *Pratt's Guide to Venture Capital Sources.* New York: Securities Data Publishing.

Comments

Comment by Margaret M. Blair: The dynamism of the venture capital market in the United States in the past twenty years has been the envy of economies all over the world. But as much as policymakers would like to be able to replicate this success story in other times and places, the truth is that neither they nor scholars know for sure what it is that we did right to encourage the growth of the sector. Was it just an accident, a product of random forces that happened to come together in a particularly propitious way in the past decade or two, especially in California? Or was it the product of some policy choices that could be adopted elsewhere?

Paul Gompers and Josh Lerner make a substantial contribution to our understanding of these questions by analyzing data on flows of investment money into U.S. venture capital funds since the 1970s. They ask whether those flows, in the aggregate, and on a state-by-state and firm-by-firm basis, can be explained by the general condition of the macroeconomy, the rate of technological change, the success of previous venture capital investments, and some specific policy variables such as tax rates and pension fund regulations.

The authors are unable to estimate a two-equation model to sort out supply-side influences and demand-side influences, because the "price" of venture capital (the ex ante expected rate of return) is not directly observable. But they make a variety of plausible arguments about why some explanatory variables would be expected to work through the supply side and some through the demand side. And in the case of one particularly ambiguous relationship—the influence of capital gains taxes—they are able to parse the data in a way that allows them plausibly to sort out supply effects from demand effects. Their

193

sorting allows them to present a fairly convincing case that the surge in the flow of funds into venture capital investments in the 1980s was largely a product of the growth in the "demand" for venture capital by entrepreneurs. The demand for venture capital, in turn, was stimulated by a growing economy, technological change (for which spending on research and development is used as a proxy), and reductions in the capital gains tax rate, all of which have made it more attractive for individuals with an entrepreneurial bent to start their own new firms.

On the supply side the authors argue that the Department of Labor's clarification of the so-called prudent man rule of the Employment Retirement Income Security Act (ERISA) in 1978 in effect gave pension fund managers permission to invest in venture capital funds as part of a balanced portfolio, which helped open the floodgates of funding into these investments. The authors also use their data (which was collected at the level of individual venture capital funds) to show evidence that a reputation for past investment success on the part of a specific venture capital firm encourages a greater flow of money into subsequent funds raised by the firm.

All of these findings are plausible, but they may not be very useful in devising policy. Consider the various factors that, according to the authors, help to stimulate the growth of venture capital funds.

The firm-level analysis tells us that venture capital organizations that have been successful in the past are more able than other firms to attract new money into new funds that they form. But this is not particularly helpful for making policy if one firm's success in attracting new investment money comes at the expense of another firm. If the policy question is how to stimulate the total amount of venture capital activity, the firm-level analysis is not really relevant. Moreover, the findings of the analysis at the aggregate level are still not very helpful because they seem to tell us little more than that to have a thriving venture capital industry there needs to be a thriving venture capital industry. Success encourages future business. This is not surprising, but it does not give a policymaker much to work with.

The other supply-side factor that the authors believe was important was the clarification of the prudent man rule. Here we have a fairly clear policy change, but the only way it is captured in the data is by a dummy variable for pre-1979 versus 1979 and later. One does not have to study figure 2 very hard to be convinced that such a variable would be significant in any regression explaining venture capital funding, because nearly all of the activity occurs after 1979. For that reason, however, one cannot say for sure that this dummy variable is picking up the clarification of the prudent man rule or some other factors that began to stimulate venture capital funding in a big way in the 1980s. The authors bolster their argument that clarifying the prudent man rule was important by noting that the flow of funding into venture capital from pension funds in particular was especially strong after 1979. Nonetheless, it seems likely that this dummy variable is proxying for other things not included in the list of explanatory variables, things that are still not well understood and that may also have been driving mergers, takeovers, and corporate restructuring and refinancing activity, all of which took off during that same period. Moreover, the clarification of the prudent man rule, while undoubtedly beneficial, was a one-time change in a rule that does not exist in very many other places. So even if it was helpful, policymakers cannot get any further mileage out of this kind of change.

The three demand-side variables that the authors found to be associated with growth in venture capital activity are overall economic growth, spending on R&D, and a reduction in capital gains taxes. There is a circularity in the logic, however, of any argument that policymakers should try to stimulate economic growth in order to encourage venture capital activity. Presumably the reason they would want to stimulate venture capital activity is, as the authors note in the first paragraph of the paper, "the importance of the venture capital sector in generating innovation and new jobs." So, yes, economic growth is great, and there are plenty of good reasons to try to stimulate economic activity for its own sake. But it does not seem particularly useful to view it as an instrument for stimulating venture capital activity because the rationale for wanting to stimulate venture capital activity is that it will spur economic growth.

The authors also present evidence that reductions in the maximum capital gains tax rate in the 1980s helped stimulate demand for venture capital. Now here is a policy tool politicians love to talk about. In the regressions explaining aggregate (nationwide) annual commitments to venture capital, the coefficient on the capital gains rate is negative in every version of the model, though it is significant (at the 90 percent level) only in the regressions on total commitments, and on commitments by pension funds, while it is not significant (at the 90 percent level) in the regressions explaining commitments by individuals, nor in the regressions in which commitments are broken out by whether they are made by a taxable or a tax-exempt entity. The authors take these results as evidence that capital gains tax rates work through the demand side by increasing the eagerness of entrepreneurial people to start their own firms, rather than by encouraging more outside investors to supply funds for venture investments.

The problem with the analysis at this point, however, is that the authors have only twenty-two observations in the regression on total commitments, and once they break it out by source of the commitments, they have only seventeen observations. But they have six explanatory variables plus a constant, leaving only ten degrees of freedom. Moreover, the capital gains rate changed in only seven of the last seventeen years of their sample period. So they do not have much power in these regressions to reject the null hypothesis that the capital gains tax rate did not matter.

The authors repeat the analysis at the state level, which significantly increases the number of observations they have to work with, and in the state-level regressions explaining venture capital activity they again find negative coefficients on the capital gains tax rate variables. The coefficient is significant in the versions of the model in which the tax rate used is the sum of state and federal rates (with the state rate adjusted for any savings in federal taxes due to the deductibility of state taxes). But when state and federal rates are broken out and entered into the regression separately, only the coefficient on the federal capital gains tax rate is significant, suggesting that it is this part of the variable that is doing all the work in the regression. There is a problem in interpreting this result, however. In a panel regression the t-statistics on a macroeconomic variable that only varies from year to year, and does not vary cross-sectionally, will be spuriously inflated because the regression methodology used assumes that there is both state-level and annual variation in all of the variables. If there is a high level of correlation across states in annual venture capital investment, the variables at the level of the macroeconomy, including the federal capital gains tax rate, pick up this cross-sectional correlation and may well be proxying for other unknown year-specific variables that affect many states at the same time.

Of course, the authors might be right that the capital gains tax rate is important in encouraging entrepreneurial activity and thus in stimulating the demand for venture capital financing. But they concede late in the paper that, even if it is, this might be a blunt policy instrument to use for this purpose.

The final factor that Gompers and Lerner consider that appears to strongly influence venture capital activity is spending on R&D, both by academic institutions and industry. Although the authors do not treat this as a policy variable, perhaps they should. During the period covered by their study (1976–94), the federal government funded nearly 30 percent of all industry spending on R&D, and federal, state, and local governments together funded more than 70 percent of spending by universities and colleges on R&D. In constant dollar terms, annual federal spending on R&D channeled through industry climbed steadily during the period from $19.4 billion (in 1992 dollars) in 1976, peaking in 1987 at $34.6 billion, and then declining to $19.3 billion in 1994. The authors' data on venture capital commmitments appear also to have peaked in 1987. Although federal funding of industry R&D has declined since 1987, federal funding of R&D at colleges and universities has climbed since 1987 from $9.1 billion to $12.2 billion in 1994 (in 1992 dollars).[1] But government spending on R&D has declined as a share of both total industry spending and total spending by colleges and universities.

The authors have found that their R&D spending variables, in their state-level regressions, are highly significant predictors of—and probably causally related to—venture capital activity. Such variables are manipulable by government policy and should be considered part of the arsenal of policy tools available to policymakers to stimulate venture capital activity. More research on this relationship is probably warranted.

Comment by Thomas Hellmann. The current paper by Gompers and Lerner is an interesting attempt at answering a question of great importance. The United States has witnessed the rise of venture capital as a unique institutional arrangement for the financing of new and innovative companies. Most people believe that venture capital plays a role in the

1. National Science Board (1998, appendix table 4–4).

competitiveness of the U.S. economy. If venture capital does play such an important role, then it seems natural to ask what determines the size of the industry. Gompers and Lerner set out to provide some answers in this paper.

A pervasive problem in studying the venture capital industry is the lack of data. Gompers and Lerner should be commended for their substantial efforts to gather data. The current paper uses not only data on the aggregate amount of funds committed to venture capital (both state and national), but also attempts to analyze fundraising at the level of the individual fund. The paper thus provides information that simply was not available before. And it is clear that there is further potential in this data beyond the current paper.

The brunt of the paper is concerned with the aggregate behavior of venture capital fundraising, so I will focus most of my comments on that. At the core of the paper is a claim that it is mainly demand and not supply factors that determine the size of the venture capital industry. Let me begin by saying that I am very sympathetic to this idea. At a theoretical level, it is hard to argue that demand considerations are of no importance. And casual observation suggests that in many countries the obstacles to investing in venture capital are relatively minor, yet there is no active venture capital market, suggesting that supply alone cannot be the problem. Instead, it is frequently argued that the lack of venture capital is due first and foremost to the lack of entrepreneurs.

From the research perspective, the obvious challenge is thus to disentangle demand and supply effects. The authors make some interesting efforts at distinguishing between these effects, but the problem turns out to be trickier than anyone can solve in a single paper. The heart of the problem is fairly simple: first, price cannot be observed, and second, good instruments have not yet been found that can isolate demand and supply effects. The authors convincingly explain why an objective price cannot be observed in the relationship between the limited and general partners. They are thus left with the measurement of the quantity of funds.[2] Without observing prices, any change in the quantity of funds

2. The paper also makes an argument that the lack of price data is not a severe omission, because the supply function is very elastic. This argument is slightly confusing: with a perfectly elastic supply function, assets exist that are a perfect substitute for venture capital investment. The authors do not identify these assets, and if there truly were perfect substitutes, then it would be more meaningful to estimate the supply

could come from shifts in the demand or supply schedules. Yet none of the explanatory variables convincingly isolates either. Clearly, the aggregate level of economic activity and the level of interest rates affect both the saving behavior of firms and households (which acts on the supply of funds), and the investment behavior of entrepreneurs (which acts on the demand for funds). Similarly the return in equity markets affects the relative returns of different asset classes (which should affect the supply of venture capital), and it is likely to be correlated with entrepreneurial opportunities (thus affecting the demand).

The only variable that holds some promise of isolating demand is the R&D expenditure by academia and industry. The authors show that R&D expenditure is correlated with venture capital fundraising at the state level (I am not sure why they do not report the equivalent regression at the national level) and suggest that this might be interpreted as evidence for a demand effect. For this to be true, one still needs to argue that the savings behavior of firms and households has no relationship to the amount of spending by firms and academia on R&D. Moreover, entrepreneurial opportunities have to be positively correlated with R&D spending, which amounts to saying that R&D and entrepreneurship are complements. But the correlation between R&D and the quantity of venture capital certainly seems encouraging for the view that demand somehow matters.

A fundamental problem occurs, however, in going further with identifying the demand for venture capital: a better understanding of the entrepreneurial process is necessary. Economists have a profound problem measuring entrepreneurial opportunity, because they tend to rely on measuring realized outcomes, which measure actual choices as opposed to opportunity sets themselves. Moreover, economists have a poor understanding of what economic conditions favor or hamper entrepreneurship.[3] Put differently, it is difficult to talk about the demand for venture capital without a good theory of entrepreneurship. This means that even conceptually it is unclear what variables should be used as instruments for the demand of venture capital.[4]

---

function of the joint asset class (or else shifts in the composition of supply might be misinterpreted as demand shocks).

3. This lack of knowledge manifested itself clearly in the very different context of transitional economies.

4. A related point is that not much is known about alternative financing mechanisms

The poor understanding of the entrepreneurial process leads to my next point. Based on the conjecture formulated by Porteba, the authors interpret their findings as evidence that capital gains taxation works through the demand for funds, rather than through supply. There are some issues with the interpretation of the empirical findings, but before I get to that, let me first question the conceptual argument that capital gains taxation is an important factor for the level of entrepreneurship and thus the demand for venture capital. I may be holding a somewhat idiosyncratic view on this matter, but it seems to me that the argument has some political sway but little economic foundation.

It is a well-known fact that capital gains taxation has distributional consequences as well as efficiency consequences. It also seems plausible to me that in a politicized debate, the parties that have an interest in a capital gains reduction would want to highlight the efficiency arguments and downplay the windfall gains. Currently, the "entrepreneurial sector" enjoys a strong political goodwill in the United States. It might thus be attractive for proponents to argue that a capital gains reduction would benefit the entrepreneurial sector.[5]

The proponents' argument is deceptively simple: lower capital gains taxes increase the rewards to successful entrepreneurs if and when they want to cash out. The problem is that it is far from clear how important this effect is. The returns to an entrepreneurial activity, especially of the type financed by venture capital, are not only highly uncertain, but also occur at a fairly distant point in time. It takes several years before a successful company goes public, entrepreneurs have holding periods after the initial public offering, and even after the holding period entrepreneurs typically realize their capital gains at a very slow rate, frequently using various techniques to delay payment of taxes. Thus the gains from a reduction in capital gains taxation ought to be heavily discounted at the time of the entrepreneurial decision. In addition, at the time of founding a company, the one thing entrepreneurs can be sure of is that by the time they cash out, there will have been at least one presidential election and probably several rounds of congressional

---

for entrepreneurs. Future research might also want to examine substitution effects between venture capital and other forms of entrepreneurial finance.

5. Never mind, also, that entrepreneurs constitute only a tiny fraction of the people (or entities) that pay capital gains taxes, yet their cause is used for a reduction of capital gains across the board.

elections, each of which might bring about changes in capital gains legislation. More generally, it is unclear how much entrepreneurs should look at the current capital gains rate as a predictor for their future tax liability.

More important, it is not clear how much entrepreneurs actually do look at capital gains. This is obviously the point where lack of knowledge about entrepreneurship (both theoretically and empirically) hurts most. In the presence of extreme uncertainty surrounding their ventures, entrepreneurs rarely seem to rely on the mechanics of discounting future cash flows, which implies uncertainty about how, if at all, they are influenced by the capital gains rate. I presume that a lot more research would be required to answer that question. At the anecdotal level, I can say that in my limited experience I have heard entrepreneurs complaining about paying too high a capital gains tax. The complaints, however, came from entrepreneurs who had already succeeded and who were pondering how to avoid paying the tax. I have yet to meet the entrepreneur who tells me about a new innovative idea, but then says the only thing preventing the enterprise from going forward is the capital gains tax the entrepreneur will have to pay in that otherwise blissful case of actual success. Put differently, I am under the impression that even (perhaps especially) in the entrepreneurial context, the distortions of ex ante investment incentives induced by capital gains taxation are of tertiary importance at best. These taxes only seem to come to people's mind once they have accumulated wealth and are directly affected by the distributional consequences.[6]

Apart from these conceptual reservations about the importance of capital gains taxation on demand for venture capital, I am still confused by the results of the paper. At the risk of simplifying, the paper seems to argue that because the data does not fit the supply story, it must be demand that is driving venture capital. This remains speculative unless demand factors can actually be identified. But even if they were, one would still need an explanation for why supply factors are not at work. Indeed, the paper suggests an interesting paradox that remains somewhat unexplored: even though there is a difference by definition in their tax treatment, taxable and tax-exempt investors do not seem to behave

---

6. Anecdotally, they also seem to matter to investors, but this is obviously on the supply side.

significantly different, and tax-exempt pension funds react even more strongly to capital gains than (presumably taxable) individuals. One possible partial resolution to the paradox might be that taxable investors imitate tax-exempt investors in their investor patterns. Institutionally it is sometimes difficult to get into a limited partnership, so it may be that investors tend to take whatever share is allocated to them, leading to fairly uniform investment behavior.[7] Future research on understanding investor behavior seems clearly warranted.[8]

Apart from my comments on the two question that I consider most fundamental, that is, demand and supply and capital gains taxation, let me briefly make a few comments about the measurement of the size of the venture capital industry. The authors take a very reasonable measure, namely, the amount of money that venture capital funds raise in a particular year. The nature of the limited partnership arrangement is such that venture capital firms raise a particular amount that is put into a ''fund.'' Over the next few year, venture capitalists then have the right to call in the monies that were committed to the fund, typically calling them in a few discrete portions. They then disburse these funds as they invest in companies. The paper recognizes that the amount of funds committed does not correspond to the amount disbursed. It would be interesting in future research to examine whether this distinction affects the analysis. My main concern is that the current measure is better at measuring the available supply of venture capital funds rather than the actual demand. Put differently, if we want to learn more about the demand factors that drive venture capital fundraising, it would seem imprudent to rely on a measure of the funds made available, as opposed to the funds actually invested in companies.

Another interesting measurement issue is the appropriate scope of asset classes. It is not clear whether institutional investors think of venture capital as the relevant unit of analysis or instead make investment decisions on the basis of a broader (or narrow) asset class. In particular, venture capital investments are often lumped together with

7. Another factor that could augment this effect would be relative performance evaluation among investors.

8. Related to this, the authors do not seem to properly recognize the contribution by Anand (1993). Anand models the preferences of the investors more carefully than the current paper, allowing for investor heterogeneity. The authors' critique of Anand's paper—being too narrowly focused on the telecommunications sector—seems secondary compared with its methodological contribution.

leveraged buyout funds and some other private equity funds into what are called ''alternative assets.'' A natural question to ask is how the supply of venture capital interacts with these related asset classes. In a similar vein, it may also be interesting to think of the quantity of venture capital not in terms of the absolute amount, but instead as a fraction of gross domestic product or some measure of savings.

Finally, let me comment briefly on the section with the disaggregate data. The comments on demand versus supply factors and on the role of capital gains taxation obviously also apply to that section. One of the interesting new questions that arises from the disaggregate data is the role of the age of the venture capital firm. Although I agree with the authors that being older may imply having a greater reputation and may also lead to succession problems, I am not yet clear on how these two effects can be isolated. Concerning distinction of early- versus late-stage funds, I echo the authors' view that understanding their differences is of great importance, especially with a view on public policy. Future research might want to investigate whether the early-stage segment of the venture capital market behaves differently from the later-stage segment and how individual venture capital firms move between those two segments.[9]

Authors' Response: We appreciate the thoughtful comments by Margaret Blair and Thomas Hellmann. Their comments at the Brookings conference significantly improved our paper, and their amended comments published in this volume suggest a variety of avenues for future research.

One point mentioned by Thomas Hellmann bears repeating: the challenges associated with empirically examining the venture capital industry. Many data series routinely collected about the public markets by government regulators and private data vendors are not available here; and much of the information available is fraught with inconsistencies and ambiguities. The example of the blurred boundary between venture capital and leveraged buyout funds highlighted by Hellmann is just one example. As the industry matures and more data is collected, these

9. For example, one could run the aggregate-level and individual-level regressions in the two respective subsamples and compare their responsiveness to the various explanatory variables proposed in the paper.

problems may be alleviated; for now, however, they are an inherent feature of empirical research into venture capital.

The reader should be aware of these limitations but should not lose sight of the broader result. The industrywide, state-level, and fund-specific analyses all suggest that public efforts to boost the demand for venture capital are considerably more effective than steps to increase the supply of funds. The findings lead us to view more favorably public efforts designed to enhance the attractiveness of entrepreneurship and the rate of technological innovation and to regard more skeptically efforts to address the supply of venture capital directly. Due to the potential for political distortions, programs that seek to stimulate the supply of venture capital by directly funding small firms must be viewed with particular caution.[10]

Commentators' References

Anand, Bharat N. 1993. "Tax Effects on Venture Capital." Unpublished working paper. Princeton. October.

Lerner, Josh. Forthcoming. "The Government as Venture Capitalist: The Long-Run Effects of the SBIR Program." *Journal of Business.*

National Science Board. 1998. *Science and Engineering Indicators.* Washington.

---

10. For one example of political distortion, see Lerner (forthcoming).

AXEL BÖRSCH-SUPAN
University of Mannheim
Center for Economic Policy Research
National Bureau of Economic Research

Capital's Contribution to Productivity and the Nature of Competition

PRODUCTIVITY RESEARCH has traditionally focused on labor productivity and treated capital intensity as one of the factors causing different levels of labor productivity.[1] Much less attention has been given to the effi-

This paper is based on research performed during the author's sabbatical year at the McKinsey Global Institute, Washington, D.C., directed by William W. Lewis. Sean Greene was project coordinator. Other team members were Raj Agrawal, Tom Büttgenbach, Steve Findley, Kathryn Huang, Aly Jeddy, and Markus Petry. The team benefited greatly from comments by the project advisory committee members: Ben Friedman, Zvi Griliches, Ted Hall, and Bob Solow. The author benefited from comments by Hans Gersbach, Jens Köke, Ulrich Schlieper, Joachim Winter, and the participants at several workshops and seminars, in particular those at the Brookings conference.

1. The literature on international and intertemporal productivity comparisons is vast. For a recent survey, see Gersbach (1997). Most work measures levels and growth of labor productivity at both the aggregate and the industry level. For manufacturing, van Ark and Pilat (1993) compiled a comprehensive set of productivity figures for Germany, Japan, and the United States based on the industry-of-origin approach; McKinsey Global Institute (1993) and Baily and Gersbach (1995) compiled productivity figures based on factory-gate purchasing power parities. More recent estimates appear in Freudenberg and Ünal-Kesenci (1994, for France and Germany), O'Mahony (1995), and Pilat (1996), which included some service industries. McKinsey Global Institute (1992) and Baily (1993) provide productivity level estimates for selected service industries. Another strand of literature investigates total factor productivity (TFP) growth. The work by Denison (1974, 1985) and Jorgenson, Gollop, and Fraumeni (1987) set up the methodology for TFP growth estimates. Based on this, the volume edited by Jorgenson (1995) and the articles by Dollar and Wolff (1988, 1994) provide a set of recent international TFP growth comparisons. There is much less work on TFP levels. Conrad and Jorgenson (1995) and Jorgenson, Kuroda, and Nishimizu (1987) show aggregate and sectoral TFP

ciency of capital management and purchase decisions. High capital intensity may be not only an implication of high labor costs relative to capital, but also a consequence of wasteful allocation of capital. This paper investigates whether the utilization of installed capital is different across the three largest economies of the world—Germany, Japan, and the United States—and if so, why. It also asks whether the amount of assets needed to produce a particular level of productive capacity differs across these three countries, and if so, what the reasons for the difference might be.

The paper synthesizes research on capital productivity carried out by the McKinsey Global Institute and published in 1996. That study is similar to earlier studies that investigated service sector and manufacturing productivity.[2] Most of the data stem from studies performed by McKinsey industry experts, who visited automotive, electric utility, food processing, retailing, and telecommunications facilities in the three countries. McKinsey Global Institute (1996) provides details on the visits, data collection, and findings. These five sectors include the three most capital-intensive sectors of the economy (telecommunications, electric utilities, and retailing) and cover roughly a quarter of the nonresidential physical capital stock in each of the three nations' markets.

The data obtained from plant visits include plant, company, industry, and market sector data. From these data, the McKinsey team computed measures of labor productivity (output per labor hour) and physical capital productivity (output per unit of capital services). Their ratio yields capital intensity, and their weighted mean, total factor productivity, or TFP.[3] Of these four productivity measures, only two are independent. The measure of overall efficiency is TFP. The second

levels in Germany, Japan, and the United States up to 1979. Dougherty and Jorgenson (1996) provide TFP-level estimates up to 1989. Capital productivity estimates are implicit in TFP and in studies that address labor productivity together with capital intensity. For instance, Baily and Schultze (1990) and van Ark and Pilat (1993) address the contribution of capital to TFP levels without actually reporting capital productivity levels. Capital productivity levels are explicitly presented in Freudenberg and Ünal-Kesenci (1994) for France and Germany.

2. McKinsey Global Institute (1992, 1993); Baily (1993); Baily and Gersbach (1995).

3. More precisely, TFP is the harmonic mean, weighted by the shares of labor and capital.

measure I focus on is capital productivity. Differences in capital productivity may indicate the result of rational choice given prices and constraints, or the inefficient use of capital. For example, low capital productivity may be a rational choice of a manager who achieves high labor productivity with a large volume of capital because labor is expensive relative to capital. Alternatively, low capital productivity could result from unwise capital investments that do not increase labor productivity. A main thesis of the paper is that relative factor prices explain only part of the higher capital intensities in Germany and Japan compared with the United States. There is some evidence that capital purchasing and management practices in these five industries also decrease capital productivity.

The paper finds strikingly large differences in levels of physical capital productivity across the three economies, both at the macroeconomic level and in the five industries that were studied in detail. In many cases low capital productivity was not offset by high labor productivity. Capital management and purchasing decisions help explain the resulting different levels of total factor productivity in the three economies. Moreover, the differences in capital productivity correlate with the rate of return generated by the corporate sectors in the three economies. The rate of return of the U.S. corporate sector, averaged over the last twenty years, was 170 to 200 basis points higher than the rates of return in Japan and Germany. Such differences have an enormous impact on the increasing share of retirement income that is drawn from pension funds.[4]

The study also shows that the nature of competition facing companies in the product market has strongly influenced the efficiency with which capital is utilized. Specifically, capital markets have reinforced product market competition by cutting off funds to unproductive companies only in the face of competitive threats.[5] Regulation and government ownership were also important causes of low productivity, both directly and indirectly through limitations of competition.

4. According to OECD (1998), about 40 percent of U.S. retirement income is currently drawn from investments on the capital market, including firm pensions, 401(k) plans, and IRAs. See Börsch-Supan (1998) for an analysis.
5. See also Kovenock and Phillips (1997), who provide empirical evidence on the plant level for this interaction.

Figure 1. Capital Productivity, Labor Productivity, Capital Intensity, and TFP

Labor productivity

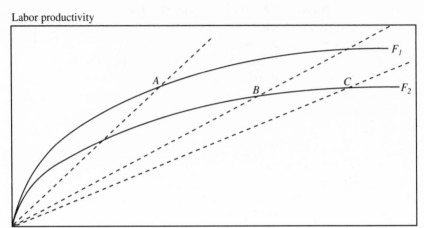

Capital intensity

Source: Author's construction; see text for full explanation.

Measurement Framework

The basic economic framework for making productivity comparisons is depicted in figure 1. For simplicity in the arguments below, I assume Cobb-Douglas technologies with identical labor shares.[6] On the axes are output per worker and capital intensity. Capital productivity is represented by a ray through the origin. Technology F_1 (dubbed, "best practice" or, "benchmark") has higher TFP than technology F_2. Industries A and B have adopted best practice with different capital intensities. Industry C represents the case I am particularly interested in: capital intensity is high and capital productivity is low without a compensating increase in labor productivity to bring the industry to top TFP.

Figure 1 also shows the fundamental identification problem in isolating causes of productivity differences. Capital and labor productivity figures do not identify whether it is capital or labor that is managed inefficiently. For example, industry C has both lower capital productivity and lower labor productivity relative to industry B, and there is no

6. A Cobb-Douglas function fits the aggregate data well; see Jorgensen, Gollop, and Fraumeni (1987) or Hall and Jones (forthcoming).

way to tell from the data underlying figure 1 whether it was bad capital management leading to a lower ray through the origin, or bad labor management leading to a lower ordinate value, or a combination of both.

The McKinsey team used microeconomic data to answer this question wherever possible. The team's research strategy was to compare companies that face the same relative prices of labor and capital, the same labor market characteristics (skill levels, costs for overtime, and so forth), but different capital productivity. For example, the team looked for companies that have low utilization rates even though other companies in the same country facing the same wage premiums for shift work run their machines longer. And they searched for instances where companies use structures and equipment of unusually high quality and quantity for a task that other companies perform with fewer assets— even though these companies face the same relative price of capital and similar constraints, such as safety and environmental standards.

In many cases, however, the management of labor and capital is so intrinsically interwoven that there is no point in attributing the corresponding change in TFP to either labor or capital. For example, a better assignment of personnel to machines increases labor and capital productivity simultaneously. Nevertheless, important insights can be gained by looking at capital's side of this joint improvement, mainly because earlier research has focused on labor management aspects, paying less attention to capital management issues. The obvious next question is why managers waste capital or manage capital and labor inefficiently. The paper goes through a checklist of potential explanations, including lack of competition, weak corporate governance, and inefficient government regulation

Data

The paper used data from four levels of aggregation: data at both the plant and company level obtained from interviews and benchmarking studies, published data at the industry level, and data for the entire market sector of each country. A consistent core set of data on output and capital was then constructed at each level of aggregation.

These data are a unique and very rich body of evidence largely untapped by academic research. The representativeness, validity, and replicability of this evidence has been discussed elsewhere.[7] In this particular study, the representativeness of some sectors is an issue. Although interviews and benchmarking studies covered most companies in concentrated sectors (automotive, telecommunications, electric utilities), such coverage was not possible in food processing and retailing. To improve the representativeness of the sample, the interview data on capacity utilization, capital expenditures, pricing, and the like were cross-checked with publicly available data sources such as industry censuses and published industry studies.

Sector Definitions

In contrast to most other studies using aggregate data, the aggregate analysis here is restricted to the market sector of each economy because there is no meaningful aggregate measure of productivity for the nonmarket sector.[8] The excluded nonmarket sector consisted of government, education, and health care services. Obtaining a consistent definition of the market sector and each industry across the three countries is not a straightforward task because sector definitions vary and because the sector definitions for output and capital stock data do not fully overlap in some industries even within a country. In these cases, more disaggregated data had to be used.[9] Nonindustry and auxiliary services, such as equipment production, were excluded from the telecommunications service industry.

Output Data

When meaningful, *physical output* was used—for example, kilowatt-hours (kWh) in electric utilities and call-minutes in the telecommuni-

---

7. Although many of the industry studies used are public (and quoted in the sources below each exhibit), benchmark studies performed by McKinsey are confidential. See the Comments and Discussion section of the Baily and Gersbach (1995) paper for a discussion of validity and replicability issues related to these data sources.

8. See the chapters by Jorgenson and Fraumeni and by Murray in Griliches (1992) for measurement of output in the education and public sectors, respectively, and Baily and Garber (1997) for an international productivity comparison of treating specific diseases.

9. For details, see McKinsey Global Institute (1996, aggregate analysis, box A1).

cations industry.[10] In the three industries in which output is heterogeneous (automotive, food processing, and retail) and at the market level, *value added* was used as the output measure.[11] Value added was converted into physical units of output by dividing it by sector-specific purchasing power parities (PPPs). The appropriate PPP for productivity comparisons are the unit prices at the factory gate of comparable products across countries.[12] Such an industry PPP was constructed from the bottom up in the automotive industry, weighting individual product PPPs to obtain an average PPP exchange rate for the industry as a whole. In the other industries and in the market sector, the relevant expenditure PPPs for taxes and distribution margins were adjusted to approximate factory-gate PPPs for the corresponding industries. The source for the PPPs was the most recent benchmark comparisons made by the Organization for Economic Cooperation and Development (OECD) in 1990 and 1993; because these benchmarks differed slightly, the 1990 and 1993 PPPs were averaged.[13] Table 1 displays the PPPs used for the large aggregates.

Capital Input Data

Because accounting conventions differ dramatically across countries with no evidence of corresponding differences in service lives, the McKinsey team did not use national accounting figures of capital stocks.[14] Instead, it applied the perpetual inventory method to time

10. Figures were drawn from the manufacturing censuses in the three countries (Germany: Statistisches Bundesamt; Japan: Economic Planning Agency; U.S.: Census of Manufactures).

11. Aggregate and industry data on value added were based on the OECD National Accounts 1981–1996 (OECD 1995, 1997, 1998).

12. There is an extensive body of literature on the usage of PPPs in international productivity comparisons. The methodology is summarized in Pilat (1994). A comparison of several approaches to approximate factory-gate PPPs can be found in Hooper (1996). See also the discussion on the papers by van Ark and Pilat (1993) and Baily and Gersbach (1995).

13. The sectoral results are published in OECD (1992, 1995). The EKS aggregation scheme was applied to the set of three countries to compute sectoral PPPs, for example, from industry to market level. More precisely, the appropriate deflators between 1990 and 1993 were applied to the 1990 benchmark prices to obtain an estimate of the 1993 PPP, and this estimate was averaged with the 1993 PPPs reported by the OECD.

14. See Blades (1991, 1993) for recent surveys of measurement issues. O'Mahony (1993) provides a bibliography on capital stock measurement.

Table 1. Purchasing Power Parities
Relative to 1993 U.S. dollar

| | Total economy | | | Market sector | |
| | | | | | |
Country	Exchange rate	Value added	Gross fixed capital formation	Value added	Gross fixed capital formation
Germany (DM)	1.65	2.10	2.27	2.47	2.38
Japan (Yen)	111	184	213	227	213

Source: Author's calculations based on OECD (1992, 1995).

series of capital expenditures at the industry, market, and total economy levels, subtracting standardized, rather than nationally defined, depreciation. The team did this separately for structures and equipment as well as for each sector. Capital expenditure time series were taken from the U.S. Bureau of Economic Analysis, the Japanese Economic Planning Agency, and the German Statistisches Bundesamt (Volkswirtschaftliche Gesamtrechnungen, Fachserie 18), starting in 1925 or earlier. The value of capital expenditures was converted to physical units by dividing structures by the OECD nonresidential structures PPP, and equipment by a general equipment PPP that was aggregated from the corresponding detailed OECD equipment PPPs.[15] The study used the "sudden death" depreciation schedule, assuming that capital services flows are evenly distributed over the entire life of the capital good. Sector-specific service lives as computed by O'Mahony were used for structures and equipment.[16] TFP and capital productivity differences are insensitive to the choice of depreciation schedule and length of service life as long as they are the same across countries. The methodology follows Maddison and O'Mahony, and the study's net capital stocks are closely comparable to their estimates in the years and sectors where the two sets of data overlap.[17] Table 2 displays the concentration of capital across the five industries studied in this paper.

Capital stocks were also converted to a measure of the *flow of capital services* used in the production process by dividing capital stocks by their service lives. Differences between stock and flow measures are

15. OECD (1992, 1995).
16. O'Mahoney (1993). I am grateful to Mary O'Mahony who provided hitherto unpublished data enabling me to compute capital stocks with a consistent definition of the market sector in each country.
17. Maddison (1987, 1993); O'Mahoney (1993).

Table 2. Capital Breakdown by Industry, 1994

Percentage of market economy

Country	Automotive	Food processing	Retailing	Telecom- munications	Electric utilities	Other industries
United States	1.4	1.4	8.4	4.8	8.2	75.8
Germany	5.1	2.0	4.4	3.9	4.4	80.2
Japan	3.5	1.3	7.4	3.5	6.1	78.2

Source: McKinsey Global Institute (1996, "objectives to approach," exhibit 12).

caused by differences in the composition of the capital stock: Germany has the highest share of structures that have a longer service life; Japan the lowest and thus a relatively smaller flow of services than equipment. The McKinsey team believes that service flow, rather than capital stock, is the more appropriate measure of capital usage in production. German flows of capital services in the market sector are closer to the U.S. flows than the corresponding stocks are; the difference is larger between Japan and the United States.

Figure 2 displays capital stocks and services in the total economy and the market sectors of the three countries, measured on a per capita basis. In the market sector, Germany exceeded the U.S. per capita level of capital stocks and services as far back as in 1970. At that time, Japan was at an earlier stage of development and had less than 40 percent of structures and about 50 percent of total capital relative to the United States. Capital grew in all three countries but faster in Germany and Japan. The speed of accumulation was particularly high in Japan during the bubble years of the late 1980s but slowed dramatically afterwards, particularly in the nonmarket sector. The United States increased equipment stocks more quickly than structures, whereas Germany and Japan grew their stocks of structures faster, leading to differing growth rates of stocks and services.

Taking 1992–95 averages, market-sector capital services in Germany and Japan were 10.3 and 16.2 percent higher than in the United States, measured on a per capita basis. During the same time, labor input per capita in the market sector, measured in hours, was 21.7 percent lower in Germany and 37.2 percent higher in Japan. This implies that the flow-based capital intensity was 41 percent higher in Germany and 15 percent lower in Japan than in the U.S. market sector. Total economy capital intensities are closer to each other. In 1992–95, flow-based

Figure 2. Capital Stocks and Services Per Capita, 1970–95

Thousands of 1993 U.S. dollars[a]

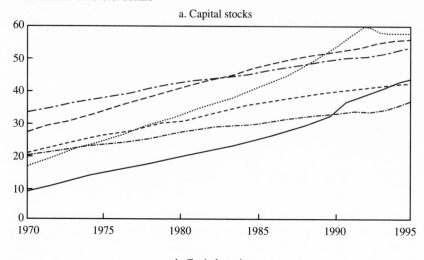

a. Capital stocks

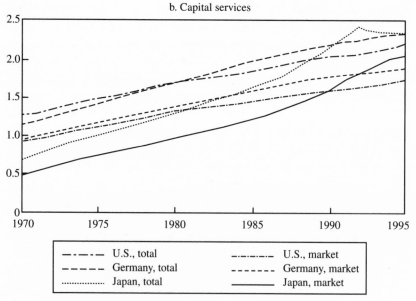

b. Capital services

—·—·—	U.S., total	—··—··—	U.S., market
—————	Germany, total	— — — —	Germany, market
··············	Japan, total	——————	Japan, market

Sources: McKinsey Global Institute (1996, 1997, 1998) and author's calculations.
a. Measured at gross fixed capital formation PPP.

Table 3. Productivity Results

Percentages relative to U.S. = 100

Country	Automotive 1991–93	Food processing 1992	Retailing 1992	Telecom- munications 1994	Electric utilities 1993	Market economy 1991–95
Total factor productivity						
Germany	70	65	95	47	73	85
Japan	120	47	55	58	57	59
Capital productivity						
Germany	65	70	110	38	78	68
Japan	100	64	65	46	49	66
Labor productivity						
Germany	75	63	90	72	66	96
Japan	130	39	50	96	101	56

Sources: Author's calculations based on McKinsey Global Institute (1996, 1997, 1998).
Notes: Labor's and capital's shares in TFP vary across industry but not across country.

capital intensity in Germany was 34 percent higher and in Japan 8 percent lower than in the United States.

Results

Table 3 summarizes productivity results for the five sectors studied and for the market economy. Productivity in Japan and Germany is lower than in the United States with two important exceptions: automotive production in Japan, and retail in Germany. In the automotive industry and the market sector, the results are averaged in order to purge business cycle effects. The variation across sectors and countries is large. Most striking is the contrast between the Japanese automotive sector and the other four industries in Japan, notably the food processing sector. German and Japanese TFP and capital productivity are remarkably low in the capital-intensive and highly regulated or monopolized telecommunications and electric utility industries.

The paper proceeds in two steps. First, it studies the market sector results in order to obtain a survey of the general situation in the three countries. It then investigates capital utilization and capital investment decisions in each of the five sectors.

Market Sector

German market sector TFP is 15 percent lower than U.S. TFP. This estimate of the gap is not much different from the estimates that were cited in the introduction, although those estimates referred to the total economy at the end of the 1980s and were based on capital stocks. The 41 percent TFP difference between the Japanese and U.S. market sectors is substantially larger than recent conventional estimates, however. For instance, Dougherty and Jorgenson reported a 16.5 percent gap for 1989, and Hall and Jones a 29.5 percent difference in 1988.[18] There are several reasons for these discrepancies. The most important reason is the inclusion of the nonmarket sector in the earlier productivity estimates. Reported value added of the Japanese nonmarket sector, relative to labor and capital inputs, is much higher than it is in the United States. Because of the problems in comparing nonmarket sector output across countries, I believe that the apparent high productivity in the government, health, and education sectors is not meaningful and that the market economy estimate is a more meaningful measure of aggregate industrial productivity. Another reason is the large Japanese investment volume before 1992 that is only partially captured in the earlier estimates and accounts for about a 5 percentage point decrease in relative TFP over the 1991–1995 period. The difference between a stock and a service-based estimate is of minor importance.

The bottom rows of table 3 separate TFP into labor and capital productivity. The market level results are graphically displayed in figure 3. Germany has a labor productivity slightly below that of the United States and a substantially lower capital productivity. Labor productivity is much lower in Japan than in the United States and Germany. Capital productivity in Japan is only slightly lower than in Germany and much lower than in the United States. Approximating the production technologies by a Cobb-Douglas function with a labor share of 0.36 produces the data in figure 3a. Germany and the United States have higher capital intensities and higher labor productivities than does Japan. These higher labor productivities might be expected from high capital investment. The comparison between Germany and the United States yields a counterexample, however: the higher German capital intensity does not yield a labor productivity higher than in the U.S. market sector.

18. Dougherty and Jorgenson (1996); Hall and Jones (1996).

Figure 3. Capital Productivity, Labor Productivity, Capital Intensity, and TFP

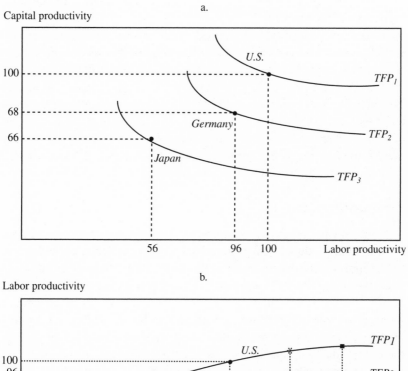

a.

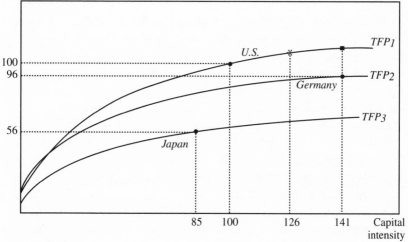

b.

Source: Author's construction.

Figure 3b shows that diminishing returns are not the only reason for low German capital productivity. The German market sector could theoretically have reached the best-practice point for its high level of capital intensity (marked by a square). At this point, capital productivity would be about 80 percent of the U.S. level. In this sense, about two-thirds of the capital productivity gap is due to diminishing returns, one-third wasted in lower TFP. The inefficient use of resources, labor, and capital is likely to have increased capital intensity if labor was relatively more expensive, however. The higher German labor costs relative to capital, as discussed later, would rationalize a capital intensity of only 126 percent of the U.S. level. At this point, marked by an asterisk, capital productivity would be at 86 percent.

Capacity Utilization

I turn now to the microeconomic evidence to understand what caused the other half of the capital productivity gap, in particular, whether part of the high capital intensity was "wasted" in inefficient capital management. Capacity utilization in the food processing and automotive industry is defined as the running time of machines. Because of maintenance, repairs and refitting, a limited number of shifts, and holiday closings, machines are not run twenty-four hours a day every day. In the retail industry, capacity may not be fully utilized because shops are closed at times when customers would like to patronize them. In the electric utilities industry, capacity utilization is the combination of grid capacity utilization (kWh per kilometer of power lines) and power generation capacity utilization (the ratio of actual generation to installed capacity). Finally, in telecommunications, capacity utilization is defined as the number of call minutes per access line.[19]

Table 4 summarizes the estimates of capacity utilization and displays capacity creation, which is defined and discussed later. Because of a lack of comparability in publicly available data, McKinsey benchmarking comparisons were used at the company and plant level and normalized by setting utilization in the United States equal to 100. Capacity utilization was lower in Germany and Japan than in the United States in almost all industries. There were, however, marked differences

19. In 1994, there were no technical capacity constraints for call minutes. Excess network capacity was actually about 60 percent in the United States.

Table 4. Capacity Utilization and Capacity Created
Percentage relative to U.S. = 100

Country	Automotive	Food processing	Retailing	Telecom- munications	Electric utilities
Capacity utilization					
Germany	75	75	96	46	90
Japan	115	62	100	44	51
Capacity created					
Germany	87	93	115	82	89
Japan	85	92	65	104	86

Source: McKinsey Global Institute (1996). See table 3 for relevant time periods.

across industries and between Germany and Japan. The difference is most striking in telecommunications and electric utilities. Capital management is potentially important in these industries because capital's share is so large (64 percent of value added in the telecommunications industry and 72 percent in electric utilities).

Japan is the benchmark in terms of TFP and also has the highest capacity utilization in the *automotive industry*.[20] Germany lags behind Japan and the United States. One component of capital utilization is plant operating hours. In 1991–93 plants in Germany operated between 3,500 and 4,000 hours a year; in the United States, 3,800–5,000 hours; and in Japan, 3,800–5,600 hours. Differences in the number of shifts account for only a small portion of these operating hour differences. Japanese and German plants uniformly ran two shifts a day, as did most U.S. plants; the exception was U.S. stamping plants, where three shifts were common. The main difference comes from fewer days worked per year in the United States and Germany, and a slightly shorter average shift length in Germany. These differences can be attributed to different labor-leisure trade-offs. There were also considerable differences in machine downtime during operating hours. These differences are important for assessing the role of capital management. Japanese plants reached an "uptime" of almost 95 percent during 1991–93, but uptime was less than 90 percent in the United States and only about 75 percent in Germany, largely because of frequent changeovers in both countries and a significantly higher rate of stopping to rework defects in German

20. The industry includes parts and assembly of cars and trucks. Parts and assembly could not be separated for Germany. U.S. plants include Japanese transplants; German plants include Ford and GM (Opel).

plants. The differences in plant operating hours and uptime imply that Japan's capacity utilization is 15 percent higher than in the United States and 40 percent higher than in Germany; in both comparisons, the overall differences were about equally divided between differences in plant operating hours and differences in machine uptimes.

These figures aggregate over important differences across segments and individual companies. Japanese auto assembly is actually less capital productive than U.S. assembly. That is offset, however, by a 20 percent capital productivity advantage in the parts segment of the Japanese automotive industry. The variation across companies is also large. Lieberman, Lau, and Williams report that in 1987 General Motors was less productive than the German auto industry, whereas Ford and Chrysler had already made major productivity improvements and had nearly attained Japanese productivity levels.[21] Similar intraindustry variation held for Japan. In 1987 Toyota had a 15 percent capital productivity advantage over Nissan, a 25 percent advantage over Mazda.

Plant operating hours and machine uptime are also the main factors determining capacity utilization in the *food processing* industry, which features large differences across plants and subindustries.[22] The comparison between the automotive and the food processing industry also shows that country patterns are by no means uniform. Whereas the Japanese automotive industry had both longer operating hours and less downtime than their U.S. and German counterparts, this pattern was reversed in the food processing industry. Thus, differences in operating hours and downtime cannot simply be attributed to countrywide labor and capital market factors. In the dairy industry, an example from the lower end of the productivity distribution across food processing subindustries, the average U.S. plant ran 18.6 hours a day, compared with 13.8 and 11.8 hours in Germany and Japan, respectively. Of that, total daily downtime was 1.5 hours in the United States, 2.2 hours in Germany, and about 5 hours in Japan. The low machine uptime in Japan was due mainly to frequent changeovers, while the difference between the United States and Germany was caused mainly by unbalanced pro-

21. Lieberman, Lau, and Williams (1990).
22. The food industry includes all foodstuff that does not go directly from the farm to the grocer. Excluded are beverages. Pet food is not included in the U.S.-Japan comparison. Differences across plants and subindustries are discussed in more detail in McKinsey Global Institute (1996).

duction lines, where congestion led to stoppages. Taking plant operating hours and machine uptime together, capacity utilization was 25 percent lower in Germany and 38 percent lower in Japan than in the United States.

In the *retailing* industry, capital utilization was the same in Japan and the United States. Restrictions on store opening hours reduced capital utilization in Germany.[23] Estimates of this effect are controversial because little is known about how much shopping during extended hours is simply substituted from other times. According to one estimate, value added in the German retailing industry would increase by about 4 percent if store hours were completely liberalized. This estimate is very conservative because it does not consider second-round effects such as a shift from low to high productivity formats in response to different shopping habits.[24]

In the telecommunications and electric utility industries, capacity utilization is more about spreading the costs of a large fixed asset base than about operating hours and machine uptime. In *telecommunications*, local calls made the main difference.[25] The United States had 2,801 local and 418 long-distance call minutes per access line in 1994, compared with Germany, which had 930 local and 401 long-distance call minutes.[26] Capacity constraints do not account for the difference—call volume in 1994 did not come close to the technical capacity in either country. German capacity utilization in the local loop was 33 percent of the U.S. level, and in total calls 46 percent.[27] In Japan, call volume was 44 percent of the U.S. level. A significant part of the lower call volume can be explained by price differentials, in particular free local calls in the United States. The telecommunications industry is an example where labor and capital productivity can be simultaneously

23. Retailing in this study is restricted to general merchandise, excluding food, car, gas, drugs, and liquor.

24. Ifo-Institut (1995). "Formats" in retailing refer to the distinction among department stores, discount stores, specialty stores, and small "mom-and-pop" retailers with fewer than five employees.

25. The telecommunications industry is defined here as public wireline and cellular operations. Not included are private networks, equipment, cable services, and bulk line leasing.

26. FCC Statistics of Communications Common Carriers, 1995; Siemens International Telecom Statistics, 1995.

27. This figure adjusts for the different service areas (local vs. long-distance) between Germany and the United States.

improved because funneling more calls through already installed access lines requires no new capital and relatively little additional labor. Because of capital's large share, however, spreading the fixed asset base is particularly important in increasing TFP.

Patterns in the *electric utilities* industry resemble the telecommunications industry.[28] Varying widely across the three countries, utilization of generation capacity is highest in Germany (50.5 percent of installed capacity), lowest in Japan (38.6 percent). The United States is in the middle (46.5 percent). This variation is attributable mainly to demand-side management, in particular peak-load pricing schemes in Germany and the United States. Utilization of the grid capacity differed even more: Germany's grid utilization was 63 percent of the U.S. utilization rate, more than offsetting the German advantage in higher generation capacity utilization. Japan had a particularly low grid capacity utilization of 36 percent of the U.S. level. Geography explains only part of these differences; the main explanation is differences in consumption. The grids are designed for similar throughputs in all three countries, but per capita electricity consumption is twice as high in the United States as it is in either Germany or Japan.

Capacity Creation

The second component of capital productivity is called capacity creation. Once capacity utilization has been measured at the plant level, capacity creation is simply capital productivity divided by the capacity utilization rate.[29] The figures for capacity created, shown in table 4, reflect output per unit of capital relative to that in the United States (which is again set equal to 100), after adjusting for differences in utilization rates. In some industries, capacity creation has a simple interpretation. In retailing, it is decomposed into two components: the value added per volume unit of goods sold, and the throughput in terms of volume units of goods sold per capital services used.[30] In telecom-

28. The industry comprises generation, transmission, and distribution. Independent power producers and autogenerators were excluded because capital expenditure data was unavailable. For detailed data sources, see McKinsey Global Institute (1996).

29. At the industry level, this relation is confounded by mix effects. See later discussion.

30. Throughput is a physical measure: sales divided by the consumer goods PPP. As opposed to most other studies of retailing, the output measure used here is value

munications, capacity created is the number of access lines; in the electric utilities industry, the amount of capacity (in megawatts) per unit of capital invested.

As a residual, the measure includes a whole range of components, of which I try to isolate the most important ones in assessing the effectiveness of capital management whenever possible. One such component is overinvestment in or "overengineering" of asset features or functions that do not contribute to an increase of output quantity or product quality for which customers pay. Another important component, related to both labor and capital management, is the defect rate. Defects reduce the ratio of output to capacity at a given utilization rate. Capacity creation is also affected by the choice of technology and by product mix. The McKinsey team isolated heterogeneity of technology by looking separately at well-defined subindustries (such as nuclear, fossil fuel, and hydropower plants) and then analyzing mix effects and product heterogeneity by applying product-specific PPPs.

There are obvious limits to the concept of capital creation as an instrument to gauge the efficiency of capital management. For instance, overengineering is clearly a capital management and purchasing decision constrained by safety and environmental regulations, whereas defect rates are functions of both labor and capital management. Moreover, capacity utilization and capacity creation are not necessarily independent from each other. For example, a higher utilization rate may come at the expense of maintenance and may therefore produce a higher defect rate.

In the *automotive industry*, the main story is "lean production": using simple machines lowers the capital requirements per line and reduces the defect rate at the same time, thus increasing net output per line.[31] For example, Japanese car makers stamp 50 percent more cars per press line than American producers, and the Japanese defect rate is 32 percent lower than in American plants and 56 percent lower than in European plants.[32] Ironically and much less known, the steep increase in automation and other capital between 1987 and 1993 in Japan sig-

---

added, which does not include intermediate service, rather than gross margin, which does.

31. The term "lean production" was coined by the MIT International Motor Vehicle Program. See Lieberman, Lau, and Williams (1990).

32. Harbour (1994).

nificantly raised the capital used per unit of production capacity, fully offsetting the Japanese advantage in higher capacity utilization. In 1987 capital intensity in the three countries was roughly comparable (91 percent of the U.S. rate in both Germany and Japan). From 1987 to 1992, capital intensity in Japan rose to 136 of the U.S. level (in Germany to 116 percent), while U.S. capital intensity remained unchanged. This increase in capital intensity drove Japanese TFP growth in the automotive industry well below U.S. TFP growth.[33]

In the German auto industry, the benchmarking studies found many instances of overengineered processes, such as higher levels of precision than tasks required. For instance, one German auto manufacturer made cylinder borings with almost double the precision of the industry standard. According to managers of this company, the additional precision neither smoothed engine movement nor prolonged engine life. After a financial crisis, the company began to make its borings with standard precision, evidently without loss of consumer satisfaction. In general, German plants typically needed more than five stamping steps to mold body panels, one of the most capital-expensive steps in car manufacturing, whereas Japanese plants require at most four. Again, major German automakers are improving their stamping process as part of the current process of restructuring.

The *food industry* was historically regionalized in all three countries, largely because of inability to transport perishable products over longer distances. After cooling technology lifted this constraint, the United States was faster to rationalize capacity by shutting down marginal plants. Japan and Germany still have excess capacity. The dairy industry is a case in point: The number of milk manufacturers in the United States fell from 4.1 per 1 million inhabitants in 1977 to 2.0 in 1992, while machine operating time increased to 18.6 hours a day, corresponding to 66 percent capacity utilization. Total factor productivity of the U.S. dairy industry increased 43 percent. In Germany, consolidation reduced the number of milk industry manufacturers from 5.4 to 3.2 per 1 million inhabitants, which was not enough to eliminate excess capacity. Machine run time was actually reduced to 11.8 hours a day,

33. For example, the decision by Honda to build a new air-conditioned assembly plant was driven by an expected boost in car sales, a need to provide amenities to an expected scarcity of laborers, and a perception of very low costs of capital. This plant severely reduced Honda's capital productivity.

corresponding to a capacity utilization of only 42 percent. TFP increased only 31 percent in Germany. Throughout the food processing industry, marginal plants in Japan spent more assets in logistics and distribution per unit of products than did larger plants in Japan, and marginal plants in Germany wasted assets in imbalanced production lines and other operational practices. Although a low utilization rate was pervasive in both countries, these wasteful practices reduced capital productivity by another 7–8 percent.

German *retailers* maximized the capacity created with a given set of assets. The main factor in retailing is floor space, and German retailers use much less floor space than do U.S. firms to generate comparable sales. German department stores, for instance, generated sales of $3,400 a square meter in 1992, U.S. department stores only $1,900. The difference is more pronounced in specialty and discount stores, less so in the small mom-and-pop stores. On average, throughput per unit of assets was 20 percent higher in the German retail industry, giving it a distinct advantage relative to the U.S. industry. At the same time, U.S. retailers achieved high capital productivity by offering more service than did retailers in Germany.[34] The U.S. value added per unit of throughput is about 10 percent higher than in Germany. Japanese retailers have about 25 percent less throughput per invested capital and about 15 percent less value added per throughput than do U.S. retailers.

In the *telecommunications* industry, Japan and the United States had roughly the same levels of capacity creation. Japan used slightly less capital per access line than did the United States. The German Telekom monopoly, however, spent 18 percent more capital per access line than Japan and the United States.[35] About half of that was spent on more costly underground wires. This difference has two components: Germany might have saved approximately 50 percent of the difference if it had adopted the U.S. aerial to underground cable mix at U.S. cable prices. Because underground cables are likely to provide more aesthetic appeal and are more reliable in preventing power outages, this component reflects a weakness in the output measure rather than a lack of

34. This effect is probably underestimated.
35. In 1994 German Telekom had a 90 percent market share in the entire industry, and a 100 percent share in wireline. In the United States, AT&T had a 24 percent share, other former Bell companies an additional 44 percent. In Japan, NTT had a 70 percent market share.

productivity. The other 50 percent, however, represents overengineering in the sense that these underground wires are unnecessarily costly: they are required to be able to withstand the full impact of being run over by a tank without losing their ability to function even though they are buried almost one meter deep. The German telecommunications industry also failed to reconfigure existing assets to free up hidden capacity as was done in the U.S. industry. Instead German Telekom provided a huge ISDN (Integrated Services Digital Network) capacity that was not used much during the 1992–94 sample period. Admittedly, the static productivity measure used here penalizes such future-oriented investments, but it is not clear whether these investments were sound. Most industry experts interviewed for this study voiced doubts and would have recommended a more phased implementation that reduced the danger of obsolescence. The developments in the wake of the German telecommunications privatization after January 1998—the usage of existing but unused parallel grids and the development of asynchronous data transmittal techniques leapfrogging ISDN—are evidence in favor of this opinion.

In the *electric utility* industry, the United States produced about 10 percent more kilowatt hours per invested assets than did Germany and Japan. According to German industry specialists, the German electric utilities tended to spend much more to produce the same amount of electricity. Examples are thicker concrete walls housing generators and unnecessarily spacious walks to rarely used devices. In Japan, several power plants were not connected to the grid by 1993. These plants were built because of a projected steep rise in demand, which did not actually materialize until 1998. This unused capacity accounts for a quarter of the capital productivity difference between Japan and the United States.

Slack in capacity utilization thus accounts for most of the capital productivity gap among Germany, Japan, and the United States.

Mix Effects

In a given industry made up of different subindustry segments, mix effects could contribute to differences in capital productivity at the industry level. In no case in practice did the mix of subindustries affect the capital productivity ranking for the overall industry. The McKinsey team, however, found significant mix effects in the food and electric utility industries. Japan's seafood industry holds a disproportionately large part of the overall food processing industry, and its capital productivity is substantially above average (81 percent versus 64 percent of U.S. level).[36] Relative productivity rankings were similar across the other food categories such as bakery, meat, and dairy. Taking these mix effects into account raised Japanese capital productivity in the food industry by 11 percent relative to a U.S.-type industry structure. Utilization, capacity creation, and relative shares of total energy production in the electric utility case differed significantly by fuel type. Germany, for instance, had more nuclear power plants than the United States and Japan, and German nuclear plants were far more capital productive than U.S. nuclear power plants.[37] The reverse was true for fossil-fuel plants. These differences approximately offset each other, however, so the mix of subindustries did not contribute much to capital productivity differences at the industry level.

Capital Management

What explains these differences in capital utilization and creation? This section explores five dimensions of capital management: operations effectiveness, product-line management, pricing, capital purchasing decisions, and industry chain management. Other dimensions, such as differences in technology, are omitted because they appear to be much less important in explaining capital productivity differences. There is one important exception discussed later—the heavy automation of the Japanese auto industry around 1990.

Operations Effectiveness

The way in which firms organize and operate their plants, stores, and networks is a critical factor in explaining differences in capital

36. The value added share of seafood is 15 percent in Japan, compared with 3 percent in both Germany and the United States.

37. Nuclear power plants supplied 27 percent of total electricity generation in Germany in 1993, 15 percent in the United States, and 20 percent in Japan. Relative to the average capital productivity of all U.S. power generators, U.S. nuclear power plants had a productivity of 46 percent, while fossil-fuel plants were at 166 percent. In Germany, productivity of nuclear power plants was 80 percent of the average U.S. level, productivity of fossil-fuel plants was 94 percent of the average U.S. level.

productivity across countries. In general, operations effectiveness improves both capital and labor productivity. Baily and Gersbach provide many examples, which do not need to be repeated here, about how a better organization of workers' functions and tasks improves output per worker.[38]

Operational effectiveness also has specific implications for capital productivity. First, better practices improve utilization by reducing machine downtime. This is most important in manufacturing industries in which downtime is a substantial determinant of capital utilization. On average, Japanese auto manufacturers set up faster during changeovers and stop machines for less time to fix process problems.[39] Second, good machine design increases the effective capacity of a line per unit of invested assets. Again, the auto industry illustrates the point. Japanese manufacturers used better design for manufacturability, as well as their continuous improvement *(kaizen)* approach, to reduce the number of production steps and lower the defect rate. In addition, one may argue that consumers recognize and pay for the higher reliability that is frequently associated with a lower defect rate in the factory. All three mechanisms are examples of capital-related management actions that raise the numerator in both capital and labor productivity.

Product-Line Management

Most types of machines can be adapted to multiple tasks. Adaptation has the advantage of spreading capital costs, but it also involves costly downtime. Product-line management refers to the trade-off between task variety and capital utilization. Effective product-line management boosts capital utilization by optimizing this trade-off.

An example is the Japanese food industry, which had three times as many different food products (measured in stockkeeping units) per unit of sales volume in 1992 than the United States. Such variety may be a good thing in principle, but the Japanese trade-off appears to be inefficient because the added variety in Japan does not result in a higher value-added food industry. At the same time, Japan's average utilization rates are less than two-thirds of the U.S. level. A particularly

38. Baily and Gersbach (1995).
39. This point is well known and has been documented; see, for example, Lieberman, Lau, and Williams (1990).

Table 5. Mix and Productivity of Retailing Formats, Japan and the United States

Category	Mom-and-pop stores	Department stores	Discount stores	Specialty stores
Mix of formats (percent of capacity)				
United States	9.8	12.1	22.6	55.5
Japan	24.9	29.9	0.4	44.8
Japanese productivity (relative to U.S. = 100)				
Capital productivity	10	80	105	120
Labor productivity	15	95	90	120
TFP	15	90	94	120

Source: McKinsey Global Institute (1996, "retail," exhibits 10, 12).

dramatic example is the Japanese dairy industry, where lines must stop for every change in container size or milk-fat content. As a result, total dairy shutdown time is about three times longer than in the United States and Germany, and changeovers occupy more than 30 percent of total operating time (compared with 9 percent in the United States and 14 percent in Germany). The benchmarking studies showed many world-class manufacturers, including some in Japan, who used market research to help them avoid excess product variety and improve the trade-off between product variety and plant utilization.

In retail, the evolution of different selling formats represents an important improvement in product-line management. The difference between Japan and the United States is particularly impressive. Specialty stores have a distinct productivity advantage in Japan, while small mom-and-pop stores fare particularly badly (table 5). This is most pronounced in terms of capital productivity. The different format mix accounts for more than 50 percent of the capital productivity difference between Japan and the United States.

Pricing

Pricing is the most important factor in explaining differences in capacity utilization in telecommunications and electric utilities. In the U.S. telecommunications industry, flat rate pricing and low price levels relative to other goods and services stimulated higher levels of demand over the largely fixed asset base, resulting in higher utilization than in Germany or Japan. To show how much pricing affects capacity utilization, the McKinsey team converted the German and Japanese pricing system to the U.S. system and applied a conservative price elasticity estimate of -0.3 for local and -0.7 for long-distance calls.[40] The difference is particularly dramatic for Germany, where a call minute is on average 60 percent more expensive than in the United States; the price differential in Japan is 20 percent. Germany would increase its call minutes per access line from 46 percent to 82 percent of the U.S. level, and Japan from 44 to 56 percent, if these countries were to switch to the U.S. pricing system with free local and cheaper long-distance calls.

In the electric utilities, capacity utilization heavily depends on the daily and annual variability of the load curve. Innovative pricing structures, such as time-of-use pricing, have proved effective in both Germany and the United States by reducing demand at peak time periods. Japan did not charge different time-of-use prices in the period under consideration. As a result, demand was much more volatile there, and average capacity utilization was low. Demand at the annual peak hour was 28.3 percent higher than average demand in Germany (26.5 percent higher in the United States); in Japan the difference was 77.7 percent. Seasonal patterns do not explain the different utilization rates. Peak demand in Germany occurs during the heating season in February, whereas peak demand in Japan and the United States is during the air conditioning season in summer. Nor is scale an adequate explanation. The United States has a much higher total demand than Japan (11,170 kWh vs. 5,029 kWh per capita in 1993). But Germany's scale (5,511 kWh per capita) is similar to Japan's, yet Germany has a much higher utilization rate.

Capital Purchasing Decisions

Several examples of unwise capital purchasing decisions were significant for the respective industries—at least in hindsight. Exaggerated demand forecasts led to too much capital investment in the Japanese electric utility industry. An overestimate of future labor shortages precipitated excessive capital-labor substitution in the Japanese automotive industry. The resulting overautomatization has been corrected in newer plants. The telecommunications industries of Germany and Japan have made huge investments in new technologies (such as ISDN and fiber-

40. Meyer (1980); Taylor (1979).

to-the-home) that are unlikely to pay back in the near and medium future. Managers in the German food processing industry did not eliminate underutilized capacity and consolidated much less than in the U.S. industry. Finally, there were many instances of overengineering in the German telecommunications and electric utilities industries.

Overengineering has two types of costs. The more obvious is the inefficiency of unused capacity. The second is that the excess capital is sometimes purchased at inflated prices. In the measure of physical capital productivity used here, most of the effects of pure price differences were removed through the application of investment goods PPPs. Although this process helps to isolate purely operational differences, it ignores the possibility that corporations in Germany and Japan could have paid less for their equipment, thereby improving financial performance. On average, capital equipment PPPs in Germany and Japan were 48 percent and 67 percent higher than the market exchange, respectively. These price differentials are striking because most equipment is tradable. In fact, interviews revealed frequent managerial biases toward locally produced equipment in both Germany and Japan. These biases were often not justified by barriers to global sourcing; rather, managers were either unaware of lower cost alternatives or were willing to pay more because of long-established relationships with local suppliers. Deutsche Telekom in Germany, for instance, paid local suppliers up to 60 percent above international prices. German auto manufacturers recognized the opportunity to reduce costs and moved to more global sourcing in the last several years. Only in some cases were local purchases at higher prices justified. In food processing in Japan, for example, some of the local price premium was offset by subsequent cost savings from local servicing and parts availability. In the automotive industry, stricter safety standards in Germany added about 10 percent to the average cost of machinery, even if imported, which, arguably, added to the utility of the German workers.

Industry Supply Chain Management

Industry supply chain management is the management of the upward linkages to providers of intermediate inputs and raw materials on the one side and the downward linkages to distributors and customers on the other side. Efficient management eliminates unnecessary interim steps, thereby saving capital in transshipping and storage facilities. The efficiency of chain management for one company is measured by comparing it to the way other companies have created higher or lower value added per capital and labor input with a different organization of the linkages with their suppliers and distributors.

Inefficient industry chain management reduced Japanese capital productivity relative to Germany and the United States. Most Japanese retailers and manufacturers employed a complicated multilayered distribution system, which in 1992 led to a three-fold higher ratio of wholesale to retail volume than in the United States, where both volumes were about equal.[41] In other words, for every hand a good went through in the United States, it went through three hands in Japan. The important point is that Japanese companies can do away with this multilayered distribution system. Most notably, the Japanese auto industry has improved capital productivity by making the management of its suppliers a critical part of its lean production system. This tactic has spread surprisingly little to the other Japanese industries in the McKinsey study, but several counterexamples in the Japanese food processing and retailing industries show it could be done. For example, Ezaki Glico demonstrated that high performance with low product variety is possible in the Japanese food processing industry. One large Japanese retailer—following the example of best-practice discount stores in the United States, which eliminated intermediaries and simultaneously reduced capital and labor costs—built up its own distribution system by reducing the capital devoted to distribution to less than half of what it had been.

Product and Capital Market Forces

Although this study has not provided a basis for a statistical test of the hypothesis, the findings are consistent with the view that pressure from product markets and capital markets increases capital productivity. Intense product market competition encourages managers to economize on the use of capital for any given level of output, in order to reduce costs and survive in the competitive environment. Pressure from

41. The ratio of wholesale to retail was about 1:1 in the United States and 3:1 in Japan.

capital markets to earn high returns also encourages effective capital management and is likely to be particularly important in utilities, where product market competition is limited. The way regulation affects product markets has a substantial impact on capital productivity.

The 1995 study by Baily and Gersbach reported a "globalization index" for auto manufacturing and food processing. They found that industries that had been exposed to competition with best practice had higher labor productivity. That correlation also holds up for capital productivity. The U.S. auto industry has faced more exposure to the best-practice Japanese industry than has the German industry, and U.S. capital productivity is higher. The German food processing industry has faced much more competition from best-practice international companies than has the Japanese industry, and German capital productivity is higher.

Of course, this finding on capital productivity is not independent of the prior results for labor productivity. Competitive pressure that encourages higher total factor productivity can increase both labor and capital productivity. But this study has drawn attention to capital management decisions that can reduce the need for capital with a given level of output and labor input. In theory, even a monopolist will minimize costs, but this study finds that in practice competitive pressure forces efficiency in capital use in a way that does not occur without such pressure.

Regulation of retailing in Japan, for example, is setting the parameters under which competition can occur. Restrictions on land use and complex and restrictive regulations that make it difficult to open large stores have limited the evolution of the industry. Highly productive formats, such as discounters, category killers, and specialty stores are restricted in order to protect the mom-and-pop incumbents. This regulation reduces capital as well as labor productivity. Product market competition is lessened because productive new entry occurs only very slowly.

Regulation is clearly important also to the electric utility and telecommunications industries. Its main impact appears to be in setting management objectives, a topic I turn to now as I look at the impact of capital markets.

Because there is no quantitative measure of the strength of capital market forces, the McKinsey team looked at several dimensions: access to capital; corporate governance mechanisms, in particular management objectives; and ownership structure. Managerial objectives and their alignment with productivity showed a high degree of variability. In most companies of the German and U.S. nonmonopoly industries, profit maximization and financial performance were the main objectives. This was different in Japan. In the auto industry, productivity itself was a main goal; in the food processing and retail industry, it was sales maximization.[42] Management objectives in the telecommunications and electric utility monopolies were mainly determined by the type of regulation. U.S. telecommunications managers faced rate-of-return (ROR) and price regulation and Japanese managers operated under a pure ROR regulation. German telecommunications managers were given a host of competing objectives—universal service for consumers, high quality and technological excellence, and profits to subsidize the postal system, which was also state-owned before the recent divestiture—that created clear objective function for managers and provided little direct pressure on them to use resources productively. In the electric utilities, ROR regulation was widespread, although the United States was first to introduce prudence reviews and price caps.

Ownership explains many of these differences. The clearest example is state ownership. In telecommunications, U.S. firms are private, common stock companies, while Deutsche Telekom and NTT (Nippon Telephone and Telegraph) are state-owned. In turn, most electric utilities in Japan and the United States are private, common stock companies, while most German utilities are either state-owned outright or have a state majority on the board. The situation in the nonmonopoly industries is more complex. German company ownership is typically interlocked in a complicated way among banks, insurance companies, and other production companies, diffusing the line of control.[43] A similar structure holds in the Japanese retail industry, where conglomerates cross-subsidize underperformers. In food processing, the German small and medium companies are mainly regional agricultural cooperatives that oppose interregional consolidation, while Japanese firms are privately held. In all of these cases, the market for corporate control is ineffective.[44]

42. This has been extensively documented; see, for example, see Kagono and others. (1985).
43. Cable (1985), Kaplan (1995), and Wenger and Kaserer (1997) provide a British, an American, and a German view, respectively.
44. See Jensen (1983, 1988) for concept and Franks and Mayer (1990) for a comparison of France, Germany, and the United Kingdom.

Capital Productivity and Financial Return

A focus on financial performance, especially prevalent among U.S. firms, did create a clear performance objective that turns out to be generally aligned with capital productivity. The argument can be formalized: under a Cobb-Douglas technology, the rate of return to capital is proportional to average capital productivity ($r = (\partial Y/\partial K = \alpha\, Y/K)$. So (physical) capital productivity is likely to be correlated with the (financial) rate of return as long as the factor of proportionality, the output elasticity of capital services, remains roughly constant. On the aggregate level, the constancy can be tested because it corresponds to capital's share of income under constant returns to scale and competition.

Empirically, physical capital productivity was indeed mirrored in financial capital performance on the aggregate level. From 1974 to 1993, financial performance in the United States was significantly better than it was in Germany and, on average, better than in Japan. Financial performance was calculated by relating the payouts from the corporate sector (interest, dividends, and capital gains) to flows into the corporate sector (debt and equity) through the corresponding internal rate of return, including the initial and final stock of financial wealth.[45] Results are displayed in figure 4.

For the twenty years between 1974 and 1993, the annualized aggregate rate of return was 9.1 percent in the United States, compared with 7.4 percent in Germany (figure 4) and 7.1 percent in Japan. These estimates are robust to changes in definition and computation period for the U.S.-German comparison. The high income share to capital in the early 1970s and the Japanese bubble at the end of the 1980s make the U.S.-Japan comparison subject to higher variance. In my view, the comparisons are meaningful only when they cover the full cycle of bubble boom and burst, that is, when they include at least some years from 1992 onward and exclude the very early 1970s, when Japan's capital market development was not comparable to the markets in the United States and Europe.

45. The computation is based on the flow of funds data in the OECD National Accounts, augmented by capital gains from Standard and Poor's 500 (U.S.); DZ-Index of all publicly listed companies (Germany); and Index of all Section 1 companies listed on the Tokyo Exchange (Japan). For details, see McKinsey Global Institute (1996).

Figure 4. Aggregate Rate of Return during Different 20-Year Windows

Percentage

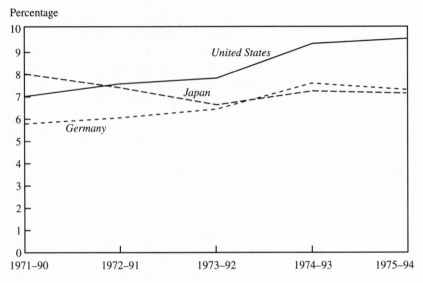

Source: McKinsey Global Institute (1996, "financial performance," exhibit A11).

This empirical relation also holds on a more disaggregated level, that is, within one sector in one country. Table 6 shows as example the U.S. retailing sector. Capital productivity and financial returns are highly correlated as more productive formats earned higher returns and created more appreciation during the 1985–94 period.

There are several reasons why the correlation between productivity and financial performance is not perfect. It is broken in product markets with low competitive intensity. For example, a monopoly such as

Table 6. U.S. Retail Capital Productivity and Financial Performance
Percent

Retail format	Capital productivity (1992) (retail average = 100)	ROIC (1985–94 average)	Change in market value (1985–93)[a]
Department	80	9.8	24
Discount	105	11.2	86
Specialty	120	15.4	82

Source: McKinsey Global Institute (1996, "synthesis," exhibit 14).
a. Defined as change in market value minus invested capital, divided by average invested capital.

Figure 5. Relative Costs of Labor and Capital, 1970–1993

1970 = 100

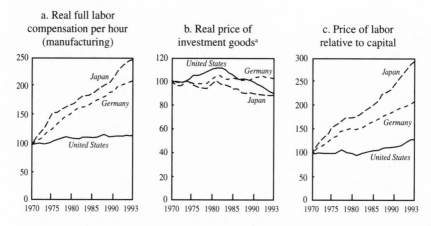

a. Real full labor
compensation per hour
(manufacturing)

b. Real price of
investment goods[a]

c. Price of labor
relative to capital

Sources: Bureau of Labor Statistics, Institut der Deutschen Wirtschaft, OECD.
a. Price index of gross fixed capital formation divided by gross domestic product deflator.

Deutsche Telekom has low productivity but high profitability through its ability to sustain high prices. Trade protection in the German and U.S. auto industry allowed the industry to earn profits despite low productivity and corporate governance that failed to apply pressure effectively until firms were close to running out of cash (General Motors in the United States, Daimler Benz in Germany). The capital market itself also introduced distortions, as evidenced by the impact of the bubble economy in Japan, which distracted retailers' attention away from operational performance in their core business to real estate speculation.

Macroeconomic Environment

The macroeconomic environment—most notably the relative price of labor and capital—plays a central role in determining capital intensity. In the simplistic Cobb-Douglas world, capital intensity is proportional to the relative price of labor to capital.[46] Figure 5 shows that the real price of capital did not change much in any of the three countries

46. The factor of proportionality is capital's share divided by labor's share.

Figure 6. Capital Intensity, Market Economy, 1970–1995

1970 = 100

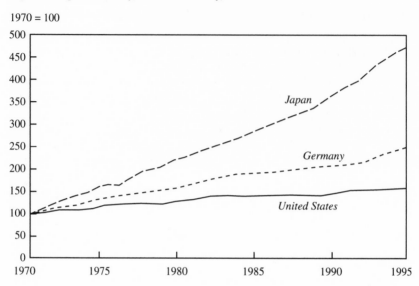

Source: Author's calculations based on data from Bureau of Labor Statistics, Institut der Deutschen Wirtschaft, and OECD.

from 1970 through 1993.[47] Real hourly labor compensation more than doubled in Germany and Japan, however, while it increased only moderately in the United States. The price of labor relative to capital increased by about 25 percent in the United States, by more than 100 percent in Germany, and by almost 200 percent in Japan (figure 5). The relative increases of the capital intensities in the three countries reflect these price changes (figure 6). Capital intensity in the market sector rose by slightly more than 50 percent in the United States, by 130 percent in Germany, and by 330 percent in Japan.

Figures 5 and 6 refer to intertemporal changes. The cross-national variation in the relative price levels of labor to capital shows a similar qualitative relation. In 1995 labor compensation per hour (measured in gross domestic product PPP) was 19 percent lower in Japan and 21 percent higher in Germany than in the United States.[48] This implies that

47. The inclusion of cross-national interest rate variation does not change this overall picture.

48. Labor compensation: Institut der Deutschen Wirtschaft, 1995, table 149. PPPs and price of capital: table 1 of this paper.

the relative price of labor to capital in Japan was 86 percent of the U.S. level, and 126 percent in Germany. These levels correspond qualitatively to the capital intensities: Japan 85 percent, and Germany 141 percent, when U.S. capital intensity is normalized to 100 percent.

The TFP differences displayed in figure 3 and table 3 show that relative factor prices do not fully explain capital intensities. Some labor and capital is used less efficiently in Germany and Japan. Because labor and capital management is interwoven in so many respects, there is no clean accounting possible of how much capital and how much labor is wasted.

Other labor market factors were not generally important in explaining capital productivity differences. For example, no evidence was found to suggest that differences in labor skills were important in explaining productivity differentials. Labor rules and unionism had only secondary influence in the food and auto cases in raising the premium required for third-shift work, primarily in Germany. The demographics of labor supply in Japan created a perception of an impending labor shortage and fueled automakers' decisions to invest heavily in automation. In no other industry, however, did demographics emerge as a factor that caused international differences in capital productivity.

The Japanese bubble economy during the second half of the 1980s had some influence on capital productivity. First, the high cost of land created by the bubble created artificial barriers to entry in the retail industry. In addition, retailers focused on speculative land acquisition in Japan, which distracted their attention from retail operations. Third, the bubble affected the level of capital spending by distorting the perceived cost and the availability of capital. This was particularly significant in the Japanese auto industry and was another factor in the excessive automation that decreased capital productivity. This contrasts sharply to the early days of the industry, in which scarce capital forced manufacturers to use existing assets extremely productively, creating lean production.

Conclusions

The five industry case studies and the aggregate analysis show that capital productivity in Germany and Japan was significantly below capital productivity in the United States for the sample period. Between 1991 and 1995 market sector capital productivity in Germany and Japan was only about two-thirds of the U.S level. Only in the Japanese auto industry and in German retail was capital productivity at par with the United States. No accounting mechanism can cleanly measure how much of this gap in capital productivity was caused by wasted capital and how much by worse labor management. But if Germany had achieved the U.S. level of TFP, its actual capital intensity should have given it capital productivity of 80 percent of the U.S. capital productivity. The main finding of this study is that part of the high capital intensity appears to have been wasted. The high price of labor in Germany relative to capital rationalizes only a lower capital intensity, at which capital productivity should have reached 86 percent of the U.S. level, rather than the 68 percent it actually attained. The Japanese market sector had a lower capital intensity, so diminishing returns are not an explanation of the low Japanese capital productivity, reflected in the even lower Japanese TFP. The case studies revealed how investment, capital management, and pricing decisions can affect capital utilization and capital productivity. Some findings, such as the importance of peak-load pricing in electric power are well known, although the magnitude of the impact across countries was revealing. Other results, such as the importance of downtime in food processing and automaking or the overengineering in telecommunications and electric power, have not been emphasized in earlier work on productivity.

The causal analysis discussed here shows the importance of a functioning combination of product market competition and capital market pressures. Without product market competition, companies can conceal their lack of productivity by raising prices. Without capital market pressure, unproductive companies will not exit even in the face of product market competition. This linkage underlines the role of financial performance. That financial returns have been markedly and consistently higher in the United States than in Germany during the last two decades invalidates claims that the U.S. focus on financial performance—as opposed to the more holistic German view—is short-term and jeopardizes long-term economic performance.

References

Baily, Martin Neil. 1993. "Competition, Regulation, and Efficiency in Service Industries." *Brookings Papers on Economic Activity: Microeconomics* 2: 71–130.

Baily, Martin Neil, and Alan M. Garber. 1997. "Health Care Productivity." *Brookings Papers on Economic Activity: Microeconomics*: 143–202.

Baily, Martin Neil, and Hans Gersbach. 1995. "Efficiency in Manufacturing and the Need for Global Competition." *Brookings Papers on Economic Activity: Microeconomics*: 307–47.

Baily, Martin Neil, and Charles L. Schultze. 1990. "The Productivity of Capital in a Period of Slower Growth." *Brookings Papers on Economic Activity (special issue)*: 369–406

Blades, Derek W. 1991. "Capital Measurement in the OECD Countries: An Overview." In *Technology and Productivity: The Challenge for Economic Policy*. Paris: OECD.

———. 1993. "Comparing Capital Stocks." In *Explaining Economic Growth*, edited by A. E. Szirmai, Bart van Ark, and Dirk Pilat. Amsterdam: North Holland.

Börsch-Supan, Axel. 1998. *Retirement Income: Level, Risk, and Substitution among Income Components*. Aging Working Paper Series AWP 3.7r. Paris: OECD.

Cable, John R. 1985. "Capital Market Information and Industrial Performance: The Role of West German Banks." *Economic Journal* 95 (March): 118–32.

Conrad, Klaus, and Dale W. Jorgenson. 1995. "Sectoral Productivity Gaps between the United States, Japan, and Germany, 1960–79." In *Productivity, vol. 2 of International Comparisons of Economic Growth*, edited by Dale W. Jorgenson. MIT Press

Denison, Edward F. 1974. *Accounting for United States Economic Growth, 1929–1969*. Brookings.

———. 1985. *Trends in American Economic Growth, 1929–1982*. Brookings.

Dollar, David, and Edward N. Wolff. 1988. "Convergence of Industry Labor Productivity among Advanced Economies, 1963–1982." *Review of Economics and Statistics* 70 (November): 549–58.

———. 1994. "Capital Intensity and TFP Convergence by Industry in Manufacturing, 1963–1985." In *Convergence of Productivity: Cross-National Studies and Historical Evidence*, edited by William Baumol and Richard R. Nelson, pp. 197–224. Oxford University Press.

Dougherty, Chrys, and Dale W. Jorgenson. 1996. "International Comparisons of the Sources of Economic Growth." *American Economic Review* 86 (May): 25–9.

Franks, Julian, and Colin Mayer. 1990. "Takeovers: Capital Markets and

Corporate Control: A Study of France, Germany, and the UK.'' *Economic Policy: A European Forum* (April): 189–231.

Freudenberg, Michael, and Deniz Ünal-Kesenci. 1994. *French and German Productivity Levels in Manufacturing: A Comparison Based on the Industry-of-Origin Method*. No. 94–10. Centre d'Etudes Prospectives et d'Informations Internationales (CEPII). Paris.

Gersbach, Hans. 1997. ''International Leadership in Productivity at the Aggregate and Industry Level.'' *Journal of Economic Surveys* 12 (1): 43–62.

Griliches, Zvi. 1992. *Output Measurement in the Service Sectors: Introduction*. University of Chicago Press.

Hall, Robert E., and Charles I. Jones. 1996. *The Productivity of Nations*. NBER Working Paper 5812. National Bureau of Economic Research, Cambridge, Mass. November.

———. Forthcoming. ''Why Do Some Countries Produce So Much More Output per Worker than Others?'' *Quarterly Journal of Economics*.

Harbour, Jerry L. 1994. *The Process Reengineering Workbook*. New York: Quality Resources.

Hooper, Peter. 1996. ''Comparing Manufacturing Output Levels among the Major Industrial Countries.'' Paper presented at Expert Workshop on Productivity, OECD, Paris. May.

Ifo-Institut für Wirtschaftsforschung. 1995. *Das deutsche Ladenschlußgesetz auf dem Prüfstand*. Berlin: Duncker und Humblot.

Jensen, Michael C. 1988. ''Takeovers: Their Causes and Consequences.'' *Journal of Economic Perspectives* 2: 21–48.

———. 1993. ''The Modern Industrial Revolution, Exit, and the Failure of Internal Control Systems.'' *Journal of Finance* 48 (3): 831–80.

Jensen, Michael C., and Richard S. Ruback. 1983. ''The Market for Corporate Control: The Scientific Evidence.'' *Journal of Financial Economics* 11: 5–50.

Jorgenson, Dale W., ed. 1995. *Productivity. Vol. 2 of International Comparisons of Economic Growth*. MIT Press

Jorgenson, Dale W., Frank M. Gollop, and Barbara M. Fraumeni. 1987. *Productivity and U.S. Economic Growth*. Harvard Economic Studies, vol. 159. Harvard University Press.

Jorgenson, Dale W., Masahiro Kuroda, and Mieko Nishimizu. 1987. ''Japan-U.S. Industry-Level Productivity Comparisons, 1960–1979.'' *Journal of the Japanese and International Economies* 1 (March): 1–30.

Kaplan, Steven N. 1995. ''Corporate Governance and Incentives in German Companies: Evidence from Top Executive Turnover and Firm Performance.'' *European Financial Management* 1 (March): 23–36.

Kagono, Tadao, and others. 1985. *Strategic vs. Evolutionary Management: A*

U.S.-Japan Comparison of Strategy and Organization. Advanced Series in Management. Vol. 10. Amsterdam: North Holland.

Kovenock, Dan, and Gordon M. Phillips. 1997. "Capital Structure and Product Market Behavior: An Examination of Plant Exit and Investment Decisions." *Review of Financial Studies* 10 (Fall): 767–803.

Lieberman, Marvin B., Lawrence J. Lau, and Mark D. Williams. 1990. *Firm-level Productivity and Management Influence: A Comparison of U.S. and Japanese Automobile Producers.* MIT Press.

Maddison, Angus. 1987. "Growth and Slowdown in Advanced Capitalist Economies: Techniques of Quantitative Assessment." *Journal of Economic Literature* 25 (June): 649–98.

———. 1993. "Standardized Estimates of Fixed Capital Stock: A Six-Country Comparison." *Innovazione e Materie Prime.* April.

McKinsey Global Institute. 1992. *Service Sector Productivity.* Washington, D.C.

———. 1993. *Manufacturing Productivity.* Washington, D.C.

———. 1996. *Capital Productivity.* Washington, D.C.

———. 1997. *Removing Barriers to Growth and Employment in France and Germany.* Washington, D.C.

———. 1998. *Productivity-led Growth for Korea.* Washington, D.C.

Meyer, John R., and others. 1980. *The Economics of Competition in the Telecommunications Industry.* Cambridge, Mass.: Oelgeschlager, Gunn, & Hain.

OECD (Organization for Economic Cooperation and Development). 1992. *Purchasing Power Parities and Real Expenditures, 1990—EKS Results.* Paris.

———. 1995. *Purchasing Power Parities and Real Expenditures, 1993—EKS Results.* Paris.

———. 1996. *National Accounts, Detailed Tables, 1981–1993.* Paris.

———. 1997. *National Accounts, Detailed Tables, 1983–1995.* Paris.

———. 1998a. *Maintaining Prosperity in an Aging Society.* Paris.

———. 1998b. *National Accounts, Detailed Tables, 1984–1996.* Paris.

O'Mahony, Mary. 1993. *"International Measures of Fixed Capital Stocks: A Five-Country Study."* National Institute of Economic and Social Research, London. September.

———. 1995. "International Differences in Manufacturing Unit Labor Costs." *National Institute Economic Review* (November): 85–100.

Pilat, Dirk. 1994. "International Productivity Comparisons—An Introduction." *Economie Internationale* 60: 11–32.

———. 1996. *"Labor Productivity Levels in OECD Countries: Estimates for the Manufacturing and Selected Service Sectors."* No. 169. OECD, Economics Department, Paris.

Taylor, Lester D. 1979. *Telecommunications Demand: A Survey and Critique.* Ballinger.

Van Ark, Bart, and Dirk Pilat. 1993. "Productivity Levels in Germany, Japan, and the United States: Differences and Causes." *Brookings Papers on Economic Activity: Microeconomics 2:* 1–48.

Wenger, Ekkehard, and Christoph Kaserer. 1997. "The German System of Corporate Governance: A Model Which Should Not Be Imitated." Economic Studies Working Paper 14. American Institute for Contemporary German Studies. Washington, D.C.

Comments

Comment by Paul Romer: One useful way to read this paper is as a coda to the cost-of-capital "crisis" that played out in the United States in the 1980s. Remember how the world looked then. Japan and Germany seemed unstoppable. Their firms had access to patient capital. Firms in the United States were hobbled by the short-term focus of equity markets. Even the firms that were trying to do the right thing and compete for the long run were forced to conform to the dictates of the market by insidious financial market innovations such as the leveraged buyout and the debt-financed hostile takeover. Serious commentators arued that the Anglo-Saxon style of corporate financing and governance had no future and that the United States needed to remake its institutions along German and Japanese lines.

Now, everybody seems to know that this diagnosis was totally off the mark. But to a worrisome extent, this 180-degree reversal in public sentiment about capital market institutions seems to be based on the same kind of signal extraction mistake that caused the misdiagnosis in the first place. People treat each temporary cyclical development as a sign of a lasting change in underlying trends. When Paul Volcker cleaned up after the monetary mismanagement of his predecessors in the early 1980s, people misinterpreted the negative side effects—a recession, high real interest rates, and an overvalued dollar—as signals of a permanent reduction in the underlying rate of growth. Germany and Japan, which did not suffer from the same sharp slowdown and benefited from the dramatic appreciation of the dollar, were perceived to have fundamental institutional advantages. Japan, in particular, was held out as the model that the United States should emulate. It experienced a long cyclical expansion and a remarkable asset price boom.

245

Now it is the United States's turn to enjoy a long cyclical expansion and a remarkable asset price boom. It is Japan's turn to clean up after previous macroeconomic policy mistakes (and, alas, to make some new ones).

We cannot make sensible judgments about fundamental institutions merely on the basis of observations on GDP growth for a few years. Nor can we use the recent behavior of a stock price index. The kind of question we must ask is whether the institutions cause inputs in production to be used efficiently. To answer this question, there is no way around the methods employed in this paper. We must measure stocks of inputs, then compare the inputs with outputs and construct a productivity estimate. The strength of this paper comes from its application of this approach at the levels of the nation, the industry, and the firm. This range of evidence helps clarify the reasons why productivity varies and offers hints about what the relevant institutional weaknesses might be. If one looks just at the level of the nation, it might be tempting to interpret total factor productivity measures as signals about things that people in white lab coats are doing and to think about institutions that will support more spending on R&D. The evidence presented here suggests that an important fraction of the variation in productivity may in fact be due to more mundane differences—the defect rate on an auto assembly line or the speed with which excess capacity is squeezed out of the dairy industry. Variation in these details may in turn be traced back to institutional differences in the competitive pressure that managers face in product and financial markets or to government regulations that keep firms from responding to competitive pressures.

Over time, other pieces of evidence can be added to the picture presented here. The paper takes a preliminary cut at one potentially rich source of evidence, financial market data. A recent paper by Albert Richards shows how this can be done for individual firms.[1] It lends support to the conclusion from this paper that competition in the market for corporate control decisively affects the efficiency with which firms manage their capital investments. The Richards paper, however, also suggests some of the difficulties that arise in any attempt to use the financial market data as a short cut without measuring inputs and outputs.

1. Richards (1998).

Richards compares Dow Chemical, a chemical company based in the United States, with BASF, a roughly comparable chemical company based in Germany. As one would expect if German capital markets are less successful at disciplining managers, the rate of return earned by BASF on its capital investment projects is systematically lower than the rate earned by Dow. Nevertheless, BASF was able to grow at about the same rate as Dow by investing a higher fraction of its income. As one would expect, the market puts a much lower valuation on BASF than it does on Dow. Dow has a total market value (debt plus equity) equal to about 120 percent of sales. BASF has a total market value equal to about 40 percent of sales. But these differences have persisted for decades. As a result, the rate of return earned by investors in the shares of BASF is about the same as the rate of return earned by investors in the shares of Dow. The basic point here is obvious but worth restating. As long as BASF invests a higher fraction of its income and pays out a smaller fraction as dividends, it can perform as well as Dow by the usual criteria. It can grow as fast and offer the same rate of return to equity holders. Yet all the while it can be wasting resources.

This example suggests that the comparison of equity market rates of return offered here needs to be interpreted with some caution. Market returns by themselves cannot answer the basic productivity question that the author raises. At the firm level, one needs to go through the same exercise as the author has done at the national level: measure capital input by cumulating investment, combine that with information about other purchased inputs like labor and materials, and compare the output of the firm with the inputs. In an indirect fashion, this is what Richards does with the available financial data for his two firms.

For citizens of the United States, the consistent and reassuring message that emerges from this paper, and from other evidence like that presented by Richards, is that competition increases efficiency, even competition in financial markets. Nobody likes operating in a competitive market, especially when times are bad as they were in the 1980s. This does not mean that competitive markets are bad institutions. Perhaps the next time that some influential group complains that our markets are too competitive, we will be a little more skeptical. Perhaps we will also take a slightly longer-term perspective and wait to see how persistent the bad times are before recommending fundamental changes in our institutions.

Economists are trained to look for a cloud to go with any silver lining. For people living in the United States, this paper has a cloud as well. As the author points out, the lesson from the Japanese auto industry is not that patient, cheap capital is the key to success. On the contrary, expensive, scarce capital was associated with the development of the lean system of production that gave Japanese producers a lasting productivity advantage. The cheap capital that became available to firms during the run-up in Japanese asset prices led to a substantial reduction in productivity. Let us hope that comparably bad investment decisions are not being made now by firms in the United States, else we may look back on the 1990s and wish that investors had been less patient and had been more focused on short-term performance.

Commentator's Reference

Richards, Alan. 1998. "Connecting Performance and Competitiveness with Finance: A Study of the Chemical Industry." In *Chemicals and Long-Term Economic Growth: Insights from the Chemical Industry,* edited by Ashish Arora, Ralph Landau, and Nathan Rosenberg, 461–511. New York: Wiley Interscience.

MARTIN NEIL BAILY
McKinsey and Company

ERIC ZITZEWITZ
Massachusetts Institute of Technology

Extending the East Asian Miracle: Microeconomic Evidence from Korea

DO THE ECONOMIES OF East Asia need to undertake fundamental economic reform to resume a path of strong economic growth? This vital question, posed in the wake of the economic crisis of 1997, has divided both economists and policymakers.

The case against major structural reform begins with the dramatic growth of these economies over the past twenty years. For example, Korea, the focus of this paper, has transformed itself into a major economic power, exporting cars and semiconductors to the world and quintupling its GDP per capita between 1970 and 1995. East Asia's achievement is all the more remarkable given that most developing countries have achieved very little development and have fallen further behind the advanced economies. Indeed, East Asia has been used as an example to understand how other countries could achieve more rapid economic development and convergence.[1]

According to those who contend that major reform is unnecessary, the crisis of 1997 was the result of macroeconomic (notably currency) mismanagement and the effects of economic crises in Thailand that created a temporary liquidity shortage. For example, Steven Radelet and Jeffrey Sachs characterize the crisis as a financial panic that shifted the countries involved from a high-investment to a low-investment equilibrium. They argue that "much of the economic activity supported by

The authors would like to thank the participants of the June 1998 meeting for their many helpful comments, and also Jim Bemowski, Cuong Do, Bob Felton, Ted Hall, and Bill Lewis.
   1. See, for example, World Bank (1993).

the capital inflows was highly productive.''[2] In short, the case against reform is that the economic fundamentals must be right because growth was so good for so long and a temporary crisis does not make the case for a major course correction.

The case for reform among Western economists has its intellectual origins in the work of Alwyn Young, Jong-Il Kim and Lawrence Lau, and Susan Collins and Barry Bosworth.[3] Their analyses indicated that the miracle growth of East Asia was primarily caused by rapid capital and labor input growth rather than rapid productivity growth. Although no one forecast a crisis based on this work, the results did suggest that growth was likely to slow unless these economies could base more of their growth on increased productivity.[4]

Like Radelet and Sachs, Paul Krugman and Giancarlo Corsetti, Paolo Pesenti, and Nouriel Roubini point to short-term confidence and liquidity problems in their analyses of the crisis.[5] But they also stress the rapid investment that has occurred in the affected countries and the declining ratios of output to capital and returns that have accompanied this rapid investment. These falling returns are said to have contributed significantly to the loss of investor confidence and to have combined with the other short-term developments to cause the crisis. The authors attribute continued investment in the face of declining returns to a moral hazard problem involving government-guaranteed lenders lending to uncapitalized but politically connected "ministers' nephews."

Advocates of reform in East Asia have included those who saw the economic systems at first hand. For example, the current president of Korea, Kim Dae Jung, wrote a book in English in 1985 pointing out

2. Radelet and Sachs (1998, pp. 2, 5). Many observers have suggested that there are moral hazard problems inherent in the lending practices of Asian financial institutions, but Radelet and Sachs are skeptical of their importance. They note that although "many borrowers did have explicit or implicit [loan] guarantees . . . a substantial number of purely private banks and firms without such insurance are now facing bankruptcy."

3. Young (1994, 1995); Kim and Lau (1994); and Collins and Bosworth (1996).

4. Debates about growth in East Asia often get caught up in the issue of how much credit these countries should get for their economic success. As we will comment later in this paper, we fully recognize that there is no easy mail-order way to increase capital and use it productively. The mobilization of resources in these countries was a major task.

5. Krugman (1998); and Corsetti, Pesenti, and Roubini (1998).

the problems in the Korean economic system and the need for economic as well as political reform.[6]

In short, the slow growth of total factor productivity in East Asia combined with problems that were widely revealed by the crisis have suggested that reform may be needed—reform of the financial sector as well as more general economic reform.[7]

This paper uses new evidence to suggest that comprehensive economic reform is essential for the Korean economy to resume sustained rapid economic growth. We do not emphasize such macroeconomic topics as the necessity for liquidity and currency stability, even though these are certainly important. Rather, the focus here is on industry-level analysis that uncovers structural problems that have limited the growth of total factor productivity, distorted the allocation of capital, reduced the return on capital, and made the economy vulnerable to crisis.

Overwhelmingly, the debate about East Asian growth and the subsequent crisis has been based on macroeconomic data.[8] These data and even conventional industry studies can provide important insights but in the end are likely to be incomplete. This paper will draw on the results of a year-long study of the Korean economy conducted by the McKinsey Global Institute and the Seoul Office of McKinsey & Company.[9] The study includes detailed microeconomic case studies of eight

6. *Mass Participatory Economy: Korea's Road to World Economic Power* was first published in 1985 (Kim Dae Jung, 1996, rev. ed.). This book was written while President Kim was in exile in the United States; Kim was aided by You Jong Keun, then a professor of economics at Rutgers and now governor of Chollabuk-do Province and a principal adviser to the president.

7. The appropriateness of macroeconomic policy in East Asia is an important part of the debate that we will not engage here. The International Monetary Fund argues that high interest rates are essential to restore stability to the currency markets, while critics argue that such high rates are unnecessary and result in severe recession.

8. An exception to this statement is *The East Asian Miracle* (World Bank, 1993), which does review some industry data and draws on industry case studies by, for example, Pack (1993).

9. This report (McKinsey Global Institute, 1998a) is the source of most of the information in this paper and will not be cited with each statement of fact. The core project team that prepared the report included Taejoon Chin, Dongchun Choi, Sungmi Chung, Jinwook Jung, Dongil Kim, Hyunsoo Kim, Chanjoong Park, Sehun Park, Jaesoo Shim, and Sanghun Yeo from Seoul, with Andrew Gomperts, Alex Schmitz, and Michael Warren from MGI. Yongsung Kim, Seungjoo Lee, and Victoria Nam were the project managers from Seoul, with Eric Zitzewitz from MGI. Vincent Palmade and

major Korean industries, measuring productivity and identifying the aspects of both the production process and the regulatory environment that cause productivity differences with best practices. The case study approach limits the use of statistical hypothesis testing but offers insights into the causes of productivity differences that are normally unavailable to academic researchers. McKinsey & Company works with clients in the industries it studies, can observe how establishments operate, and has experts that know each industry worldwide.

This industry-level analysis yields insights that are more difficult to reach using aggregate information. First, we find much stronger evidence of overinvestment than is suggested by aggregate data. Whereas the aggregate Korean capital-labor ratio is only 34 percent of that in the United States, it is 57 percent in the manufacturing sector, which has better access to domestic and foreign capital. Within manufacturing, we found industries that have reached or exceeded U.S. levels of capital intensity have done so despite having only about 50 percent of U.S. total factor productivity. Low returns in the most indebted part of the economy have been the natural result. Second, moral hazard in lending only partly explains overinvestment. Moral hazard may have affected the incentives of some lenders, but we found many examples of poor investments made by borrowers with substantial equity interest. Korea appears to have suffered from an unfortunate coincidence. It deregulated its capital markets and increased the availability of capital just when overall growth slowed and land price inflation ended, making profitable investment much less automatic. Korean firms did not develop capital management skills quickly enough to cope with this new environment. Other emerging economies that are deregulating their capital markets may face the same problem. Finally, our case studies in services reveal the tangible effects of sector-specific barriers that limit growth and the ability of these industries to absorb workers displaced in manufacturing.

Jaana Remes from MGI contributed to the synthesis and writing the final report. The project was directed by Cuong Do, William Lewis, Jim Bemowski, Robert Felton, and Martin Baily. The outside advisory committee was chaired by Robert Solow, with Richard Cooper, Sangyong Park, and Ted Hall.

Figure 1. GDP and Total Factor Inputs per Capita, and Total Factor Productivity, United States, Japan, and Korea, 1970–95

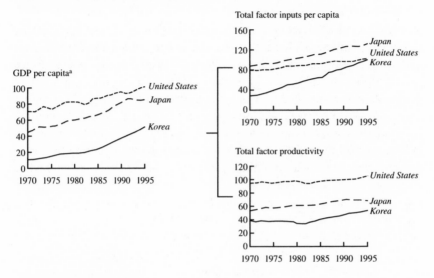

Index: United States 1995 = 100

Source: McKinsey Global Institute (1998a, ''Aggregate Analysis,'' p. 1).
a. Excludes residential real estate.

Aggregate Analysis

Korea has been among the fastest growing economies since 1970, increasing its GDP per capita fivefold to US$12,600 in 1995, about half the U.S. level. We carried out our own growth accounting exercise and confirmed that the impressive growth has been largely driven by increases in total factor inputs (figure 1). Input growth accounts for 77 percent of the output growth from 1970 to 1995, driven by a capital stock that grew at 12 percent a year. Total factor productivity growth accounts for the remaining 23 percent.[10] We did not treat increases in

10. Our aggregate capital data are estimated using a perpetual inventory method with sudden death depreciation and standardized asset lives for all countries (forty years for structures, fifteen years for equipment). We developed our own aggregate estimates in order to be consistent with the methodology used in the cases (see the appendix). Our aggregate estimates do not yield significantly different results from those in the literature: we estimate total factor productivity (unadjusted for ''labor quality'') growth of 3.2 percent in the 1980s versus 3.4 percent in Young (1995). Estimates of TFP levels vary

years of schooling as input in either our aggregate growth accounting or our cases. We prefer instead to assign all the contributions of intangible capital to increases in total factor productivity—education, technology, and improvements in business systems. In part this reflects skepticism among McKinsey's industry experts about the contribution years of schooling makes to productivity. They do not see a direct connection between much of what is learned in school and what is required on the job. And they observe high-productivity establishments operating despite low education levels, provided there is good training. It is not necessary to agree with this judgment, however.[11] The speed with which Korea created an educated work force (accounting for years of schooling in the traditional manner) only strengthens the conclusion that growth has been input driven.[12]

Figures 2 and 3 summarize the Korean development path and the level of income the country has reached. The United States, Germany, and France followed a productivity-oriented path, with much higher levels of GDP per capita at each level of inputs. By 1995 Korea and Japan had reached or exceeded the levels of inputs of the three Western economies, but on a flatter, lower productivity path. Korea's GDP per capita of about 50 percent of that in the United States in 1995 was achieved with about the same level of inputs, albeit with a very different mix—more labor and less capital. The overall capital-labor ratio in Korea was 34 percent of the ratio in the United States in 1995.

---

more, but our estimate of 42 percent for the United States is between the estimates of 34 percent and 58 percent by Pilat (1994) and Hall and Jones (forthcoming), respectively.

11. In a study of Brazil, the average level of education was far below that in the United States, but some establishments with average work forces used U.S.-style business systems and achieved productivity comparable to that in the United States. In Korea we were told that the increase over time in the educational level of the work force was of very limited value in the steel industry. We recognize the weight of evidence linking education to market-determined wages, however, and we believe that some reasonable level of education is required for a modern high-productivity economy—not to mention a democratic society. The econometric evidence linking education to economic growth is sketchier than is often thought, though. For example, Mark Bils and Peter Klenow (1998) have found that growth causes schooling more than the other way around. And Jess Benhabib and Mark Spiegel (1994) found that in a regression of growth on capital, labor, and human capital inputs, the human capital or education variable entered with a coefficient of essentially zero.

12. The shares of the work force with high school and university education increased from 14 percent and 3 percent in 1970 to 44 percent and 19 percent in 1995 according to recent data from the Korean National Statistical Office (Pilat 1994).

Figure 2. GDP and Labor and Capital Inputs per Capita, Five Countries, to 1995

Per capita GDP

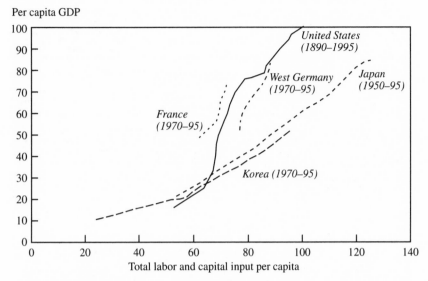

Total labor and capital input per capita

Percent of U.S. 1995 level

Source: McKinsey Global Institute (1998a, "Aggregate Analysis," p. 6). Residential real estate excluded.

With a capital-labor ratio that is still little more than a third of the U.S. level, it is not obvious that Korea has overinvested or should expect a low rate of return to capital. Aggregate capital productivity (the ratio of output to capital) has declined rapidly in Korea since 1970, but by 1995 it was still 5 percent above the U.S. level. The aggregate rate of return on capital, as measured by the Organization for Economic Cooperation and Development, has fallen from 22 percent to 14 percent between 1984 and 1994, but is still within a percentage point of the average for the European Union.[13] Signs of trouble emerge, however, when one looks at the sector level. Figure 4 shows how unevenly the capital has been applied. Manufacturing in Korea has absorbed much of the investment and by 1995 had a lower capital-productivity ratio than the United States had. As capital productivity declines, the pool of resources from which to pay returns to capital is squeezed. Using

13. The European Union is used as a comparison because the OECD has stopped publishing figures on rates of return on capital for the United States. The 1994 figure for Japan was about 13 percent.

Figure 3. Components of GDP per Capita, United States, Japan, and Korea

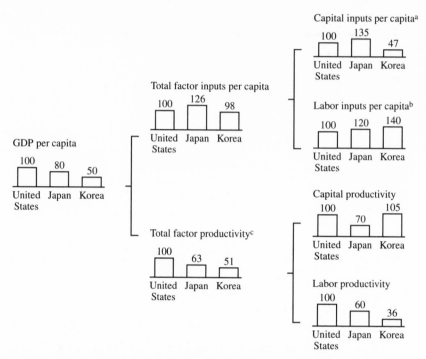

Index: U.S. 1993–95 average = 100; 1995 U.S. dollars at purchasing power parity

Source: McKinsey Global Institute (1998a, "Aggregate Analysis," p. 6).
a. Excludes residential real estate in GDP and dwellings in capital stock.
b. Hours worked.
c. Based on Cobb-Douglas production function with labor share of 66 percent.

Bank of Korea data, figure 5 shows the return on invested capital in industrial companies, excluding capital gains on land. Measurement difficulties for such data are acute, but they suggest that returns have been below the cost of debt for most of the period from 1981 to 1995.[14] Land appreciation may have helped justify investment in manufacturing during the 1980s, but since 1991 land values have been flat or decreasing. The recent profitability of the top thirty *chaebol* (individual conglomerates in Korea), which are predominantly involved in manufac-

14. The returns and interest cost are in nominal terms and hence could be misleading if inflation is changing. Notice the consistent gap in the United States, however, despite variations in the inflation rate.

Figure 4. Estimated Components of GDP per Capita for Manufacturing and Services in Korea, 1995

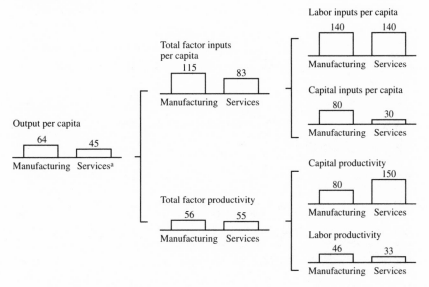

Index: United States in 1995 = 100

Source: McKinsey Global Institute (1998, ''Synthesis,'' p. 5).
a. Includes agriculture and construction.

turing, is also below the cost of debt according to Seung Jung Lee.[15] Manufacturing accounts for 38 percent of the total Korean capital stock; low returns on so large a portion of Korean capital seem consistent with a loss of investor confidence.

The aggregate data whet the appetite for more detail, and we provide this now by reviewing eight case studies, four in manufacturing and four in services and construction.

Manufacturing Cases

We studied the automotive, food processing, semiconductor, and steel industries in Korea and compared them with those in Japan and the United States. Of these four, two of the industries contain subseg-

15. Lee (1997).

Figure 5. Return on Invested Capital and Cost of Debt in Industrial Companies, United States, Japan, and Korea, 1981–95

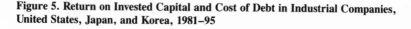

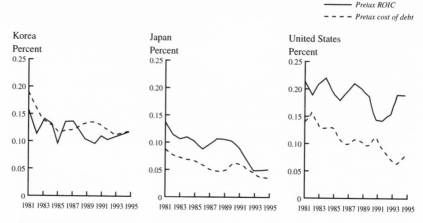

Source: McKinsey Global Institute (1998a, "Aggregate Analysis," p. 9). Land purchases included in invested capital at book value. Land appreciation excluded from earnings. Cost of debt estimated from financial statements (interest expense divided by debt outstanding).

ments that are different enough to merit separate consideration. In food processing, most of the industry has capital intensity levels that are close to those of the United States. In most cases these levels have been reached only very recently: the capital intensity of the whole sector rose from about 30 percent to 72 percent of the U.S. level from 1987 to 1995. Some processed food industries, such as milling, noodles, and preserved fruits and vegetables, never received this investment and remain at less than 50 percent of U.S. capital intensity. In steel, although both the integrated producers and the minimills have high capital intensity, the integrated producers have world class productivity, but the minimills are only 65 percent as productive as minimills in Japan.[16] In total then, we surveyed six manufacturing industries or subindustries: automotive, semiconductors, high- and low-capital-intensity food processing, integrated steel mills, and minimills.

Of the six, four resemble the manufacturing averages in terms of

16. Integrated steel mills produce steel from iron ore and coking coal in blast furnaces and basic oxygen furnaces, whereas minimills produce steel from scrap steel in electric arc furnaces. Minimills are a newer technology and, as the name suggests, can produce efficiently at much lower scales than integrated facilities (less than 1 million tons as opposed to 5 million to 10 million tons a year).

Table 1. Capital Productivity and Return on Capital Investments, Selected Industries, Korea, 1995

Index: United States = 100

	Capital intensity[a]	Capital productivity	Rate of return on capital investments[b]
Semiconductor	96	54	64
Automobile	100	48	57
Confectionery	112	42	50

Source: McKinsey Global Institute (1998a, ''Synthesis and implications,'' p. 22).
a. Capital inputs per labor hour.
b. Production rate of return = capital productivity × (PPP (output) ÷ PPP (investment goods)) × (share of capital in value added).

capital intensity and total factor productivity: automotive, semiconductors, high-capital-intensity food processing, and minimills. These industries have near best-practice capital intensity but roughly 50 percent of best-practice productivity and have earned low returns on their capital (table 1).

We discuss these industries first before turning to the two outliers, low-capital-intensity food processing and integrated steel mills. The first four cases help explain the overall result for Korean manufacturing—that investment in best-practice capital intensity has not produced best-practice productivity. The last two cases provide instructive exceptions to this general result.

Automotive

The automotive industry is still fairly young in Korea. In 1980 the country produced about 100,000 vehicles, mostly from licensed designs and for domestic consumption. By 1996 output had grown to nearly 3 million domestically designed vehicles, about 40 percent of which were exported. During this period capital intensity increased from less than 50 percent of that in the United States in 1985 to the same as that in the United States in 1995. Total factor productivity in Korea has grown 11.5 percent a year since 1985, but despite high capital intensity it remains less than 50 percent of that in the United States and 40 percent of that in Japan (figure 6). The overall productivity figures are consistent with plant-level data. Korean producers have similar numbers of robots per worker and have automated their stamping, welding, and painting to the same extent as producers in the United States, but hours worked per vehicle are twice as high.

Figure 6. Automotive Productivity, the United States, Japan, and Korea, 1985–95

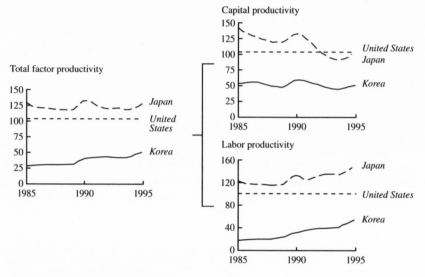

Index: United States = 100

Source: McKinsey Global Institute (1998a, "Automotive Industry," p. 6).

In Japan both the assemblers and the parts producers have invested very heavily, so that part of the labor productivity advantage of this industry over both the United States and Korea comes from a higher level of automation.[17] For the most part, however, high productivity is achieved in Japan through a system known as "lean production," which has been partially transferred to the United States by Japanese-owned transplants and through its adoption (often in modified form) by U.S.-nameplate producers. Lean production has not fully transferred to Korea, and this is the main source of the productivity gap. Lean production differs from traditional mass production in three main areas: design for manufacturing, the conduct of supplier relationships, and the organization of production.

17. Very low interest rates and high labor costs in Japan have led to more automation than in the U.S. industry. In 1991 the U.S. and Japanese industries had similar capital intensity, but by 1995 Japanese capital intensity was 45 percent higher than that in the United States. Given the extreme factor price ratios in Japan, this extra automation is not necessarily surprising, but the fact that Korean capital intensity is equal to that of the United States despite lower wages and higher interest rates is surprising.

—Design for manufacturing. Japanese designers increase productivity by designing cars that share common parts, often by producing multiple models from the same "platform" (chassis and power train), and that are easy to assemble. Korean cars have much less parts commonality and are rated as being among the most difficult to assemble. The average Korean OEM (original equipment manufacture) has more platforms than Honda despite producing one-third as many models and vehicles.[18]

The Japanese have been able to design manufacturable cars with shorter lead times in part due to strong project management that resolves conflicts between different functions early in the process. U.S. producers have shifted to this approach, but the Korean producers have maintained a traditional, functional development process. When the Korean OEMs have attempted to match Japanese lead times, they have produced a lower-quality product.

—Supplier relationships. Japanese OEMs also achieve productivity gains by collaborating with suppliers in the design of products and by helping suppliers lower their costs. The Japanese use a tiered supplier system. The limited number of top-tier suppliers receive engineering and R&D help in exchange for participating in product development and maintaining high standards of quality. Korean producers have been less successful in collaborating with their suppliers. Fewer parts are collaboratively designed, and parts design lead times are longer.

—Organization of functions and tasks. Lean production has been successful in generating continuous improvements along two dimensions: reductions in wasted time and labor during production and improvements in quality. Cycle times, the time required for a worker or team to complete activities on a car before it moves down the assembly line, are 50 percent longer in Korean plants for comparable tasks. Indirect labor per car produced is twice as high as in Japan, and a precrisis study by a Korean OEM suggested that the work force could be reduced 15 percent without any substantial reorganization.[19] Strong

---

18. In 1996 Honda had six platforms, produced three models per platform, and averaged 300,000 cars per platform. Hyundai had seven platforms, produced just 1.4 models per platform, and averaged 157,000 cars per platform. Kia produced only 58,000 cars per platform.

19. The use of more labor in a lower-wage country like Korea may have been justified if the labor were substituting for capital, but in fact Korean companies are using

unions in the automotive industry have made layoffs of excess workers impossible; unions have even prevented a reduction in hours worked per employee from the current 2,700 a year.

Product quality is a major issue in Korean plants; defects per car are 2.5 times the Japanese average. Hyundai owners report twice as many problems as Toyota owners to J. D. Power and Associates while Kia owners report almost five times as many. Due mainly to these quality problems, Korean cars sell for 20 percent less than comparable Japanese cars in the United States, the major market in which the two industries compete. Because producing low-quality cars requires basically the same materials, labor, and capital as producing high-quality cars, the effect of quality problems on productivity and returns is severe. Despite this, Korean automakers have focused more on increasing volume and sales and less on quality (and thus productivity and returns). Unlike their counterparts in Japan and the United States, Korean plant managers are evaluated almost exclusively on volume produced.

The automotive industry is probably one of the most difficult manufacturing industries to learn. The U.S. industry had considerably more experience than Korea in 1980, and the U.S. industry has not caught up with the best Japanese producers either in labor or total factor productivity. Toyota had a twenty-year head start on Hyundai, and therefore one might argue that it is unsurprising that Hyundai is still behind. There is reason to believe, however, that the Korean industry could have caught up more than it actually did. Auto industry productivity growth in Korea in the past twenty years has been significantly lower than in the comparable period for Japan's industry. Hyundai makes fewer cars per worker today than Toyota or Nissan did in the early 1970s (27.9 in 1996, compared with 44.7 for Toyota and 35.5 for Nissan in 1974). In addition, the Korean OEMs did not have to develop lean production on their own; they could have continued and deepened the joint ventures with world-class producers that existed in the 1960s and 1970s, rather than attempting to be self-reliant. Self-reliance was a priority for nationalistic reasons, but it is surprising that it was maintained in the face of returns that have been well below the cost of debt since 1988. It is also surprising that the Korean industry would invest

---

more workers with basically the same capital input per worker as in the United States. Japan's higher total factor productivity also indicates greater efficiency.

so aggressively given its significant productivity gap. A safer strategy may have been to attempt to match at least the United States in total factor productivity before matching it in capital intensity.

Semiconductors

The semiconductor industry is another industry recently added in Korea. From a negligible base in the early 1980s the Korean industry has grown to become the third largest in the world. It constitutes a much larger share of the Korean economy than it does in the United States or Japan—about 15 percent of exports, 15 percent of manufacturing GDP, and an even larger share of manufacturing capital stock. It also accounted for more than half the 1995 domestic value added of Samsung, Hyundai, and LG, the three largest *chaebol* and the major participants in the Korean semiconductor industry. The Korean economy is very exposed to changes in semiconductor prices. High DRAM (dynamic random access memory chips) prices helped fuel the economic boom in 1995, and falling prices in 1996 and 1997 (as well as large semiconductor-related capital investments) contributed to the widening current account deficit.

The Korean industry has focused on producing DRAMs, which account for 76 percent of its sales. Producing these is very capital intensive and requires manufacturing and process control capabilities, but not the design capability required to produce microprocessors and other specialized chips. This industry has not been an attractive one for investment anywhere. Aside from Intel, the semiconductor industry has not earned its cost of capital consistently. This is particularly true of DRAM production, where high fixed costs, lumpy investment requirements, and undifferentiated products have combined to produce highly volatile returns that have been lower on average than those in the rest of the industry. This is even true of Micron, which despite a 50 percent productivity advantage in DRAMs over Korean, Japanese, and other U.S. producers, has underperformed the Standard & Poor's 500.

Korean total factor productivity is roughly 50 percent of that in the United States (figure 7), despite the fact that the overall capital intensity of the Korean industry rose from 50 percent to 100 percent of the U.S. level from 1991 to 1996. Korean productivity is lower for three main reasons. The most important is product mix: DRAMs have less value

Figure 7. Semiconductor Productivity, United States, Japan, and Korea, 1991–96

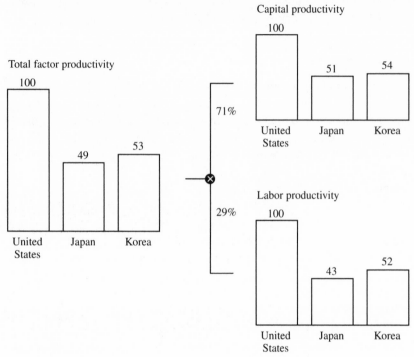

Index: United States = 100

Source: McKinsey Global Institute (1998a, "Automotive Industry," p. 7).

added per unit input than the average product produced in the United
States. This is mainly due to the disadvantageous market structure of
the DRAM industry and the advantageous market structure of the mi-
croprocessor industry. Intel alone accounts for one-fifth of the U.S.-
Korea productivity gap.[20] The second reason is that Korea has a higher
share of chip assembly activities, which are lower-productivity activities than chip fabrication and thus bring down the Korean average. The
final reason is the difference in operational performance of the U.S.
and Korean producers. This gap is due to the non-DRAM Korean pro-

20. Our analysis includes 1996. Since 1996, Intel's market position has weakened
somewhat, although microprocessors have remained a more profitable and higher-
productivity (high value added per unit of total factor input) product than DRAMs.

duction; Korean DRAM producers have caught up with the average U.S. producer, although not with such best-practice producers as Micron. The Korean average hides substantial differences in DRAM productivity among the three companies; Samsung is within 15 percent of Micron, while Hyundai and LG have achieved 60 percent and 45 percent of Micron's productivity, respectively.

The entry of Korean companies into semiconductor production has been cited as an example of successful entry into a technologically advanced industry.[21] And there is no question that the achievement of establishing this industry and becoming one of the world's leading producers has been considerable. Transferring the technology and developing the production skills were challenging. But despite this success, overall Korean productivity and returns on investment have been disappointing, raising the question of whether the heavy investments in this industry have been wise economic and business decisions.

One defense of Korea's investment decisions is that it may be too early to judge the returns. The Korean producers may ultimately win the technology race and reap high profits. Alternatively, one could argue that the decision to enter this industry was sound; but like all investments these were subject to uncertainty, and events have not turned out as expected. It was not as easy to see in the mid-1980s as it is in hindsight that the profitability of the DRAM industry would be so low, that the spillover benefits to the rest of the economy would be so limited, or that the escalation of investment would require Korea to become so dependent on its big bet in semiconductors.

In our judgment, however, this defense of the decision to invest heavily in this industry does not hold up. First, even precrisis market valuations of semiconductor companies suggested that investors did not believe that this would be a profitable industry any time soon. Second, it is hard to argue that this was an early mistake, made before the status of the industry was revealed. Almost half the total Korean investment in semiconductors has been made since 1995. Despite the deteriorating performance of the industry, Korean investment plans were accelerating until the financial crisis forced their postponement. This suggests the explanation lies with the corporate governance and investment decisionmaking of Korean firms, a theme to which we return later.

21. See, for example, Kim (1997).

Steel Minimills

Steel minimills account for about one-third of the Korean steel industry. Unlike integrated mills, which produce a wide range of products from iron ore and coking coal, minimills produce a narrow range of commodity long products (for example, wire rod, reinforcement bar) from scrap sheet that is melted in an electric arc furnace. The minimum efficient scale is much lower for minimills, and capital requirements per ton are also lower. In Korea the government-owned Pohang Iron and Steel Company (POSCO) is the only integrated producer; the minimills are almost all privately owned.

Unlike POSCO, which has productivity slightly above the Japanese average, Korean minimills have only 65 percent of Japanese labor productivity despite roughly equivalent capital intensity.[22] Best-practice minimill producers such as Tokyo Steel and U.S.-based Nucor have achieved high productivity by taking advantage of the simple product mix and small scale of minimills to streamline management and processes. Nucor manages more than 4,000 employees with only four management layers, compared with up to ten in a traditional integrated producer. Fewer management layers combines with the small size of a typical minimill (200 to 500 employees compared with 5,000 to 10,000 at large integrated plants) to increase accountability of both production workers and management. Both Nucor and Japanese minimills have adopted practices such as cross-training workers to handle multiple tasks, limiting the number of products produced in a given mill to reduce change over time, and using continuous improvement programs to increase productivity.

Korean minimills have lower productivity mainly because they have not adopted Japanese and U.S. best practices. For example, Korean mills make less use of multitasking. In Japan the three main production tasks of sampling, handling, and inserting scrap steel into the electric arc furnace are handled by one person, whereas Korean minimills use three. Korean companies also attempt to produce a mix of products in each minimill, while Japanese minimills specialize in particular prod-

---

22. Because of data limitations, we are not able to estimate separate capital and total factor productivity measures for minimills and integrated producers. Most of the capital in a minimill is in the furnace, caster, and rolling mills, and there is little scope for varying capital intensity to match factor prices.

ucts.[23] In some cases, antilayoff laws have prevented Korean minimills from making feasible productivity improvements. In addition, there are some small differences in the automation of materials handling. These reduce Korean labor productivity, but not necessarily total factor productivity, compared with plants in Japan.

Despite their low productivity, Korean minimills have earned returns that are above their cost of debt.[24] Unlike POSCO, which under government direction sells its (mainly flat) products domestically at an average of 12 percent less than world prices, minimills are able to take advantage of tariffs and transport costs to charge prices that are about 10 percent above world prices.

This pricing difference helps the minimills earn acceptable returns despite low productivity. POSCO is implicitly forbidden from entering the product segments of the private minimills, which prevents it from putting them under more competitive pressure.

Food Processing

To provide a complete picture of manufacturing, it was important to include a large domestic consumer goods industry, and we selected food processing. Given the diversity of products involved, we focused on two minicases within the sector, choosing both a high-capital-intensity segment—confectionery—and a low-intensity segment—wet corn milling. The outputs of these industries were reasonably comparable among the comparison countries.

CONFECTIONERY. The confectionery sector has 42 percent of U.S. total factor productivity despite a capital intensity equal to 112 percent of that in the United States. It is the largest of the processed food subindustries in Korea, accounting for 15 percent of processed food value added and is representative of a large number of subindustries such as bakery goods, seasoning, and fats and oils that have high capital intensity but low productivity—confectionery is roughly equally

---

23. Small industry size does not account for the lack of specialization in Korean minimills. They produce 13 million tons a year (compared with 26 million in Japan and 25 million in the United States), which makes the industry large enough to have plants efficiently specialize.

24. Minimills earned a return on invested capital of 16 percent from 1985 to 1995, compared with a cost of debt of 14 percent. POSCO earned 8 percent compared with a (subsidized) cost of debt of 7 percent.

Figure 8. Estimated Labor and Capital Productivity Differences in Confectionery Industry, United States and Korea, 1995

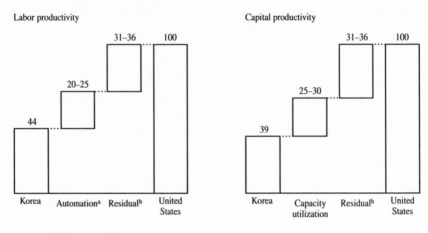

Index: United States = 100

Source: McKinsey Global Institute (1998a, ''Processed Food Industry,'' p. 8).
a. Packaging lines.
b. Includes marketing and organization of functions and tasks.

divided into chocolate and candy, cookies (biscuits), and ice cream. In confectionery, capital intensity has risen 11 percent a year from 1987 to 1995, the same rate as for the industry as a whole.

Total factor productivity is low despite high capital intensity because of three main problems: misallocation of capital (resulting in overinvestment in some areas but inadequate automation in others), low capacity utilization, and poor organization and marketing (figure 8). Packaging is much less automated than in the United States, which increases labor requirements by 50 percent in an activity that accounts for about half of total labor. Despite this automation gap, the Korean industry has more capital per worker hour overall because of very low capacity utilization. A typical Korean production line operates 40 percent fewer hours a week than a line in the United States; capacity utilization in Korea was an estimated 37.5 percent in 1997, compared with 62.5 percent in the United States. Most of this difference is due to insufficient demand for the products that the lines are designed to produce.[25] Most of these lines were built

25. This conclusion was reached based on interviews made in early 1997, before the current crisis. Managers told us that this problem existed to roughly the same extent in 1995, the most recent business cycle peak.

to produce poorly researched products that did not sell as expected. U.S. producers avoid these overcapacity problems by conducting more careful market research and producing products on more flexible, less dedicated production lines until the products are proven successful.

In addition to creating overcapacity, poor execution of the marketing function has directly created productivity problems. Korean firms have produced large numbers of poorly differentiated products, in many cases producing "me-too" copies of competitors' products rather than developing original high-value products. Sales per product are one-tenth as large as in the United States, which creates scale-related productivity penalties. Sales and market share goals rather than profitability or shareholder returns have driven Korean product development. Representative comments from interviews include: "Our key performance measurement has been sales growth rather than profit growth," "we often produce 'me-too products' to protect our market share even though these products may negatively impact long-term profit performance," and "as we have been focusing on sales growth, we have not been very good at eliminating dead products."

WET CORN MILLING. We chose wet corn milling because it is the largest subsegment of milling, which is in turn the largest of the low-capital-intensity food processing industries. The industry produces products such as starch, high-fructose corn syrup, and glucose. The capital intensity of wet corn milling is 24 percent of the U.S. level and total factor productivity is 44 percent. Unlike most of the rest of food processing and manufacturing, wet corn milling has not invested to developed-country levels.

The industry is in a situation similar to that of other Korean processed food industries before rapid investment in them began about ten years ago. Most corn milling plants in Korea are more than twenty years old, have outdated equipment, and are unable to produce products with higher value added. Plant scale is on average one-fifth of that in the United States. Korean plants are overstaffed compared with U.S. plants, and product yields are lower.

Globally, wet corn milling is handled by multinationals that transfer best practices into plants in Latin America, Africa, and elsewhere in Asia. The Korean industry consists of only five companies, entry by foreign companies was prohibited until 1996, and import quotas were in place on major products. As with other low-capital-intensity processed food industries (such as noodles and corn oil), large Korean companies have been prohibited from entering the sector. Wet corn milling is the only manufacturing industry we studied from which the *chaebol* were absent, which may help explain its less than average capital intensity.

Integrated Steel Mills

Integrated steel mills are the one highly productive industry we studied. Interestingly, this sector consisted entirely of a government-owned company, POSCO. The company owes its high productivity to modern, large, and efficiently laid out facilities at Kwangyang and Pohang. Unlike older steel plants, such as those in the United States, which grew gradually and contain older casting technology and furnaces and rolling mills that are smaller than efficient scale, the POSCO facilities are well planned, use the latest technology, and are laid out in a manner that minimizes materials handling effort. Unlike many of the other Korean manufacturers we studied, POSCO has tried to match its labor productivity against that of the best Japanese producers and has increased it steadily.

How did a government-owned company accomplish what few private Korean companies were able to? Much of the credit is probably due to Taejoon Park, who was chairman of POSCO from 1968 to 1994. Park, a former general, accepted his position on the condition that there be no government interference in the company's procurement and staffing decisions. He then instituted modern Japanese and Western management practices that were absent in other Korean companies. POSCO continuously matched itself against world best practice, conducted an assessment based on net present value of new investment projects, and sourced its capital equipment globally. The company has a strong anti-corruption ethic and has demanded very high performance from its suppliers. The government helped keep the pressure on POSCO by requiring that it sell steel domestically at less than world prices. Whereas many steel industries in emerging countries (including the Korean minimill industry) price at import parity (the world price plus tariffs and transport costs), POSCO has priced at export parity, the price below which domestic customers could export its steel at a profit.[26]

26. Amsden (1989).

That POSCO has been well run makes it something of an exception among state-owned enterprises we have studied in many countries. Its leadership has likely been a special case that tests the usual rules. Moreover, it is an exception among Korean industries in that it has consistently earned its cost of capital. Although its capital costs are subsidized, this subsidy is more than repaid through the low prices the company charges domestic customers. Allowing POSCO to charge world prices on its domestic sales would increase its return on invested capital (ROIC) by roughly 6 percent, and allowing it to charge import parity prices like the private minimills would increase it by another 5 percent. If import parity is viewed as the opportunity cost at which Korea could have acquired steel had POSCO not existed, the company's true return on invested capital over the past ten years is roughly 19 percent, well above even a nonsubsidized cost of capital.

The success of POSCO, of course, is not final. Chairman Park has retired, and it is possible that the company will revert to performance more typical of state-owned enterprises. This is part of the rationale for the government's plan to privatize POSCO and potentially even divide it in order to achieve domestic competition. It is also essential that the company avoid overbuilding capacity the way Japan did in the early 1970s. Experience has shown that domestic demand for steel grows rapidly until GDP per capita reaches about $10,000 and then slowly declines. Japan continued to build capacity as its GDP per capita grew past this level; the result was massive excess capacity, which has destroyed its returns and forced painful restructuring (figure 9). Exporting its excess steel production became less viable as labor costs increased. Even without considering the effects of the financial crisis, Korea is now nearing the point where domestic steel demand will begin to slow, and it needs to manage its capacity carefully.

Services and Construction Cases

Services and construction together employ twice as many workers as manufacturing. Although industry-level capital data are more difficult to obtain in the service sector, aggregate data suggest that services as a whole have about 20 percent of U.S. capital intensity, compared with 57 percent for manufacturing, and that average capital productivity is

Figure 9. Crude Steel Production and Capacity per Capita, Korea and Japan

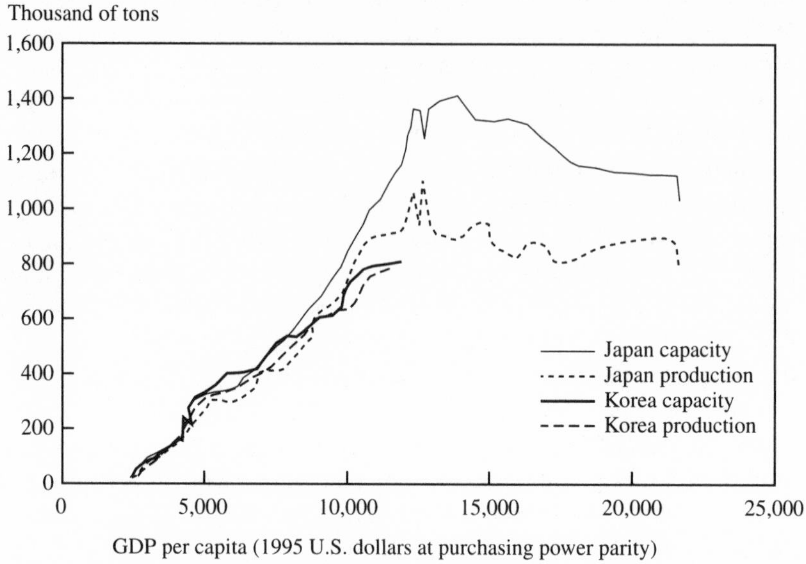

Thousand of tons

GDP per capita (1995 U.S. dollars at purchasing power parity)

Source: McKinsey Global Institute (1998a, ''Steel Industry,'' p. 14).

much higher in services and construction. Given this difference in average (and presumably marginal) productivity, why has so little investment been made in the nonmanufacturing sector?

To answer this question, we examined four industries that cover about one-third of total market employment in the nonmanufacturing sector. Given the diversity of the sector, it is hard for any sample to be fully representative, but analysis of these four industries gives both a range of reasons for the successes and failures of this part of the economy and uncovers common themes that help explain the overall result.

General Merchandise Retailing

The retail industry is a large employer in any economy; in Korea it accounts for 12 percent of service and construction employment, so it is an important for the country's overall economic performance. In addition, retail employment often expands as economies grow and can create new jobs at a time when employment is declining in other industries.[27] Our productivity analysis focused on general merchandise (non-food) retailing, the larger and more complex segment of the industry. Hereafter, *retailing* will refer only to general merchandise retailing.[28]

In all developed and middle-income countries, retailing is evolving from traditional mom-and-pop stores to more productive formats such as department stores, discounters, and specialty stores. These formats achieve high productivity (high value added per unit of input) either by providing goods to consumers efficiently (high sales per unit of input) or providing a shopping service for which customers are willing to pay extra (high ratio of value added to sales).[29] Discounters such as Wal-Mart or Costco tend to focus on high efficiency, while department stores and specialty chains provide a high level of service by supplying attractive surroundings and knowledgeable sales personnel (Nordstrom) or a range of goods targeted on a limited group of consumers (J. Crew). All of these advanced formats use information technology and the advantages of a large-scale firm (not necessarily large-scale stores) to achieve more productive logistics and purchasing and to better target customers' needs.

In Korea the evolution toward higher-productivity stores has been slower than would be expected given the country's income level. Korean stores are much smaller than those in the United States or Japan,

27. Retail employment has not expanded in France and Germany because of high labor costs and product market barriers such as strict (and often anticompetitive) application of zoning laws. This is a major contributor to the unemployment problem in these countries. See McKinsey Global Institute (1997).

28. The sectors in the three countries were adjusted in order to achieve comparability. Specifically, eating and drinking, gasoline service stations, and automotive dealers in the United States; gasoline service stations in Japan; and personal and household goods repair in Korea were all excluded from our study.

29. With cross-country comparisons, it is difficult to determine if low ratios of value added to sales reflect low real service levels or a low price of retailing service (because of low minimum wages, for example). Ideally, one would want to convert value added to a common currency using a double-deflated PPP for retailing service, but we have found this impossible given available data. For this study we used the PPP for private consumption expenditure as a proxy. In our studies of retail productivity in the United States, France, Germany, and the Netherlands, we have experimented with other methodologies, such as assuming that workers in the same format have identical productivity across countries or that workers in a given multinational store (Ikea, for instance) have the same productivity in all countries. In general we found that the results varied by about 10 to 15 percent depending on the methodology; an error of this magnitude would not affect the conclusions drawn from the U.S.-Korea comparison. See Baily and Zitzewitz (1998) for details.

Figure 10. Estimated Retail Store Labor Productivity, by Type of Store, United States and Korea, 1992

Productivity by format
U.S. 1992 average labor productivity=100

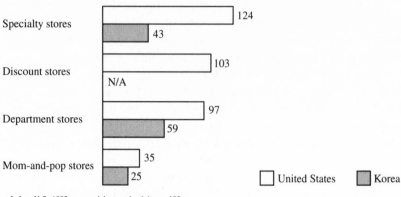

Index: U.S. 1992 average labor productivity = 100

Source: McKinsey Global Institute (1998a, ''Retail Industry,'' p. 8).

with 2.2 employers per store compared with 4.7 in Japan and 8.0 in the United States, and 99 percent of all retail stores operate as single units, not as part of a chain. More than 70 percent of the workers in Korean retail stores are proprietors or unpaid family members. Korean retail is composed mainly of traditional, low-productivity, mom-and-pop stores, whereas the U.S. sector is 80 percent advanced formats (figure 10). As a result, Korean labor productivity is only 32 percent of the U.S. level (figure 11) because of lower efficiency (ratio of sales to input) and lower ratios of value added to sales.[30]

In addition to the different format mix, advanced Korean formats are less productive than their U.S. counterparts. Korean department stores achieve only 59 percent of U.S. department store productivity, while

30. Because value added data were not available in all countries, we use gross margin as a proxy for value added. Gross margin causes problems in that it includes purchased services, which could bias the results in favor of stores with disproportionate purchases of services such as advertising. At least for a subset of Korean stores for which we had both figures, however, this bias was very small. Another data problem is that the retailing censuses on which our results are based are not conducted in the same years in all countries; our comparison uses different base years—1993 for Korea, 1992 for the United States, and 1994 for Japan.

Figure 11. Retail Sector Labor Productivity, United States, Japan, and Korea

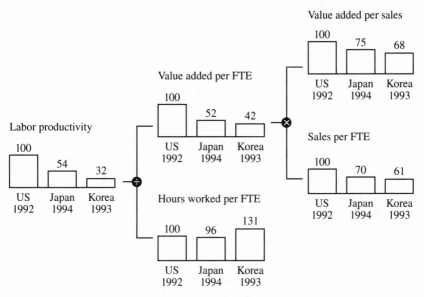

Index: United States = 100

Source: McKinsey Global Institute (1998a, "Retail Industry," p. 7). Value added calculated using consumption purchasing power parity. FTE is full-time equivalent employees.

specialty stores reach just 43 percent.[31] The McKinsey Global Institute's review of work practices in Korea found that department and specialty stores did not deploy their work forces efficiently, providing low levels of service despite large numbers of staff on the floor. There was ineffective use of point-of-sale information, and merchandising was not best practice, as seen, for example, in the lack of category management skills.

The main reason advanced formats have emerged only slowly and foreign retailers have not transferred best practices (as they have in Brazil and other middle-income countries) is Korea's land use policies. Land in Korea is scarce, and intricate zoning and land development laws govern both its availability and use. Until 1993 the National Land

31. A productivity comparison for discount stores is not included because there were no discount stores in Korea during the year of our study. Some of the gap in specialty store productivity may be explained by format mix within categories: many Korean specialty stores were mom-and-pops, while U.S. specialty stores were more advanced category killers such as Home Depot or Circuit City, which are highly productive.

Usage Management Act prohibited stores larger than 1,000 square meters from operating in any area outside the urban zone. The Urban Planning Act and the Construction Act again restricted the commercial area that could be used for retail formats larger than 1,000 square meters. Known as urban commercial areas, these zones are conveniently located to generate very high sales traffic. Unfortunately, the available locations are often already occupied by retailers or office buildings or too small to accommodate department stores, discounters, or the shopping malls that make advanced specialty stores viable. Retailers could have redeveloped these attractive commercial locations in urban areas by buying smaller buildings, tearing them down, and building a large store. However, many retailers pointed out that redeveloping existing retail stores is a cumbersome option because of the long, complex negotiations required to get agreement from multiple owners.

Land use policies also contribute to the high cost of urban land by concentrating the population in city centers and preventing the development of edge cities. This problem is made worse by the policy-related pressure on the population to concentrate in Seoul. Only 0.2 percent of the land area in Korea is designated for commercial use, suggesting that policy, not intrinsic factor endowments, is the larger problem.

Special land use policies have restricted the entry of advanced foreign retailers. Most advanced formats need at least 5,000 square meters to operate efficiently. Before 1984, only retail outlets less than 200 square meters and selling only one type of product were allowed to enter Korea. In 1984 shop sizes of 700 square meters and selling multiple product types were allowed. In 1991 the first step of a three-stage deregulation allowed foreign investment in up to ten stores less than 1,000 square meters in lot size. The second step in 1993 allowed store sizes of up to 3,000 square meters, and the number and sizes of stores was completely deregulated in 1996. Thus until 1996 foreign retailers were effectively limited to subscale discounters and the few small specialty stores that could survive outside of shopping malls. Even now, foreign retailers face the same land use laws as domestic firms.

A host of additional regulations, such as restrictions on *chaebol* involvement in retail activity and an arduous, bureaucratic store-opening evaluation process contributed to Korea's low productivity. These regulations were established with the objectives of protecting mom-and-pop stores, discouraging consumption, and promoting more investment in manufacturing industries. Figures on capital intensity and productivity for the entire trade sector suggest that the policies were successful in diverting investment: capital intensity in trade is only 21 percent of that in the United States, while capital productivity is roughly 150 percent, double that of Korean manufacturing. By diverting capital from trade to manufacturing, Korea diverted capital to low-productivity investments and closed off potentially high-return investments in retail.

There are parallels between retailing in Korea and in Japan. In previous work on this sector, we found that land use and other restrictions had prevented the evolution of retailing in Japan, just as it has done in Korea.[32] More recently, Japan has opened up the sector to some extent to foreign retail chains and has allowed the development of Japan-based discounters, thereby increasing productivity.[33]

Construction

The construction industry in Korea accounted for 16 percent of GDP and 8.5 percent of employment in 1995. In the past ten years, construction has experienced compounded annual growth of 17 percent in value added and 8 percent in employment. Most of this growth has occurred since 1989 when the government announced that it would construct 2 million houses to resolve the housing shortage and relaxed industry entry restrictions.[34]

The construction industry can be divided into three segments: residential, nonresidential, and heavy construction, each accounting for roughly one-third of sales and employment. Residential construction includes both private and public housing construction, nonresidential includes commercial and industrial structures, and heavy construction includes infrastructure such as bridges and roads. Although we report productivity estimates for all three types, our analysis focuses on residential construction.

Based on value added at purchasing power parity (PPP), overall

32. McKinsey Global Institute (1992).
33. Because of its very restrictive land use policy, Japan may find that discounters and category killers drive out the mom-and-pop stores, but the lost employment is not replaced by specialty retailing. This type of retailing requires the development of shopping malls, or some equivalent mechanism, to generate customer traffic.
34. The compounded annual growth rate of value added from 1989 to 1995 was 27 percent.

Figure 12. Labor Productivity in the Construction Industry: Value Added per Hour Worked, United States and Korea, 1995

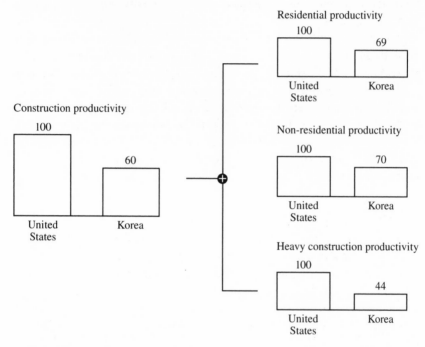

Index: United States = 100

Source: McKinsey Global Institute (1998a, ''Construction Industry,'' p. 5).

Korean labor productivity is 60 percent of that in the U.S. industry, with residential construction productivity at 69 percent of U.S. value added per hour worked (figure 12).[35] For residential construction we also computed a physical measure of output (square meters) and found that Korean physical productivity—square meters per hour—is 93 percent of the U.S. level, but the value added for each square meter built is only 75 percent of the U.S. level. The value added per square meter is constrained by regulation. Government regulations have set a price ceiling for units in apartment buildings, which encourages developers to design small units with poor-quality fixtures and few appliances. It

35. The best available residential construction PPP was from the 1985 UN International Comparisons Project, which was updated using national construction GDP deflators.

is common practice in Korea for a purchaser to immediately renovate a newly constructed unit to upgrade the contents. The price cap also keeps net margins low (0.7 percent as opposed to 5.0 percent in the United States), which discourages larger-scale developers from consolidating the industry. We estimated that the inefficiencies associated with the price cap account for 10 percent of the productivity gap.

In addition, land use policy in Korea shifts the mix of units toward multifamily housing. Although these units allow the construction of more square meters per hour worked, single-family housing generates higher value added per square meter. Copying the U.S. mix of single-family homes may be impractical because of Korea's higher population density. But other similarly populated countries, such as the Netherlands, have achieved high productivity and higher shares of single-family and medium-density housing while preserving green space. (Residential construction productivity in the Netherlands is the same as in the United States).

Korean productivity is also lower because of the absence of operational best practices. Based on interviews with industry participants, the problems most commonly cited were:

—Less standardization. Housing construction in the United States and the Netherlands is usually handled by developers who manage a number of large projects. This allows standardization in designs and in the sizes and quality of construction materials and allows firms and workers to benefit more from learning by doing. Residential construction is much more fragmented in Korea.

—Poor project management, especially in the design phase. Unlike in the United States and the Netherlands, where a lead contractor with proper incentives manages projects from design to completion, in Korea the process is again more fragmented. This leads to communication problems and more frequent revision of designs.

—Less productive construction methods. Many construction methods used in Korea require more steps and labor hours. For example, Korean housing often has in-floor heating, which takes 30 percent longer to install than standard heating. Korean housing also usually has concrete walls instead of drywall, and concrete walls take almost twice as long to construct.

Like retail activity, residential construction is a sector in which productivity, output, and investment have been limited by both land use regulations and the absence of large companies that have adopted modern business practices. However, residential construction, at 69 percent of U.S. productivity, does appear to be more advanced than retail.

Telecommunications

Although the Korean telecommunications industry was deregulated in 1996, like many recently deregulated industries, it is still dominated by the state-owned former monopoly. Korea Telecom accounts for 80 percent of industry revenue, but even though it still has a local monopoly, it has faced competition from DACOM in international calling since 1991 and domestic long distance since 1996. Mobile services have experienced more deregulation: the market already has two national cellular companies and three mobile telephone providers. The government issued thirteen additional licenses in 1996. The Korean government still owns 71 percent of Korea Telecom, but it plans to reduce this share in the coming years.

The Korean telecommunications industry has achieved a network development that ranks among the world's fastest. The number of access lines per hundred inhabitants, grew from 3.0 in 1975 to 41.5 in 1995, an average annual increase of 14 percent. Most of this growth was in fixed lines, but recent growth in the number of mobile subscribers has been extremely rapid. Korea has also taken major steps to improve the quality of its network: the share of digitally switched lines has increased to 63 percent.

Korea combined this rapid network growth with fairly high labor productivity. Since its rapid network growth began in the late 1970s, access lines per employee have been comparable to those in the United States (figure 13). The experience of other developing countries reveals that this achievement is not automatic (Brazil), nor is it final (Mexico, Hong Kong). The Korean telecommunications industry has captured much of the productivity benefit of new technology, rather than applying the new technology while maintaining staffing levels as other telecommunications industries have done. This has been made easier by rapid network growth; the country has been able to increase productivity by limiting its employment growth rather than having to lay off workers who were hired to staff a lower-technology network.

Although the number of access lines per employee is higher than in

Figure 13. Telecommunication Access Lines per Telecommunications Employee, Five Countries, 1975–95

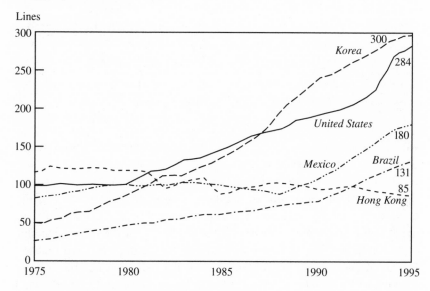

Source: McKinsey Global Institute (1998a, ''Telecommunication Services Industry,'' p. 17). Telecommunications employment as reported to the International Telecommunication Union.

the United States, labor productivity overall is only 83 percent of that in the U.S. industry, mainly due to longer hours worked in Korea (table 2). Interviews suggested that the long working hours (2,700 a year) were unnecessary and could be reduced without affecting service quality. Long hours appear to result from internal evaluation procedures that emphasize ''face time'' (time spent at work) rather than quality of

Table 2. Telecommunications Productivity, 1995

Index: United States = 100

Country	Labor productivity Access lines, call minutes per FTE	Capital productivity Call minutes per U.S. dollar capital service	Total factor productivity
United States	100	100	100
Japan	82	39	51
Brazil	41	77	62
Korea	83	58	66

Source: McKinsey Global Institute (1998a, ''Telecommunication Services Industry,'' p. 7).

Table 3. Average Use Per Access Line, 1995

Country	Local calls[a]	Long distance[a]	International and mobile	Annual calls per line	Call minutes per capita	Average minutes per call
United States	5,703	2,037	280	8,020	5,955	2.70
Japan	1,822	1,428	206	3,456	1,983	2.64
Brazil	6,278	1,288	102	7,668	779	2.80
Korea	3,662	1,429	90	5,181	2,376	1.51

Source: McKinsey Global Institute (1998a, "Telecommunication Services Industry," p. 7).
a. The definition of local and long distance calls (in terms of distance covered) differs by countries and regions.

work. The fact that most employees are salaried makes the problem less obvious to top management.

The larger issue, however, is capital productivity. Network utilization (call minutes per unit of capital stock) is only 58 percent of the U.S. level, mainly because of fewer call minutes per access line. Koreans make fewer and shorter calls and more local than long distance calls (table 3). The conclusion is similar to the one we have reached for Japan and many European countries: the United States has greater network utilization than most countries. Many factors influence demand for and use of telecommunications services, and isolating their impact is empirically difficult. We have found in past studies that U.S. demand is significantly influenced by sophisticated and aggressive marketing, low marginal pricing of calls, and the availability of services that promote call initiation and completion.

In Korea the factors that drive high U.S. demand appear to be absent. Marketing activity has been limited. In fact, during the 1980s, when Korea was focused on expanding its network to meet demand, Korea Telecom actually encouraged low usage: "Tonghwa nun kandan hee" ("Call brief") was one of its slogans. The company prices local calls by the minute rather than providing free local calls for a fixed monthly charge. Business use of the telephone has not been promoted, and uses such as telemarketing, teleconferencing, toll free calling, and electronic transactions are much less common. Some of the lower business and residential telephone usage may be due to lower income levels, but the contrast in the marketing and pricing strategies of U.S. and Korean carriers suggest that income is not the whole story.[36]

36. Korean telecommunications use, and therefore productivity, may also depend on the age of the industry. The United States developed its telephone network more than

In addition to low network utilization, Korean capital productivity is also reduced by its higher capital cost per access line. The government encouraged Korea Telecom to work closely with domestic equipment manufacturers to develop advanced switching technology. The government viewed the development of domestic switching technology as a means to reduce dependence on foreign equipment makers and to provide a source of exports. Korea achieved some success in duplicating overseas technology, but at a cost. Korean investment per line was 12 percent higher than it was in the United States. Detailed data on switch prices in Korea were not available, but industry experts estimated that Korean prices were 10 to 20 percent higher than those in the United States.

The Korean telecommunications industry is a mixture of good and not-so-good performance. In some respects it resembles the integrated steel industry. Development of a modern telecommunications network was seen as a priority for the country, and a state-owned industry was established with access to capital and a mandate for rapid growth. Korea's relatively late economic development allowed it to take advantage of best practices and new technologies.[37] The country was able to engage in extensive knowledge and technology transfers with the more developed countries. In addition, interviews with Korean service providers indicate that they actively sought telecommunications experts from the more advanced economies and attempted to learn from their experience. Unlike steel, however, Korea Telecom did not export and did not have to provide service at international prices. Also unlike steel, promoting high output (network usage) was not a priority, and marketing and pricing reflect that. Interviews suggested that despite deregulation efforts, Korea still views Korea Telecom as a national asset, suggesting that although some formal barriers to competition have been

---

a generation before the world's other advanced economies. As a result, calling patterns in the United States may be more mature than those in other countries. America has developed a culture of phone use that does not currently exist in Korea and has oriented its economic activity around telecommunications to a greater extent. In telecommunications there are positive network externalities (for instance, the value of the network to subscribers, and the likelihood they will use it, increases with the size of the network). U.S. subscribers may demand comparatively more telephone service because of the country's larger network, and Korea's use may increase as its network expands.

37. The advantage may be offset, however, by more developed markets and usage patterns in the United States.

removed, competitive intensity is still restrained by policies favoring the company.

Retail Banking

The Korean government has historically used the banking sector to advance its overall development goals by encouraging high personal savings rates, capturing the savings within the formal banking system, and channeling them to high-priority industries. The government nationalized the banks in the 1960s, and although they have since been privatized, government influence remains strong. In the 1960s time and savings deposits in the formal banking system increased from 1.8 percent to 20.7 percent of GDP, mainly due to changes in interest rates that encouraged saving and attracted savings away from informal lenders. Saving was also encouraged by the restriction of consumer finance; Koreans were encouraged to save for a home through the Korean Housing Bank because mortgages were difficult to get. Banks were prohibited from lending to certain industries, such as leisure and real estate, and were encouraged to lend to export-oriented sectors such as manufacturing and overseas heavy construction.[38]

Banks have a dual function in modern economies. First, they allocate saving to finance business and consumer investment, presumably in a way that makes good use of a country's scarce capital. Second, they make payments, maintain deposit and loan accounts, and provide other banking services to retail business customers. This case study examines how productive Korean banks are in providing services. To understand how well they have done in allocating savings, we look at capital productivity and allocation in the whole economy.

To measure productivity in providing banking services, we used a physical output methodology based on the approach used by the U.S. Bureau of Labor Statistics. This methodology forced us to focus on retail banking. We measured productivity separately in the three key activities of retail banking: transacting payments, managing deposit accounts, and managing loan accounts. Korea has higher labor productivity than the United States in deposits but lower productivity in pay-

---

38. Industries in which lending was formally banned accounted for 25 percent of the establishments operating in Korea in 1991.

Table 4. Personal Financial Services Labor Productivity, by Country
Index: United States = 100

Country	*Transacting payments and disbursing cash*[a] *(number of transactions per hour of labor input)*	*Managing deposit accounts (adjusted number of deposit accounts per hour of labor input)*[b]	*Managing loan accounts (adjusted number of deposit accounts per hour of labor input)*[c]	*Total*[d]
Netherlands (1995)	140	n.a.	n.a.	n.a.
United States (1994)	100	100	100	100
Korea (1995)	65	138	57	76

Source: McKinsey Global Institute (1998a, ''Personal Financial Services Industry,'' p. 4).
n.a. Not available.
a. Includes wholesale payment transactions and wholesale payment staff.
b. Labor weight: checking/current account = 4; savings account - 1; time deposit; 1.5, MMDA - 2; others - 1.
c. Labor weight: overdraft - 1; credit card - 1; car loans - 3; mortgage - 10; installment credits - 3; other consumer loans - 1.
d. Labor weights: payments 54 percent; deposit accounts 19 percent; loan accounts 27 percent.

ments and loans (table 4).[39] Both Korea and the United States have lower payments productivity than the Netherlands. Overall Korean productivity is 76 percent of that in the United States.

Korean productivity in payments is weak because of a less efficient mix of electronic and manual payments, a denser branch network, and less efficient utilization of labor. The Netherlands makes much greater use of electronic payments than the United States or Korea (table 5); these payments have labor requirements that are two to ten times lower than checks and paper-based transfers. In addition, Koreans conduct a much greater share of payment transactions at the teller. The Netherlands also derives a productivity advantage from its fewer branches per capita, in part because of high population density. Korea also has a high population density, but it has not rationalized its branch network.

After adjusting for the mix of payments and density of branch networks, the United States has the most efficient utilization of labor. U.S. banks aggressively use part-time tellers to avoid the problem of peak demand periods (figure 14). When one U.S. bank increased the share of part-time tellers from 25 to 50 percent, it was able to reduce total full-time-equivalent employees by 20 percent without impairing service

39. Capital input is very difficult to estimate for banks because it is very hard to separate the fixed assets that are used to provide banking services from those that are held as real estate investments. We therefore are limited to measuring labor productivity.

Table 5. Financial Services Payments, by Country and Type, 1994–95
Percent of total[a]

Type of Payment	Netherlands (1995)	United States (1994)	Korea (1995)
Total electronic transactions	88	28	31
Paperless credit transfer	50	2	7
Direct debits	18	1	4
Credit and debit cards[b]	7	16	6
Cash withdrawals at ATM	13	9	14
Total paper transactions	12	71	70
Paper-based credit transfer	3	0	9
Checks	5	68	27
Cash withdrawal at teller	4	3	34

Source: McKinsey Global Institute (1998a, "Personal Financial Services Industry," p. 6).
a. Total number of transactions in millions: Netherlands, 15,838; United States, 90,053; Korea, 3,629.
b. No debit card for Korea in 1995.

quality. Korean banks have less flexible working hours and do not use incentive-based compensation, which further affects productivity.

In lending, Korean branches are managed as a series of little banks. Credit decisions are made in each branch through manual and hierarchical processes. Larger loans also require hierarchical review at head offices. Lending officers cannot be given incentives to sell loans because of their dual responsibility for reviewing credit. They are instead personally penalized for defaults. This leads the officers and branch

Figure 14. Branch Bank Staffing, by Type of Employee, United States and Korea, 1994

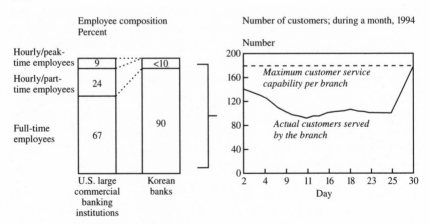

Source: McKinsey Global Institute (1998a, "Personal Financial Services Industry," p. 8).

managers to review loan applications in a painstakingly careful manner, which has created a credit approval process that takes days or weeks and requires much more labor. In the United States, banks have centralized lending decisions, allowing branches to focus on selling loans and creating the scale needed to implement credit scoring. This has reduced the time required for lending decisions to minutes or hours, and has reduced labor requirements by up to 50 percent.

Korean banks are productive in taking deposits. The highly regulated banking environment has effectively made increasing deposits the natural focus for banks. As a result, they have streamlined taking deposits while minimizing the amount of advice provided to depositors. Opening an account is done at the teller, directly in the banks' computer systems. All deposit handling is, therefore, as easy as handling transactions.

It is not hard to see the relation between the structure and goals of the banking industry, as influenced by government policy, and the industry's performance. The banks are not intended to encourage spending and borrowing but rather to encourage saving, which is then directed to industrial development.

Competition among the banks is limited. Because interest rates on deposits and loans are regulated, banks cannot compete in payments and lending, but only through branch expansion to gain access to deposits. The government also controls entry to the banking industry, so that specialized competitors, such as Countrywide in the United States, are not able to compete for specific bank activities. (Until recently, securitization of mortgages or consumer loans was also not available.) The exit of poorly performing banks has also been controlled by the government. Strong ties between government and the industry seem to have created beliefs among bank managers and customers that banks will never go bankrupt. Deposit insurance was only introduced in 1996, but in fact no Korean banks have gone bankrupt or merged for the past fifteen years. The only merger in the history of the banking industry (between Seoul Bank and Korea Trust Bank) was led by the government in 1976.

Unions and labor rules have also affected banks' performance. All Korean banks including the Central Bank are unionized and subject to rules that make layoffs difficult or impossible, restrict flexible staffing, and discourage incentive pay. These practices are also a barrier for mergers and acquisitions because these usually involve layoffs.

Synthesis of the Results

Most developing countries would be delighted to have experienced the growth in GDP per capita that Korea experienced from 1970 to 1995. To have mobilized such large amounts of capital and labor and educated its work force at such speed was an amazing achievement. Several of our industry case studies have shown how Korea accomplished the growth. In steel, POSCO purchased plants that incorporated best-practice technology, managed plant construction efficiently, and staffed at best-practice levels. The telecommunications industry created an efficient high-technology network. In the semiconductor industry, Korean companies were able to acquire the engineering knowledge needed to achieve relatively high productivity in DRAMS. By successfully transferring best-practice capital technology, Korea succeeded where many other developing countries did not.[40]

At the same time, the case studies also suggest why the growth in Korea was not achieved with higher productivity.

—Korea has been able to acquire best-practice engineering and technical knowledge but not best-practice managerial knowledge.[41] It has been able to transfer best-practice technology when the technology has been embodied in capital goods. The country has also successfully acquired engineering knowledge and managed capital building projects. In the case of integrated steel mills, that was enough to create a best-practice industry. Automotive manufacturing has not been able to transfer the intangible capital (total quality management, continuous improvement, design for manufacturing) required for lean production. The semiconductor industry has not been able to transfer the design skills needed for higher-value-added chips.

40. Our projects on Brazil (McKinsey Global Institute, 1998b) and Latin America (McKinsey Global Institute, 1994a) show how other developing countries have failed to efficiently transfer best-practice capital technology. Unlike POSCO, the steel industries in Brazil, Mexico, and Argentina built small, poorly laid out plants that they dramatically paid too much for (corruption was a major problem) and overstaffed. The same was true in telecommunications.

41. Dollar and Sokoloff (1990) found a different dichotomy. Using 1963–79 data, they found that within manufacturing total factor productivity growth had been high in textiles and other light and medium industries and low in such heavy industries as steel and chemicals. This suggests that as of 1979, Korea had mastered some engineering challenges, but not all of them. We find that by 1995 Korea had acquired the remaining engineering knowledge but still lagged in managerial knowledge.

It is very hard to transfer certain types of intangible capital. The U.S. auto industry has not caught up to Japanese industry in productivity because it has not fully transferred lean production to all its products and plants. Aside from Intel, profits have been scarce in the semiconductor industry worldwide. As well as its strong design skills, Intel, like Microsoft, has an advantage it inherited from IBM. It sets the industry standard. It is thus not surprising that Korea found it difficult to catch up to best practice in many sectors, particularly when it decided not to allow foreign direct investment.

—Capital has been misallocated within and among industries. Government policy has strongly affected the allocation by controlling or influencing the banks, making funds available to some industries and discouraging borrowing by others. In some cases this worked. In steel the investments earned a high rate of return and (until the crisis) there was no overcapacity. In telecommunications an efficient network was set up. However, in autos, semiconductors, and confectionery, the *chaebol*'s access to funds encouraged overinvestment. Cronyism and outright fraud undermined the efficiency of the government-controlled capital allocation system. In addition, direct industry regulation prevented some profitable investments from being made and distorted others. Regulation prevented investments in modern retailing. In milling, automation investments with very short estimated payback periods were not made because of regulations that inhibited the consolidation of the industry.

Even taking the regulatory environment as given, companies did not always make economically rational decisions. Access to bank lending may have encouraged overinvestment, but the *chaebol* generally had the owners' funds at risk and still retained an incentive to make wise investments. In practice, we found from interviews and from working with companies that their decisions were based on gaining market share, not on profitability. We have noted the overcapacity in auto manufacturing and the large investments in semiconductors despite very uncertain profit prospects. In confectionery, companies overinvested in new production lines but did not make investments with good payoffs in packaging automation. Banks used information technology much less than would have been justified on profitability grounds.

Our findings about the structure of financial institutions and the misallocation of capital suggest some causes for the financial crisis. The crisis had several elements, including an overvalued exchange rate and contagion effects from other Asian economies. But the case studies have revealed some more fundamental problems that made the Korean economy vulnerable.

The reason the crisis in Korea occurred in 1997, instead of earlier or later, is that a crisis in Thailand in 1997 spread to other Asian countries. Crises are often associated with a shortage of liquidity, and this was certainly the case in Korea, where foreign lenders refused to roll over loans because they perceived the risk as being too great. Indeed, some observers have likened the crisis to a speculative panic that spread to different countries in the way that panic selling on the stock market will drag down most or all companies. And there is some truth to this; a shift in investor expectations certainly took place.

But blaming the crisis in Korea entirely on panicky overreaction to events elsewhere in Asia is not plausible. Following the crisis in Thailand, only a handful of countries around the world were forced into crisis. Why some and not others? The crisis in Korea did not occur for some months after Thailand's, and not until there were bankruptcies among the *chaebols* (most notably Hanbo steel where $5 billion was lent to finance a minimill that would have cost $1.5 billion in the United States). Certainly, events elsewhere in Asia changed the assessment of risk, but there were deeper problems.

The crisis in Thailand spread because it forced a reappraisal of the risks of lending in East Asia.[42] Banks in the West and especially in Japan had believed the risk of lending to these countries was very low because of their rapid growth and the support the governments were giving to the banks. Once lenders started looking seriously at the fundamentals, they found severe problems, problems that had in fact existed for some time. A 1994 McKinsey Global Institute study of capital markets reported:

> "The case of Korea illustrates the cost of providing large amounts of credit that are not allocated by the market. . . . Directed credit has led to very high levels of non-performing assets in the banking system. In 1993, Korea had a ratio of non-performing assets to total assets of 10

---

42. We said earlier that Japan and Korea are on very similar growth paths. Japan may well show how an economy with some of the same fundamental problems in lending and investment decisionmaking as Korea can have a financial crisis without having a liquidity crisis.

percent, versus just over 1 percent in the United States. . . . Even at the peak of the savings and loan crisis in the United States during the late 1980s, this ratio was less than 2 percent of total assets.''[43]

From a limited number of case studies we cannot prove an argument, but our observations strongly suggest why there were nonperforming loans. The rate of return on capital in many industries had been driven down, and this was not because the overall capital intensity of the economy had become particularly high. Rather it was that capital investment had been concentrated in certain industries so that their capital intensity had reached or exceeded U.S. levels while productivity remained weak. Moreover, even within companies capital use was often poor. Thus capital productivity and the return to capital were low. Specifically, we found in autos, semiconductors, and confectionery that capital intensity was about the same as in the United States but productivity was much lower and the gross return to capital was only one-half to two-thirds that in the United States.

The concentration of investment in export-oriented manufacturing was clearly encouraged by the government, in part through its influence over the lending decisions of banks. Individual lending decisions were politically influenced and in some cases involved outright corruption, as with the Hanbo loan. The careers of top bank officials were determined more by politics than by their lending performance, and bank officers were rotated so frequently that there was limited accountability. These factors made possible companies' poor investment decisions. Properly regulated, profit-maximizing lenders would have demanded that better investments be made.

And yet the entire explanation does not lie with the lenders. The owners of the *chaebol* that made poor investment decisions had significant amounts of their own money at stake. Although Korea's 1995 debt-to-equity ratio of 3:1 for manufacturers is high compared with the 1.7:1 average for the United States, this still means that owners of Korean companies were contributing 25 percent of the firm's capital.[44]

43. McKinsey Global Institute (1994b, chap. 2, p. 8). Nobody likes the smart aleck that says ''I told you so,'' but in fact we, and no doubt others, did tell them so. There was a Global Institute presentation in Seoul in March 1994 on problem loans.

44. The companies that went bankrupt recently (among them Hanbo, Sammi, Jinro, and Kia) were probably more highly leveraged than average when they made their ill-fated investment decisions and thus more prone to moral hazard. But investments with

It is hard to see how it was in their interests to overinvest just because banks were willing to lend them the money. Furthermore, with the important exception of DRAM manufacturing, most of the over-investment does not appear to have involved gambles that went wrong. It is hard to see how investments involving excessive product proliferation in processed food and those focusing on volume instead of quality in the automotive industry would have paid off even in a Panglossian world. And even though the focus on DRAM chips was a gamble, the companies involved had substantial equity in other businesses, which they were putting at risk.

If Korean companies had such a strong incentive to make good investment decisions, why were their decisions so bad? One culprit is the absence of capital management skills. Measures such as return on invested capital and economic value added were not used by Korean firms. Financial statements tracking the true contributions and returns earned by individual subsidiaries, business units, and products were not available, even internally. Few companies measured their operational performance, especially their capital productivity, against best practice.

The high-growth environment in Korea from the 1960s through the 1980s reduced the need for these management techniques and thus crippled the incentive to acquire them. If capital could be obtained from banks (often at negative real interest rates), it was not hard to find a profitable investment. Overcapacity problems were solved with a few years' growth, and land appreciation was rapid enough that even otherwise uneconomic investments could be justified on the grounds that they created an excuse to speculate in land. At the same time that capital availability increased in the 1990s, the conditions that had helped make investments profitable changed: land appreciation ended in 1991, and GDP growth slowed in 1996.

Alternative Growth Paths

These results raise two important questions. First, could Korea have grown as fast or faster if it had adopted a different development strat-

---

low returns were made by almost every large Korean firm, including the most financially sound.

egy? Second, what should it do to enhance its growth prospects? We have some thoughts on the first of these questions, but not a clear answer. We believe that there is a clear answer to the second question, however. We estimate Korea's future growth potential under different policy approaches.

Reviewing the Past

Korea has followed the Japanese path of input-driven growth with long hours of work, high rates of saving with funds channeled into the industrial sector, a strong export orientation, strict limits on "nonessential" imports and direct foreign investment, and strict zoning laws and other restrictions on the distribution system. These characteristics describe both economies' approach to development.[45]

This path carries penalties for productivity, illustrated by Korea's experience.

—Limiting direct foreign investment forces domestic industries to attempt to master best-practice technologies on their own. For best practices in the automotive industry (lean production), semiconductors (design of non-DRAM chips), processed food and telecommunications (marketing, capacity management), and banking (credit risk assessment), this has proven very difficult.

—Channeling funds into priority sectors is easy to overdo. Industrial policy and government control of bank lending may be helpful in the early stages of economic development, particularly when capital markets are undeveloped. Whether or not this is the case, Korea retained a directed approach too long and overinvested in favored industries while restricting or discouraging investments elsewhere.

—Exposure to best-practice competitors can be beneficial. In earlier work for the McKinsey Global Institute we found that exposing companies to best-practice competitors encourages them to be more productive. Limiting foreign competition in Korea meant that many domestic companies did not feel the pressure to be more productive.

Although we suspect that Korean consumers would have been better

---

45. There are of course differences between the two economies. Japan developed its own first-rate capital goods industry, reducing the import requirements for growth. It also has large foreign exchange reserves and has avoided a currency crisis, although it is facing a banking crisis.

off with a less restrictive policy environment, we do not have enough evidence to replay Korea's history. We do not know whether the long hours of work and the high savings could have been mobilized in a more open and consumer-oriented economy. We do not know whether more direct foreign investment or imports competing against infant industries would have encouraged greater productivity or have led to infanticide.

Alternative Growth Policies for the Future

In this section we describe alternative growth scenarios that Korea might achieve under different policy regimes. We take 2000 as our starting point, with the idea that the current crisis will have passed by then and that reform legislation could have been implemented.[46] We estimate the growth potential for ten years through 2010.

We are not making forecasts, and we have excluded many important variables, such as monetary and demand-side variables, as well as social factors. The main novelty and contribution of this exercise is to use the case study results and McKinsey's knowledge of industries worldwide to make rough estimates of potential labor productivity growth. In the alternative scenarios we assess the extent to which alternative policies would or would not allow this potential to be realized. We are not looking for precise estimates but rather a quantitative judgment as to whether policy differences are significant. Given space constraints we cannot do justice to the material. Readers are referred to the full Korea report.[47]

The policy scenarios we examined follow.

—Scenario 1: Assumes no fundamental reform and that the government continues to be a significant factor in directing economic development. We estimate that GDP per capita growth would drop to 3 percent a year, and Korea would remain vulnerable to another financial crisis. This growth path would represent a continuation of the Japanese path, where per capita growth dropped from 7.5 percent in 1964–74 to 3 percent in 1974–84.

46. Using 2000 to start gives us a dilemma because the most recent actual data we have is for 1995. Therefore, we simply assume that the state of the economy that existed in 1995 prevails in 2000. To the extent that this is not true, our estimate of the future would have to be adjusted.

47. McKinsey Global Institute (1998a).

—Scenario 2: Assumes the financial and manufacturing sectors are reformed but not services and construction. We estimate that growth would be higher, at 4 percent a year for GDP per capita, and that the risks of another financial crisis would be averted. Employment in manufacturing would decline by about 20 percent over ten years as firms faced competitive pressure. However, there would be a lack of good jobs opening up in services, so workers would be forced either into low-productivity or subsistence employment.

—Scenario 3: Assumes reforms to services and construction as well as manufacturing. We estimate that per capita growth could be as high as 6 percent and that services would provide employment opportunities for displaced manufacturing workers. Manufacturing growth would actually be higher than under scenario 2 because the greater income growth generated in services would increase the demand for manufactured goods.

Our first step then was to figure out the growth potential in each of the case study industries under different policy regimes. In no case did we assume new technologies or formats were developed. Instead, we examined the likely diffusion of best practices. More specifics are given later and in the McKinsey Global Institute report, but the idea was to use the experience of other countries to see how rapidly diffusion occurs in a less regulated environment and then modify this to reflect different factor endowments of land or skilled labor. In scenarios 1 and 2 we estimated how continued restrictions would slow this diffusion process. Using the cases as a guide, we then extrapolated to the broader sectors of the economy to estimate potential productivity growth by broad sector of the economy.[48]

To move from potential productivity growth by sector to overall growth requires an estimate of how expenditure is allocated by sector as income growth proceeds. In a general equilibrium exercise, estimating income and price elasticities for the outputs of the different industries could do this. Instead, we took a simpler approach and looked at current and historical data on the distribution of output by industry in other countries as they passed through the levels of income that Korea

48. Real GDP in 2010 is measured in 2000 (actually 1995) relative prices (except for semiconductors). This means that even if one of our scenarios were to play out exactly as described, the actual measured growth 2000–2010 would be slower than the rates given here.

would reach in each scenario. We then used this historical experience to provide a benchmark for the likely changes in Korea's distribution of output as it grows. In doing this we recognized that Korea's emphasis on heavy industrial development will affect its future even if the policy environment changes. In short, Korea will not look exactly like the United States looked at a similar level of income.

The level of aggregate labor input is based on current forecasts of labor force growth plus an assumption that hours per worker decline by 1 percent a year, as occurred in Japan when its income reached comparable levels. Given the productivity estimates and the output distribution, there is an implied distribution of employment.

One approach on the capital input to growth would be to estimate the likely saving rate in Korea and thus the availability of capital. We took a different approach. We made estimates of the capital requirements for each sector of the economy, taking into account, for example in retailing, the investment in new construction needed as modern retail formats are introduced. This may miss some nuances of capital-labor substitution as factor prices change, but it draws on the pattern of investment seen historically elsewhere. We then aggregated up to an estimate of the amount of capital required in each of the growth scenarios. We assumed that this much capital will either be available through domestic saving or foreign borrowing. If too much saving is available, it will flow into foreign lending.[49]

To illustrate the approach, we look at the specifics for scenario 3. We then summarize how scenarios 1 and 2 differ.[50] Table 6 illustrates the estimates made of the potential for growth in the case study industries. The exhibit shows where the industry would stand relative to the United States in 2000, where it would reach in 2010, and the implied growth rate over time.

McKinsey has detailed knowledge of all the major steel plants around the world. The nature of best practices in each element of steelmaking can be assessed. The 5 percent growth assumed for the Korean industry is in line with the rate of increase this industry has achieved in the recent past. In scenario 3 we assume that productivity is increased in

49. In a similar study on Brazil we also examined the foreign exchange and skill requirements for growth. In Korea our judgment was that these factors should not constrain growth.

50. Additional detail can be found in McKinsey Global Institute (1998a).

Table 6. Estimated Labor Productivity Growth, by Selected Industry, Scenario 3
Index: U.S. 1995 productivity = 100

Industry	Level in 2000	Level in 2010	CAGR (Percent)
Steel	108	180	5
Automotive	48	120	10
Confectionery	43	110	10
Wet corn milling	24	100	15
Semiconductors[a]	52	70	3
Telecommunications	64	120	7
Retail banking	76	120	5
Housing construction	69	100	4
Retail	32	75	9
Average	53	94	6

Source: McKinsey. CAGR means compound annual growth rate.
a. Five-year forecast

this industry by greater competitive pressure on the minimills that results in improved product mix and increased automation. In the automotive industry, direct foreign investment by best-practice competitors and the spread of best practice as a result of more competition should encourage the industry to maintain 10 percent productivity growth for ten years ahead. At that point it would still be well below where the Japanese industry is likely to be in 2010. In confectionery we assume direct foreign investment improves operational efficiency and marketing. It forces a rationalization of the product range and of plants. In wet corn milling, competition is assumed to cause industry consolidation around two large plants (compared with fifteen currently). In semiconductors we assume that the Korean industry does not try to move into more advanced chips. Instead, the weaker DRAM manufacturers exit the industry.[51]

In telecommunications the main improvement results from increased utilization as privatization brings greater emphasis on marketing and overall incomes increase. In retail banking it is assumed that the industry moves toward electronic funds transfer and that specialized players introduce higher-value-added products. Both construction and retailing evolve as a result of opening up zoning and the ability of the industries

51. In the semiconductor case we use Bureau of Economic Analysis deflators, which imply massive productivity growth for both the U.S. and Korean industries. The 3 percent growth reported here is relative to the U.S. level of productivity.

Table 7. Estimated Labor Productivity Growth, by Sector, Scenario 3
Index: U.S. 1995 productivity = 100

Aggregate sectors	Level in 2000	Level in 2010	Last 10-year CAGR (Percent)	2000–10 CAGR (Percent)
Personal services	30	70	4	9
Business services	40	70	1	6
Utilities and transportation	55	100	7	6
Trade	30	70	4	9
Construction	60	100	3	4
Manufacturing	40	85	7	7
Agriculture	15	30	5	7
Total	36	73	6	7

Sources: OECD; McKinsey. CAGR means compound annual growth rate.

to attract funds. The construction industry builds more single-family homes and higher-value-added multifamily homes. Retailing moves to a combination of discounters and high-service formats

Table 7 shows the estimated extrapolation to the broader sectors of the economy. The potential growth in personal services and wholesale and retail trade were both assumed to be similar to that in the retail trade case. Growth in business services was taken from the retail banking case. Utilities and transportation were assumed to reach the 1995 U.S. level by 2010. The results from the telecommunications case were used as a guide in setting this assumption. Growth in construction was based on the housing construction case, while the manufacturing cases were used as the guide to potential growth in overall manufacturing. Productivity growth in agriculture was assumed to be more rapid than in the past because of the pull of workers out of this sector, with rapid employment growth in services occurring under scenario 3.

Figure 15 shows the predicted distribution of output if the productivity growth by sector given in table 6 is realized. This implies an 80 percent increase in GDP per capita over the ten years and would put Korea at about the same level as the United States was in 1988. We explored the output distributions of a variety of countries and found enough similarity in the pattern that we felt confident in using an adjusted U.S. distribution as the benchmark for this scenario. We adjusted the assumed 2010 Korean distribution away from the 1988 U.S. output distribution because of the starting point, giving a somewhat larger

Figure 15. Per Capita Output Growth Potential, Korea Scenario Three

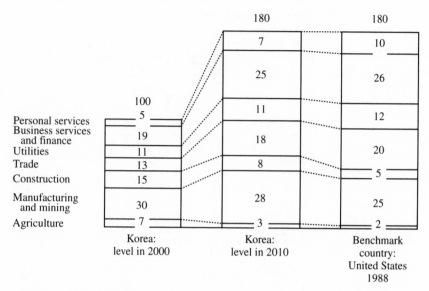

Index: Korean GDP = 100 in 2000

Sources: Organization for Economic Cooperation and Development; and McKinsey. Based on nominal GDP shares in relative prices of the initial period.

share of output to agriculture, manufacturing, and construction and correspondingly smaller shares to the remaining sectors.

Table 8 shows the assumption made about capital productivity (the output-capital ratio). We suggest that capital productivity on average would stay the same in the economy, at slightly above the U.S. level. This reflects the increase of output per unit of capital in the manufacturing and industrial sectors, where there has been overinvestment and misallocation, and the decrease in service sectors where there has been underinvestment.

Table 8. Estimated Capital Productivity Estimate by Sector, Scenario 3
Index: U.S. 1995 = 100

Sectors	Level in 2000	Level in 2010
Manufacturing and utilities	80	100
Services sectors	150	110
Total	105	107

Sources: OECD; McKinsey.

Figure 16. Korean Investment Requirement, Capital Stock per Capita

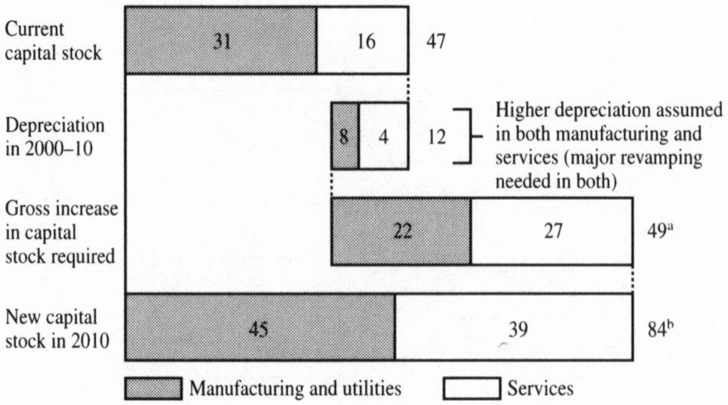

Index: United States 1995 = 100

Sources: Organization for Economic Cooperation and Development; and McKinsey.
a. Thirty percent investment rate required (18 percent business investment rate). Investment in residential housing (8 percent of GDP) and government investment (4 percent of GDP) are assumed to remain constant.
b. Based on generalization of capital productivity estimates.

Figure 16 translates these findings into an investment rate, taking depreciation into account. There is a dramatic shift in the location of the capital implied in these numbers. Whereas the current business capital stock is split roughly two-thirds manufacturing and one-third services and construction, the 2010 stock is split close to half and half. The business investment rate required for this scenario is 18 percent of GDP; more than half of the new investment would be in services and construction. The overall investment rate would be around 30 percent.

The message from scenario 3 is fundamentally positive. We find that Korea has the *potential* to increase its GDP per capita by 80 percent over ten years. It has the ability to absorb large additions to its capital stock without running into diminishing returns. Indeed it needs to maintain a very high investment rate to realize its potential for growth.

This does not mean that Korea will actually follow this path. It may find that its saving rate falls once regulations on the economy are lifted. It may decide not to attempt such a comprehensive program of deregulation. It may run into political conflict as some companies shed workers—indeed, this has already happened. Scenarios 1 and 2 provide our estimates of what might happen with less reform.

If there is no fundamental change in Korea (scenario 1), we would expect much slower growth. In manufacturing, productivity growth slows sharply in the capital-intensive sectors as the gains from investing in leading-edge equipment are exhausted.[52] We assume that productivity growth in large labor-intensive industries that we did not study explicitly, such as apparel and light electronics, would continue at about their recent growth rate. Overall we would expect manufacturing productivity growth to be 4 percent a year. For similar reasons, banking productivity growth would slow as investment opportunities are filled within an unchanged industry structure. Continued tight zoning laws would restrict the development of more productive retailing and residential construction industries.

Extrapolating to the broader economic sectors, we estimate that the potential for labor productivity growth in the market economy as a whole is 4 percent a year. That is not bad compared with the growth of economies at the leading edge. There would still be some catch-up going on. But it is well short of the potential with comprehensive reform.

Without any change in the environment, capital productivity would continue to fall, from 5 percent above the current U.S. level to 15 percent below it. With declining capital productivity and declining growth of output, the business investment share of GDP required for this scenario is very high, around 20 percent. The overall investment share would then be 32 percent. To avoid confusion resulting from everything changing at once, we keep the path of labor input the same as in scenario 3, even though income growth is lower. By 2010, GDP per capita would be 35 percent above its starting level, an increase of 3 percent a year.

Although we describe the specifics of this "no change" scenario, we believe that it may not be feasible. Very high investment levels would continue despite falling returns to capital. The chances of another financial crisis would be considerable. And given that there has already been one crisis, savers might be unwilling to provide the capital to continue in the same way. It may not be possible for Korea to go as far down the Japanese path as Japan did.

If there were reforms of the financial and manufacturing sectors but

52. Industry by industry specifics are given in McKinsey Global Institute (1998a). In the case of semiconductors, we assume that Korean companies will try unsuccessfully to move into higher-value-added chips.

no reforms in services and construction (scenario 2), the outcome would be both better and worse than in scenario 1. There would be more productivity growth in manufacturing (we estimate 6 percent a year) as greater openness, combined with improved lending procedures, would result in more transfer and adoption of best managerial practice and less misallocation of capital. And there would be more productivity growth overall (at 5 percent compared with 4 percent). With less wasteful capital spending, capital productivity would remain stable, and the share of business investment in GDP would fall to 15 percent. The total investment share would be 27 percent. This scenario has the largest share of GDP available for consumption or for net foreign investment.

These figures are calculated on the assumption that the level of labor input that applied to the other scenarios—unemployment at about 5 percent—remains the same. However, the release of labor resulting from increases in manufacturing productivity would be substantial. With growth in modern services choked off by regulation, workers would be forced either into agriculture or low-productivity services, notably retailing formats such as stalls, kiosks, and street markets.

In practice, labor input in this scenario might not be comparable to that in scenarios 1 and 3. Instead, unemployment might rise. If there were increases in unemployment insurance and other transfers to the point that the available low-wage jobs became unattractive, or if minimum wage rates made such jobs unavailable, workers released from manufacturing or new entrants to the labor force would remain unemployed.

The lesson that we draw from the three scenarios is that comprehensive reform is by far the most attractive policy option. It allows the country's growth potential to be realized. It reduces the chance of another crisis. It creates new employment opportunities and pulls workers out of subsistence agriculture. The alternatives run the risk of either allowing a new crisis or creating increased underemployment or unemployment.

Conclusion

We find four main lessons from this microeconomic approach to understanding industries in Korea.

—Korea's rapid growth has included a mixture of successes and failures, with a distinct pattern to the different outcomes. In integrated steel, telecommunications, and DRAMs Korean industries were successful in purchasing and efficiently operating best-practice capital technology. In this respect, Korea succeeded where other developing countries such as Brazil had failed. Korea was less successful in acquiring the design, marketing, and organizational practices essential to high productivity in the automotive, processed food, and banking industries. And even in the "success" industries of semiconductors and telecommunications, the lack of design and marketing skills was a constraint on performance. To some extent this problem occurred because acquiring design and managerial skills is difficult, but it was made more difficult by Korea's strategy of self-reliance and restrictions on foreign direct investment.

—Low productivity and low returns contributed to the crisis. Although other macroeconomic factors no doubt contributed, Korea's recent economic crisis is at least partly due to the low returns that resulted from the low productivity and concentration of capital in manufacturing. Thus we agree with Paul Krugman's view that despite Korea's low overall capital-labor ratio, rapid investment and declining capital productivity helped cause the crisis.[53] We would disagree, however, at least for Korea, with his attribution of overinvestment to a moral hazard problem involving uncapitalized borrowers with nothing to lose from making risky investments. We found numerous examples of poor investments made by companies with substantial equity interest.

—Korea needs comprehensive reform to encourage a return to rapid growth. Regulation that protects health and safety, encourages competition, and deals with externality problems can work to make markets more efficient. The case studies of Korean industry identified more intrusive and distorting forms of regulation that have caused a misallocation of resources and prevented the productive evolution of industries.

In all the countries we have studied, economic growth involves a decline in agricultural employment and at a certain point a decline in the share of employment in manufacturing. If Korea is to continue to grow rapidly, it must open up the nonagriculture and nonmanufacturing

53. Krugman (1998).

part of the economy, particularly services. This would create new jobs and new investment opportunities. Unless restrictions are lifted in services, particularly land use restrictions, the rise of productivity in manufacturing and formal agriculture will release labor that will either become unemployed or will be forced into subsistence activities.

—Opening up the economy to international trade and investment will encourage reform in banks and companies and will transfer skills. Korea appears to have suffered from an unfortunate coincidence. It deregulated its capital markets and increased the availability of capital at precisely the time at which a slowing of growth and of the inflation of land prices made profitable investing much less automatic. To resolve this problem, bank loan officers must be trained in loan assessment skills and evaluated on the basis of how well their portfolios perform. Business managers must move away from the goal of maximizing market share and instead use cost and profitability as criteria for success. How are these things to be accomplished? Legal and regulatory frameworks can do much. A crucial mechanism, however, is to force domestic companies to compete against international best practice.

Appendix

Our methodology for measuring total factor productivity at both the aggregate and industry levels was to assume a Cobb-Douglas net production function with factor shares reflected by the shares of labor cost and gross return to capital (EBITDA) in value added. For the aggregate we excluded both GDP and capital input associated with residential real estate. Output and labor and capital input were measured as follows.

We made cross-country output comparisons either by converting value added to a common currency using an industry purchasing power parity or by using a single or composite physical measure of output. For the aggregate, as well as for automotive, processed food, semiconductor, retail, and construction industries, we used the approach of value added at PPP. The PPPs for the aggregate and construction were from the UN International Comparisons for 1985 updated using national deflators. For processed food we constructed our own PPP by surveying prices in supermarkets in both the United States and Korea, then adjusting the prices for distribution margins and taxes to get a factory-gate PPP. For the automotive industry, we used census data on the value of factory shipments and number of vehicles shipped to estimate the average factory-gate price of a car, and then adjusted for size, content, and quality to get the average price of a comparable car. Our quality adjustment came from comparisons of the U.S. prices of comparably sized and equipped U.S., Japanese, and Korean cars. Semiconductors are a global commodity. Our industry practice claimed that domestic prices of semiconductors do not differ from world prices, so we used the average market exchange rate as a PPP.

In banking, telecommunications, and steel, we used physical output measures. In steel we weighted the tons produced of individual products by the average value added per ton of that product, then adjusted for cross-country differences in the extent of vertical integration. For banking we used a methodology based on one developed by the U.S. Bureau of Labor Statistics. We measured the number of payments transacted and deposit and loan accounts maintained and weighted the number of accounts using industry estimates of their labor intensity. We then calculated separate productivity measures for the employees in the three functions and calculated overall productivity weighing by the employment share of the country in the numerator of the functional productivity measures. This produces the same result as if we had weighed the three functional outputs using their labor requirements in the denominator country.[54]

In telecommunications we used a similar approach for measuring labor productivity. Eighty-five percent of telecommunications labor requirements are driven by network size and 15 percent are determined by call volume. So our labor productivity measure is close to access line per hour worked. In contrast, almost all telecommunications capital is used to produce calls, not maintain access lines. So our capital productivity measure is call minutes per unit of capital stock, which can be decomposed into call minutes per line (network utilization) and lines per unit capital stock.

Labor input was simply hours worked. As was discussed in the aggregate analysis, we did not adjust for years of schooling.

We measured aggregate and industry capital input using a perpetual inventory method (PIM) with sudden death depreciation and standard-

---

54. See Baily and Zitzewitz (1998) for details.

ized asset lives for all countries. The asset lives for the aggregate were forty years for structures and fifteen years for equipment. For industries we estimated asset lives based on interviews and industry knowledge. In banking and construction we were unable to calculate capital input because we could not separate assets used in the production process from those held by producers as investments. In steel we had access to a proprietary McKinsey database containing information on all steel capital equipment in the countries studied that allowed us to value the steel assets at current replacement costs. This database yielded results similar to a PIM for the United States and Korea, but yielded a lower result for Japan, probably because it correctly captures the retirement of excess capacity in Japan since the early 1970s.

References

Amsden, Alice H. 1998. *Asia's Next Giant: South Korea and Late Industrialization.* Oxford University Press.

Baily, Martin Neil, and Eric Zitzewitz. 1998. "Service Sector Productivity Comparisons: Lessons for Measurement." NBER-CRIW conference paper. National Bureau of Economic Research, Cambridge, Mass.

Benhabib, Jess, and Mark M. Spiegel. 1994. "The Role of Human Capital in Economic Development: Evidence from Aggregate Cross-Country Data." *Journal of Monetary Economics* 34 (October): 143–74.

Bils, Mark, and Peter J. Klenow. 1998. "Does Schooling Cause Growth or the Other Way Around?" NBER Working Paper 6393. National Bureau of Economic Research, Cambridge, Mass.

Collins, Susan M., and Barry P. Bosworth. 1996. "Economic Growth in East Asia: Accumulation versus Assimilation." *Brookings Papers on Economic Activity* 2: 135–91.

Corsetti, Giancarlo, Paolo Pesenti, and Nouriel Roubini. 1998. "What Caused the Asian Currency and Financial Crisis?" Unpublished manuscript, Yale University.

Dollar, David, and Kenneth Sokoloff. 1990. "Patterns of Productivity Growth in South Korean Manufacturing Industries, 1963–1979." *Journal of Development Economics* 33 (October): 309–27.

Hall, Robert E., and Charles I. Jones. Forthcoming. "Why Do Some Countries Produce So Much More Output than Others?" *Quarterly Journal of Economics.*

Kim, Dae Jung. 1996. *Mass Participatory Economy: Korea's Road to World Economic Power.* Latham, Md.: University Press of America.

Kim, Jong-Il, and Lawrence J. Lau. 1994. "The Sources of Economic Growth of the East Asian Newly Industrialized Countries." *Journal of the Japanese and International Economies* 8 (September): 235–71.

Kim, Linsu. 1997. *Imitation to Innovation: The Dynamics of Korea's Technological Learning.* Harvard Business School Press.

Krugman, Paul. 1998. "What Happened to Asia?" Unpublished manuscript, MIT.

Lee, Seung Jung. 1997. "The Financial Crisis in Korea." Unpublished manuscript cited in Corsetti, Presenti, and Roubini.

McKinsey Global Institute. 1992. *Service Sector Productivity.* Washington, D.C.: McKinsey & Co.

———. 1994a. *Latin American Productivity.* Washington, D.C.: McKinsey & Co.

———. 1994b. *The Global Capital Market: Supply, Demand, Pricing, and Allocation.* Washington, D.C.: McKinsey & Co.

————. 1997. *Boosting Dutch Economic Performance.* Washington, D.C.: McKinsey & Co.

————. 1998a. *Productivity-led Growth for Korea.* Washington, D.C.: McKinsey & Co.

————. 1998b. *Productivity—The Key to an Accelerated Development Path for Brazil.* Washington, D.C.: McKinsey & Co.

Pack, Howard. 1993. "Industrial and Trade Policies in the High-Performing Asian Economies." Background paper for World Bank, *The East Asian Miracle.*

Pilat, Dirk. 1994. *The Economics of Rapid Growth: The Experience of Japan and Korea.* Aldershot, U.K.: Elgar.

Radelet, Steven, and Jeffrey Sachs. 1998. "The Onset of the East Asian Financial Crisis." Unpublished manuscript, Harvard University.

World Bank. 1993. *The East Asian Miracle: Economic Growth and Public Policy.* Oxford University Press.

Young, Alwyn. 1994. "Lessons from the East Asian NICs: A Contrarian View." *European Economic Review* 38 (April): 964–73.

————. 1995. "The Tyranny of Numbers: Confronting the Statistical Realities of the East Asian Growth Experience." *Quarterly Journal of Economics* 110 (August): 641–80.

Comments

Comment by Barry Bosworth: This paper has two major objectives. First, it uses some industry-level data and case study work of McKinsey and Co. to extend the macroeconomic framework of growth accounting Second, it seeks to provide some insights into the causes of the 1997–98 economic crisis and the policies needed for recovery. The industry-level analysis is a major extension of previous studies of Korean economic growth. It takes a more negative view of Korea's accomplishments in arguing that although the overall rate of capital investment has been very high, significant portions have been misallocated with a resulting large decline in the rate of return. I was less convinced by the second argument that the declining return to capital was a major cause of the economic crisis.

Previous studies, based on aggregate data, concluded that despite the extraordinarily high rates of economic growth achieved in Korea over the past quarter century, the contribution of gains in total factor productivity (TFP) has been surprisingly modest. Instead, the growth in output per worker has resulted primarily from rapid increases in capital per worker. The emphasis on capital formation as the primary source of growth and the modest contribution of TFP are surprises because one would think that countries that begin with levels of technology far below best practice would find it easier to concentrate on copying the technologies of more advanced economies. Capital accumulation, in contrast, is hard work—it requires sacrifices of foregone consumption that are not easy to achieve in poor societies. In addition, the stress on capital formation would not appear to be sustainable because ultimately it will drive down the rate of return.

Baily and Zitzewitz argue that the emphasis on capital accumulation

309

has already reduced the rate of return to capital to a low level that threatens future growth prospects. In addition, they maintain that the low rates of TFP growth are reflective of structural problems that have distorted the allocation of capital. Those same structural problems contributed to the economic crisis. The conclusion is that comprehensive economic reform is a precondition for a return to high growth in the future.

A major strength of this paper is the measurement of outputs and capital inputs in comparable international prices. This makes it possible to make cross-national comparisons of the level, as well as the rate of growth, of labor productivity and TFP. For example, Korea has about the same level of total inputs (capital plus labor) per capita as the United States, but it generates only about half the level of gross domestic product. The mix of inputs is also quite different as Koreans work longer hours than Americans, but the amount of capital per worker is still well below the U.S. standard. The comparisons with Japan and the United States suggest that Korea has been able to obtain best-practice capital and technology on international markets at competitive prices, but it has been far less successful in applying best-practice management skills.

The microeconomic analysis of eight Korean industries reinforces the conclusions of the aggregate analysis in finding consistent evidence of modest gains in TFP, but it goes beyond that research in documenting cases of poor investment choices. Levels of capital per worker in some industries are close to the U.S. levels, but the corresponding estimates of TFP lag far behind. Some of the results, however, contrast sharply with conventional wisdom. The government-owned integrated steel mills appear to be world class, whereas the privately owned minimills are quite inefficient. Similarly, the telecommunications industry is still dominated by a state-owned firm, yet it has a relatively efficient network. The number of access lines per worker is comparable to the United States, but the utilization of those lines is far below that of the United States. The authors trace the difference to the reliance on per minute pricing of local calls in Korea compared with fixed monthly rates in the United States—Koreans spend much less time on the telephone than do Americans.

I do have some reservations about the results, however. The microeconomic extensions do raise a question of whether they are representative of Korean industry as a whole. How were they chosen? Are these simply industries for which past studies of McKinsey and Co. had developed data? Certainly they do not represent balanced samples of the overall economy. Second, microeconomic studies have difficulty fitting the analytical framework of the aggregate analysis with the data available at the industry level. Information on investment and the capital stock is particularly limited at the level of individual firms and industries.

In addition, I would question the emphasis placed on measures of output per unit of capital, that is, capital productivity. Many past studies have focused on labor productivity because of its close link to real wages and living standards. Also, the change in output per worker can easily be partitioned between the two critical components of the growth process: the contribution of increased capital per worker, and gains in TFP—the efficiency with which the inputs are used. The same logic does not apply to the concept of capital productivity. The general message of the paper is that capital is poorly utilized in Korea as measured by the low average ratio of output to capital. But, by that same measure, the productivity of capital is estimated to be higher in the service sectors of Korea than in the United States (see the authors' figure 4). The scarcity of capital in the service sector should not be interpreted as evidence of efficiency in its use. If a measure of capital is available, it seems preferable to focus on changes in TFP and the amount of capital per worker, and not on the ratio of output to capital.

Finally, the authors place great emphasis on a low return to capital in Korea as evidence of excessive reliance on capital formation. However, although the OECD data they cite show a decline from a very high level in the mid-1980s, the rate of return is still comparable to that in other industrial countries. During the same period, the real return on debt instruments has remained basically unchanged, suggesting a large decline in the risk premium in Korea. That should be seen as a positive development. Korea cannot sustain its high growth in the future by relying on growth in the capital stock that exceeds growth of output without driving the rate of return to low levels; but that return is not yet at a crisis point. Capital per labor hour in Korea is still only about a third of that of the United States and Japan.

Korea does have a very high ratio of debt to equity, but that is an inevitable consequence of its extraordinarily high growth. Individual enterprises cannot finance high growth solely out of internal funds. Yet, in all countries debt, not equity, issues are the dominant source of external finance. The debt-equity ratio is low only in countries with relatively low growth rates, such as the United States, that have only limited need for external finance.

I am particularly doubtful that the falling rate of domestic profit and a loss of investor confidence played a major role in Korea's economic crisis. The economy was growing rapidly in the months before the currency collapse, and there was little evidence of investor concern in financial markets. The suddenness of the collapse is more reflective of a liquidity crisis triggered by the crises in other parts of Asia. Korea had an extraordinarily low level of reserves relative to its short-term foreign liabilities. The exchange rate collapse initiated in turn a sharp fall of domestic demand; and when the government increased interest rates in an effort to support the exchange rate, highly leveraged enterprises went into default on their loans, bringing down the banking system. The crisis and subsequent recession seem much more reflective of failures in the financial system than the real sector.

Comment by Larry E. Westphal: This is a particularly timely and especially valuable contribution to our understanding of the performance and prospects of the Korean economy.[1] The authors have given us a unique perspective on Korean development, one derived from painstaking and carefully conducted microeconomic empirical work of the sort that one wishes could more often be done for diagnostic purposes as well as to inform theoretical analysis. I have no reason whatsoever to doubt the essential validity of the findings with respect to the TFP (total factor productivity) levels and growth rates of the industries studied, or to question the detailed portrayals of their comparative strengths and weaknesses. Of course, one might reasonably wish that the sample of industries were more diverse—for example, that other important manufacturing industries having somewhat different characteristics, such as textiles, had been sampled. But one has to agree that the sampled industries include several that have been considered key to Korea's success in the manufacturing realm, certainly by those commentators who have lauded Korea's approach to development.

1. Thanks are due to Howard Pack for helpful reactions on the draft of these comments.

The authors motivate their analysis by asking if the economies of East Asia "need to undertake fundamental economic reform to resume a path of strong economic growth?" Their answer, for Korea at least, is a resounding "Yes." In support of their answer, they marshal a considerable body of evidence pointing to allocative and managerial deficiencies, and they deploy alternative policy scenarios that suggest the need for major changes in development strategy and economic policy. Although the evidence surely compels agreement that there is substantial scope for improving the productivity of the Korean economy, the scenario analysis is, to my mind, at best only weakly suggestive for those who were not a party to its construction. I will accordingly have nothing further to say about it. Rather, I will focus my comments on the context in which the authors place their analysis. Although I concur with the view that major reforms are warranted, I do not agree with the authors' principal arguments in support of this conclusion.

The context of the authors' analysis is decidedly neoclassical. This is clear from its general tenor as well as from the judgments made in relation to specific findings about the impact of various government policies in the promotional and regulatory spheres. The pursuit of more liberal policies would, in the authors' view, have avoided the apparent deficiencies without, in all likelihood, seriously sacrificing any of the past growth. Perhaps this is so; surely many economists of liberal persuasion would agree with the authors in this regard, and I do wonder if anything I could say here would convince them otherwise. Be that as it may, my reading of comparative development performance persuades me that such deficiencies are a generally inescapable transitional cost of the pronounced structural changes that typically accompany fast-paced growth. This is not in any way meant to deny their existence or to minimize their magnitude; nor is it meant to imply that Korea's performance could not have been better in at least some respects. But it is to argue that one should not gauge Korean performance against an unattainable ideal of complete allocative and managerial efficiency.[2] Unless one believes that the transfer of technology can be costlessly undertaken and its complete assimilation immediately achieved, this

---

2. A considerable body of research employing frontier production functions shows that this ideal is not even achieved in the advanced countries—in all industries many firms use other than best-practice technologies.

ideal is all the more implausible when applied to an economy that has been engaged in catching up to the global technological frontier.

There is surely no point in time over the past three decades for which a similarly conducted empirical investigation would not have uncovered deficiencies of comparable extent, magnitude, and seemingly probable cause. Thus a neoclassical reading of the authors' empirical findings effectively proves too much; that is, it does unless one is persuaded, as many analysts are not, that Korea's past development success occurred largely in spite of, rather than significantly because of, its government's interventionist practices.[3] In short, such investigations cannot by themselves be legitimately used as the basis for arguing the necessity of "fundamental economic reform," which I take to mean reform that is systemic in the sense of radically changing the nature of the policy regime and the institutions that importantly guide resource allocation. To be compelling, the argument for so sweeping a change in development strategy requires the weight of vastly more evidence than is afforded by such an investigation, which is far more directly and immediately relevant to gauging the need for modest adjustments within the framework of an established development strategy.

But the authors do not simply focus on microeconomic departures from efficiency in stating their case for fundamental economic reform. They also importantly rely on the view that Korea has experienced disappointingly slow TFP growth insofar as factor accumulation has been the principal source of its growth. That they do so is particularly apparent in their introductory discussion, but the view is pervasive throughout their analysis. Has Korea's TFP growth performance in fact been disappointing? The answer, not surprisingly, depends on one's perspective. Considered comparatively, it can not fairly be termed at all disappointing. In the mainstream's consensus assessment, which reflects crosscountry estimates by Young and by Collins and Bosworth, Korea's TFP growth rate (whether aggregate or in manufacturing) over the 1960s through mid-1990s is seen to have been distinctly above the average in comparison to both developing and developed countries, but it is not seen to have been at all extraordinary or atypical.[4] As they

3. The World Bank's (1993) report on the East Asian miracle is one of many studies that argues the efficacy of the government's practices; others, as shown by Wade (1994), find that the Bank's report seriously understates their contribution.
4. Young (1995); Collins and Bosworth (1996). Nelson and Pack (forthcoming)

note, the authors' TFP growth estimates are broadly in line with this assessment. Accordingly, their view of disappointing performance cannot be considered consistent with the mainstream understanding of comparative TFP growth experience; Korea has distinctly not been an underachiever in terms of productivity growth relative to other countries. Their view is consistent, however, with the widespread and seemingly plausible expectation that developing countries have the potential to experience atypically rapid TFP growth.

This expectation flows from old notions of "economic backwardness" a la Gershenkron as well as from contemporary growth theorizing. The central proposition is that developing countries can experience exceptional productivity performance by successfully exploiting the vast backlog of modern technology that is readily available for their use. But is there any evidence that this is in fact so? No, there is not, at least not insofar as one accepts the mainstream understanding of comparative TFP growth performance. In particular, the possibility of extraordinary TFP growth appears to be contradicted by the consensus view of East Asian experience. If, as in the mainstream perception, none of the East Asian "miracle economies" has experienced exceptional productivity growth, then shouldn't this be taken as compelling evidence against its possibility? Where else is one to look for confirming evidence? Considering the contemporary period (from the end of World War II to the present), there are no other cases of similarly remarkable development success sustained over three and half decades.

There are two possible objections to the foregoing argument that the record of contemporary development experience contradicts the hypothesis positing the possibility of extraordinary TFP growth. One is that the mainstream's consensus assessment of comparative TFP growth performance is invalid; in particular, that it considerably understates the TFP growth that has been experienced by at least some of the East Asian economies. This is very probably so, but it is not pertinent to argue the contention in any detail here. Suffice it to say that my reading of the relevant literature has led me to the conclusion there are very strong reasons for being agnostic about our ability to comprehend sat-

argue that above-average TFP growth should in fact be seen as extraordinary because it was achieved in the context of an exceptionally rapid rate of capital accumulation. My argument later in these comments about the impossibility of extraordinary TFP growth given the mainstream appraisal complements rather than contradicts theirs.

isfactorily the truth about comparative TFP growth experience; not only are the available data problematic and most likely inadequate, the tools of analysis are also probably insufficiently discriminating in important respects.[5] As an agnostic in this matter, I have no particular reasons for not accepting, for the sake of argument, the mainstream perception. Moreover, the authors' analysis is clearly premised on this perception and can thus legitimately be appraised within it.

The other objection to the denial of the possibility of extraordinary TFP growth is that East Asian experience would not be pertinent if technological development in these economies could in any way be considered inadequate, such that they failed in attempting to realize the potential gains from technology transfer. But a careful reading of the reasonably extensive, albeit largely qualitative, body of research on technological development among developing countries leads one to exactly the opposite conclusion.[6] Seen comparatively, the East Asian economies—Korea, Singapore, and Taiwan in particular—have been atypically very attentive to technological development and have pursued what appear in most respects to have been atypically very sensible approaches at the national as well as enterprise levels. Reasoning from the mainstream perception of comparative TFP growth performance, it would thus appear that exceptional productivity performance (at least in the contemporary world) is a chimera, comparable to the ideal of complete efficiency. Why might it be so; where is the flaw in reasoning leading to its expectation? It must lie in a mistaken view of the costs of technology transfer relative to its potential benefits. In fact, a reasonably large body of microempirical case study research does show that the costs are far from being trivial.[7]

To summarize the foregoing: Taken at face value and in light of the comparative record of development performance, the authors' evidence does not support their view that there is something fundamentally wrong with the Korean economic system. To see Korea's TFP growth performance as disappointing, or disappointingly slow, is to be inconsistent with the historical record, both comparatively and (within the mainstream perception) expectationally. In turn, where the authors prefer to

5. See Nelson and Pack (forthcoming) on the latter point.
6. See, for example, Hobday (1995) and Kim (1997) on East Asia in comparison with Lall (1987) on India.
7. Evenson and Westphal (1995).

appraise the evidence from a particular set of ideas about the nature of successful development, it is consistent with the inadequate state of our understanding of the development process simply to take the evidence as providing rich documentation about certain aspects of arguably successful development. We lack a sufficient, empirically well-grounded theory of successful development from which to reach strong evaluative conclusions on the basis of a single set of observations. Embedded within this general critique is a narrower observation: the authors seriously underplay the many cases of remarkable microeconomic TFP performance that they have uncovered, giving them only rather begrudging acknowledgment. In this respect the authors appear to be far more attentive to the allocational deficiencies than to the productivity achievements that are surely no less at the heart of the development process.

The authors are highly circumspect in relating their empirical findings to the severe crisis that overtook Korea in 1997. Given their neoclassical predisposition, one should not doubt that they would have argued the necessity of fundamental economic reform even absent the crisis. One might wonder, though, if their argument would have been so forcefully expressed. But this is of lesser concern than the likelihood that some readers will believe that the crisis somehow confirms the authors' analysis. Such a conclusion would be doubly wrong. Insofar as the authors' findings pertain to underlying systemic problems in the operation of the Korean economy, they are not really relevant to understanding the nature of the crisis. In turn, as argued above, the evidence of such problems is not to be found simply in the authors' detailed appraisals of productivity performance, but rather in the full details of Korea's contemporary economic history. The authors' appraisals form but one small, yet nonetheless extremely valuable, contribution to the overall understanding of that history.

It is by now well appreciated that there was no single cause of the Korean crisis; analysts agree in recognizing multiple sources but differ in the relative weights that they attach to each. Nonetheless, most agree with the authors in assigning considerable importance to overinvestment as a proximate cause.[8] But was excessive investment the result of systemic maladies; was it secular or cyclic in nature? While it is true that

8. See Chote (1998) and the references cited by the authors.

Korean economic management at both the macroeconomic and enterprise levels has long been characterized by a bias toward excessive
investment, the degree of overinvestment that was experienced in the
several years prior to the crisis was highly aberrational. In the authors'
most telling observation about the relationship of the crisis to overinvestment, they note that nearly half of Korea's total investment in
semiconductors by the time of their study had been made since 1995.

In the light of much other evidence (which the authors could very
usefully have surveyed insofar as they chose to focus on the crisis)
suggesting greatly excessive investment during this period relative to
plausible estimates of demand growth in various sectors, one could well
conclude that Korean economy was caught, as were many other East
Asian economies, in a frenzy of manic investment behavior fueled by
the hubris engendered by past success and global expectations of more
to come. This is essentially correct; the crisis is best understood in
terms of the periodic cycles of boom through fragility to bust that seem
still to bedevil capitalist economies in their vigorous youth if not beyond. In short, there is nothing singularly unique about the Korean
crisis that would tie it significantly to systemic problems in the economy's operation. The crisis was prototypically cyclical in nature; it was
not the consequence of secular tendencies.

Nonetheless, the Korean economy has for some time been infected with
systemic weaknesses that warranted resolute attention even though they
remained largely benign.[9] They were first manifested in Korea's big push
to develop the so-called "heavy (largely metals and engineering-related)
and chemical industries" in the mid-1970s, which led to an economic
crisis spanning roughly 1979 to 1981 (Korea's only other post-1960 crisis
of major proportions). Excessive, misdirected investment also played a
major role in this earlier crisis, but with an important difference; the cause
was largely the government's highly overt, interventionist direction of the
investment. The crisis led to a serious effort of systemic reform in many
areas that was at best only somewhat successful in accomplishing the
stated objectives, which were entirely liberal in character. Even so, activist
government intervention in the direction of investment was very greatly
reduced. Continued recognition of the need for further reform effort in all

9. SaKong (1993) and Soon (1994) well state the case that this is so.

of the initial areas resulted in a series of only partially successful reform undertakings that continued up to the present crisis.

What has made fundamental systemic revision so very difficult in the Korean setting is the critically consequential interaction between policy and institutional changes. This is well seen in the attempts to reform the highly problematic financial system and (not unrelated) *chaebol* structure of enterprise management and functioning. In both cases the central problem lies in the inability to generate appropriate institutional structures from those that already exist. Policy reform in the absence of radical institutional change can easily lead to severe difficulties; this is no better illustrated than by the other cause of the current crisis to which considerable importance has been generally as-signed—the reckless short-term borrowing that was enabled by the relaxation of capital controls in an institutional setting of repressed financial development and insufficient prudential oversight. In short, institutional change is the essential element, one seemingly not easily achieved in the Korean context.

I am thus far less sanguine than are the authors that the liberal recipe for fundamental economic reform—however right it may be in terms of the proper direction, if not extent, of systemic change—can achieve the complete extension of the East Asian miracle in the Korean case. To put the same point another way: in watching for signs of the resto-ration of the Korean miracle, I will be far more attentive to institutional than to policy changes. Here is where the major contribution of the authors' empirical investigation is to be found. In highlighting Korea's deficiencies in the transfer of "managerial knowledge," the authors have identified and given meaningful substance to a multidimensional institutional failing of obviously great importance in gauging Korea's strategic needs. Although they do not draw particular attention to it in their summary discussions, the authors have also documented serious problems of a more general nature in the areas of labor management and labor relations, which equally merit strategic attention. Finally, the authors' investigation importantly identifies Korea's services sector as being an area to which considerable investment should be directed. Whatever the changes finally made in Korea's development strategy, they should surely address these elements uncovered by the authors' diagnosis of the deficiencies of Korea's precrisis development strategy.

Authors' Response: Both Bosworth and Westphal are skeptical of the role low returns to capital played in the recent crisis in Korea, noting that returns on average were comparable to those in other OECD countries. Our paper, however, highlights several large manufacturing industries that had high capital intensities and low returns. *These were the industries that were borrowing (directly or through intermediaries) from abroad.* We recognize that many factors contributed to the crisis and argue simply that poor investment decisions made Korea more vulnerable to crisis. Bosworth objects to the use of the concept of capital productivity. The ratio of output to capital is a standard one, reported routinely by the Bureau of Labor Statistics for the United States (see the bureau's Web site). It can be misunderstood, as indeed can the concept of labor productivity, but it can also be useful, particularly in understanding returns to capital. Westphal takes issue with our implication that total factor productivity growth in Korea could have been faster, even though it was already well above average for a developing country. We acknowledge fully in the paper that Korea has performed better than most developing countries. An advantage of our detailed case studies, however, is in allowing us to see where Korean industries have had problems and where a new policy environment might alleviate those problems. Whether this environment is interventionist or liberal is much less important than the need for a shift in focus—away from promoting rapid investment concentrated in specific sectors and toward encouraging productivity growth and broader-based investment.

Commentators' References

Chote, Robert. 1998. "Financial Crises: The Lessons of Asia." In *Financial Crises and Asia,* CEPR Conference Report 6, 1–34. London: Center for Economic Policy Research.

Collins, Susan M., and Barry P. Bosworth. 1996. "Economic Growth in East Asia: Accumulation versus Assimilation." *Brookings Papers on Economic Activity* 2: 135–91.

Evenson, Robert E., and Larry E. Westphal. 1995. "Technological Change and Technology Strategy." In *Handbook of Development Economics,* edited by Jere Behrman and T. N. Srinivasan, 3A, 2209–99. Amsterdam: North Holland.

Hobday, Mike. 1995. *Innovation in East Asia: The Challenge to Japan.* Brookfield, Vt.: Edward Elgar.

Kim, Linsu. 1997. *Imitation to Innovation: The Dynamics of Korea's Technological Learning.* Boston: Harvard Business School Press.

Lall, Sanjaya. 1987. *Learning to Industrialize: The Acquisition of Technological Capability in India.* Macmillan.

Nelson, Richard R., and Howard Pack. Forthcoming. "The Asian Growth Miracle and Modern Growth Theory." *Economic Journal.*

SaKong, Il. 1993. *Korea in the World Economy.* Washington, D.C.: Institute for International Economics.

Soon, Cho. 1994. *The Dynamics of Korean Economic Development.* Washington, D.C.: Institute for International Economics.

Wade, Robert. 1994. "Selective Industrial Policies in East Asia: Is the East Asian Miracle Right?" In *Miracle or Design? Lessons from the East Asian Experience,* edited by Albert Fishlow and others, 55–79. Policy Essay 11. Washington, D.C.: Overseas Development Council.

World Bank. 1993. *The East Asian Miracle: Economic Growth and Public Policy.* Oxford University Press.

Young, Alwyn. 1995. "The Tyranny of Numbers: Confronting the Statistical Realities of East Asian Growth Experience." *Quarterly Journal of Economics* 110 (August): 641–80.

JEREMY BULOW
Stanford University

PAUL KLEMPERER
Nuffield College, Oxford University

The Tobacco Deal

Q. Could you please explain the recent historic tobacco settlement?

A. Sure. Basically, the tobacco industry has admitted that it is killing people by the millions, and has agreed that from now on it will do this under the strict supervision of the federal government.

Dave Barry[1]

ON JUNE 20, 1997, the largest cigarette companies, most state attorneys general, and trial lawyers agreed to a comprehensive settlement of tobacco litigation: the tobacco resolution. By settling litigation largely in return for tax increases on cigarettes, the resolution was a superb example of a win-win deal. Agreeing to a tax increase that would cost the companies about $1 billion a year in lost profits and yield the government about $13 billion a year in revenues made all the parties to the deal happy. The companies would settle lawsuits cheaply, smoking would decline because of the price increase, state governments would raise taxes under the name of "settlement payments," and the lawyers would be able to argue for contingency fees based on tax collections instead of the much smaller cost to companies. Only consumers, in whose name class action suits were filed, would lose out.

We thank Ian Ayres, Jonathan Baker, Jack Calfee, Jonathan Gruber, Peter Reiss, our colleagues and seminar participants, and members of the Brookings Panel on Microeconomic Activity for their comments. After this paper was completed, Bulow was named Director of the Bureau of Economics, Federal Trade Commission. The views expressed here are his and Klemperer's and do not reflect those of the FTC or its commissioners.
1. David Barry, "Tobacco Road's Toll; Except for Lawyers, It'll Go Up in Smoke," Knight-Ridder Newspapers, August 10, 1997.

In effect the resolution facilitated collusion among the companies to raise prices. (That the proceeds were used to buy off the states and lawyers is irrelevant to this point.) The only problem was that antitrust authorities might challenge the resolution's collusive pricing and the related provisions deterring market entry for new companies, provisions needed to maintain collusive prices.[2] Therefore these terms of the deal and others, especially the protections against future litigation, required congressional legislation. The Senate Commerce Committee approved the National Tobacco Policy and Youth Smoking Reduction Act, better known as the McCain bill, after its chief sponsor Senator John McCain. The McCain bill was based on the resolution, but it evolved into anti-tobacco legislation after lobbying by antismoking groups, which had declined to participate in the settlement negotiations. The companies fought back with television ads, denouncing the bill as a huge tax increase, and it was killed on June 17, 1998, to be replaced in part by a scaled-down agreement reached in November 1998 between the states and the tobacco companies.

This paper analyzes the major economic issues raised by the resolution and bill. We do not debate whether dramatically increasing cigarette taxes is good social policy.[3] Nor do we address whether giving companies protection from class action suits is a good idea. Instead, without taking sides on the major normative issues, we assume certain objectives for the major players and ask how a better deal could be achieved for them all.

We assume that the companies focus on maximizing shareholder value, public health officials on reducing the adverse health conse-

2. The FTC did object strongly to a provision in the resolution that would have given the deal antitrust immunity. See U.S. Federal Trade Commission (1997).

3. See, for example, Gravelle and Zimmerman (1994), who conclude that 33 cents a pack, an amount considerably below current excise taxes, was both the best and median estimate of studies that have estimated the externalities involved in smoking. Also see Viscusi (1994), who contends that although tar and nicotine yields are about 25 percent of what they once were, most mortality calculations have been based on epidemiological studies going back to the 1950s and 1960s and on smokers who spent years puffing cigarettes much more toxic than those that are now on the market. Viscusi concludes that smokers actually saved society money by dying younger and represent a break-even proposition if claims about the effects of secondhand smoke are taken at face value. Hanson and Logue, however, contend that smokers do not rationally assess the damage that cigarettes cause to them and that a tax of $7.00 or more a pack should be imposed to force them to make correct calculations about smoking.

quences of smoking, and the government on enacting a politically popular bill that raises tax revenues subject to a constraint on the cost to
the firms. Aiming for political popularity means placing a special emphasis on reducing (or seeming to reduce) smoking among young people. The trial lawyers want to maximize their take.

The paper begins with some background on the economics of the
industry in 1997, followed by a brief description of the legal environment. In this context we then discuss the economic issues.

We first review the kinds of taxes imposed by the bill and argue that
very different kinds would have better served all parties' purposes. The
bill's unusual fixed-revenue taxes yield lower prices and raise less tax
revenue at a *higher* cost to the firms than ordinary specific taxes would
yield. Ad valorem taxes would probably have been an even better
choice, especially to combat youth smoking. And public health advocates, at least, should prefer to tax tar and nicotine rather than the
volume of cigarettes.

We next address the proposed damage payments and legal protections. The distribution of damage payments demonstrates clearly that
the settlement reflects a negotiation based on companies' differing abil-
ities to pay rather than a punishment based on their relative responsi-
bilities for tobacco-related problems. We also focus on the perverse
incentive effects of the proposed legal protections, which would have
produced a further bonanza for lawyers.

We challenge the proposition that the bill was primarily focused on
youth smoking. Many widely proposed youth smoking measures were
never adopted or were even relaxed during the amendment process.
Although a focus on overall smoking rather than youth smoking makes
sense from a public health standpoint, it is inconsistent with the lan-
guage of the bill and the surrounding rhetoric.

We also challenge the conventional wisdom on the importance of
youth smoking to the companies. Certainly companies compete aggressively to win new smokers because smokers tend to be very brand loyal.
But this competition increases costs and holds down prices, so the
present value of profits from new smokers is very small. Therefore the
marketing restrictions included in both the resolution and the bill would
have reduced youth smoking at very little cost to the companies' shareholders.

We consider the fees proposed for the lawyers (Texas's lawyers alone

Table 1. Cigarette Sales and Profits, by Major Company, 1997

Company	Unit sales (billions of cigarettes)[a]	Market share (percent)	Operating revenues (millions)	Operating profits (millions)	Profits as percent of revenue
Philip Morris	235	49.2	10,663	4,824	45
RJR	117	24.5	4,895	1,510	31
Brown and Williamson	77	16.2	3,114	801	26
Lorillard	42	8.7	1,915	777	41
Liggett	6.5	1.3	235	20	9
Industry	478	100	20,822	7,932	38

Sources: Company 10k reports for all but Brown and Williamson. Operating profits are reported profits plus reported settlement costs deducted from profits. For example, Philip Morris reported domestic tobacco operating profits of $3,267 million. Brown and Williamson data are from its Web site, www.bw.com. Go to site index and then to B&W annual review. B&W operating profits are from a phone conversation with Sanford C. Bernstein analyst Gary Black. Column 5 is calculated as column 4 divided by column 3.

a. There are twenty cigarettes to a pack.

have claimed $2 billion) and the equally remarkable exemption for Liggett that would have produced more than $400 million a year in pretax profits for a company with a presettlement market value of about $100 million. Although Liggett's turning "state's evidence" may have been a significant turning point in the battle against "big tobacco," we question the bases on which these rewards were calculated.

We next discuss the individual state settlements that were modeled on the national resolution but were the only deals left after the failure of the national legislation. As collusive agreements that effectively impose federal excise taxes for the exclusive benefit of one plaintiff, these deals set very dangerous precedents. The multistate settlement of November 1998 is equally bad.[4] After offering some radical solutions, we conclude with views about how a better deal for all parties might be negotiated.

The U.S. Tobacco Industry

The tobacco industry in 1997 was a tight oligopoly dominated by four highly profitable firms controlling about 98 percent of the market—

4. Most of this paper was written in early summer 1998 after discussion at the June 1998 meeting of the Brookings Panel on Economic Activity: Microeconomics. The section on the multistate agreement was written in November 1998, but, as we argue here, this agreement resolved little and does not affect our analysis and conclusions about the earlier resolution and bill.

Table 2. Product Mix, by Major Tobacco Company and Market Shares across Segments, 1997

Percent

Company	Sales in premium segment	Sales in branded discount segment	Sales in generic and private label segment	Market share, premium segment	Market share, discount segments
Philip Morris	86	12	2	58	26
RJR	63	31	6	21	34
Brown and Williamson	43	51	6	10	35
Lorillard	94	6	0	11	2
Liggett	25	15	60	0.5	3.5

Sources: Column 1, for Philip Morris and RJR, company, 10k reports. For Brown and Williamson, Lorillad, and Liggett, Federal Trade Commission (1997, table 7). Breakdown between columns 2 and 3, Federal Trade Commission (1997). Columns 4 and 5 are taken from the 10k reports of Philip Morris, RJR, and Liggett. Column 4 for Lorillard is from the Loews' Corporation 10k report. Column 5 for Lorillard is based on the Federal Trade Commission (1997, table 7). Columns 4 and 5 for Brown & Williamson are calculated from the company's market share and Federal Trade Commission (1997, table 7).

Philip Morris, RJR, Brown and Williamson, and Lorillard. A fifth firm, Liggett, had a 1.3 percent share of the market.[5] Advertising restrictions—tobacco advertising has been banned on TV and radio in the United States since 1971—and the prospect of becoming embroiled in the industry's legal woes severely hindered entry on a major scale. Further deterrents to entry were the declining size of the market and the strong brand loyalty of most customers (see the section on the value to the companies of the youth market). There are also some economies of scale, but these are not too large at the scales of the major firms. Philip Morris, which has half the market, has average costs that are just 5 cents a pack lower than fourth-ranked Lorillard, which has less than 10 percent of the market. Given the enormous profitability of the major companies, scale economies cannot be the primary barrier to large-scale entry.[6] Table 1 briefly summarizes the size and profitability of the five leading firms.

The market was divided into premium, discount, and deep discount cigarettes. Table 2 shows the companies' different positions in these segments, and table 3 shows the implications for their profitabilities.

5. In addition to these five companies, more than one hundred fringe firms held in aggregate perhaps 0.1 percent of the market when the settlement was reached (Federal Trade Commission, 1997, p. 1). These fringe firms were growing rapidly, attaining an estimated 1.1 percent of the market by 1998. See Black and Rooney (1998).

6. Economies of scale, including economies in distribution, may be more important in hindering smaller-scale entry, however.

Table 3. Product Mix and Profitability, by Major Tobacco Company, 1997

Company	Percent of sales in premium segment	Revenue per pack (cents)	Costs per pack (cents)	Profits per pack (cents)
Philip Morris	86	91	50	41
RJR	63	84	58	26
Brown & Williamson	43	81	60	21
Lorillard	94	92	55	37
Liggett	25	73	67	6
Industry	73	87	54	33

Sources: Federal Trade Commission (1997, table 7) and calculations from table 1.

Although average costs of manufacturing premium and discount cigarettes vary by only a few cents, wholesale prices for premiums are 18.5
cents a pack higher than for discounts and 34 cents a pack higher than
for deep discounts.[7] These price differentials mean that most of the
market's profits are earned on the premium brands. This explains why
Lorillard, with a market share of less than 10 percent, is almost as
profitable as Philip Morris, while RJR and Brown and Williamson, with
intermediate market shares, lag behind in profitability. Liggett's much
poorer profitability seems due both to the company's much weaker
position in the more attractive market segments and to its higher costs.[8]

Because different firms have different presences in the premium and
discount segments, they have a conflict of interest on pricing. Table 4
presents an abbreviated history of price changes since 1990 and shows
a striking change in the relative prices of the three market sectors in
1992–93. In April 1992 premium cigarettes sold for $1.10 a pack at
wholesale, discounts at 97 cents, and deep discounts at 36 cents. The
discount segments grew to 36 percent of the market. Philip Morris and
RJR aggressively attempted to increase their market shares and took 60
percent of the business in those segments. They then tried to increase
prices. When adequate cooperation from Brown and Williamson and

7. For example, according to the company's 10k report filed with the Securities and
Exchange Commission, Liggett's average costs for its discount cigarettes are about 3.7
cents a pack less than its costs for its premium cigarettes.

8. One contributing factor to these higher costs is that Liggett's chief executive
officer pays himself about 25 percent more than the CEO of Philip Morris, even though
Philip Morris's market value and profitability are 500 times as great as Liggett's. His
pay comes to considerably more than a penny a pack. See the company 10k reports filed
with SEC.

Table 4. Prices of Premium and Discount Cigarettes, Selected Months, June 1990–August 1998

Cents per pack

Month and year	Premium	Discount	Deep discount
June 1990	89.3	65.0	35.5
December 1990	94.3	70.0	40.5
January–February 1991	94.5	70.2	40.7
March 1991	96.0	75.2	40.7
June 1991	99.5	83.2	43.2
November 1991	105.0	88.7	45.7
April 1992	110.5	96.7	35.75
July–August 1992	115.5	75.7	39.75
November 1992	121.0	81.2	43.75
January 1993	121.2	81.4	43.95
February 1993	121.2	81.4	51.9
March 1993	123.2	83.4	56.9
August 1993	83.9	83.4	56.9
November 1993	87.9	83.4	60.9
May 1995	90.9	83.4	63.9
April–May 1996	94.9	83.4	67.9
March 1997	99.9	83.4	67.9
September 1997	106.9	90.4	74.9
January 1998	109.4	92.9	77.4
April 1998	112.4	95.9	80.4
May 1998	119.4	100.9	85.4
August 1998	125.4	106.9	91.4

Source: Authors' calculations based on data from U.S. Department of Agriculture. Premium brand prices can be found at *http://www.econ.ag.gov/briefing/tobacco/Table8.htm*. Includes leading brands. A 3 percent discount is made for payment within ten days or 2 percent within fourteen days. Discount and deep discount prices (including federal excise taxes) can be found at http://www.econ.ag.gov/briefing/tobacco/Table7.htm.

Liggett was not forthcoming, Philip Morris announced a cut of 40 cents a pack in the price of Marlboros on April 2, 1993, dubbed "Marlboro Friday." After Marlboro Friday premium cigarettes sold for 84 cents, discounts for 83 cents, and deep discounts for 57 cents. By March 1998, before a series of price increases to offset the effect of state settlements went into effect, prices had risen to $1.00 for premiums, remained at 83 cents for discounts, and had risen to 68 cents for deep discounts. Predictably, the combined share of the discount and deep discount market has fallen steadily since 1993 to about 27 percent; the deep discount segment in particular has collapsed to about 4 percent.[9]

9. Prices in this paragraph and the current size of the deep discount market are from table 4. Market share numbers are from Eben Shapiro, "Cigarette Burn: Price Cut on

The higher price of deep discount cigarettes sold by the five largest firms has encouraged some small-scale entry at the low end. Smaller firms now have about 1 percent of the market, selling mostly discount cigarettes at wholesale prices of about 34 cents a pack.[10]

Although the industry is highly profitable, it is clear that full cooperation among the players would lead to much higher prices still: the demand elasticity is widely estimated to be around -0.4.[11] Sales are declining over time. Consumption has fallen by about 25 percent since 1981, from 640 billion cigarettes a year to 480 billion. This decline has come about because the number of smokers has decreased approximately 10 percent from its peak, and the number of cigarettes consumed per smoker has also decreased. As a result, per capita adult consumption, which peaked at 4,345 in 1963, fell to 2,423 by 1997 (table 5).

Manufacturers sell their cigarettes to thousands of jobbers, who then resell to retailers. Retail sales are divided primarily among convenience stores (47 percent), supermarkets (17 percent), and cigarette-only stores (13 percent). The remaining 23 percent is split among "the vending industry, restaurants, mass merchandisers, warehouse clubs, Indian reservations, and traditional gasoline service stations."[12] One implication is that convenience store owners are a force opposing cigarette tax hikes and rules that would restrict where cigarettes can be sold.

A rough breakdown of the cost of the average pack of cigarettes at retail is given in table 6. Of manufacturing costs, 8–9 cents are for leaf and 3–4 cents for packaging, while fixed manufacturing costs represent only about 2 cents.[13] Although some administrative and marketing ex-

---

Marlboro Upsets Rosy Notions about Tobacco Profits," *Wall Street Journal,* April 5, 1993, p. A1; and Philip Morris 1997 10k report.

10. See Black and Rooney (1998).

11. Traditional estimates have been in the range of -0.3 to -0.5; see National Cancer Institute (1993). The FTC in its analysis used -0.4. Martin Feldman of Salomon Smith Barney stated that his point estimate was -0.47, although he used -0.36 in some of his calculations. See "Statement of Martin Feldman before the Senate Commerce Committee," March 19, 1998 (available at http://www.tobaccoresolution.com/ctrans/feld03.html). Townsend (1993) cites some higher estimates. The tobacco industry cited a recent study by Becker, Grossman, and Murphy (1994) that estimates a short-run elasticity of -0.45 and a long-run elasticity of -0.75. The FTC, however, cites studies using a similar approach that indicate less elasticity. For example, Chaloupka (1991) estimates -0.27 to -0.37.

12. National Association of Convenience Stores (1998).

13. See the report on Philip Morris by David Adelman, Investment Report 2651147, Morgan Stanley, Dean Witter, March 3, 1998, table 5.

Table 5. Total and Per Capita Consumption of Cigarettes, Selected Years, 1900–97

Year	Total consumption (billions of cigarettes)	Per capita consumption (age eighteen and older)
1900	2.5	54
1905	3.6	70
1910	8.6	151
1915	17.9	285
1920	44.6	665
1925	79.8	1,085
1930	119.3	1,485
1935	134.4	1,564
1940	181.9	1,976
1945	340.6	3,449
1950	369.8	3,552
1955	396.4	3,597
1960	484.4	4,171
1963	523.9	4,345[a]
1965	528.8	4,258
1970	536.5	3,985
1975	607.2	4,122
1980	631.5	3,849
1981	640.0[a]	3,836
1985	594.0	3,370
1990	525.0	2,826
1995	487.0	2,515
1996	487.0	2,483
1997	480.0	2,423

Sources: 1900–95: Centers for Disease Control Web site *http://www.cdc.gov/nccdphp/osh/consump1.htm*, which cites the following sources: U.S. Department of Agriculture (1987, 1996); Miller (1981, p. 53); and 1996 and 1997 from U.S. Department of Agriculture Economic Research Service, (1998, tables 1 and 2).
a. Peak year.

penses are subject to economies of scale, the barriers to entry are not on the production side. Therefore the industry will be vulnerable to entry in the generic segment if new entrants are given a substantial cost advantage over incumbents as the outcome of litigation or legislation.

The final major firm involved in tobacco litigation in the United States is UST, which sells smokeless tobacco. This business is, if anything, even more profitable than cigarettes. UST's gross tobacco revenues in 1997 were $1.2 billion and its operating margin was approximately 60 percent.[14]

14. UST 10k reports to the Securities and Exchange Commission.

Table 6. Breakdown of Cigarette Prices, 1997 (Cents per pack)

Retail price	190	
− State excise tax		(32)
− Trade margin		(47)
= Wholesale price	111	
− Federal excise tax		(24)
= Operating revenue	87	
− Advertising & marketing		(23)
− Other marketing		(5)
− Manufacturing costs		(20)
− Legal		(2.5)
− Other		(2.5)
= Operating profit	33	

Sources: Retail price, state excise tax, federal excise taxes: Federal Trade Commission (1997, table 8). Advertising, marketing; table 10. Operating revenue per pack and operating profit per pack calculated from table 1. Trade margin calculated as Retail price − State excise tax − Federal excise tax − Operating revenue. Wholesale price calculated as Operating revenue + Federal excise tax. Manufacturing costs: David Adelman (Morgan, Stanley, Dean Witter March 3, 1998 INVESTEXT Report Number 2651147 report on Philip Morris estimates manufacturing costs at 18 cents per pack. Liggett 10k report implies manufacturing costs of about 17 cents a pack for discount cigarettes and 21 cents a pack for premiums. Other marketing and Legal: Estimated from Gary Black, "Tobacco Industry: U.S. Profitability by Manufacturer," Sanford C. Bernstein, INVESTEXT report number 1917209, May 2, 1997, p. 4. Other calculated as operating revenue − advertising & marketing − other marketing − manufacturing costs − legal − operating profit.

Litigation

The three major categories of domestic tobacco litigation are individual personal injury, class action personal injury, and health care cost recovery (mostly brought by governments and unions). Litigation has mushroomed in all three categories. The number of cases Philip Morris was defending rose from 185, 20, and 25 in the three categories on December 31, 1996, to 375, 50, and 105 at the end of 1997. Seventeen of the individual cases and 6 of the class actions involved environmentally transmitted smoke (ETS, or second-hand smoke). RJR was defending 540 cases as of March 3, 1998, versus 54 at the end of 1994.[15]

The current flood of lawsuits, starting in 1994, is called the "third wave" of tobacco litigation. From 1954 to 1965, the companies faced a first wave of tort litigation, generally based on warranty and failure-to-warn claims.[16] The second wave, which ran from 1983 to 1992,

15. The number of cases are from the 10k reports for 1997 filed by the two companies. In addition to its domestic cases, Philip Morris also faced class actions in Brazil, Canada, and Nigeria.

16. Some authors use slightly different dates. Two concise summaries of tobacco tort litigation are Robert L. Rabin, "Tobacco Tort Litigation in the United States,"

again involved individual lawsuits against the companies. Claimants were operating in a more favorable legal environment, but failure-to-warn claims became less credible in light of the health warnings that were displayed on every pack of cigarettes after 1964. These lawsuits were played out as in the Kreps-Wilson-Milgrom-Roberts model of entry deterrence: cases arrived sequentially, most smokers never brought suit, and those who did faced companies that would never settle and would pay millions to fight (and win) each case, staunching the flow of future suits.[17]

Obviously a large contributory factor to the third wave is that the tobacco companies (and smokers in general) have become so despised. But several other factors have tipped the balance against the companies and made suing them far more attractive. For example, Merrell Williams, a paralegal, stole some 4,000 pages of sensitive documents from Brown and Williamson and traded them to Richard Scruggs, a trial lawyer who is the brother-in-law of Trent Lott, the Senate Majority Leader, for a job and some gifts, including the funds to purchase a $109,600 house for cash. Because the documents were stolen, Scruggs could not introduce them directly into a case, but they were copied and distributed widely and anonymously, and University of California Professor Stanton Glantz posted the documents on the World Wide Web on July 1, 1995.[18] These documents, which indicated that the tobacco companies had hidden information about the health effects of smoking, helped plaintiffs erode the defense that health warnings have been posted on cigarette packages since 1965. They helped win an individual case in Florida in August 1996 and have probably led to the discovery of many documents since.[19]

The recent certification of class actions has greatly increased the potential payoff to plaintiffs' lawyers from filing suits. The first such case was *Castano et. al.* v. *The American Tobacco Company et. al.*, in which sixty-five leading law firms together filed a class action suit in

available at www.cnr.it/CRDS/rabin.htm, and Mark Gottlieb, ''Chronology,'' available at www.tobacco.neu.edu/TobaccoTalk/disc1/00000009.htm.

17. Kreps and Wilson (1982); Milgrom and Roberts (1982).

18. Mollenkamp and others (1998, pp. 12, 41, 46, 47).

19. *Carter* v. *American Tobacco Company et al.* No. 95-934-CA Fla Cir Aug. 9, 1996. The American Tobacco Company is now part of Brown and Williamson. The Carter verdict was overturned in the spring of 1998.

March 1994 charging that the tobacco companies had failed to warn smokers adequately about the addictive properties of cigarettes.[20] Although this suit was thrown out as unwieldy by the Fifth Circuit Court of Appeals in May 1996 (after having been approved by a federal district judge), by then the trial lawyers were ready to file individual state class actions.[21]

It became common to argue that despite the health warnings on cigarette packs, there were no adequate warnings of addiction. The state suits to recover health care costs also circumvented the problem that smokers knowingly contributed to their illnesses. Florida's Medicaid Third-Party Liability Act of 1994 represented a new type of legislation, which allowed the state to sue the manufacturer of an allegedly harmful product for the medical expenses of a group, relying on statistical evidence instead of proving causation and damages in each case. This legislation was said to have been conceived by the Inner Circle, "an exclusive group of 100 personal injury lawyers."[22] The statute barred the assumption-of-risk argument, imposed joint and several liability, and allowed the courts to order damages on the basis of market share, regardless of the brands used by medicaid patients. The legislation was made retroactive, and several other states are in the process of enacting similar legislation.[23]

A turning point in the legal war came in early 1996 when Liggett broke ranks with its rivals and settled with five states.[24] Liggett's position was far different from that of its rivals because it had a market share of less than 2 percent and was teetering on the edge of bankruptcy. It was therefore able to negotiate a light deal in return for handing over secret industry documents that would be damaging to the other companies.[25] It also agreed to admit the dangers of smoking and conceded

20. The law firms each agreed to contribute $100,000 a year to fund the litigation.

21. It would have been difficult to consolidate cases from different states with different fraud and negligence laws as well as different evidentiary laws.

22. Junda Woo, "Tobacco Firms Face Greater Health Liability," *Wall Street Journal*, May 3, 1994, p. A3.

23. See Larry Rohter, "Florida Prepares New Basis to Sue Tobacco Industry," *New York Times*, May 27, 1994, p. A1.

24. Liggett settled with the attorneys general of Florida, Louisiana, Massachusetts, Mississippi, and West Virginia on March 15, 1996. It settled with seventeen more states on March 20, 1997, four states plus the District of Columbia and the Virgin Islands during the rest of 1997, and fourteen states on March 12, 1998.

25. The terms included payments of $1 million a state to be spread over ten years,

that the industry was liable for damages. Settling early, and in effect turning state's evidence, also offered the possibility of a much larger reward for assisting in the other companies' defeat.[26]

Market Valuation of Litigation Risk

The companies now faced a tremendous amount of risk: except for BAT (the owner of Brown and Williamson), which is not a U.S. firm and has most of its assets outside the United States, there was some prospect that companies would ultimately be bankrupted if the lawsuit barrage was left unabated. By early 1997 the stock market appeared to value future domestic tobacco profits at little more than the present value of settling present and future domestic litigation. The market value of RJR illustrates this: on March 31, 1997, the company had non-Nabisco long-term debt of $5.2 billion, $1.5 billion of preferred stock outstanding, and a common stock value of $8.7 billion for a total enterprise value of $15.4 billion. Against this, RJR owned Nabisco shares worth $8.7 billion. This left a residual value for the combined domestic and foreign tobacco businesses of $6.7 billion. The foreign business earned $670 million before taxes in 1997. According to Gary Black of Sanford C. Bernstein, perhaps the leading industry analyst, RJR's foreign business could be sold for approximately 8.5 times pretax earnings, implying a value of $5.7 billion.[27] Therefore the net value of the domestic business cum legal liabilities was approximately $1 billion, or less than the expected operating income for the remainder of the year.[28]

---

plus a share of Liggett's currently nonexistent pretax profits (set at 7.5 percent for the first five states, then raised to 27.5 percent after forty-one states settled).

26. Liggett's imaginative legal strategy led to an options grant of 1.25 million shares to its lead attorneys, Marc Kasowitz and Daniel Benson. See Liggett's 10k report. It is possible that Liggett may have realized that settlements with the major companies would be financed largely by increases in cigarette taxes and, as we show later, even a partial exemption from such taxes could enable Liggett to become extremely profitable.

27. Telephone conversation with Black, June 4, 1998. The calculation was based on the market valuation of comparable European manufacturers such as Gallagher and Imperial.

28. Similarly, in explaining RJR Nabisco's eagerness for a settlement, CEO Steven Goldstone stated, "I do not have to tell you that the continuing controversy surrounding our domestic business has caused investors to give that business no value—and I mean zero value when you add up all the components of RJR Nabisco stock. When you realize that today that business earns $1.4 billion operating earnings a year and it has no value

Settlements

The low stock market values of the companies and the increasingly hostile legal environment, combined with new leadership at Philip Morris and RJR, pushed the four large companies to the bargaining table in April 1997. They negotiated simultaneously with two groups of plaintiffs, the state attorneys general who had filed medicaid suits, and the class action lawyers, known collectively as the *Castano* lawyers, who were fighting on behalf of smokers rather than states.[29] There was considerable mistrust between the two groups of contingency-fee attorneys, those representing the states and the *Castano* lawyers. Perhaps as a counterweight to the political connections of Scruggs, who repre-

---

from the stock market, there clearly is some up side." Remarks at an October 27, 1997, conference sponsored by the Investor Responsibility Research Center, available at www.irrc.org/profile/tis/conf97/goldston.htm.

The market's valuation of potential litigation losses has created an incentive for firms to spin off their domestic tobacco assets from the rest of their businesses as a way of shielding other assets from litigation. BAT recently announced a spin-off of its tobacco operations from its financial operations, and its stock rose by about 25 percent in one month. According to one investment report, "B.A.T.'s ability to move forward with the spin-off is the envy of its American counterparts, which relish the chance to break up their own conglomerates in an effort to raise shareholder value. Tobacco litigation stands in the way of these moves by U.S. companies. Plaintiffs, who want to prevent the companies from taking any action that may diminish their ability to pay future claims, are prepared to charge them with fraudulent conveyance of assets if they try to break apart." *Investors' Tobacco Reporter*, vol. 2, July 1998, published by the Investor Responsibility Research Center and available at http://www.irrc.org/profile/tis/itr_iss6/page3.htm. A spin-off would not guarantee a company legal immunity. For example, Fortune Brands, the parent of the American Tobacco Company from 1904 to 1994, is a party to ninety-seven lawsuits. (BAT, which purchased American, is contractually obligated to reimburse Fortune for all related legal expenses and damage payments; see Fortune Brands 10k report.) Of course, in this case Fortune spun off its tobacco businesses. Nontobacco assets might be a little more protected from litigation if, say, RJR Nabisco spins off Nabisco than if it spins off R. J. Reynolds.

In early November 1998, the *Financial Times* reported that RJR Nabisco shares "surged by more than 20 percent in recent days amid speculation that the company is about to sell or spin off . . . its overseas tobacco business. . . . [W]orries that antitobacco litigants would sue to prevent a spin-off [seem] likely to ease in the near future because U.S. tobacco companies are close to settling the biggest lawsuits pending against the industry—those brought by the states." Richard Tomkins, "RJR Shares Surge 20 Percent: Speculation Over Sale of Overseas Tobacco Business," *Financial Times*, November 4, 1998, p. 17.

29. As of June 1998, forty-one state suits were outstanding. A little fewer than half were filed after the settlement negotiations began. For a comprehensive list of filing dates, see "State Suit Summary," available at http://www.stic.neu.edu/summary.htm.

sented Mississippi and several other states, the *Castano* group added Hillary Clinton's brother, Hugh Rodham, even though he had never tried any major cases and had been only an assistant public defender in Florida.[30] The lead attorney general was Mike Moore of Mississippi. On June 20, 1997, a settlement, the tobacco resolution, was announced.

Because of its terms, the resolution required congressional approval. While awaiting legislation, the four major companies settled state suits with Mississippi (July 1997), Florida (August 1997), Texas (January 1998), and Minnesota (May 1998) on terms modeled after the resolution. The Senate Commerce Committee passed S.1415, the McCain Bill, on April 1, 1998. But the parties to the resolution had made a major tactical blunder by not explicitly including the congressional leadership in the negotiations and by not recognizing the importance of achieving widespread support in the public health community for any settlement.[31] The bill was considerably less favorable to the companies than the resolution and was subsequently amended many times by the Senate, magnifying the costs to the companies and, in the end, eliminating their benefits. The companies then lobbied and advertised heavily against the bill, and on June 17, 1998, the Senate voted against cloture, dooming the legislation. A scaled-down version of the resolution, settling only the states' medicaid claims, was signed on November 23, 1998.

The Tobacco Resolution

The resolution brilliantly satisfied the needs of the tobacco companies for legal protections, the attorneys general for a political win, and the lawyers for big transfers on which to base legal fees. Described as a $368.5 billion deal over twenty-five years, it included a projected $358.5 billion in tax increases, plus $10 billion in lump-sum damage

30. Mollenkamp and others (1998, p. 74).
31. The public health community had largely declined to participate in the negotiations. The exception was Matt Myers of the National Center for Tobacco-Free Kids, but most public health interest groups said that "there's no negotiating with killers" and that using the courts would be a more effective way to achieve their goals. Mollenkamp and others (1998, pp. 188–90).

payments by the companies.[32] Specific taxes were to be increased by 35 cents a pack immediately and by 62 cents after five years, with adjustments for inflation. These tax increases would effectively apply to all U.S. tobacco sellers, not just the settling companies, so that new companies would not find it profitable to enter the market.[33] The resolution would have settled the state claims and eliminated state class action suits (*Castano* claims) and punitive damages for past actions. Individual claims against the industry were to be capped at $1 billion a year, with a four-for-one matching fund set up to subsidize plaintiffs who won judgments against and settlements from the companies.[34] The companies also agreed to significant marketing restrictions and ratified Food and Drug Administration (FDA) regulation of tobacco.[35]

The central trade-off was that the companies would accept an increase in cigarette taxes in return for liability protection. Given standard industry demand elasticity estimates of -0.4 and a current retail price of approximately $2.00 a pack, a 62-cent tax would reduce sales by about 12 percent. Assuming that average profit margins would remain

32. This estimate ignored the inflation adjustment in the tax rate, set at a maximum of 3 percent a year plus the rate of increase in the Consumer Price Index, and ignored the effect on tax revenue of projected declines in smoking. The projection was a simple sum, undiscounted.

33. Nonsettling firms who did not wish to participate in the settlement would have been required to escrow as a bond against future legal claims (for thirty-five years) 150 percent as much money as they would have had to pay in new excise taxes. Furthermore, any distributors and retailers who handled nonsettling firms' products would lose the proposed exemptions from civil liability suits. As a practical matter, the purpose was to force other cigarette producers to "voluntarily" agree to pay the same excise taxes as the four largest firms.

34. A rough calculation of the cost of the resolution to the companies is that the taxes would cost them about $1 billion a year, the $10 billion in lump sum damages are roughly equivalent in cost, settling lawsuits would cost at most $1 billion a year, and the other aspects of the deal would not be very costly (see, for example, the section "Marketing Restrictions"). So, given the firms' domestic pretax profits of $8 billion, the total corresponds to perhaps 40 percent of their value absent any litigation liability. The widespread prediction of securities analysts that passage of the resolution would help tobacco stocks was probably accurate (see the section "Market Value of Litigation Risk").

35. The FDA claimed the right to regulate tobacco in 1996. On August 14, 1998, after the McCain bill collapsed, a federal appeals court ruled that the FDA does not have the authority to regulate cigarettes and smokeless tobacco. See Barry Meier, "Court Rules FDA Lacks Authority to Limit Tobacco," *New York Times*, August 15, 1998, p. A1.

about 33 cents a pack,[36] pretax profits would decline by about $1 billion a year, while the bill would raise about $13 billion a year.[37] This leverage was the primary driver behind the resolution. Effectively, the resolution created a collusive agreement among the companies. By agreeing with the attorneys general that each of the companies would pay a per-pack tax, the companies would push the price of cigarettes closer to the monopoly level, enabling them to pay the states and the attorneys about twice as much as their annual pretax profits without being badly damaged.[38] The fact that the proceeds of the companies' agreement were to be used to buy legal protections does not in any way alter the collusive nature of the arrangement.

36. This assumption is the most important one here. The assumption of constant margins is consistent with log-linear demand in a Cournot model. More generally, in a Cournot model the pass-through rate is equal to $N/[N-1+$ (slope of industry marginal revenue curve $\div$ slope of demand curve)], where N is the number of firms in the industry. This is a simple generalization of the monopoly analysis in Bulow and Pfleiderer (1983). That is, for linear demand, where the marginal revenue curve is twice as steep as the demand curve, the pass-through rate is less than 100 percent, while for constant-elasticity demand the pass-through rate is more than 100 percent. This matters. For example, if 110 percent of a tax is passed through to consumers, it will probably increase operating profits.

The issue is further complicated by the two-tier industry price structure. Specific taxes of the kind proposed by the resolution probably favor the premium brands and may aid profitability (see the section on specific versus ad valorem taxes).

Jobber and retailer margins are less important, but the FTC assumed that they would be essentially unchanged, which is roughly consistent with empirical studies that indicate a pass-through rate of slightly more than 100 percent of state taxes at the retail level. See, for example, Sumner (1981) and Merriman (1994). The industry, which had incentive to say taxes would be costly, argued that at least 112 percent of any company's price increase would be passed on at retail; see Bozell Sawyer Miller Group (1997). But MIT economist Jeffrey E. Harris calculated that real retailer margins fell by 1.3 percent a year from 1994 to 1997, whereas real manufacturer revenues per pack rose by 4.7 percent. See "Prepared Statement before the Senate Democratic Task Force on Tobacco," table 1, available at http://www.mit.edu/jeffrey/harris/.

37. The resolution scaled taxes so that if sales remained constant, new tax revenues would be $15 billion a year. A 12 percent reduction in sales would reduce this amount to $13 billion. Additionally, current state and federal cigarette excise taxes are about $14 billion a year. Those revenues would also fall by 12 percent. Furthermore, the increase in excise taxes would leave smokers with less money to spend on other goods, ultimately reducing income tax revenues. Allowing for a conventional estimate of a 25 percent offset on income tax collections, the net effect of the resolution on total state and federal revenues would have been an increase of about $8 billion a year.

38. Assuming a current per-pack price of $2, a current profit margin of 33 cents, and a demand elasticity of -0.4, linear demand would imply a monopoly price of about $4.34, while log-linear demand would imply a monopoly price of $6.67.

We are concerned, more broadly than in just this case, that negotiating collusive price increases to settle lawsuits will seem a great way to benefit plaintiffs, lawyers, and defendants at the expense of consumers.[39] This kind of deal would clearly violate the antitrust laws if the companies worked out an equivalent arrangement on their own, and the prospects for mischief with these kinds of settlements are enormous. For example, with a little tinkering the resolution could be restructured to raise prices enough to increase tax revenues still further *and* boost industry profits. Raise the tax to $1.10 a pack but give each company an exemption equal to 10 percent of base year sales. The increase in specific taxes would reduce sales and profits by about 20 percent.[40] But because of the exemption, the companies would increase their pretax profits by about $1 billion a year.[41] Tax revenues net of the exemption would be about $17 billion instead of the $13 billion under the resolution.

For political reasons the per pack payments were called ''settlement payments'' rather than taxes. The states had an incentive to frame their actions as a victory over ''big tobacco'' rather than a tax increase on smokers. The contingency-fee attorneys could get fees as a percentage of ''damage payments'' but maybe not as a percentage of tax increases. And the companies wanted to describe their concessions as being painful rather than admit to having sold out their customers by agreeing to cigarette tax hikes in return for protection from lawsuits.[42]

39. Of course, the class action suits were theoretically filed on behalf of consumers, so the consumers were the plantiffs and suffered a financial loss in the settlement. Their attorneys, however, represented themselves very aggressively.

40. This estimate assumes a log linear demand curve with a current elasticity of -0.4 and a current price of $2. It further assumes that prices will rise by the amount of the tax increase.

41. The lost sales would reduce current profits of $8 billion by $1.6 billion. The rebate of $1.10 on 10 percent of a current 24 billion packs sold each year would increase profits by $2.6 billion, for a net gain of $1 billion.

42. Furthermore, according to the industry's official Web site,

—Under budget-scoring conventions, excise taxes raise only 75 percent of the actual amounts received because of an offset for lost income taxes. (Simplistically, if you spend a dollar on goods and services, someone else will receive a dollar in income and have to pay an average of 25 cents in income taxes.) Settlement payments would not suffer from this offset if they were treated as fees paid to the federal government. So avoiding the tax terminology would allow the federal government to increase spending by more.

—Excise taxes are scored on the ''mandatory'' side of the budget and thus cannot

The resolution required congressional approval for several reasons. First was the requirement that the terms apply to nonsettling companies. Second were the restrictions on future litigation. Third was the collusive nature of the deal. The resolution specifically included an antitrust exemption for the companies. Whether such collusive price agreements would be legal without national legislation has yet to be tested. This issue takes on greater relevance now that the bill has died but state settlements, modeled on the resolution, remain.

Tax Increases

Although the tobacco deal's overall strategy of substituting taxes for damages seems brilliant (from the point of view of the parties involved), the detailed execution of this strategy seems less well done. The differences between the kinds of taxes that the resolution and bill proposed, and between these and other possible tax instruments, are critical to whether the parties' objectives would be likely to be met. In fact, the taxes started out rather badly designed (in the resolution) and managed to get worse (in the bill).[43]

"Fixed-Revenue" Taxation versus Specific Taxes

The resolution proposed standard specific taxes (taxes at a fixed rate per pack).[44] Instead of setting a tax per pack, however, the McCain bill

be used for discretionary spending items unless a 60 percent super majority votes to waive budget rules. Settlement payments can be treated as user fees that offset discretionary spending.

It was also particularly important for the Senate Commerce Committee not to refer to the payments as taxes, since it has no jurisdiction over tax issues. (Similarly, in the state settlements, avoiding the tax terminology may allow the attorneys general to both negotiate the "damages" and decide how to spend them without consulting the state legislatures—currently a hot political issue in Texas.) See www.tobaccoresolution.com. Click under "The Real Story," "Issue Briefs," and "Why Not an Excise Tax" to find a document labeled "'Excise Tax' Treatment for Industry Payments Is Inappropriate."

43. Economists at the Treasury Department and the FTC made some improvements in the bill.

44. The proposed taxes were an increase of 35 cents a pack the first year, rising to 62 cents in the fifth year. These amounts would then be increased annually by the maximum of 3 percent plus the rate of inflation as measured by the consumer price index. They were set so that if volume remained at 24 billion packs, revenue would equal $8.5 billion in year one, $9.5 billion in year two, $11.5 billion in year three, $14 billion in year four, and $15 billion in year five and later.

specified a total tax bill for years one to five, to be apportioned according to market share. The taxes were set at $14.4 billion in year one (1999), rising to $ 23.6 billion in year five.[45] For year six and thereafter, the original bill specified a switch to a per pack tax, the amount of the tax to be determined by dividing a fixed sum by sales in year five, but this last provision was particularly perverse and was later changed.[46]

It is worth thinking through the impact of the McCain bill's fixed-revenue taxation system. For a monopoly, this would be a lump-sum tax. But the industry "only" earns about $8 billion a year before taxes. Therefore, if the industry were a perfectly functioning cartel, the McCain bill would have put it out of business.[47] However, all estimates of the demand elasticity for cigarettes imply that the market price is well below the monopoly price, so a tax increase would lead to a much smaller loss in profits, and we must think through the McCain fixed-revenue tax program for an oligopoly.

The most salient feature of fixed-revenue taxation is that companies' marginal tax rates will generally be less than their average tax rate. Let the average tax rate per pack be t and the market share of a firm be s. If the firm makes an additional sale that would otherwise have been made by a competitor, its marginal tax rate is just t, because the tax burden on its other sales is unaffected. If selling the additional pack does not affect other companies' sales, however, the firm will have to pay t in taxes on the new pack, but the industry tax burden on inframarginal packs will be reduced by t. Because the firm's market share is s, its tax burden on inframarginal packs is reduced by ts, so the firm's marginal tax rate becomes $t(1 - s)$. Note that for a monopolist the marginal rate is zero, and for a competitive (or very small) firm the marginal rate is equal to the average rate.

45. Before the bill died, the number of years with fixed payments was reduced to three, thanks in part to economists at the Treasury Department and the FTC. Discussion with Jonathan Gruber (Treasury) and Jonathan Baker (FTC).

46. Another provision of the original bill that was subsequently eliminated would have imposed a per pack fee of 2 cents on all overseas sales. Philip Morris, RJR, and Brown and Williamson all have substantial international businesses, with Philip Morris's international volume about three times its domestic volume.

47. Even if we were to assume that the industry colludes on a monopoly price to maximize the rents available in the market and then dissipates some of those rents through marketing competition, the magnitude of the McCain tax would drive the industry out of business. That is, gross revenues net of manufacturing costs but before other nontax expenses are about $16 billion, which is less than the McCain tax.

There are several important implications. First, fixed-revenue taxation gives firms an incentive to focus on building sales through expanding the market rather than by stealing share from competitors. If the goal of the legislation is to reduce smoking, this form of taxation clearly provides the wrong incentives. Second, fixed-revenue taxes give larger firms lower marginal tax rates than smaller firms, and so result in bigger differences in market shares between firms than do ordinary specific taxes. That is, Philip Morris will have a larger market share under fixed-revenue taxation than under specific taxation.[48] Third, because fixed-revenue taxation gives lower marginal tax rates, it results in lower pass-through to prices than does specific taxation. In a Cournot model the pass-through of a small fixed-revenue tax increase in an N firm industry is $(N-1)/N$ times the pass-through of a specific tax increase that yields the same average tax per pack.[49]

The last point has very severe consequences for profitability. Making the conventional assumption that industry demand for tobacco is log-linear, specific taxes are passed through dollar for dollar. So a $1.10 (average) tax increase, the level the McCain bill proposed, imposed through fixed-revenue taxation on a four-firm industry implies only an 82.5 cent pass-through or a five-sixths reduction in current industry margins. In other words, the model (taken literally) implies that fixed-revenue taxation that yields the same per pack rate as a given specific tax reduces industry profits to one-sixth of the level achieved by the specific tax, and of course also yields higher sales of cigarettes than the specific tax.[50] Obviously the parties to the deal, governments who want

48. Under the conventional assumption that demand for tobacco is log linear, a Cournot oligopolist with lower costs than the (unweighted) industry average gains market share under fixed-revenue taxation, but its market share is unchanged under specific taxation. With inelastic constant-elasticity demand, however, a low-cost firm loses market share under either kind of taxation.

49. Because price in a Cournot model depends only on the (unweighted) average of firms' marginal costs plus marginal tax rates, and the average firm has share $s = 1/N$, hence marginal tax rate $[1 - (1/N)]t = [(N - 1)/N]t$ under fixed-revenue taxation. See appendix A for more details. The result in the text also holds true for nonmarginal tax increases with standard demand curves including linear, log linear, constant elasticity, and so forth.

50. Of course, a given average tax rate imposed as a fixed-revenue tax yields a higher tax take (because of the higher sales) than a specific tax imposed at the same rate. Unless the taxes would yield prices above the (no-tax) monopoly price, however, a given total tax take can be raised at a lower cost to firms' profits and at higher prices (thus less smoking) through a specific tax than through a fixed-revenue tax.

taxes, firms who want profits, and public health advocates who want lower smoking, can all do better with specific taxes. Appendix A gives more details of these points.

The quantity adjustment after year five in the bill involved a less subtle mistake. With the tax per pack for the future to be determined by sales in year five, firms were given a significant incentive to sell as much as possible in year five through promotions and by moving sales back from year six and forward from year four. This flaw was ultimately corrected.

The best explanations for the fixed-revenue taxation are that Congress wanted revenue certainty for budgetary purposes and wished to understate the change from the resolution.[51]

Distributional Issues

Because cigarettes are an inferior good—people smoke less as their incomes rise—taxes on cigarettes are highly regressive. Table 7 illustrates the distributional consequences of the original McCain proposal when fully implemented in 2003. The bill would have increased taxes by 9 percent for the average household making less than $30,000 (in 1998 dollars). Consumers with incomes in excess of $30,000 would face a tax increase of less than 1 percent, and taxes for consumers with incomes in excess of $100,000 would increase less than 0.1 percent.[52]

Both the resolution and the bill were careful to deal with the distributional consequences for other interest groups such as tobacco farmers, vending machine owners, quota holders, and even sports events that had been receiving tobacco sponsorship.[53]

51. All of the revenue estimates for the resolution and the bill were made by taking the undiscounted sum of revenue over twenty-five years, assuming no inflation adjustment and no decline in sales, even though volume was likely to fall substantially. By fixing taxes paid each year rather than adjusting for lower sales, the bill's authors could raise the real tax rate without changing the bill's reported size.

52. These distributional effects might have been somewhat mitigated by the primary amendment to the bill, which would have used a third of the revenues to reduce the "marriage penalty" tax on two-income households, particularly those earning less than $50,000 a year. This Republican-sponsored amendment was criticized by some public health advocates who wanted all the revenues to be allocated to public health and antismoking programs. It was also criticized by some Republicans, who opposed the tobacco bill and were concerned that bundling in the tax cut would increase the chance of passage by attracting more Republican support.

53. According to the FAQ page produced by the Senate Commerce Committee,

Table 7. Distributional Effects of the Tobacco Payment Provisions of S. 1415, Calendar year 2003

Income category[b]	Change in federal taxes[c]		Federal taxes under present law[c]		Federal taxes under proposal[c]		Effective tax rate[d]	
	Millions	Percent	Billions	Percent	Billions	Percent	Present law (Percent)	Proposal (Percent)
Less than 10,000	2,544	44.6	6	0.4	8	0.5	6.9	10.0
10,000 to 20,000	3,911	12.3	32	2.0	36	2.2	7.5	8.4
20,000 to 30,000	4,170	5.4	78	4.8	82	5.0	13.2	13.9
30,000 to 40,000	3,796	3.3	114	7.1	118	7.2	16.2	16.7
40,000 to 50,000	2,675	2.2	120	7.4	123	7.5	17.6	18.0
50,000 to 75,000	4,109	1.5	280	17.3	284	17.3	19.5	19.8
75,000 to 100,000	1,884	0.7	252	15.6	254	15.5	22.6	22.8
100,000 to 200,000	446	0.1	351	21.7	351	21.4	24.9	25.0
200,000 and over	65	e	383	23.7	383	23.4	29.3	29.3
All taxpayers	23,600	1.5	1,614	100.0	1,638	100.0	20.8	21.2

Source: Joint Committee on Taxation, (1998). Available at http://www.house.gov/jct/x-40-98.htm. Columns may not add because of rounding.

a. Includes gross payments by tobacco companies distributed equivalent to an excise tax.

b. The income concept used to place tax returns into income categories is adjusted gross income (AGI) plus tax-exempt interest, employer contributions for health plans and life insurance, employer share of FICA tax, worker's compensation, nontaxable social security benefits, insurance value of medicare benefits, alternative minimum tax preference items, and excluded income of U.S. citizens living abroad. Categories are measured at 1998 levels.

c. Federal taxes are equal to individual income tax (including the outlay portion of the earned income credit, employment tax (attributed to employees), and excise taxes (attributed to consumers). Corporate income tax is not included due to uncertainty concerning the incidence of the tax. Individuals who are dependents of other taxpayers and taxpayers with negative income are excluded from the analysis. Does not include indirect effects.

d. The effective tax rate is equal to federal taxes described in table note c divided by income described in table note b plus additional income attributable to the proposal.

e. Less than 0.02 percent.

Taxes on Tar and Nicotine Consumption

The bill and the resolution both taxed all cigarettes at the same rate. There was no financial incentive for consumers to switch to cigarettes with less tar or nicotine, and almost none for firms to develop safer cigarettes.

If one makes extreme assumptions that the tar in cigarettes causes all the health problems and that nicotine is the sole cause of addiction, a rational addiction model along the lines of Becker and Murphy's would imply that tar is what should be taxed.[54] It is clear, however, that the public health goals are not based on such a model. If consumers, especially young consumers, are myopic and fail to understand how addictive cigarettes are, nicotine levels are critical to lifetime consumption and should also be taxed.

Taxes should perhaps not just be proportional to a (weighted) sum of tar and nicotine: Smoking low tar and nicotine cigarettes may contribute to an addiction to smoking rather than an addiction to nicotine and, of course, cigarettes may contain other dangerous ingredients. Furthermore, it is often claimed that the machines that the Federal Trade Commission (FTC) uses to determine tar and nicotine levels in cigarettes understate the consumption of real smokers, particularly for low

---

"The bill contains legislation drafted by tobacco state Senators to provide comprehensive assistance to farmers and rural communities. Congress is committed to ensuring that innocent, hardworking American farmers and tobacco dependent rural communities will receive the support and assistance they need." The page goes on to say, "The Committee believes the tobacco vending machine companies and employees should be compensated if their industry is adversely affected by a tobacco settlement. The tobacco bill passed by the Commerce Committee would create a non-profit corporation that includes tobacco vending machine industry representatives, to provide payments to vending machine companies. The amount of compensation provided to individual vending companies would be determined by this non-profit Board. The vending machine industry strongly supported this proposal and urged the Committee to include the provision in the bill." Available at http://www.senate.gov/commerce/legis/tobfaq.htm.

Furthermore, quoting from the resolution, title VII A (5): "Beginning in the second year, $75,000,000 [will be allocated] annually for a period of ten (10) years to compensate events, teams or entries in such events, who lose sponsorship by the tobacco industry as a result of this Act."

54. Becker and Murphy (1988). The argument here assumes that health effects are linear in consumption. If smoking twice as much is more than twice as bad, then taxing nicotine might serve as a proxy for taxing heavy smokers disproportionately more. But if smokers can get their nicotine fix from gum and patches, tar and nicotine become less closely tied and the argument for taxing nicotine becomes less compelling.

tar and nicotine brands (although ideally tests should be developed to measure accurately the effects of cigarettes on smokers). A straightforward solution is a tax on cigarettes of the form *Tax* = *a* + *b* Tar* + *c* Nicotine*.[55] In any case, it is hard to see the health reason for taxing all cigarettes at the same rate.

There was some implicit recognition of this principle in the resolution and the McCain bill. Title I, Section E5A of the resolution limited cigarettes to a maximum of 12 milligrams of tar based on current testing methods. Both the resolution and the bill continued requirements for publishing tar and nicotine ratings, presumably because that information is useful to consumers. The quantity restrictions, however, would have done nothing to encourage the development of safer cigarettes.[56]

Specific Taxes versus Ad Valorem Taxes

A further issue is whether the taxes should have been ad valorem (proportional to the pretax price, like a value added tax) rather than specific (additive to the pretax price). Currently all taxes (except state sales taxes) on cigarettes in the United States are specific, which is appropriate if the taxes are meant to correct an externality. However, if one imagines that the purpose of the bill was, as stated in its title, youth smoking reduction, ad valorem taxes merit consideration.

Write a firm's profits absent taxes as $\pi = p \cdot q - c$, in which p is the firm's price, q its quantity, and c its total costs. A specific tax of s then

55. One could imagine more complex taxes, but these are problematic if smokers use multiple brands.

Although we are assuming the use of specific taxes in our discussion, a similar formula could be used with ad valorem taxes.

56. Other clauses in the resolution may be detrimental to innovation. For example, the requirement that any safer cigarette technology be cross-licensed across the industry at "reasonable" prices may discourage R&D. The bill contained a provision making it difficult for a company to get approval from the secretary of health and human services that a cigarette was "reduced risk." According to section 913 (2) (B) "the Secretary shall take into account (i) the risks and benefits to the population as a whole, including both users of tobacco products and non-users of tobacco products; (ii) the increased or decreased likelihood that existing users of tobacco products will stop using such products including reduced risk tobacco products; (iii) the increased or decreased likelihood that those who do not use tobacco products will start to use such products, including reduced risk tobacco products; and (iv) the risks and benefits to consumers from the use of a reduced risk tobacco product as compared to the use of products approved under chapter V to reduce exposure to tobacco."

results in profits $\pi_s = p \cdot q - (c + s \cdot q)$, while an ad valorem tax of $100t$ percent results in profits $\pi_t = [p/(1 + t)] \cdot q - c$, which can be rewritten as $\pi_t = \{1 - [t/(1 + t)]\}[p \cdot q - (1 + t)c]$. So while a specific tax corresponds to a fixed increase in marginal costs, an ad valorem tax can be thought of as the sum of a profit tax and a multiplicative tax on *all* costs. A specific tax causes substitution from the taxed attribute (quantity) to other attributes (quality).[57] Relative to a specific tax, an ad valorem tax greatly reduces the incentive to spend on advertising and promotion and gives a strong incentive to cut (pretax) price, because it effectively multiplies a firm's perceived elasticity by $(1 + t)$.[58]

In short, specific taxes encourage firms to produce and market high-priced and highly promoted premium brands, while ad valorem taxes encourage the sale of low-priced generics. Figure 1 shows how pretax prices vary with the level of specific taxes across the European Union.[59]

The advantage of specific taxes, then, is that they will lead to higher average prices, which would lead to lower consumption, other things being equal.[60] But correspondingly higher ad valorem taxes can achieve the same price levels without the same level of promotional activity; ad

57. Barzel (1976).

58. A specific tax has little effect on advertising and promotion activities that increase the price that can be charged for a given output, but it does reduce activity that increases sales.

59. There is a wide variation between similar countries. For example, as of January 1998, Sweden had an unavoidable tax of $3.45 a pack and a proportional tax rate of 0.61 while its neighbor Finland had an unavoidable tax of $1.04 a pack and a proportional rate of 2.14. By proportional tax, we mean $(1 + \text{ad valorem rate}) \times (1 + \text{VAT rate}) - 1$. Delipalla (1995) and Delipalla and O'Donnell (1998) also study the European industry. See Keen (1998) for discussion of the substantial shift toward specific taxation in the 1980s in the Netherlands, which also seems to have favored more expensive brands.

Several papers, including Barzel (1976), Johnson (1978), Sumner and Ward (1981), and Sobel and Garrett (1997), have examined the claim that specific taxes favor premium brands by exploiting the variation in taxes across states in the United States. Limitations include lack of variation in the data, firms' difficulty in producing different products for different states, and their use of national advertising and promotional campaigns. In a very recent contribution, however, Sobel and Garrett (1997, 884) estimate that "for approximately every 3 cents of state [specific] tax there is an increase of one percentage point in the market share of premium brands [in that state]," while the effect of ad valorem taxes on the share of premiums as opposed to that of generics is "insignificantly different from zero."

60. Even if the higher prices reduce total youth consumption, the number of youth smokers may not be greatly reduced if the product is made more glamorous, so the effect on future addiction rates may be limited.

Figure 1. Pretax Prices versus Specific Taxes in the Fifteen European Union Countries as of January 1, 1998

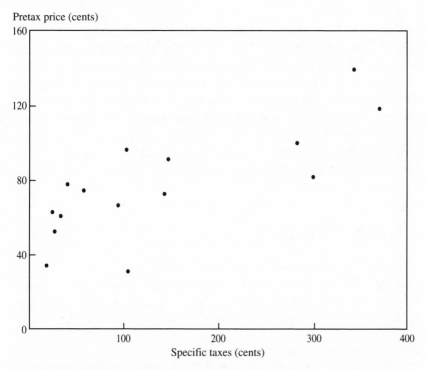

Pretax price (cents)

Specific taxes (cents)

Source: Authors' calculations based on data from U.K. Tobacco Manufacturers' Association and Confederation of European Community Cigarette Manufacturers. Specific taxes are total unavoidable tax per pack (tax at pretax price of zero). EU taxes consist of a fixed per-cigarette tax, a proportional ad valorem tax that is calculated on the sum of the pretax price and the fixed tax, and a value-added tax that is then calculated on the sum of all the foregoing. The total unavoidable tax per pack equals [(fixed) × (1+ ad valorem rate) × (1+VAT rate)]. Note that by contrast with our terminology the fixed tax is generally referred to as the specific tax. Pretax price is the price of the most popular price category.

valorem taxes that favor deglamorized generic products may support continued sales to old addicted smokers but fail to attract so many new young smokers.

Another way to view the argument for ad valorem taxes is that it is similar to that for taxing nicotine content. As noted earlier, ad valorem taxes effectively tax all costs; that is, they tax the advertising as well as the contents of a cigarette. This is appropriate if the advertising helps get youth smokers addicted.[61] Ad valorem taxes are also preferable for

61. There is some evidence that youth smokers are less interested than adults in

350 Brookings Papers: Microeconomics 1998

distributional reasons because they reduce the relative taxes on cheaper products.[62]

The major argument against ad valorem taxes is that they would probably be far worse for firms' profits.[63] There are other ways to compensate the companies, however. For example, instead of setting average and marginal taxes equal, marginal rates could be set above average rates—exactly the opposite of what would have happened under the McCain bill's fixed-revenue taxation. This can be done, for example, by allowing all companies an annual tax exemption on one pack for every five or ten sold in 1997. These adjustments could be further tailored to account for the current differences in firms' mixes between premium and discount cigarettes.

Lump-Sum Damages

Both the resolution and the bill specified that the industry would pay damages of $10 billion in rough proportion to the relative market values of the companies. The way these payments were to be split proves that the settlement was based on the relative bargaining power of the various

---

generics. Although only 72.5 percent of cigarette sales are of premium brands, youth smokers report that more than 90 percent of the cigarettes they smoke are premium cigarettes. See Centers for Disease Control and Prevention, Tobacco Information, "Comparison of Advertising to Brand Preference in Adolescents and Adults, 1993." Available at http://www.cdc.gov/nccdphp/osh/brndtbl.htm. Specific taxes are less undesirable if all advertising and promotional activities can be completely banned, but we fear that cigarette companies may continue to find ways to market their brand images.

62. This conclusion assumes that poorer people are relatively more likely to buy generics. Some believe that the poor view premium cigarettes as one of their few "affordable luxuries," but Townsend, Roderick, and Cooper (1994) provide evidence from Great Britain that lower socioeconomic groups are much more sensitive to cigarette prices than are higher socioeconomic groups.

63. Ad valorem taxes are worse for profits for any given rate (cents per pack) of tax, but they are better for a monopoly (or sufficiently collusive oligopoly) for a given amount of tax raised. See Keen (1998) for a summary of the literature.

A practical concern is that specific taxes may give more precise control of the market price (and tax revenues) than ad valorem taxes do. A senior U.K. treasury official argues that specific taxes provide less scope for fraud (private conversation). The United Kingdom has the highest specific taxes in the European Union: total "fixed" taxes were $3.71 a pack in January 1998. Finally, by favoring premium brands over generics, specific taxes may also tend to favor home producers over inexpensive imports.

Table 8. Share of Tobacco Sales since 1950 versus Lump-Sum Damage Payments
Percent

Company	Current market share	Share of tobacco sales since 1950	Share of lump-sum damage payments
Philip Morris	49.2	23.0	68
RJR	24.5	31.0	7
Brown and Williamson	16.2	30.0	18
Lorillard	8.7	8.5	7
Liggett	1.3	7.5	0

Sources: Tobacco sales were calculated from FTC data on market shares over time (Federal Trade Commission, 1997) and U.S. Department of Agriculture Economic Research Service estimates of tobacco consumption in cigarettes. Damage payments were calculated from the McCain bill. Actual amounts were $6.58 billion for Philip Morris, $660 million for Reynolds, $1.73 billion for Brown and Williamson, $710 million for Lorillard, and $320 million for US Tobacco. Percentages were calculated excluding US Tobacco.

firms rather than on any measure of the damages for which they were responsible.

Table 8 compares the relative amounts of tobacco sold by the five major tobacco companies since 1950 with the percentages of the lump-sum payments they were to make. If firms' lump-sum payments were set in proportion to damage to today's sick smokers, RJR and Liggett would probably be liable for even more than their share of tobacco sales since 1950. There are three reasons, all relating to these companies having larger market shares in the early years. First, the amount of tar and nicotine in cigarettes per pound of tobacco has declined over time. Second, sick smokers are predominantly older smokers who have disproportionately smoked the declining brands. Third, one might wish to assign liability disproportionately to the brand that the smoker began smoking when young, if one believes that addiction caused by youth smoking is at the root of smoking problems. Philip Morris's market share when most of today's sick smokers started smoking was closer to 10 percent than 50 percent. This explains why RJR faces more individual suits than Philip Morris.

In fact, the payments were based on deep pockets: they were to be directly proportional to companies' equity valuations. This is the outcome one would anticipate from a negotiation in which there are bimodal expectations for tobacco litigation: either litigation in the absence of a deal will generally fail, or it will be so successful that it will put all the companies into bankruptcy. It is also consistent with the focus in bill negotiations on whether future suits could be brought only against the domestic tobacco subsidiaries of the companies or against the conglomerates.[64]

So RJR's leveraged buyout in 1989 by Kohlberg, Kravis and Roberts, which left it with less equity and more debt, reduced its payments. Philip Morris's tremendous growth, its dominance of the premium markets, and its ownership of Miller Brewing and Kraft increased its payments. The allocation of these damages were even less "fair" than the tax increases that allocated companies' costs in proportion to their current and future, but not past, market shares.

The $6 billion after-tax cost of these lump-sum damages is about 4 percent of the market value of the equity of the firms but perhaps 13 percent of what their domestic tobacco businesses would be worth were there no prospective litigation costs.[65] The lump-sum damages would have been roughly as costly to the firms as the resolution's proposed $358.5 billion in tax increases. So although economic theory can explain the allocation of the lump-sum payments, we have more trouble explaining their existence; they seem less desirable for all parties than tax increases that can raise more money at a much lower cost to companies, while seeming to the general public to be more punitive, and also having the public health advantage of raising prices. The negotiators now better understand this point, as we will show when we describe the multistate settlement of November 1998.

Legal Protections

In return for the tax increases and lump-sum damages, the resolution banned all punitive damage suits based on the companies' past actions

---

64. The bill at first protected the nondomestic tobacco assets of the companies, but antitobacco forces loudly protested this provision.

65. Calculation by Gary Black, based on approximately $8 billion in industry earnings before interest and taxes in 1997 before the costs of settling state litigation, a multiple of 6 times pretax earnings for Philip Morris and a 15 percent discount for the rest of the industry, corresponding to about 10 times unlevered aftertax earnings for Philip Morris and 8.5 times unlevered aftertax earnings for other firms. See Gary Black, "Philip Morris/RJR/UST Company Report," INVESTEXT Report 1896658. March 31, 1997.

as well as class action suits.[66] These legal protections are the reason, apart from the taxes, that federal legislation was required to implement the resolution.

The resolution capped the amount of damages the companies would have to pay out in any one year to $1 billion. Specifically, the resolution placed a cap of $5 billion on the amount that could be awarded in judgments each year and gave the companies "coinsurance" of 80 percent by paying 80 percent of the judgments from the tax revenues collected.

This coinsurance produces two obvious incentive conflicts. First, the governments and public health agencies that were the financial beneficiaries of the resolution would effectively pay 80 percent of any verdict against a tobacco company, so they would have more at stake than the companies in trying to defeat the suits. Second, and probably more important, is simply that it would be less costly for a company to settle a suit for $1 million than it would be to spend $250,000 fighting and winning in court. This would greatly counter the companies' reputational incentive not to settle individual suits and would probably lead to more suits.[67]

Further incentive problems might arise if the companies came to feel that the cap would be reached every year. There would then be little point in defending against suits, except that some suits might provide disproportionately large claims against one firm or another, so negotiations could be over which suits to settle first. Litigation is usually thought of as having social value in discovering information and in punishing the guilty, but if the companies gave up on trying to keep payments below the cap, the lawsuits would generate neither of these benefits.

The original McCain bill included an 80 percent coinsurance clause, as in the resolution, but provided a cap of $6.5 billion instead of $5 billion. A more significant difference is that McCain provided no protection against class actions and punitive damage cases, so there was a much greater likelihood of large payments.

66. Although it seems unlikely that a federal class action could proceed, based on cases like the Supreme Court asbestos case, *Amchem Products* v. *Windsor*, 117 S. Ct. 2231, 2249–50 (1997), the resolution was meant to ban state class actions.

67. Of course, the companies might currently have an excessive incentive to fight for reputation reasons, so coinsurance might in that way actually improve incentives.

An important provision in the early drafts of the McCain bill was that companies' liability was limited to their domestic tobacco assets.[68] Because the market value of the domestic businesses was roughly equal to the companies' legal liabilities, this provision in itself should have been enough for the deal to be a good one for stockholders. Antitobacco forces objected to the provision, however.[69]

Although the public health community and the antitobacco lawyers wanted all of the companies' assets to be available for paying damages, actually putting them into bankruptcy might be disastrous. If the companies were placed in chapter 11, their brands and factories might be sold to new companies that would have no liability for the past actions of the tobacco manufacturers. Facing much less potential legal liability, the new firms would have much less incentive to trade marketing restrictions and tax increases for litigation protection.[70]

By the time the Senate had finished amending the McCain bill, essentially all of the companies' legal protections—the carrots that induced the companies to make a deal in the first place—had been removed.

68. This provision was not included in the resolution but was not really needed there because the resolution effectively eliminated the risk of bankruptcy from lawsuits. It was important in the McCain bill because even the original draft specified some circumstances in which the damage caps would be lifted and later drafts abandoned the caps.

69. Daynard and others (1998), available at http://www.tobacco.neu.edu/Congress/McCain/index.html#EXECUTIVE. As is clear from our analysis of the allocation of the lump-sum damage payments across companies, as well as of the stock market discounts of the companies, the vulnerability of domestic nontobacco and foreign tobacco assets to U.S. lawsuits affected the companies' bargaining power.

70. Jeffrey Goldberg, "Big Tobacco's Endgame," *New York Times Magazine,* June 21, 1998 p. 36. "According to Steven Goldstone of RJR, 'This is what would happen if we had to go into reorganization. . . . Any judgment against us would be stayed, the states wouldn't get their money, the shareholders of the company would suffer, all of the lawsuits against the industry would grind to a halt. The only thing that will still be going the day after is that we'd still be making cigarettes. . . . What have these public-health people achieved in 40 years? They think they'll end smoking by bankrupting us, but believe me, that's not going to happen.'" Goldberg goes on to say, "Goldstone argues that bankruptcy is a real possibility—and that a bankrupted industry could mean the formation of new tobacco companies with no history, and therefore no liability for past practices. Goldstone sounds almost gleeful when he mentions that scenario."

Youth Smoking

Everyone would like to end youth smoking, and it was a major focus of attention. On the one hand, the stated purpose of the bill was to reduce youth smoking; on the other hand, the companies are often said to regard young smokers as "tomorrow's cigarette business."[71] But the truth is that the value to the companies of the youth market is tiny: most of the present value of future tobacco profits resides in the lungs of smokers who are currently older than age eighteen. Nor is it so clear that the public health community is, or should be, focused primarily on youth smoking, although the political value of referring to smoking as a children's disease is not lost on anyone. It is in these contexts that we discuss the provisions of the resolution and bill that were advocated as youth smoking measures.

The Value to the Companies of the Youth Market

Even if all smokers were equally profitable, the present discounted value of all future smokers would probably be only one-sixth, at most, of the present value of all current and future smokers.[72] But this calculation ignores smokers' strong brand loyalty. Many smokers seem to become addicted to a particular brand; only about 10 percent switch brands in any year.[73] Assuming new smokers are relatively uncommit-

71. Steve Lohr and Barry Meier, "Cooperation and Miscalculations on Shaping Tobacco Legislation," *New York Times,* April 11, 1998, p. 1, quoting an RJR memo from 1974 making this vacuous comment.

72. To compute this, observe that the current quit rate of all smokers is 2.5 percent a year. Given the long-term downward trend of more than 0.5 percent a year in the number of smokers, this implies entry of no more than 2.0 percent a year. Discounting all future profits by 8.5 percent and allowing for a 1 percent decline in cigarette purchases per smoker, the present value of future profits from current smokers is current profits divided by 0.12, while the present value of future profits including future smokers is current profits divided by 0.10. The discount rate was chosen to give the companies a price-earnings ratio of 10 in the absence of future litigation costs (summing the discount rate and the decline in annual sales and assuming that profits per pack would remain constant), which is broadly consistent with how the firms are valued (see note 65).

The value of the youth market is even lower if we use the alternative estimates that the combined quit and death rate of smokers is 3.5 percent while the "smoker formation rate" is 2.2 percent, resulting in a decline of 1.3 percent a year. See National Association of Convenience Stores (1998). These figures are attributed to analyst Gary Black.

73. Department of Health and Human Services (1989, p. 503). Similarly, "only about 10 percent of [cigarette smokers] switched annually, and then often to brands of the same manufacturer" (Kluger, 1996, p. 632). Note, however, that prices of brands

ted to any particular brand, the value of new customers is relatively tiny compared with the value of mature smokers. As we show in appendix B, the competition to capture youth smokers dissipates most of the future profits from them. The argument is that if price discrimination were possible, firms would be willing to cut prices substantially to new potential customers. But if price discrimination is impossible, firms will still cut prices to all customers a little to capture the youth market. Although it will then appear from an accounting perspective that the new customers are as profitable as any others, short-run profits will be lower and long-run profits will not be much higher than if there were no new customers.

The Public Health Significance of the Youth Market

Youth smoking is one of the serious public health issues monitored by the Youth Risk Behavior Surveillance System sponsored by the Centers for Disease Control and Prevention. Table 9 puts the problem in perspective. According to the Department of Health and Human Services, "more than 80 percent of all adult smokers had tried smoking by their 18th birthday and more than half of them had already become regular smokers by that age."[74] But these facts do not necessarily imply that more effective deterrence of youth smoking will lead to a proportional reduction in adult smoking.[75] For example, black high school senior smoking rates have averaged less than half of white rates over the past twenty years, but because of dramatically lower quit rates among African American adults, their current smoking rate is slightly higher than the smoking rate among white adults.[76]

---

within a category are very similar, which does not encourage switching; that perhaps 70 percent of smokers have a second-choice brand; and that about 25 percent regularly buy more than one brand each month. See Sullum (1998, p. 102).

74. U.S. Department of Health and Human Services, "Children's Future at Risk from Epidemic of Tobacco Use," press release, August 23, 1996, available at http://www.hhs.gov/news/press/1996pres/960823d.html.

75. Of course, it is true that many young people who become addicted to smoking would never have started if they could have been deterred until age 18. But extreme versions of the argument are reminiscent of the claim that because historically very few women married after age 25, a structural change that made marriage before that age much less likely would result in tens of millions of permanently unmarried women.

76. Department of Health and Human Services, "Tobacco Use Among U.S. Racial/Ethnic Minority Groups" A Report of the Surgeon General," 1998, available at www.cdc.gov/nccdphp/osh/sgr-min-fs-afr.htm.

Table 9. Major Youth Risk Behaviors, Grades 9–12, 1995

Percent

Risk factor	Lifetime participation	Current participation	Frequent participation
Tobacco	71.3	34.8	16.1
Alcohol	80.4	51.6	32.6
Marijuana	42.4	25.3	4.6
Cocaine	7.0	3.1	. . .
Sex	53.1	37.9	17.8
Pregnancy	. . .	6.9	. . .
Carry a gun	. . .	7.6	. . .
Attempted suicide	. . .	8.7	. . .
Drink and drive	. . .	15.4	. . .

Source unless otherwise cited: Centers for Disease Control "Youth Risk Behavior Surveillance-United States, 1995," *Morbidity and Mortality Weekly Review* 45 (no. SS-1996): 1-86. Data available at CDC Web site, *ftp://ftp.cdc.gov/pub/ Publications/mmwr/ss/ss4504.pdf*. Definitions: For all categories, lifetime participation means one or more experiences. For tobacco, current participation means one or more cigarettes in the past thirty days. Frequent participation means one or more cigarettes on twenty of the past thirty days. For alcohol, current participation means one or more drinks in the past thirty days. frequent participation means five or more drinks on at least one occasion in the past thirty days. For marijuana, current participation means at least one smoke in the past thirty days. Frequent participation is for daily use, cited in Rhonda L. Rundle, "Smoking Marijuana, Crack Cocaine Linked to Increased Lung-Cancer Risk," August 19, 1998. *Wall Street Journal*, August 19, 1998 p. B5, citing a paper in *Journal of the National Cancer Institute*. For cocaine current participation means at least one use in the past thirty days. For sex, current participation means sexual intercourse within the previous three months. Frequent participation means four or more sexual partners during lifetime. Pregnancy refers to the percentage of students who had either been pregnant or gotten someone pregnant. Carry a gun refers to the past thirty days. Attempted suicide refers to the past year. Drink and drive refers to the past thirty days as a driver.

Look-back penalties would have been based on daily, rather than monthly, uses.

Furthermore, youth smokers make up only 2 percent of consumption, and their primary death risk is perhaps forty years distant. Much may change in that time to make cigarettes safer, quit rates generally higher, and medical care more effective. In addition, there is some evidence that the health risks of smoking increase more than proportionally with years of smoking.[77] So getting an extra 35-year-old to quit smoking seems at least as important as preventing an 18-year-old from becoming a regular smoker. Therefore, although youth smoking is a serious problem, there would still be public health concerns if it ended tomorrow.

A disproportionate emphasis on youth smoking is warranted if it is easier to stop young people from becoming regular smokers than it is to get an equal number of adults to stop, but whether this is true is unclear. Until recently, most studies indicated that youth smoking is more elastic than adult smoking, improving the case for classifying tax hikes as youth smoking measures.[78] But some recent studies have argued the

77. Peto (1986); Townsend (1993).
78. For example, the Congressional Budget Office estimates that the youth partici-

opposite.[79] As a theoretical matter, if youth smokers mistakenly assume that they can and will easily quit in a few years, a price increase will deter them from starting to smoke less than it will persuade an addicted adult that quitting will provide a significant financial benefit.

Of course, many people would argue that adults should make their own choices about smoking, and governments should do no more than correct externalities,[80] so any bill should be targeted at underage smoking. However, we believe that the real (and appropriate) goal of the public health community is to reduce smoking in all age groups and that this explains many aspects of the bill, including the emphasis on smoking cessation programs and high taxes. A problem with the youth smoking rhetoric is that if a bill narrowly focused on youth smoking is passed now, it may become harder to pass broader antismoking legislation later.

Nonprice Youth Smoking Measures

The resolution and the bill both contained marketing restrictions that could be construed as youth smoking measures and that we show later to be a sensible part of any settlement. In other ways, though, the bill moved away from its stated purpose of curtailing youth smoking. For example, it reversed the resolution to prohibit color advertising in adults-only outlets. To the extent that adults-only outlets are less likely to be sources of underage tobacco purchases, one might wish to en-

---

pation elasticity is in the range of -0.50 to -0.75, implying that a \$1.10 tax increase would drop consumption by about a third. See U.S. Department of the Treasury, "Background on Youth Smoking Elasticity Estimates," April 20, 1998. Addiction theory (Becker and Murphy, 1988) would also seem to predict a higher elasticity among people who are not yet addicted. The U.S. Treasury report noted that Canadian youth smoking fell by almost 50 percent from 1981 to 1991 as real prices rose by about 100 percent. Townsend (1993) reported that teenage smoking in Britain increased "from 20 percent to 25 percent [in] 1988–90 when the relative price of cigarettes was falling," but youth smoking participation (one cigarette a week or more for those aged 11 to 16) rose from 8 percent to 13 percent in 1988–96 despite a 26 percent increase in real prices (statement of Martin Feldman, March 19, 1998, before the Senate Commerce Committee, citing Office of National Statistics data).

79. Most notably, DeCicca, Kenkel, and Mathios (1998).

80. In this case taxes should be lowered, not raised. See note 3. This is especially true now that smoking has been banned in so many places that much of the secondhand smoke problem is between spouses, where presumably the Coase theorem applies.

courage their growth.[81] Similarly, an amendment to the bill eliminated a provision that gave the Food and Drug Administration (FDA) authority to prohibit cigarette sales in specific categories of retail outlets.[82]

Because the marketing restrictions in the bill would have largely tied the companies' hands, and because the new taxes meant the states' share of tobacco revenues would be much greater than the companies' share, strong provisions to encourage states to curtail youth smoking would seem desirable. We would advocate giving the states greater financial incentives to enforce existing laws and to develop other innovative solutions to curb youth smoking. Perhaps states should be subject to performance penalties if their youth smoking rates fail to fall as much as those in other states.[83]

In fact very few requirements were placed on states.[84] Nothing in the resolution or bill required any jurisdiction to increase the legal age for

81. Adults-only tobacco stores grew from 1 percent of the market in 1992 to 13 percent in 1998. See Barnaby J. Feder, "Tough Climate May Benefit Smoke Shops; Catering to Adults Only Is Becoming Bigger Plus," *New York Times,* August 5, 1997, D1.

82. These changes were made at the behest of the convenience store lobby. See "Thank You NACS Members! Grassroots Outpouring Helped Secure Changes in Tobacco Bill," *National Association of Convenience Stores Washington Report,* vol. 13, June 1, 1998, available at http://www.cstorecentral.com/REGISTER/RESOURCE/washrep/rf25.htm, under "past issues." The report says that it became clear that the FDA would eliminate convenience stores as a "class of trade" eligible to sell tobacco and that the provision exempting tobacco-only and adults-only stores from restrictions would have been potentially disastrous. Senator Spencer Abraham, a Republican from Michigan, is especially thanked for killing these provisions.

83. Of course, both the states and the companies might argue that youth smoking is affected by exogenous factors. Pringle (1998, p. 174) cites a 1988 in-house study by Philip Morris noting that high school students older than the age at which they were allowed to drive sharply cut back smoking when the price of gas rose in the late 1970s, but those under the driving age did not change their consumption. Pringle quotes from the report, "When it comes to a choice between smoking cigarettes or cruising around in his car, the average red-blooded American male would probably choose the latter." (So raising gasoline prices might therefore be a better way to cut youth smoking than raising cigarette prices and would have the additional benefit of reducing global warming, arguably a greater environmental hazard than environmental tobacco smoke.) A larger point is that income effects may be important for youth smoking. Townsend and others (1994) provide evidence from U.K. data that income elasticities are much larger than price elasticities for young men.

84. The main requirement was that each state should perform 250 random checks a month per million residents on retail smoking outlets for illegal sales to minors. Assuming that these checks cost a generous $50 apiece to perform, this imposed a nationwide burden of $40 million a year.

smoking, use scanner technologies to show proof of age, or put in practice several other youth smoking measures.[85] Although we do not know enough about these commonly suggested proposals to know whether they would make good policy, they have the advantage of discriminating against youth smokers much more heavily than would taxes.

"Look-Back" Penalties

The resolution included "look-back" penalties that would have increased taxes by about 8 cents a pack if youth smoking participation rates failed to fall by 35 percent over ten years.[86] A company that complied with the resolution, however, would be eligible for up to a 75 percent reduction in these penalties.[87] Because even the maximum tax, if applied to the whole industry, would not hurt the companies very much, the real problem for a company would be if it had to pay 8 cents when its competitors only had to pay 2 cents. Therefore the primary effect of the resolution's look-back penalties would have been to enforce compliance with its marketing restrictions.[88]

The much larger look-back penalties in the bill moved significantly away from a genuine youth smoking focus. If youth smoking participation fell by less than 38.4 percent over ten years, the excise tax on cigarettes would rise by 28 cents a pack plus inflation.[89] For perspective,

85. For a range of such measures, see the Tobacco Retailer Responsibility Initiative at http://stic.neu.edu/trri. See Chaloupka and Grossman (1996) and Chaloupka and Pacula (1998) and the references they cite for discussion of the effectiveness of various measures to reduce youth smoking.

86. The maximum penalty was described as $2 billion if sales remained at the current level of 24 billion packs, with reductions proportional to quantity declines. Youth smoking participation was to be measured by the University of Michigan's Monitoring the Future survey data.

87. Specifically, companies would be eligible "if they could thereafter prove to FDA that they had fully complied with the Act, had taken all reasonably available measures to reduce youth tobacco use, and had not taken any action to undermine the achievement of the required reductions."

88. Because the penalty rate per pack increased with the number of youth smokers, the companies' marginal tax cost of an extra youth smoker would have exceeded the average rate, creating some small distortions similar to the much larger ones we discuss in our analysis of the bill's look-back provision.

89. Penalties were to begin if youth smoking participation fell by less than 60 percent, reaching a maximum of about 17 cents a pack if the decline was less than 38.4 percent. Because the penalties were not tax deductible, the maximum penalty translated to an excise tax increase of about 28 cents a pack.

the maximum penalties would have been imposed even if the number of young people who regularly smoke tobacco fell to less than half the number who now smoke marijuana every month.[90] Some penalties would be imposed even if the number fell below the number who claim to have carried a gun in the previous month or attempted suicide in the previous year. Of course, the credibility of youth surveys may be doubted, but that is another reason to question their use in determining tax rates.

So the most likely effect of these look-backs would be an increase in the tax rate on all smoking, with no marginal incentive to reduce youth rates. If, however, youth participation were to decline by more than 38.4 percent, firms' incentives would become bizarre, as we now show.

The look-back penalty per pack was increasing in youth participation in the range in which youth participation was between 38.4 and 60 percent of its base level, so the marginal tax rate on a pack of cigarettes therefore would exceed the look-back rate.[91] For example, if ten years from now Philip Morris sold an extra 100 million packs of Marlboro and this created 18,000 extra youth participants, the look-back rate would rise by about 1 cent.[92] If Philip Morris were selling 6 billion

90. In 1995, 27.6 percent of students in grade 11 had smoked marijuana in the previous thirty days; Centers for Disease Control, "Youth Risk Behavior Surveillance—United States, 1995," *Morbidity and Mortality Weekly Review*, vol. 45, no. SS-4 (1996), pp. 1–86. Data available at CDC Web site, www.cdc.gov/nccdphp/. In the same year, 21.6 percent of 12th graders reported smoking one or more cigarettes a day (CDC table, "Smoking status of high school seniors—United States, Monitoring the Future Project, 1976–1996," available at the same web site.) See also table 9, which implies that daily youth smoking would have to fall to 40 percent of monthly marijuana use to avoid maximum penalties.

The Joint Committee on Taxation estimates that penalties at or near the maximum would be paid. See Joint Committee on Taxation, "Description and Analysis of Revenue-Related Provisions of S. 1415 Relating to National Tobacco Policy as Modified by the Manager's Amendment," JCX-45-98, June 3, 1998.

91. Assuming, of course, that youth participation is increasing in total sales.

92. This estimate assumes a decline in youth smoking of between 38.4 and 50 percent and initially 3 million youth smokers, based on a population of 19 million and a daily participation rate of about 16 percent (see table 9). The penalty would increase by 1 cent for each 1 percent, or 30,000 participants, but adjusting for the nondeductibility of the penalties makes the rate 1 cent for every 18,000 participants. Marlboro sales were 8.2 billion packs in 1998 (Philip Morris 10k report), and Marlboro was estimated to have 60 percent of the youth market, implying 22,000 youth smokers for every 100 million packs. See "Comparison of Advertising to Brand Preference in Adolescents and

packs by then, the cost to the company of this increase in the look-back rate would be $60 million, making the marginal tax rate on Marlboro about 60 cents above the average look-back rate.[93] But if youth participation were equally sensitive to an increase in the sales of Lorillard's Newport, Lorillard's marginal rate would be only 10 cents above the look-back rate, because Lorillard is only a sixth the size of Philip Morris.[94] Because the largest firms would have marginal costs that are furthest above average, they would tend to lose market share in equilibrium. The reasoning is the mirror image of that for fixed-revenue taxation, where the large firms benefited (in terms of market share) by having marginal costs that were the furthest below average.

Because prices reflect marginal rather than average taxes, more than 100 percent of the look-back penalties would be passed through to consumers. So if the decline in youth participation did exceed 38.4 percent, the look-backs would probably raise industry profits.[95]

The bill also contained company-specific look-backs, which would have had very different effects. Within ten years companies would have to pay $1,000 (not tax deductible) for every estimated youth smoker in excess of 40 percent of their starting amount. So if there are currently 3 million youth smokers and youth participation fell by 30 percent, the companies would be liable for the equivalent of $1.5 billion in pretax profits, or 12.5 cents a pack if overall volume were 12 billion. Again,

---

Adults, 1993,'' cited in full in note 61. This source claims that 60 percent of youth smokers report preferring Marlboro, 13.3 percent Camel, and 12.7 percent Newport.

93. Total smoking was estimated to fall 46 percent between 1999 and 2007, to 12.3 billion packs, by the Joint Committee on Taxation, "Description and Analysis of Revenue-Related Provisions," JCX-45-98, June 3, 1998. If Philip Morris's sales fell by the same percentage, it would sell about 6 billion packs.

94. For example, if the look-back penalty were 20 cents, the marginal tax cost to Lorillard of selling an extra pack of Newport would be 30 cents in all. But each extra pack of Newport that Lorillard sold would cost Philip Morris 60 cents.

95. The companies would benefit most if youth smoking fell 38.4 to 50 percent. If youth smoking fell by 50 to 60 percent, the marginal impact of an extra smoker on the tax rate would be much lower than if the rate fell by less than 50 percent, so the difference between marginal and average rates would be less. The FTC recognized that look-backs could facilitate higher industry prices and profits (conversation with Jonathan Baker, director of the Bureau of Economics). There might be a strong incentive for firms to collude to get youth smoking to decline by more than 38.4 percent to create this large wedge between marginal and average taxes. The companies' protests about these penalties is an indication, however, that they did not believe that the maximum penalties would be avoided.

marginal rates could be very different from average rates—probably higher but possibly lower, depending on the elasticity of youth partici- pation with respect to overall volume.[96]

The penalties would also have a tremendously different impact across companies. Philip Morris would probably have to pay hundreds of millions of dollars a year, while Brown and Williamson (which would be unlikely to have to pay any penalty because of a de minimis exemp- tion) would see its profits soar as Philip Morris raised its prices in response to its penalties.[97]

Although taxing young people's favorite brands more heavily seems a good idea in principle, this plan has problems. First, the way the penalties are calculated makes them closer to fines than taxes. The penalties would undoubtedly be challenged by Philip Morris, Lorillard, and RJR if they were passed without a global settlement.[98] Companies could reasonably argue that if they are not breaking any laws about selling to youth (they sell only to jobbers), they should not be subject to such fines.[99] The companies could also contest whether a survey of high school students was adequate evidence to impose the large penal-

96. For example, if Marlboro gained 18,000 youth smokers from selling an extra 100 million packs, its marginal tax rate would be 30 cents a pack. That is, 18,000 smokers times 1,000 dollars divided by 100 million packs equals 18 cents nondeductible, which is the equivalent of a 30 cent excise tax. The marginal rate would certainly exceed the average rate if the elasticity of youth participation with respect to overall consump- tion were 0.6 or greater but might be lower if consumption and youth participation had little relation. Specifically, if youth participation fell by $100X$ percent, $X < 0.6$, the marginal rate would equal the average rate times $(1 - X)/(0.6 - X)$ times the elasticity of youth consumption with respect to overall consumption. So, for example, if youth smoking fell by 40 percent, the marginal rate would exceed the average rate as long as the elasticity was greater than 0.33.

97. The de minimis exemption would apply because very few youth smokers claim Brown and Williamson's discount products as their "usual brands." With its competi- tors' average costs increasing, and their marginal costs increasing even more, Brown and Williamson would be well positioned to increase both its margins and its market share. For example, if its competitors passed on cost increases of 12.5 cents a pack, Brown and Williamson could choose to go along, raising its profits from about 20 cents to 32.5 cents a pack. An ardently antitobacco senior congressional staffer, arguing for even stronger brand-specific penalties, claimed that he had talked to Brown and Wil- liamson and that they considered such penalties "very reasonable" (private telephone conversation).

98. Brown and Williamson and Liggett would effectively be exempted from the company-specific penalties by de minimis rules.

99. If the companies violate the marketing restrictions, they would be liable for the penalties prescribed for those violations.

ties in the bill. For example, if about 50,000 students are surveyed (as is currently the case) and 19 million youths are in grades 8 through 12, then on the margin a company would owe $380,000 for each additional young person who said he or she usually smoked one of its brands.[100] Beyond that, if smokers typically smoke a ''usual'' premium brand but sometimes smoke discount and less popular premium brands, the penalties on the leading brands will be disproportionate to the fraction of youth smoking that their brands account for. Finally, if companies are left with any nonprice weapons to affect sales, their incentives will be as much to get youths to switch to other brands as to get them to quit smoking.[101]

Given the marketing restrictions in the bill, the main effect of the company-specific look-backs would have been to raise further the price of certain brands of cigarettes.[102] But this could probably could have been done in a more straightforward manner. For example, ad valorem taxes might have a broadly similar effect without the problems. It is our belief that the designers of the look-back penalties had other agendas besides youth smoking: a desire to raise cigarette taxes even higher and to punish the most profitable manufacturers. The badly flawed design of these provisions relates to the political decision to cast them in terms of their impact on youth smoking.

Marketing Restrictions

Both the resolution and the bill contained marketing restrictions roughly along the lines of earlier proposals by the Food and Drug Administration. These restrictions seem to be a good idea. If youth participation is highly sensitive to promotion, marketing restrictions are

100. Antismoking teenagers could do little to hurt the industry more than falsely reporting that they smoked one of the leading brands.

101. The analysis is similar to Ayres and Levitt's (1998) comparison of The Club and Lojack as systems to reduce car theft. The Club, a metal bar locked to the steering wheel, is a device to encourage criminals to steal someone else's car. Lojack, a hidden device that enables police to find stolen vehicles quickly, discourages overall theft. Company-specific penalties create Club-like incentives. Of course, companies will be most concerned with affecting reported, rather than actual, youth smoking.

102. If the bill had dropped the resolution's marketing restrictions, or if they had been overturned in court, the company-specific look-backs could also have been important in discouraging youth-oriented marketing.

Table 10. Cigarette Marketing Expenditures, by Category, 1996
Millions of dollars unless otherwise specified

Category	Industry expenditure	Percent of total
Promotional allowances	2.15 billion	42.1
Coupons and retail value added promotions (e.g., free lighters)	1.31 billion	25.6
Specialty item distribution (e.g., branded clothing)	544.3	10.7
Outdoor advertising	292.3	5.7
Point-of-sale ads	252.6	4.9
Magazines	243.0	4.8
Public entertainment	171.2	3.4
Direct mail	38.7	0.8
Transit advertising	28.9	0.6
Sampling distribution	15.9	0.3
Newspapers	14.1	0.3
Internet	0.4	0
Testimonials	0	0

Source: Federal Trade Commission (1998, table 3E). Available at http://www.ftc.gov/os.1998/9803/index/htm#17. The FTC also collects data on expenditures on sporting events, which may be allocated among several categories. The total in 1996 was $85 million. No money was spent on having cigarettes appear on television or in movies. No money has been spent on testimonials since 1988 (U.S. Department of Agriculture 1997, tables 3C, 3D).

a good way to target youth consumption, and the companies will not lose much because the profits from the youth market are largely competed away by advertising. Indeed, if marketing expenditures serve largely to redistribute a fixed supply of new customers, the restrictions may actually raise company profits.[103] Also, marketing restrictions do not have the adverse distributional consequences of a tax increase.

Table 10 shows the FTC's breakdown for industry spending in 1996 on advertising and promotion. The proposed restrictions affected virtually every category listed other than the first two. The resolution banned tobacco brand names, logos, and selling messages on non-tobacco merchandise; prohibited sponsorship of sporting and cultural events in the name, logo, or selling message of a tobacco product brand; and restricted tobacco advertising to black text on white background except in adult publications and adult-only facilities. It required tobacco advertising to carry a statement of intended use (''nicotine delivery

103. Of course, if marketing simply redistributes a fixed number of customers between the discount and premium segments and does not affect youth smoking, the marketing restrictions will serve no public health purpose and may hurt the profits of the premium producers.

device'') and banned offers of nontobacco items or gifts (t-shirts, gym bags, caps) based on proof of purchase of tobacco products. It also banned human images and cartoon characters like the Marlboro Man and Joe Camel in all tobacco advertising and on tobacco product packages; all outdoor tobacco product advertising, including advertising in enclosed stadiums and indoor advertising directed outdoors; and tobacco product advertising on the Internet unless designed to be inaccessible in or from the United States. Finally, it limited point-of-sale advertising to black-on-white, text-only signs and regulated the number and size of signs (except in adult-only facilities). The McCain bill was similar to the resolution, except that it also extended some of the restrictions on other outlets to adult-only stores.

Based on the list of current advertising vehicles employed by the industry, very little would be left other than free cigarette lighters, black-and-white point-of-sale and magazine advertising, some color ads in adult-only facilities, and promotional allowances and coupons. Although promotional allowances and coupons are the largest categories of ''marketing expenditures,'' they are really forms of price cuts that the companies use to price discriminate among retailers and consumers, respectively, and the effect of banning them seems unclear.[104]

In principle, there are many reasons to promote cigarette brands. Companies may wish to steal customers from other brands or defend their current customers from other brands, but if these were the primary motivations, companies would gain from (and not object to) marketing restrictions.[105] They may wish to deter entry or promote new brands,

---

104. The literature about the effects of permitting price discrimination is mixed in its conclusions. For a monopoly firm selling to segmented markets, Varian (1989) shows that price discrimination has ambiguous effects on total output, and if demand curves are linear, price discrimination leaves total output unchanged. In the case of oligopoly, which is more relevant here, the effects of price discrimination are still ambiguous, but there seems a greater presumption that price discrimination may increase total output. For example, Corts (1998) proposes a duopoly model in which price discrimination causes all prices to fall (thus output rises). Armstrong and Vickers (1998) analyze a duopoly model in a Hotelling framework and show that price discrimination causes total output to increase whenever the products are sufficiently close substitutes. Futhermore, banning price discrimination may facilitate collusion by improving price coordination among the oligopolists. See Ordover and Panzar (1980) for discussion of quantity discounts to retailers. Recent work by Morton (1997) and Elzinga and Mills (1997) on prescription drugs also suggests that banning price discrimination may raise prices.

105. Although some individual companies might object, we would not expect in-

but neither of these activities looms large given the current state of the industry and the ban on radio and television commercials for smoking. There may also be a desire to influence the media and social culture generally, but free-riding would make marketing for this purpose unlikely for any company except Philip Morris.[106] The most compelling reason why marketing restrictions might harm shareholders is that marketing can help maintain a brand's premium status, allowing it to continue charging a premium price.[107]

Firm managers may oppose marketing restrictions because the firms are marketing-driven organizations and the managers wish to retain their jobs and empires, but that is is no reason for shareholders to value marketing. Similarly, marketing may be important for attracting new customers, which is a further reason for executives who value their future jobs to fight to defend it. As we showed earlier, however, there is likely to be little net profit gain to the industry in being able to advertise for new customers because the marketing competition will dissipate a lot of the profits that the new customers generate.[108]

Ironically, the more sensitive youth smoking is to youth-oriented marketing, the larger the fraction of the present value of profits from

---

dustry associations to object to restrictions. But in fact the U.K. Tobacco Manufacturers' Association, for example, objects very strongly to marketing restrictions.

106. Warner, Goldenhar, and McCaughlin (1992) show that magazines' coverage of the health risks of smoking is negatively related to the proportion of advertising revenues derived from tobacco advertising (and not merely related to the binary variable of whether tobacco advertising is accepted or not, which suggests the direction of causation may not only be from magazines' attitudes to choice of advertising). The Smee report (U.K. Department of Health, 1992) argues that it is likely that some magazines have modified their stance in deference to tobacco advertisers.

Marsh and Matheson (1983) show that 44 percent of smokers and 26 percent of nonsmokers agree with the statement that "smoking can't be really dangerous or the Government would ban cigarette advertising," despite the government's health education program. See also the Smee report. Tobacco advertising and tobacco company sponsorship of sports and other activities may also increase the social acceptability of smoking.

107. When marketing a brand to increase the willingness to pay of consumers who already prefer that brand, a firm is in the position of a monopolist, and there may thus be less dissipation of rents than when the oligopolists compete for a new customer. Of course, the distinction between different kinds of marketing is very fuzzy.

108. See the section on the value to the companies of the youth market. So the traditional argument that companies oppose marketing restrictions because of the impact on recruiting new customers (see, for instance, Tye, Warner, and Glantz, 1987), would seem to have to rely on the agency-theory argument of the previous sentence.

today's youth smokers that will be competed away through the marketing competition. So even if advertising is very important for recruiting new customers, restrictions that eliminate the competition for youth smokers are likely to reduce the market valuations of the companies only slightly and will also increase short-term profits. Of course, if the industrywide number of new smokers is insensitive to marketing efforts, firms may actually gain if youth marketing is banned. These results are consistent with the tenor of negotiations over the resolution, in which the companies agreed to give up Joe Camel and the Marlboro Man after the very first day of meetings.[109] We develop these points further in a simple model in appendix C. The bottom line is that strong marketing restrictions oriented against youth smoking are an efficient part of any deal.[110]

Special Interests

The bill, in particular, catered to a variety of special interests with a host of economically unjustifiable provisions. The most notable among these were provisions rewarding Liggett, small manufacturers, and the trial lawyers involved in the deal.

Liggett

Liggett argued that it should be rewarded because it had in effect turned state's evidence by settling early with the state attorneys general and turning over secret industry documents. The amended version of the bill accordingly exempted it from the taxes so long as its market share remained under 3 percent (more than twice its share at the time). Assuming cigarette sales would be about 19 billion packs once the tax of $1.10 a pack is instituted, the exemption is potentially worth $630 million a year. Because Liggett's market share is well below 3 percent, it would have to raise prices by a little less than $1.10 to benefit

109. See Mollenkamp and others (1998, p. 137). For perspective, the negotiations took about two and a half months overall (April 4–June 20).
110. We are assuming marketing is undesirable from the standpoint of public health. Marketing could be very desirable if it were to facilitate entry of new, less-toxic products.

maximally from its tax break.[111] Liggett's state settlements require it to turn over 27.5 to 30 percent of its pretax profits to the states, so the net pretax benefit to the company would perhaps be closer to $400 million a year.[112] Still, this is a remarkable annual payment for a firm with a total market value of around $100 million presettlement.[113]

We suspect this provision could only have passed because of confusion between the concepts of exempting Liggett from being economically punished by the bill, and exempting Liggett from paying the "damages" or "settlement payments," a confusion that would be less likely if the payments had been referred to honestly as taxes. If the aim were to exempt Liggett from punishment, a simple solution would be to treat it as a new manufacturer. This would imply exempting it from the $10 billion up-front payment and giving it a tax credit for any amounts it pays to the states under its state settlement agreements. A more generous approach—it is arguable that Liggett's betrayal of its competitors was a crucial turning point in the war against Big Tobacco—would be to reward it out of the payments that would otherwise be paid to the attorneys for their part in the victory.

From an economic viewpoint Liggett should probably be closed down (or merged into another firm). Its costs are much higher and its average quality lower than the those of the big four, implying substantial deadweight losses, and few appear concerned about maintaining price competition in this industry.[114]

111. The company has claimed that it will raise its list prices along with the other manufacturers, but obviously it will have an enormous incentive to provide retailers with whatever incentives it takes to get to a 3 percent share. Given the large market share of deep discount cigarettes before Marlboro Friday, it seems likely that Liggett can return to 3 percent of the market while increasing its prices by close to a dollar.

112. The primary beneficiary would have been Bennet LeBow, a controversial businessman who controlled Brooke Group, which owns Liggett. On LeBow, see Laurie P. Cohen, "Ready Credit: Head of Brooke Group Draws on Its Coffers to Tune of Millions," *Wall Street Journal*, July 30, 1993, p. A1.

Liggett's state settlements are available at http:///www.ag.ohio.gov/agpubs/Tobacco/liggett1.htm.

113. It would have been much cheaper to buy control of Liggett, photocopy its secret papers, and close it down, writing off the cost as part of the litigation expense, than to give the company even a fraction of the proposed subsidy.

114. In any case, giving Liggett a fixed market share removes the company as a force for holding down profit margins, because the rest of the firms then know that they will end up with 97 percent of the market, no matter what.

More generally, mergers in this industry might be less undesirable than usual, al-

Small Manufacturers

The Senate Commerce Committee version of the bill gave small companies a 75 percent tax reduction on the first 150 million packs they sold and a 50 percent reduction on the next 150 million packs.[115] The implication is that a new manufacturer (or an importer) could market 150 million packs of generic cigarettes at an 80 cents a pack advantage over Philip Morris. This incentive would have swamped the market with billions of packs of generic cigarettes from small labels. The Treasury and FTC noticed this problem and persuaded the Senate to cut back the provision to apply only to the Kentucky chewing tobacco companies it was originally designed to protect.

Lawyers' Fees

Because it was widely agreed that even the smallest amount of money the trial lawyers would ask for would seem outrageous, neither the bill nor the resolution quantified fees but instead left them to be determined by arbitrators.[116] State settlements adopted the technique of announcing a settlement with lawyers' fees to be paid in addition, so that the governments could disclaim spending the billions of dollars. Knowing that if the trial lawyers were not bought off, the whole deal might fall apart, the companies offered to pay the lawyers an annuity of up to $500 million a year, presumably in proportion to each company's sales, as part of any national settlement.[117]

Jeffrey E. Harris, an MIT economist and longtime industry critic, who has served as plaintiffs' expert witness in three major cases, including the Florida medicaid suit, proposed a scheme under which lawyers from the states that have contingency fee agreements would receive 12.9 to 14.6 percent of the revenues that would go to those

---

though an argument could be made that Liggett is valuable because it mostly sells discount brands, if those brands have less appeal to youth smokers.

115. See section 403(d)(B).

116. There would be three arbitrators, one chosen by the lawyers, one by the companies, and one jointly. Smokers, who would pay most of the costs, would have no say.

117. See Milo Geyelin, "Tobacco Firms Quiet on Fees to Be Paid to Plaintiffs' Lawyers under Settlement," *Wall Street Journal,* December 15, 1997, p. B16.

states.[118] These rates were consistent with the fees that had already been negotiated in the Texas and Minnesota state cases.[119] The Harris plan would cost at least $15 billion in present value based on the bill's taxes and would be financed by a "lawyer's tax" of 8 cents a pack.[120] Put another way, it would amount to an average of more than $30 million apiece for 470 class action lawyers for a deal that yields smokers no money.[121]

The week the bill died Republicans succeeded in putting caps on legal fees. The cap for lawyers who filed suit before December 31, 1994, was $4,000 an *hour*.[122] Richard Scruggs, who would have had his fees very sharply reduced by this limitation, argued that the provision was unconstitutional.[123] Richard A. Daynard, chairman of the To-

118. Jeffrey E. Harris, "Written Testimony Before the Subcommittee on Courts and Intellectual Property, Committee of the Judiciary, U.S. House of Representatives, Oversight Hearing on Attorneys Fees and the Proposed Global Tobacco Settlement," available at www.mit.edu/people/jeffrey.

119. In Texas a 15 percent contingency fee for the lawyers, projected to be about $90 million a year forever, adjusted for inflation, has been ruled reasonable by Judge David Folsom; see Scott Baldauf, "Texas-Size Lawyers' Fee Rankle in State Tobacco Suit," *Christian Science Monitor,* April 13, 1998. One calculation indicated that these fees come to as much as $92,000 an hour; see Barry Meier and Jill Abramson, "Tobacco War's New Front: Lawyers Fight for Big Fees," *New York Times,* June 9, 1998, p. A1. These fees mean that if the Texas settlement holds, every pack sold anywhere in the United States will include a ⅜ cent tax for select members of the Texas plaintiffs' bar. In Minnesota, Attorney General Hubert Humphrey has already defended a proposal to award plaintiffs' attorneys $565.9 million in fees and expenses over five years; see David Shaffer, "Minneapolis-Based Law Firm to Collect Millions from Tobacco Settlement," *St. Paul Pioneer Press,* June 2, 1998. Although this fee was widely reported as 7 percent, the lawyers would be paid over five years while the state would be paid over twenty-five years. Discounting payments at 10 percent, the lawyers' fee was closer to 17 percent. In both cases the amounts were effectively financed by raising the national excise tax.

120. This estimate assumes a tax rate of $1.10 a pack, Harris's estimates of lawyers' fees of 6.65 to 7.14 cents a dollar, and Harris's estimates of the present value based on the resolution's taxes. It also assumes that firms would divide fee payments by future market shares, effectively turning them into a national excise tax.

121. The estimate of 470 lawyers comes from Paul A. Gigot, "$50 Million Men: Tobacco Lawyers Become Sultans," *Wall Street Journal,* June 27, 1997, p. A14.

122. The caps were $2,000 an hour for those who filed before April 1, 1997; $1,000 an hour for those who filed before June 15, 1998; and $500 an hour for those who filed after June 15.

123. Jeffrey Taylor, "Senate Votes to Selectively Limit Fees of Trial Attorneys in

bacco Products Liability Project at Northeastern University School of Law, argued that the caps would "protect the tobacco cartel by effectively quashing tobacco litigation forever."[124]

The Senate was surely right to place some limits on fees: We believe there are crucial differences between litigation, under which the lawyers' contingency fee contracts would apply, and legislation. In particular, in a conventional class action lawsuit, parties can choose not to participate in the class. Would Kentucky be allowed to opt out of the bill, its citizens not paying the tax increase and the state not receiving its share of the tax revenues?[125] No. Could a settlement make as yet unborn companies be liable for damages of $1.10 for every pack of cigarettes they sell, a crucial component of the bill? Of course not. Because most of the payments would be taxes rather than damages, and all would be the result of legislation rather than litigation, the contingency agreements seem to be of limited relevance.[126] Furthermore, as a general principle, we are very troubled by the prospect of a group of private citizens getting paid a percentage of a tax increase they helped pass.

Tobacco Cases," *Wall Street Journal*, June 17, 1998, p. A4. Scruggs is in line for contingencies from more than twenty states.

124. See Tobacco Products Liability Project, "Law Professor Says Senate Bill Would Protect Tobacco Cartel by Effectively Quashing Tobacco Litigation Forever," press release, June 17, 1998, available at http://www.tobacco.neu.edu/Congress/GortonPR.htm. Daynard was a member of the trial lawyer team in Florida, where attorneys have been asking for fees with a present value of $1.3 billion just for that state settlement. About that controversy, Daynard said, "If the money is being distributed, I want my share, but I'm not going to get involved" in fee disputes. See John D. McKinnon, "State's Lawyers Battle over Tobacco-Suit Fees," *Wall Street Journal*, September 10, 1997, *Florida Journal*, p. F2.

125. Similarly, an individual smoker who was part of the *Castano* class action would not be allowed to withdraw from the "settlement," and avoid the $1.10 per pack tax increase in return for forgoing the "free" smoking cessation materials that would be provided in the bill. Smokers might regard the situation as Orwellian: "their" lawyers would be claiming a great victory with a net financial cost to the clients of several hundred dollars a year. States can refuse their share of settlement revenues but cannot avoid taxes on their citizens.

126. If the bill maintained its fixed-revenue taxation, part of the cost to firms would probably not have been passed through to consumers, and that part might reasonably be regarded as damage payments.

Individual State Settlements

Before the demise of the bill, settlements modeled on the resolution were negotiated in Florida, Minnesota, Mississippi, and Texas. These deals all included scaled-down marketing restrictions, lump-sum payments, and national excise taxes, called "damage payments," as in the national tobacco resolution. That is, the revenues for each state would be collected nationally even though they would be distributed only to plaintiffs in that state.[127] Congress, of course, has the right to legislate a national tax that is economically equivalent to a collusive agreement. And Texas, for example, has the right to raise prices within its own state.[128] But the idea that Texas should be able to impose taxes on cigarettes manufactured in Virginia and sold in Kentucky seems a terrible precedent.

Another unappealing feature of states being able to impose national taxes on cigarette companies is that other state legislatures will feel compelled to pass laws similar to Florida's Medicaid Third Party Liability Act and sue the companies so that they can get their fair shares of national tobacco taxes.[129] Maryland and Vermont rapidly did exactly that.[130] States that do not wish to sue the industry, or that are unwilling to distort their state constitutions to improve their bargaining power in this case, will find their residents paying new tobacco taxes but not benefiting from the revenues. Similarly, judges who have to face elections will have an incentive to bias their rulings in favor of the state.[131]

127. In fact all firms raised national prices after the Florida and Mississippi deals and again on the days after the Texas and Minnesota deals.

128. Although an agreement that raised prices throughout Texas would still be collusive if the "damages" were not interpreted as a tax, it might fall under the principle of "state action," which is what allows cities and taxi owners to fix fares without running afoul of the federal antitrust laws.

129. Even North Carolina Attorney General Michael Easley called on his state's legislature to repeal a law that he says makes it virtually impossible for the state to sue the industry. See "However Unhappily, Easley Does His Duty," *Wilmington, N.C. Sunday Star-News*, July 26, 1998, p. 6E. The dismissal of Indiana's suit in state court increased the pressure.

130. Those states "also stripped the industry of its traditional defenses, such as that smoking carries well-known risks." See Tara Parker-Pope and Milo Geyelin, "Tobacco: Without Legislation, Price Rises Could Ease," *Wall Street Journal*, June 19, 1998, p. B1.

131. For example, in Minnesota the companies were not allowed to argue that the state estimates of medicaid costs were overstated because they did not allow for the

A further troubling aspect of the state cases is that they are negatively related to any losses the states might be suffering because of smoking. Table 11 lists taxes state by state, as well as whether the state had sued the tobacco companies by June 1998. Not surprisingly, states that already charged higher taxes to smokers were the ones filing these cases, which are then settled for yet higher taxes on smokers.

Why were the state deals structured as national taxes? First, each state would like nothing better than to get its tax revenue from the residents of other states if it could. Second, because the states demanding the damages already had high taxes, new state taxes to finance the deals would increase smuggling between states.[132] Third, a crucial difference between the individual state settlements and the resolution is that the state deals apply only to the four large firms, and not to Liggett (because of its prior settlement) or to any new entrant. If the state deals were financed exclusively by in-state damage payments, they would create a large cost advantage for Liggett and the fringe firms relative to the major companies and would enable aggressive entrants and Liggett to dominate the generic business and seriously damage the premium segment for the major companies. By basing damages on national sales the deals have given Liggett and the fringe a small, nondisruptive national advantage of a few cents a pack.

An implication is that while the four state deals were not enough to

---

premature deaths of smokers. They were also not allowed to argue that the state should be allowed to sue only for its part of medicaid expenses, rather than for the federal government's part as well. A reasonable case can be made (at least to an economist) that these rulings were flawed, particularly because what was really being negotiated was a tax hike on smokers, rather than liability payments by the companies. One might not want to reduce a company's liability based on the "savings" from smokers who die early, but it is quite another thing to tell smokers who are being asked to pay for the externalities they create that their shorter life expectancy should not be credited. The presiding judge was removed from the case shortly after the settlement was announced. See Associated Press, "Fitzpatrick Removed from Tobacco Case," *Minneapolis Star Tribune*, June 10, 1998, p. B3.

132. In the United Kingdom, where smuggling in contraband is relatively difficult, tobacco smuggled from foreign countries accounts for about 20 percent of cigarette consumption and about two-thirds of hand-rolled tobacco consumption. See Richard Tomkins, "Failing to Kick the Habit," *Financial Times*, June 26, 1998, p. 22; and John Willman, "Customs to Clamp Down on Smuggling," *Financial Times*, July 29, 1998, p. 8. In the United States the classic example of interstate smuggling is between New Hampshire and Massachusetts. For example, in 1996 taxes (including sales taxes) were 63 cents a pack lower in New Hampshire than in Massachusetts; per capita sales were 74.6 packs in Massachusetts and 158.0 in New Hampshire.

Table 11. State Cigarette Taxation 1996, and Propensity to Sue

Cents per pack

State	Excise tax	Sales tax	Consumer price	Suing as of June 1998
Alabama	16.5	7	167.4	No
Alaska	29	0	214.4	
Arizona	58	11	222.0	
Arkansas	31.5	8	181.3	
California	37	14	200.3	
Colorado	20	0	174.4	
Connecticut	50	13	208.5	
Delaware	24	0	171.9	No
Florida	33.9	11	182.7	
Georgia	12	5	158.9	
Hawaii	60	9	242.8	
Idaho	28	9	184.4	
Illinois	44	12	198.7	
Indiana	15.5	8	156.3	
Iowa	36	10	189.3	
Kansas	24	8	171.3	
Kentucky	3	9	145.6	No
Louisiana	20	7	166.9	
Maine	37	11	190.2	
Maryland	36	10	190.7	
Massachusetts	76	12	244.6	
Michigan	75	14	233.8	
Minnesota	48	14	216.8	
Mississippi	18	12	168.6	
Missouri	17	7	163.4	
Montana	18	0	164.9	
Nebraska	34	9	184.8	No
Nevada	35	13	198.5	
New Hampshire	25	0	176.6	
New Jersey	40	12	194.6	
New Mexico	21	9	176.0	
New York	56	9	222.5	
North Carolina	5	6	152.0	No
North Dakota	44	12	194.1	No
Ohio	24	8	166.8	
Oklahoma	23	8	172.0	
Oregon	38	0	197.6	
Pennsylvania	31	11	176.5	
Rhode Island	61	15	217.0	
South Carolina	7	8	153.9	
South Dakota	33	7	181.7	
Tennessee	13	13	161.1	No
Texas	41	12	189.8	
Utah	26.5	9	186.2	
Vermont	44	10	201.9	
Virginia	2.5	7	159.6	No
Washington	82.5	17	265.1	
West Virginia	17	10	160.9	
Wisconsin	44	10	200.7	
Wyoming	12	0	164.1	No

Sources: first 3 columns, Tobacco Institute (1997). Data are as of November 1, 1996. Data for last column from the State Tobacco Information Center Web site at *www.stic.neu.edu.*

a. The average tax in states with suits is 45 cents. The average tax in nonsuing states is 24 cents.

encourage entry, the companies could not make similar deals with all fifty states unless smaller firms and new entrants could be required to participate.[133] The companies probably settled the first four state claims to minimize bad publicity while a national deal was pending, but this concern became less salient once the McCain bill was killed.[134] Furthermore, state settlements could not provide any protection from *Castano* cases, so any deal negotiated jointly by the remaining states would have to be more modest than either the resolution or the bill.

The November Multistate Agreement

On November 23, 1998, the attorneys general of all the remaining states signed a reported $206 billion settlement of their medicaid claims against the tobacco industry. Moving in our suggested direction of reducing lump-sum payments, the deal actually consists of just $2.4 billion to be paid in proportion to the firms' market values, followed by a national cigarette tax that will ultimately settle at about 35 cents a pack.[135] Marketing restrictions are weaker than in the resolution, resembling those negotiated earlier in the individual state deals.[136] There are

133. The entry problem would be even more severe if entrants were able to buy the rights to the names of premium brands while maintaining their tax advantages. In this situation the firms might escape their liabilities by selling off their trademarks and liquidating themselves. Liggett is already structured so that its trademarks are owned by separate, wholly owned subsidiaries. Therefore it would be necessary to make transferred brands still liable for tax.

134. During this period the companies also settled the *Broin v. Philip Morris* suit concerning environmentally transmitted smoke, although the scientific evidence behind such claims is much weaker than the evidence on direct smoking. In addition to the companies' desires to avoid negative publicity, the willingness of the attorneys to accept a settlement that gave the plaintiffs no money was crucial, as was the companies' agreement not to contest the lawyers' fees at the hearing to determine the fairness of the settlement. The lawyers, a husband-and-wife team, received $49 million. See Richard Tomkins, "Justice Is Blind," *Financial Times,* July 17, 1998, p. 21.

135. See Gary Black and Jon Rooney, "AG Settlement: Less Onerous Payment Stream Could Fuel Positive Revisions. 43–45 States In." November 16, 1998. Available at www.tobacco.org.

136. The marketing restrictions include bans on billboards and transit signs, on promotional merchandise with brand logos, on product placements in movies, and on cartoons in advertising (including Joe Camel); a limit of one sports sponsorship per company per year; and a limit on the size of indoor and outdoor signage to 14 square feet. See Gary Black and Jon Rooney, "New AG Settlement: Critical Investment Question–Not When, But How Many," November 11, 1998. Available at www.tobacco.org.

no look-back provisions. At the same time, the companies receive relief only from the state cases and not from private litigation.

The artifice of describing the tax increase as ''damages'' implies that without further action, the payments would apply only to the Big Four. New entrants and smaller rivals, most prominently Liggett, would have a 40-cent advantage (including the earlier similar settlements with Florida, Minnesota, Mississippi, and Texas) on a product that costs only 20 cents to manufacture.[137] Therefore, significant sections of the agreement focus on alternately providing carrots and sticks to encourage the small companies to sign.

On one hand, a small company that voluntarily subjects itself to the tax increase will be allowed to keep for itself all tax revenues on sales up to 125 percent of 1997 levels.[138] Given current wholesale prices of about 34 cents a pack for small firm generics, this subsidy will significantly exceed current annual revenues for these firms, so their profits will exceed their current sales.[139] The deal gives Liggett alone the right to receive this subsidy on 400 million packs a year.

On the other hand, the states are to pass model statutes requiring small companies that do not sign the agreement to make alternative ''trust fund'' payments, nominally as a bond against future legal claims, designed to bankrupt any nonsignatories.[140] States that do not pass the model statute risk forfeiting their entire share of the tax revenue; any who pass the law but whose state courts declare it invalid will lose up to 65 percent. So states have a significant incentive to appoint judges who will rubber-stamp this provision of the deal.

---

137. By the time of the deal, the smaller rivals held a little more than 2 percent of the market. See note 5.

138. There was talk of changing the base period for the small firms' tax subsidies to 1998, which would give these firms an incentive to give away as many cigarettes as possible during the last five weeks of 1998. See Gary Black and Jon Rooney, ''Philip Morris/Liggett Deal: Has Philip Morris Re-Armed the Enemy?'' November 23, 1998. Available at www.tobacco.org.

139. See Gary Black and Jon Rooney, ''The Renegade Rift: Why RJR and B&W Will Come Back to the Table,'' August 28, 1998. Available at www.tobacco.org.

140. Payments would equal the same amount per pack as the taxes under the deal, but would be nondeductible. A payment of 35 cents a pack would require a price increase of about 55 cents a pack, putting a nonsignatory at a 20-cent price disadvantage. Furthermore, the trust fund payments would cover all packs sold rather than just those in excess of 125 percent of base sales. The approach is similar to that in the resolution; see note 33.

Liggett argued that if it became a nonsignatory, it should be exempt from the "trust fund" payments, because of its earlier settlement with the states. If Liggett had won this argument in court, it would have been tremendously damaging to the settlement. So Philip Morris agreed to pay Liggett $150 million to sign the deal, and another $150 million for three brands that were probably worth about half that amount. In addition, Liggett retained its annual tax subsidy of more than $100 million a year.[141]

Small cigarette companies are likely to flood into any state, including any of the four that are not parties to the current deal, that does not successfully enact a model statute. To insure the industry against this, the states have promised to pay the Big Four as much as $1.00 a pack a year for any market share lost to nonsignatories beyond 2 percentage points, up to 18⅔ points. The senior claims against this money will be 40 cents a pack for the companies that actually lose share (most likely, RJR and Brown and Williamson), up to $300 million per firm per year, while the remainder of the payments will be made in proportion to market share.[142]

Lawyers will be paid a total of $750 million a year for five years and then $500 million a year indefinitely.[143] The present value of the fees

141. Technically, the deal was structured as a $300 million purchase of the Chesterfield, L&M, and Lucky Strike brands (in the United States), with Liggett getting to keep $150 million if the FTC rejected the deal. Gary Black estimated the 1998 sales of the three brands at 40 million packs. Generously assuming that these declining brands earn the industry average of 35 cents a pack and are worth 5.1 to 6 times pretax earnings (see note 65), their value would be $71 million to $84 million. See Bloomberg News, "Brooke Sells 3 Brands to Philip Morris, Joins Accord (update 1)," November 22, 1998, 3:47 p.m., and Gary Black and Jon Rooney, "Philip Morris/Liggett Deal: Has Philip Morris Re-Armed the Enemy?" November 23, 1998, available at www. tobacco.org.

142. There is some reallocation between Lorillard and Philip Morris that has the effect of making the value of Lorillard's claims on the rebates proportional to its market share, assuming that its sales and market share do not rise too dramatically. Compare the 40 cents per pack promised to firms that lose share with RJR and Brown and Williamson's operating profits of about 25 and 20 cents per pack, respectively. So these firms, which are most likely to lose market share, might benefit from medium-scale entry by nonsignatories and may even be encouraged in some circumstances to raise prices as a means of losing share. Certainly, the terms of the deal would make it much easier for the industry to sustain high prices in the face of nonsignatory entry. See Section IX of the agreement.

143. Robin Topping and Harry Berkowitz, "Big Payday in Tobacco Settlement," *Newsday*, November 17, 1998, p. A52.

is about $8 billion, or six to seven times the amount of actual damages that will be paid to the fifty percent of the states that hired outside counsel.[144]

It would make much more economic sense to negotiate a deal that included the marketing restrictions and damage payments plus an agreement that the companies would not fight an increase of up to 35 cents in any state's cigarette excise tax. But taxes defined as such would sound less attractive politically and would surely require legislative approval. Furthermore, such taxes could be based only on state-by-state sales because the attorneys general and the state legislatures have no authority to pass taxes based on national sales. But on that basis, many states, particularly those that had no desire to sue the industry, like North Carolina, would not have joined the deal.[145] By imposing de facto national taxes the deal coerces these reluctant states into participating; if North Carolina did not join, its consumers would still be hit with the tax hike, so its only option is whether or not to accept its share of the revenues. Finally, the trial lawyers had a multibillion dollar incentive to promote the deceptive labeling of the payment as damages rather than as taxes.

Because of its byzantine structure, the signing of the multistate settlement represented a beginning rather than an end. There will be debates in every state over whether to pass the model statute. Some legislators may ultimately understand the economics of the whole deal and fight to have it overturned. Even if most states pass the model statute, it is likely that some will not. For example, the four states that settled earlier have no incentive to pass the statute. There may well be new companies that start by selling in states without statutes, and as they grow, they may have an incentive to fight to overturn the statutes in other states. An organization focused on consumer, but not trial

144. This estimate assumes a 7 percent discount rate and fees continuing indefinitely. Some lawyers are complaining about their treatment under the deal, See, for example, Dan Morain and Henry Weinstein, "Dispute Brewing over Private Attorneys' Fees in Tobacco Lawsuits Litigation," *Los Angeles Times*, November 22, 1998, p. A26, detailing the complaints of William Lerach, one of the country's most politically powerful trial lawyers.

145. The North Carolina state legislature voted in 1996 to prohibit a suit against the industry, but the state's attorney general, Michael Easley, was a major player in the settlement. See Bob Williams, "2 Who Forged Tobacco Accord," *Raleigh News and Observer*, November 23, 1998, p. A1.

lawyer, interests could object to the structure of the multistate settlement, as might anyone disturbed by the prospect of one or more states being able to get together to pass a national tax. And of course the deal leaves us where we were at the beginning of 1997 in terms of the class-action *Castano* suits. So very little has been truly resolved.

Radical Solutions

This paper has focused mostly on the provisions in the bill and resolution and how they could be improved. This section looks at two ideas that were not seriously considered but perhaps should have been.

A more radical approach to a tobacco deal would be for the federal government to buy the companies' domestic tobacco businesses. Applying McCain-like taxes to pay the cost, the debt incurred in a fully debt-financed purchase could be paid off in about two years.[146] Tobacco policy could then be determined without any input from tobacco executives and shareholders. The disadvantage of this option is political: there would be no more industry villains to kick around, and the government would have to take responsibility if demand failed to decrease adequately. If there is one thing that government monopolies are traditionally good at, however, it is deglamorizing their products and making them as consumer-unfriendly as possible.[147]

As another alternative, if concern over public health focuses on the amount of cigarette smoking, why not regulate quantity directly instead of price? That is, a fixed and declining number of licenses could be sold each year to cigarette makers, analogous to tradable pollution

146. Assuming a price-earnings ratio of 10 for the domestic tobacco industry ex litigation expenses, the industry would be worth about $50 billion. The resolution showed that the companies would be willing to give up at least a third of that value to settle litigation claims, and the firms' market values show that shareholders would take much less. Excluding the lump-sum payments, the McCain bill would have collected $29.8 billion in tax revenues in its first two years. Combined with the operating profits from the acquired companies (perhaps another $13 billion), this should be enough to pay off a fully debt-financed purchase.

147. One possibility might be to ask Bob Tisch, one of the brothers who controls Lorillard and a former Postmaster General, to run the monopoly and institute post-office worst-practice marketing reforms.

permits.[148] Firms would still have an incentive to market so that they could raise prices, but the marketing would have no first-order health consequences. An advantage of this approach is that it sidesteps the disputes between the government and the firms about the sales impacts of different taxes. Of course, the usual issues about quantity versus price regulation would apply. But even if setting quantity targets is desirable, it may not happen because of politics: the rhetoric has all been about reducing youth smoking while allowing adults to smoke. Setting quantity levels for overall cigarette sales (as opposed to the quantity targets for youth participation in the look-back rules) might be too difficult to defend as a youth smoking policy.

The Way Forward

It is not possible to make a deal that would satisfy both the tobacco industry and its most ardent critics. David Kessler, former head of the Food and Drug Administration, says of the companies: ''I don't want to live in peace with these guys. . . . If they cared at all for the public health, they wouldn't be in this business in the first place. All this talk about it being a legal business is euphemism. They sell a deadly, addictive product. There's no reason to allow them to conduct business as usual.''[149] What is possible is a deal that would sharply reduce smoking, youth smoking in particular, in return for reducing the companies' exposure to lawsuits. This was the concept behind the resolution and the early draft of the bill, and some steps in this direction are taken in the badly flawed multistate settlement. In this concluding section we summarize the main ways in which such a deal should be structured.

Cigarette taxes should be set so that firms' marginal rates are greater than or equal to their average rate, preferably greater. An easy way to do this is to exempt a small fraction of each firm's current sales from the taxes. The resolution set marginal and average rates equal; the bill set marginal rates below average.

In the context of this legislation, there is no good rationale for setting

148. The licenses could relate to tar and nicotine content as well as to number of cigarettes.
149. See Jeffrey Goldberg, ''Big Tobacco's Endgame,'' *New York Times Magazine*, June 21, 1998.

the same tax rate on all cigarettes. One might argue that government's role is to make sure that citizens have adequate information to decide what to eat, drink, and smoke and to set taxes based on the externalities imposed on others. But if that is all, cigarette taxes should be lower than they already are. Higher taxes must be justified by assuming that smokers do not adequately internalize their risks to themselves. If so, taxes should be higher the more tar and nicotine there is in a cigarette. This approach would be consistent with the provisions in both the bill and resolution to set maximum levels of tar in cigarettes. Basing taxes on tar and nicotine would also give the companies an incentive to develop safer cigarettes. If youth smokers are attracted by heavily marketed brands, there is also a rationale for imposing ad valorem taxes. Such taxes reduce the incentive to market premium cigarettes and would discriminate against youth smoking.

We support tough marketing restrictions. Such restrictions should reduce smoking, youth smoking in particular, without proportionally reducing profits. The argument that few smokers switch brands, and therefore the reason that companies wish to continue to advertise is to attract youth smokers, is simply wrong. Companies will aggressively fight for new customers, but in doing so will dissipate much of their future profits. It is not surprising that they were willing to sacrifice Joe Camel and agree to other marketing restrictions on the first day of negotiations over the resolution.

The look-back penalties in the resolution were a useful mechanism for enforcing the marketing restrictions. The look-back penalties in the bill were simply another poorly designed tax on cigarettes, having little to do with youth smoking. Restrictions on where tobacco can be sold and increases in the minimum legal age would make more sense than look-backs as youth smoking measures. Given the bill's hand-tying marketing restrictions on the companies, the incentives for reducing underage smoking should be directed at state governments, which would be responsible for the efficacy of antismoking programs and would have the police power to enforce rules against the illegal sale and consumption of cigarettes. That said, we believe that regardless of the rhetoric, the public health community is more concerned, and appropriately so, with reducing overall smoking than with reducing youth smoking participation rates.

Whether or not the companies' past actions should make them liable for damages, we support including protections from lawsuits in any deal. It is the one thing that can be offered to the companies to make them acquiesce to all the other provisions that will be in any legislation. Congress could pass an antismoking bill, but if there are no legal protections, it would have to be done over the vigorous opposition of the industry, which succeeded in defeating the current bill after its protections were removed.[150]

If the litigation against the companies were focused on truth seeking and a fair calculation of damages, we would be less enthusiastic about legal protections. But none of the parties seems particularly concerned about relating payments to damages. That is why the up-front damage payments were based on how deep each company's pockets were and not on its contribution to disease. Similarly, the coinsurance provisions that made it as cheap for a company to give a plaintiff $5 million as it would be to spend $1 million fighting off an invalid claim hardly seem designed to push the legal system to get at the truth. We do not advocate lump-sum payments made in proportion to market value, nor do we advocate the coinsurance scheme.[151]

We have enormous problems with the individual state settlements. The collusive nature of these agreements, which effectively impose national excise taxes on the industry to settle the claims of an individual state, will set a terrible precedent for other litigation if the agreements are allowed to stand without explicit congressional approval. These settlements also create a common pool problem; each state now has the incentive to pass laws making it easier to sue tobacco and other industries as a way to tax consumers in other states.

The flaws in the multistate agreement illustrate how inaccurately describing taxes as damages generates huge windfalls for special interests, including trial lawyers and smaller companies.

In the end, whether a comprehensive deal occurs may depend on how important it is to the antitobacco forces to punish the companies. The companies can be bargained into accepting higher taxes and marketing bans and paying some money. They cannot be bargained into bankruptcy. Without a full national settlement they may be forced to

150. Furthermore, the marketing restrictions and look-back penalties were likely to be challenged in court if Congress passed a bill without industry acquiescence.

151. We would not object so much to lump-sum payments made in rough proportion to a company's responsibility for damages.

pay more money, maybe even forced into bankruptcy. But bankruptcy would not make the cigarette industry disappear, and the restructured companies that arose from chapter 11 would be less vulnerable to lawsuits than the current firms. If the goal is to cut smoking and to do it quickly, a deal makes sense.

Appendix A: Fixed-Revenue Taxation versus Specific Taxes

This appendix shows that relative to specific taxes, fixed-revenue taxation results in lower pass-through and yields more dispersed market shares.

Let firms $i = 1,...,N$ have marginal costs c_i, and choose outputs q_i. Let $Q = \sum_{i=1}^{N} q_i$, and assume a conventional tobacco demand specification $\ln Q = a - bp$, or equivalently $p = \alpha - \beta \ln Q$, in which p is the industry price.

Assuming Cournot behavior and a specific tax of t, each firm, i, sets

$$c_i + t = \frac{d}{dq_i}(pq_i) = \alpha - \beta \ln Q - \beta s_i = p - \beta s_i,$$

in which s_i is i's market share. Aggregating over all N firms yields $Np - \beta = \sum_{i=1}^{N} c_i + Nt$, which implies $p = c^* + \beta/N + t$, in which c^* is the (unweighted) average cost of the firms.

However, a fixed-revenue tax $T = tQ$, allocated in proportion to market share, implies that the individual firm's first-order condition becomes $c_i + (1 - s_i)t = \frac{d}{dq_i}(pq_i) = p - \beta s_i$, and aggregating over the N firms yields $p = c^* + \dfrac{\beta}{N} + \dfrac{N-1}{N}t$.

This result, that the derivative of price with respect to the average tax is only $(N - 1)/N$ as great with a fixed-revenue tax, is independent of the specification of demand, but it does depend on the Cournot assumption. We chose the log-linear distribution to illustrate because it is commonly used to estimate cigarette demand.

Log-linear demand also has the nice feature that specific tax increases are passed on dollar for dollar with no changes in industry market shares. With the fixed-revenue tax, solving for market share yields $s_i = \dfrac{1}{N} + \dfrac{c^* - c_i}{\beta - t}$, which has the intuitive implication that market shares will become more dispersed if a fixed-revenue tax is instituted, because the largest firms will face the smallest incremental marginal costs from the tax.

Again, it is not too hard, although algebraically messier, to check that the result that a firm with costs below (above) c^* has a larger (smaller) market share under fixed-revenue than under specific taxation is independent of the specification of demand.

The results are qualitatively the same but not as strong outside the Cournot model. In a Cournot model, a firm's actions do not affect its competitors' sales. In the extreme where industry demand is completely inelastic, a firm's marginal tax rate under fixed-revenue taxation will be equal to the average rate of t. If activity that leads to one extra sale for the firm leads to an increase of δ in industry sales, then the effective marginal tax rate under fixed-revenue taxation is $t(1 - \delta s_i)$, and the projected pass-through rate is $\dfrac{N - \delta}{N}$ times the pass-through rate of a specific tax.

Appendix B: The Value of the Youth Market: Price Competition

This appendix describes a simple model of price competition in which the inability to price-discriminate between old and young consumers does not affect the value of the youth market, and the value of young consumers is small because the profits earned from them after they have developed brand loyalty are dissipated by competition for those profits.

Begin with a single-period N-firm market in which each firm i has a privately known marginal cost c_i independently drawn from a common distribution $F(\cdot)$.[152] Each firm has $\left(\dfrac{n}{N}\right)$ "old" brand-loyal customers

---

152. This assumption allows us to analyze the effects of asymmetries in firms' costs while maintaining a symmetric model structure.

who have reservation price R for consuming its brand, but a high cost of switching to any other brand.[153] There are also m "youth" consumers who have reservation price R for consuming *any* brand and so will buy the cheapest brand.[154] Firms are risk neutral and independently and noncooperatively choose prices p_i.

To analyze this model let $d_i = R - p_i$ be the "discount" below the reservation price that firm i offers. Think of the firm that offers the highest discount as the winner of a prize worth $m(R - c_i)$, that is, the low-price firm wins the youth market, which is worth $m(R - c_i)$ to it before accounting for the discount. The winning firm pays $\left(\dfrac{n}{N} + m\right)d_i$ in discounts while nonwinners pay $\left(\dfrac{n}{N}\right) d_i$ in discount costs.[155] It now follows from the Revenue Equivalence Theorem that the expected profits of the firms in this "discount auction" equal their expected profits if they were bidders in any standard auction mechanism that allocates the same prize.[156] But if an auctioneer simply ran an ascending auction for the prize, raising the asking price until just one bidder remained, the winning bidder would be the lowest-cost firm and would pay the price at which the second-lowest-cost firm (call its actual cost c_2) quits,

153. We assume this "switching cost" is so high that no firm finds it profitable to price low enough to sell to other firms' old customers. Obviously, we do not intend this model to be taken literally. See Klemperer (1987a) for discussion.

154. An alternative model would have these consumers buying from the best-advertised brand. The results would be similar. It is trivial to relax the assumption that the youth consumers have the same reservation prices as the older ones.

155. All firms additionally make profits of $\left(\dfrac{n}{N}\right)(R - c_i)$ on their old customers.

156. The Revenue Equivalence Theorem states that if each of N risk-neutral potential buyers has a privately known value, v_i, independently drawn from a common, strictly increasing, and atomless distribution for a prize, then any mechanism in which the object always goes to the buyer with the highest value and any bidder with the lowest-possible valuation expects zero surplus yields the same expected revenue to the auctioneer and results in a buyer with value v_i making the same expected surplus. Here, $v_i \equiv m(R - c_i)$. We assume the assumptions of the theorem hold and note that a bidder with the highest possible cost sets $d_i = 0$, so earns zero surplus from the competition to serve the youth market. For other examples of using the Revenue Equivalence Theorem to efficiently analyze situations that are not obviously auctions, see Bulow and Klemperer (1994, 1999). See Klemperer (forthcoming a, b) for further discussion.

$m(R - c_2)$. That is, since each firm has the lowest costs, say c_1, with probability $\dfrac{1}{N}$, its expected profits from the auction are $\left(\dfrac{m}{N}\right)E(c_2 - c_1)$, and its expected total profits are $\left(\dfrac{m}{N}\right)E(c_2 - c_1) + \left(\dfrac{n}{N}\right)E(R - c_i)$. [157]

But if firms could price discriminate, each firm would make the same expected profits, $\left(\dfrac{m}{N}\right)E(c_2 - c_1)$, from Bertrand competition for the youth market, and $\left(\dfrac{n}{N}\right)E(R - c_i)$ from its old customers.

Of course, the youth consumers of today become old customers tomorrow: let the market last for M periods, demand in the first period remain as above, and consumers always repeat-purchase from their previous suppliers in all subsequent periods. To keep things simple, assume there are no new consumers after the first period. Then all firms' prices after period one will be R, so the prize of winning the youth customers in the first period equals $Mm(R - c_i)$, that is, M times larger than in the single-period model, before accounting for the discounts. So firms will discount their first-period prices M times further below R, and expected profits from the "auction" and total profits are just M times larger than previously. As before, the incremental value to the firms of the youth consumers is exactly their value in a model of (re-

---

157. To compute the expected market price without price discrimination, use the Revenue Equivalence Theorem to observe that the auctioneer's expected receipts from the ascending auction, $E[m(R-c_2)]$, equal his expected receipts from the "discount auction,"

$$E\left[\left(\frac{n}{N} + m\right)d_1 + \sum_{j=2}^{N}\left(\frac{n}{N}\right)d_j\right],$$

in which d_1 is the highest discount actually offered. Note that the former expression equals $E[(n + m)\bar{d}]$ in which $\bar{d}$ is the firms' average actual discount weighted by their sales. This equals $(n+m)(R-\bar{p})$ in which $\bar{p}$ is the expected average price in the market weighted by sales. Reorganizing yields

$$\bar{p} = \frac{nR + mE(c_2)}{n + m}$$

which, as expected, varies continuously from $E(c_2)$ for a pure youth market, to R for a market with no youth segment.

peated) Bertrand competition without brand loyalty; the monopoly profits they generate after the first period are dissipated by the correspondingly low prices that are set in period one to attract them.

A full model of many periods in which youth consumers enter in
every period raises many more technical issues but yields the same
messages. Although from an accountant's perspective youth smokers
pay the same prices as anyone else, they are responsible for older
customers paying less than they otherwise would. The value attributable
to current and future youth smokers approximates their present value
absent brand loyalty effects, while the value of old smokers is their
value taking their brand loyalty into account.[158]

Computing the share of market value attributable to youth smokers
requires assumptions about the nature of competition absent brand loyalty effects. Our simple model assumed winner-take-all Bertrand competition (and monopoly pricing for old consumers) and so implies a
particularly low relative value of the youth market.[159] The advertising
model in Appendix C involves less cut-throat competition (as would a
model with Cournot competition or with some exogenous product dif-
ferentiation) and yields a somewhat higher value of the youth segment.[160]

The truth probably includes elements of both these models and lies

---

158. In such a model, firms set prices that trade off their conflicting desires to capture
new consumers and exploit old consumers in every period, and in symmetric steady
state the price is the same in every period and for every consumer. The richest available
model of multiperiod competition in which brand loyalty is developed endogenously is
perhaps the model with switching costs in Beggs and Klemperer (1992). See also Farrell
and Shapiro (1988) and Padilla (1995) for other multiperiod models, and Klemperer
(1987a, 1987b) for simple two-period models with switching costs. The effects that
these models demonstrate suggest this discussion may have *slightly* underestimated the
value of the youth market, but the magnitude of the necessary correction is probably not
large, and even its sign is ambiguous. See Klemperer (1995) for more discussion.

159. A figure of perhaps 2 percent of the present value of the whole market is
obtained, making the assumptions in note 72, using a generous estimate of the profitability of Bertrand competition with differing costs (say 5 cents a pack), a conservative
estimate of the current value of the old customers to a monopolist (say \$35 billion,
which is consistent with linear demand and a demand elasticity of -0.4) and assuming
10 percent of smokers switch every year (and then act like new consumers).

160. See appendix C. Also observe that our calculations are really valuing current
nonsmokers, who include some above-age future smokers but exclude underage smokers
who are already hooked. But the value of the underage segment cannot be very different.

somewhere between them and the case without brand-loyalty effects.[161] So although future smokers may account for a sixth of the present value of future revenues, their contribution to future profits is much lower. If industry executives seem to value the youth segment, it is probably due more to concern for their own future jobs than concern for their shareholders.

Appendix C: The Value of the Youth Market: Advertising Competition

This appendix describes a very simple model of advertising competition in which, although firms may advertise heavily to attract young consumers, the value to them of being able to do so may be small; and the more sensitive to advertising young consumers are, the larger the fraction of the future revenue from these consumers that is dissipated.

Assume firms $i = 1, \ldots, N$ independently choose marketing expenditures A_i that generate a flow of new consumers into the industry, $y = \left(\sum_{j=1}^{N} A_j \right)^{\eta}$, normalized so that the mass of current smokers is 1. Firms' shares of new smokers are proportional to their shares of current advertising expenditures, and smokers stick with their original firm until they quit the market at rate λ. Assuming a discount rate r, and that each consumer generates profits at rate $Xe^{-\beta\tau}$ at time τ for the company from which he buys (representing a constant real profit per pack and a secular decline of 100β percent in consumption per smoker), the present value of profits from a youth smoker is $X/(r + \lambda + \beta)$.

Firm i thus maximizes

$$\left[\frac{A_i}{\sum\limits_{j=1}^{N} A_j} \left(\sum_{j=1}^{N} A_j \right)^{\eta} \frac{X}{r + \lambda + \beta} \right] - A_i,$$

161. For the latter case, which yields a value of the youth market at most equal to one-sixth of the value of the whole market, see the main text.

taking other firms' advertising levels as given, so in equilibrium

$$NA_i = y\left(\frac{N - 1 + \eta}{N}\right)\frac{X}{r + \lambda + \beta}.\text{[162]}$$

So fraction $(N - 1 + \eta)/N$ of the future profits from youth smoking is dissipated in advertising costs. This fraction is increasing in the elasticity, η, of youth consumption with respect to advertising expenditures.

Current industry profits are X without advertising, and $X - NA_i$ with advertising; the market value of the industry is $X/(r + \lambda + \beta)$ without advertising, and $(X - NA_i)/(r + \lambda + \beta - y)$ with advertising. To take a simple example, if $y = 0.02$, $\beta = 0.01$, $\lambda = 0.025$, $r = 0.085$ (which are all consistent with the data in note 72), and $\eta = \frac{1}{2}$, then current profits rise by 7/41, and the industry's present value falls by only 1/41 if advertising, and hence youth smoking, is eliminated.[163] Extending the model to allow some brand switching would increase the value of the youth market because firms would spend less money trying to attract customers who might later be diverted to another firm.

162. We assume symmetric Markov-perfect equilibrium, thus ruling out "punishment strategies" which might allow more "collusive" equilibria to be supported in this dynamic game.

163. For example, if current pretax profits were $8.2 billion, marketing expenditures would be $1.4 billion. Eliminating those expenditures would increase short-run profits to $9.6 billion. But the gradual erosion of the customer base would mean that, assuming a 40 percent tax rate, the market value of the domestic tobacco industry would fall from $49.2 billion to $48 billion.

References

Armstrong, Mark, and John Vickers. 1998. "Competitive Price Discrimination." Unpublished manuscript, Oxford University. March.

Ayres, Ian, and Steven D. Levitt. 1998. "Measuring Positive Externalities from Unobservable Victim Precaution: An Empirical Analysis of Lojack." *Quarterly Journal of Economics* 113: 43–77.

Barzel, Yoram. 1976. "An Alternative Approach to the Analysis of Taxation." *Journal of Political Economy* 84 (December): 1177–97.

Becker, Gary, Michael Grossman, and Kevin Murphy. 1994. "An Empirical Analysis of Cigarette Addiction." *American Economic Review* 84 (June): 396–418.

Becker, Gary S., and Kevin M. Murphy. 1988. "A Theory of Rational Addiction." *Journal of Political Economy* 96 (August): 675–700.

Beggs, Alan, and Paul D. Klemperer. 1992. "Multiperiod Competition with Switching Costs." *Econometrica* 60 (May): 651–66.

Black, Gary, and John Rooney, "The Renegade Rift: Why RJR and B&W Will Come Back to the Table," *Sanford C. Bernstein Report*, August 28, 1998, available at www.tobacco.org.

Bozell Sawyer Miller Group. 1997. "Impact of the Proposed Resolution on the U.S. Cigarette Industry." Report for the tobacco industry. Washington, D.C. October 9.

Bulow, Jeremy, and Paul Klemperer. 1994. "Rational Frenzies and Crashes." *Journal of Political Economy* 102 (February): 1–23

———. Forthcoming. "The Generalized War of Attrition." *American Economic Review*.

Bulow, Jeremy, and Paul Pfleiderer. 1983. "A Note on the Effect of Cost Changes on Prices." *Journal of Political Economy* 91 (February): 182–85.

Centers for Disease Control and Prevention. 1993. "Smoking Cessation during Previous Year among Adults: United States, 1990 and 1991." *Morbidity and Mortality Weekly Reports*. 42 (26): 504–7.

Chaloupka, Frank J. 1991. "Rational Addictive Behavior and Cigarette Smoking." *Journal of Political Economy* 99 (August): 722–42.

Chaloupka, Frank J., and Michael Grossman. 1996. "Price, Tobacco Control Policies, and Youth Smoking." NBER Working Paper 5740. Cambridge, Mass.: National Bureau of Economic Research.

Chaloupka, Frank J., and Rosalie Liccardo Pacula. 1998. "Limiting Youth Access to Tobacco: The Early Impact of the Synar Amendment on Youth Smoking." Working Paper. University of Illinois, Chicago Circle. March.

Corts, Kenneth. 1998. "Third-Degree Price Discrimination in Oligopoly: All-Out Competition and Strategic Commitment." *RAND Journal of Economics* 29 (Summer): 306–23.

Daynard, Richard A., and others. 1998. "An Analysis of Selected Provisions of the McCain Committee Bill (S. 1415): Working Paper 8 in a Series on Legal Issues in the Proposed Tobacco Settlement." Tobacco Control Research Center, Northeastern University.

DeCicca, Philip, Donald Kenkel, and Alan Mathios. 1998. "Putting Out the Fires: Will Higher Taxes Reduce Youth Smoking?" Unpublished manuscript, Cornell University. August.

Delipalla, Sophia. 1994. "Specific Versus Ad Valorem Taxation: Empirical Evidence from the European Cigarette Industry." Unpublished manuscript. University of Wales Swansea, United Kingdom. November.

Delipalla, Sophia, and Owen O'Donnell. 1998. "The Comparison between Ad Valorem and Specific Taxation under Imperfect Competition: Evidence from the European Cigarette Industry." Working paper. University of Kent, United Kingdom. February.

Elzinga, Kenneth G., and David E. Mills. 1997. "The Distribution and Pricing of Prescription Drugs." *International Journal of the Economics of Business* (November): 287–300.

Farrell, Joseph, and Carl Shapiro. 1988. "Dynamic Competition with Switching Costs." *RAND Journal of Economics* 19 (Spring): 123–37.

Federal Trade Commission. 1997. "Competition and the Financial Impact of the Proposed Tobacco Industry Settlement." Washington. September 22.

———. 1998. "Federal Trade Commission Report to Congress for 1996, Pursuant to the Federal Labeling and Advertising Act." March 17.

Gravelle, Jane G., and Dennis Zimmerman. 1994. *Cigarette Taxes to Fund Health Care Reform: An Economic Analysis.* Congressional Research Service.

Hanson, Jon. D., and Kyle D. Logue. 1998. "The Costs of Cigarettes: The Economic Case for Ex Post Incentive-Based Regulation." *Yale Law Journal* 107 (March): 1163–361.

Johnson, Terry R. 1978. "Additional Evidence of the Effects of Alternative Taxes on Cigarette Prices." *Journal of Political Economy* 86 (April): 325–28.

Joint Committee on Taxation, U.S. Congress. 1998. "Distributional Effects of S. 1415, as Reported by the Senate Committee on Commerce, Science, and Transportation." JCX 40-98. May 18.

Keen, Michael. 1998. "The Balance between Specific and Ad Valorem Taxation." *Fiscal Studies* 19 (February): 1–37.

Klemperer, Paul 1987a. "Markets with Consumer Switching Costs." *Quarterly Journal of Economics* 102 (May): 375–94.

———. 1987b. "The Competitiveness of Markets with Switching Costs." *RAND Journal of Economics* 18 (Spring): 138–50.

———. 1995. "Competition When Consumers Have Switching Costs." *Review of Economic Studies* 62 (October): 515–39.

———. Forthcoming a. "Auction Theory: A Guide to the Literature." *Journal of Economic Surveys.*

———, ed. Forthcoming b. *The Economic Theory of Auctions.* Cheltenhem, U.K.: Edward Elgar.

Kluger, Richard. 1996. *Ashes to Ashes.* Knopf.

Kreps, David M., and Robert Wilson. 1982. "Reputation and Imperfect Information." *Journal of Economic Theory* 27 (August): 253–79.

Marsh, Alan, and Jil Matheson. 1983. *Smoking Attitudes and Behaviour.* London: Her Majesty's Stationary Office.

Merriman, David. 1994. "Do Cigarette Excise Tax Rates Maximize Revenue?" *Economic Inquiry* 32 (July): 419–28.

Milgrom, Paul, and John Roberts. 1982. "Predation, Reputation, and Entry Deterrence." *Journal of Economic Theory* 27 (August): 280–312.

Mollenkamp, Carrick, and others. 1998. *The People vs. Big Tobacco.* Princeton, N.J.: Bloomberg Press.

National Association of Convenience Stores web site. 1998. "Tobacco Update: Facts to Consider." March 9. Available at http://www.cstorecentral.com/register/resource/tobupdate981.htm.

National Cancer Institute, National Institutes of Health. 1993. *The Impact of Cigarette Excise Taxes on Smoking among Children and Adults,* Summary Report of a National Cancer Institute Expert Panel.

Ordover, Janusz A., and John C. Panzar. 1980. "On the Nonexistence of Pareto Superior Outlay Schedules." *Bell Journal of Economics* 11 (Spring): 351–54.

Padilla, A. Jorge. 1995. "Revisiting Dynamic Duopoly with Consumer Switching Costs." *Journal of Economic Theory* 67 (December): 520–30.

Peto, R. 1986. "Influence of Dose and Duration of Smoking on Lung Cancer Rates." In *Tobacco: A Major Internatational Health Hazard,* edited by D. G. Zarridge and R. Peto, 23–33. Lyon: International Agency for Research on Cancer.

Pringle, Peter. 1998. *Cornered: Big Tobacco at the Bar of Justice.* Holt.

Scott Morton, Fiona M. 1997. "The Strategic Response by Pharmaceutical Firms to the Medicaid Most-Favored-Customer Rules." *RAND Journal of Economics* 28 (Summer): 269–90.

Sobel, Russell S., and Thomas A. Garrett. 1997. "Taxation and Product Quality: New Evidence from Generic Cigarettes." *Journal of Political Economy* 105 (August): 880–87.

Sullum, Jacob. 1998. *For Your Own Good: The Anti-Smoking Crusade and the Tyranny of Public Health.* Free Press.

Sumner, Daniel. 1981. "Measurement of Monopoly Behavior: An Application to the Cigarette Industry." *Journal of Political Economy* 89 (October): 1010–19.

Sumner, Michael T., and Robert Ward. 1981. "Tax Changes and Cigarette Prices." *Journal of Political Economy* 89 (December): 1261–65.

Tobacco Institute. 1997. *The Tax Burden on Tobacco* 31 (1996). Washington.

Townsend, Joy. 1993. "Policies to Halve Smoking Deaths." *Addiction* 88 (January): 43–52.

Townsend, Joy, Paul Roderick, and Jacqueline Cooper. 1994. "Cigarette Smoking by Socioeconomic Group, Sex, and Age: Effects of Price, Income, and Health Publicity." *British Medical Journal* 309 (October): 923–27.

Tye, Joe B., Kenneth E. Warner, and Stanton A. Glantz. 1987. "Tobacco Advertising and Consumption: Evidence of a Causal Relationship." *Journal of Public Health Policy* 8 (Winter): 492–508.

U.K. Department of Health. 1992. *Effect of Tobacco Advertising on Tobacco Consumption: A Discussion Document Reviewing the Evidence.* Economics and Operational Research Division, London. October.

U.S. Department of Agriculture. 1987, 1996, 1998. *Tobacco Situation and Outlook Report.*

U.S. Department of Health and Human Services. 1989. *Reducing the Health Consequences of Smoking: 25 Years of Progress.* Report of the Surgeon General.

U.S. Federal Trade Commission. 1997. *Competition and the Financial Impact of the Proposed Tobacco Industry Settlement.*

Varian, Hal. 1989. "Price Discrimination." In *Handbook of Industrial Organisation*, vol. 1, edited by Richard Schmalensee and Robert D. Willig, pp. 597–654. Amsterdam: North Holland.

Viscusi, W. Kip. 1994. "Cigarette Taxation and the Social Consequences of Smoking." NBER Working Paper 4831. National Bureau for Economic Research, Cambridge, Mass. October.

Warner, Kenneth E., Linda M. Goldenhar, and Catherine G. McLaughlin. 1992. "Cigarette Advertising and Magazine Coverage of the Hazards of Smoking: A Statistical Analysis." *New England Journal of Medicine* 326 (January 30): 305–9.